Saveur Cooks Authentic French

SAVEUR
COOKS

AUTHENTIC
FRENCH

BY THE EDITORS OF
SAVEUR MAGAZINE

CHRONICLE BOOKS
SAN FRANCISCO

Library of Congress Cataloging-in-Publication
Data available.

ISBN 0-8118-2564-7

Printed in Hong Kong.

Designed by Jill Armus, Michael Grossman, and
Amy Henderson
Typeset in Bernhard Gothic, Della Robbia, and
Garamond 3

Distributed in Canada by
Raincoast Books
8680 Cambie Street
Vancouver, British Columbia V6P 6M9

10 9 8 7 6 5 4 3 2 1

Chronicle Books
85 Second Street
San Francisco, California 94105

www.chroniclebooks.com

Acknowledgments

FRANCE HAS BEEN the source of so many of our most memorable stories, of so many of our most memorable meals. What if—we wondered—we were to assemble in one volume all the French classics we love to cook? Not only would this save us from frantically rifling through five years of issues for a favorite recipe, it would also affirm our reverence for this venerable (and lately overlooked) cuisine. Et voilà! *Saveur Cooks Authentic French* appears just a year after our first book, *Saveur Cooks Authentic American*, and is brought to you by the same merry band—the people who turn out every issue of SAVEUR magazine: Colman Andrews, Editor (and award-winning writer); Christopher Hirsheimer, Executive Editor (and acclaimed photographer); our crack conceptual design team: Michael Grossman, Creative Director; Jill Armus, Art Director; María Millán, Photography Editor; and to keep us all in line, the wonderful Ann McCarthy, Assistant Managing Editor. We're grateful for the help of Meg Matyia and Victoria Rich, Assistant Photography Editors; Amy Henderson, Designer; Christiane Angeli, Copy Editor; Gabrielle Hamilton, recipe tester; Melissa Moss and Zoë Pellegrino, who demand the highest production quality; and, above all, our superb project editor in France, Megan Wetherall. Others in our group were drafted into service: Catherine Whalen, Melissa Hamilton, Shoshana Goldberg, Mindy Fox, Sophie Cramer, Marina Ganter, Toby Fox, Julie Pryma, Chad Tomlinson, Jenny Chung, Robin Malik, Johanna Guevara, and Samantha Smith. Our team's high spirits and commitment to excellence is evidenced on every page. I am profoundly grateful for their generosity.

Most of the recipes in this book have been researched in the kitchens of the French cooks who prepared them. We cover the country (see map, page 20) from populous (and popular) cities to tiny hamlets, from three-star kitchens to humble home stoves, always looking for the memorable story that connects each recipe to its origins. To tell these stories, we have drawn on the work of the great photographers and writers who regularly appear in our magazine. Photography credits are listed on page 310. The writers are: R.W. Apple Jr., Michael Balter, Michael Bateman, Claudia M. Caruana, David Case, David Downie, Judy Fayard, Jacqueline Friedrich, Eric Goodman, Richard Goodman, Mireille Johnston, Marie-Pascale Lescot, Connie McCabe, Kevin McDermott, Thomas McNamee, Colette Rossant, Sally Schneider, Warren Schultz, George Semler, William Sertl, Elaine Sterling, Corinne Trang, Lucian K. Truscott IV, John Willoughby, and Clifford A. Wright.

More thank-yous are due to Cullen Stanley, our agent at Janklow & Nesbit, for her loyalty and smarts; to Bill LeBlond, our trusty editor at Chronicle Books, and to Chronicle's Laura Lovett and Shona Bayley as well. To our leaders, Chairman Chris Meigher and President Doug Peabody; to SAVEUR Publisher John McCarus and Marketing Director Stephanie Sandberg; and to all our colleagues at Meigher Communications: We're delighted to present you with another Christmas gift.—DOROTHY KALINS, *Editor-in-Chief*, SAVEUR

Table of Contents

SAVEUR
COOKS
AUTHENTIC
FRENCH

INTRODUCTION

THREE OF US sat down to lunch one

day, not long ago, at a pretty little restau-

rant in the pretty little French wine town

of Chablis. We'd just arrived in France that

morning, two of us from New York and

In a Parisian bistro, left, where hearty food is served family style, the proprietors enjoy ample portions of their own cuisine. The year is 1953.

Some French Essentials

Picking wine grapes in front of a windmill in Bussac, in the Dordogne, in the early 1940s, top. Above, an array of cheeses on an early-20th-century poster advertising Fromageries Ch. Dayot, a chain of cheese shops. Right, outside an artisanal bakery in rural France in the early 1920s. The French, it is said, consume more bread than the citizens of any other country in the world; this photograph purports to show the quantity of bread eaten by the average peasant family every three or four days.

one from Moscow, and we were hungry, both physically and emotionally, for the succor that a good French meal can provide. We expected to be well fed…but when we took our first bites of our appetizers—snails in a buttery, garlic-accented parsley sauce (see page 130), chicken liver terrine with chablis-based gelée, and sautéed medallions of foie gras with apples and red currants— something extraordinary happened: In an instant, we rediscovered French food. All of us had traveled and eaten extensively in France for decades, and would have claimed to know the country's cuisine very well. Yet those first flavors were somehow a revelation to us—an epiphany. Maybe it was jet lag; maybe it was too many months of silly "fusion" cooking in America—but for whatever reasons, we were dazzled. What we had on our plates, we realized, wasn't just ingredients arranged; it was *cooking*—and it reminded us (though these may be fighting words in today's culinary climate) that good French food can be the best food in the world. It sent us this message so strongly, so immediately, in fact, that we pretty much decided then and there that our next SAVEUR book had to celebrate the cuisine of France.

French cuisine is far more than just a collection of recipes. It's a philosophy, an aesthetic, an attitude towards life. It is a way of preparing food—which is to say, a way of approaching (and assimilating) the natural world—

The Art of Food Shopping

A fashionably dressed and coiffed Parisian picks out non-French fruit at a stand in Montparnasse, probably in the 1950s, top. Above, the open-air market called the Marché des Innocents, on the rue St-Denis in Paris, around 1840, as depicted in a lithograph by one W. Parrott. Facing page, a covered food market somewhere in France, filled with shoppers on the first day of January 1950.

based on an immensely complex and sophisticated system of complementary, interlocking bases, part chemical, part mathematical, part artistic. French cooking can certainly involve trickery (marinating lamb to resemble venison, for instance), but at its best, it acknowledges and respects an old and surprisingly coherent canon, even when it sometimes deviates from it in pursuit of creativity. (French chefs are trained draftsmen even when they're painting abstract canvases, and it shows.) It is also a remarkably accommodating cuisine, capable of borrowing from other kitchens without compromising its own identity. Why is French cuisine ultimately greater than that of, say, China? Because it can adopt ingredients and techniques from the Chinese and remain true to itself, while the converse is not true.

For so many of us Americans, French food started it all. It was our introduction to the whole idea of cooking as an art, and to eating as an ennobling experience. Whether we learned to make it ourselves at home from Julia Child or Richard Olney or first experienced it in France itself, French was our first Cuisine with a capital C. But it is a cuisine that has been very much out of fashion in America in recent years. It is heavy and unhealthy, we are told. Italian food (it is said) is better—celebrating the integrity and purity of impeccable raw materials, while French food is culinary obfuscation,

based on sauces probably invented to cover up the stink of rotten meat. Oh, and by the way, the Italians taught the French to cook in the first place….

These are mindless libels. French food is rich, its flavors concentrated, but it can satisfy in small amounts. No one eats cassoulet every day, and none but the most voracious have a second helping. But that one serving, once in a while, is a treasure house of flavors, resonant of good living; it feeds the soul as well as the body. And it implies no disrespect to the gastronomic glories of Italy to say that, apart from introducing some ingredients to their Gallic neighbors, the Italians have taught the French little about cooking (historians have long since disproven the myth about Catherine de Médicis bringing haute cuisine to France). As for culinary ingredients, the French are absolutely fanatical about them, at least as much so as their peninsular neighbors—but while Italian food tends to be intentionally simple and accessible, the French seem more concerned with the extension of possibilities. They approach their foodstuffs with an almost Augustinian conceit, as if they are saying to each succulent guinea fowl or earthy truffle or juicy pear: "God made you, thus imbuing you with a certain natural perfection. Now, what can you become?"

France is a vast hexagon at the heart of western Europe—a nation of about 54 million inhabitants (those

The French at Table

An engraving from the late 18th century, top, suggests that food, drink, music, and love were all on the menu at a French country auberge. Above, Parisians gather at a café in the Quartier Latin in 1986. Facing page, vineyard workers moisten the remains of their soup with red wine (see page 74) at a harvesttime lunch in 1993—though this scene could have taken place a century or two ago.

famous "50 million Frenchmen [who] can't be wrong"), covering some 212,918 square miles and encompassing an immense variety of geography, from Alpine fastnesses to farmlands rippling with grain, from craggy Atlantic coastlines to Mediterranean hillsides covered with vines and olive trees. Despite the legendary chauvinism (in the original sense) of the French, France is a country, too, of many accents—German in Alsace, Flemish in Nord-Pas-de-Calais, Celtic in Brittany, Italian on the Côte d'Azur, Spanish in parts of Provence, Catalan in the Pyrenees. France's larder is thus abundant and diverse, and its cuisine is polyglot—even when it doesn't look to China.

But at the core of French cuisine are two parallel traditions: One is that of a rigorous classical culinary culture, descended from the kitchens of royalty and the nobility by way of men like Taillevent (who wrote the first French cookbook, back in the 1370s), Beauvilliers (who opened what was probably the world's first real restaurant, in 18th-century Paris), Carême (who once famously remarked that pastry making was a branch of architecture; see page 308), and Escoffier (the first "modern" chef, and the great encyclopedist of French recipes). The other tradition is that of home cooking, the food of ordinary Frenchmen and, even more so, Frenchwomen (like the famous *mères* of Lyon), who follow no rules but those of making-do and of nourishing a family as best

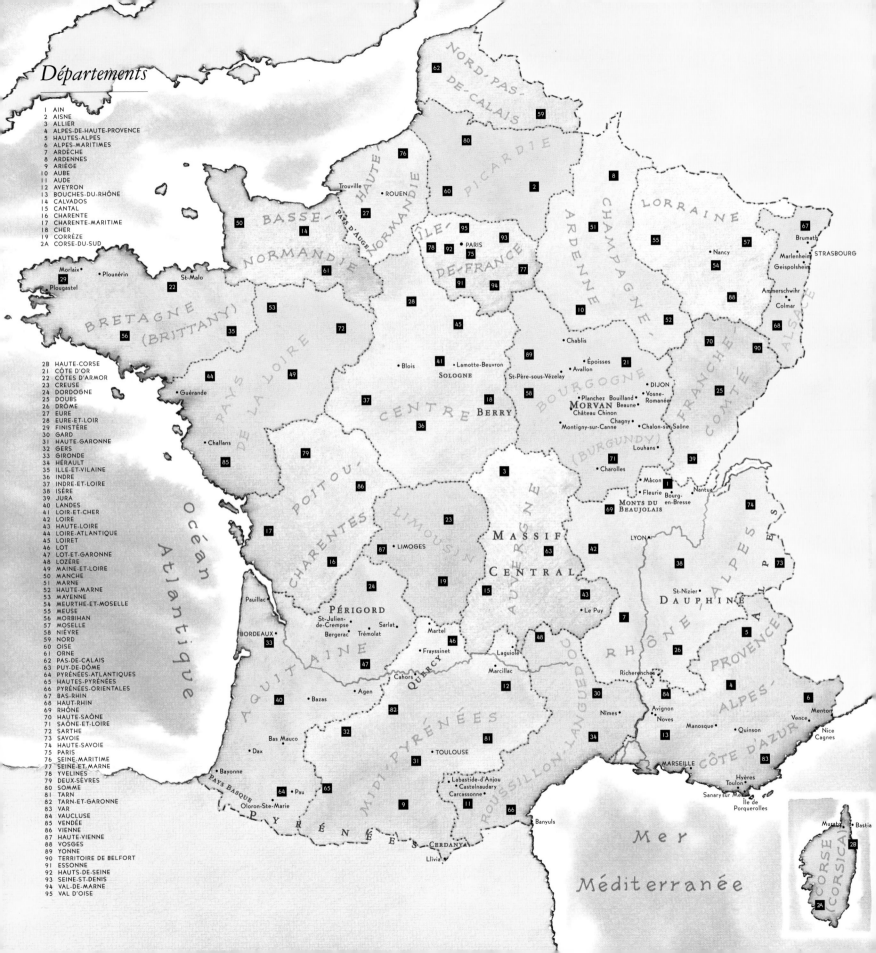

Départements

1 AIN
2 AISNE
3 ALLIER
4 ALPES-DE-HAUTE-PROVENCE
5 HAUTES-ALPES
6 ALPES-MARITIMES
7 ARDÈCHE
8 ARDENNES
9 ARIÈGE
10 AUBE
11 AUDE
12 AVEYRON
13 BOUCHES-DU-RHÔNE
14 CALVADOS
15 CANTAL
16 CHARENTE
17 CHARENTE-MARITIME
18 CHER
19 CORRÈZE
2A CORSE-DU-SUD
2B HAUTE-CORSE
21 CÔTE D'OR
22 CÔTES D'ARMOR
23 CREUSE
24 DORDOGNE
25 DOUBS
26 DRÔME
27 EURE
28 EURE-ET-LOIR
29 FINISTÈRE
30 GARD
31 HAUTE-GARONNE
32 GERS
33 GIRONDE
34 HÉRAULT
35 ILLE-ET-VILAINE
36 INDRE
37 INDRE-ET-LOIRE
38 ISÈRE
39 JURA
40 LANDES
41 LOIR-ET-CHER
42 LOIRE
43 HAUTE-LOIRE
44 LOIRE-ATLANTIQUE
45 LOIRET
46 LOT
47 LOT-ET-GARONNE
48 LOZÈRE
49 MAINE-ET-LOIRE
50 MANCHE
51 MARNE
52 HAUTE-MARNE
53 MAYENNE
54 MEURTHE-ET-MOSELLE
55 MEUSE
56 MORBIHAN
57 MOSELLE
58 NIÈVRE
59 NORD
60 OISE
61 ORNE
62 PAS-DE-CALAIS
63 PUY-DE-DÔME
64 PYRÉNÉES-ATLANTIQUES
65 HAUTES-PYRÉNÉES
66 PYRÉNÉES-ORIENTALES
67 BAS-RHIN
68 HAUT-RHIN
69 RHÔNE
70 HAUTE-SAÔNE
71 SAÔNE-ET-LOIRE
72 SARTHE
73 SAVOIE
74 HAUTE-SAVOIE
75 PARIS
76 SEINE-MARITIME
77 SEINE-ET-MARNE
78 YVELINES
79 DEUX-SÈVRES
80 SOMME
81 TARN
82 TARN-ET-GARONNE
83 VAR
84 VAUCLUSE
85 VENDÉE
86 VIENNE
87 HAUTE-VIENNE
88 VOSGES
89 YONNE
90 TERRITOIRE DE BELFORT
91 ESSONNE
92 HAUTS-DE-SEINE
93 SEINE-ST-DENIS
94 VAL-DE-MARNE
95 VAL D'OISE

they can, but who seem to have an unerring sense of flavor and of culinary harmony, and who ultimately inspire formal cuisine much more than they are influenced by it.

From the first issue of our magazine, SAVEUR—whose name is French for "flavor" or "savor"—in the summer of 1994, we've made the food and wine of France a specialty. We've introduced readers to the gloriously simple cooking of "hidden" Provence; revealed the culinary secrets of modest bistros in Lyon and three-star restaurants in Paris; celebrated the wonderful food of Nice, Alsace, Burgundy, Brittany, and more. We've gone to the source to learn the truth about black truffles, foie gras, dijon mustard, and walnut oil. And we've deconstructed and then reproduced such definitive French dishes as bouillabaisse, boeuf à la bourguignonne, ratatouille, cassoulet, and soufflé au chocolat (all of which appear in this book), among many others. Along the way, as we tested recipes for this book—as aromas from simmering pots filled our offices and samples of French cooking made grown editors swoon—we became ever more enamored of this exquisite cuisine, and ever more convinced of its continuing importance, its eternal viability. There's a lot of talk these days about getting back to the culinary basics. These, in the Western world at least, are indisputably, and authentically, French. —COLMAN ANDREWS, *Editor*, SAVEUR

Gastronomy and Gourmandise

The staff of Mère Poulard, the famous omelette restaurant in Mont-St-Michel, in northwestern France, top. Above, an undated lithograph captures the moment of the toast at a formal dinner party. Facing page, Julia Child, who introduced so many Americans to real French food, on a visit to a Parisian kitchen in 1967.

Our France

THERE ARE good things to eat in every part of France, but we find ourselves returning time and again to the food of certain regions—Burgundy, Alsace, the Southwest, Provence, and few others—and in so doing, we find ourselves drawing our own map of France, defined by flavor and aroma more than geography. These are its essential compass points.

HORS D'OEUVRES

"Curving sinuously around the Baie des

Anges, about 20 miles west of the Italian

border, the ancient city of Nice, capital of

the Côte d'Azur, has a palpable Italianate flavor—especially in the city's southeastern quarter, between the Vieux Port and the Promenade des Anglais. Here, the architecture is baroque, the language (Nissart, a dialect of Provençal) has a peninsular accent, and family names tend to end in vowels. Indeed, the old quarter, Vieux Nice, resembles an Italian hill town more than a French village. Streets are overhung with narrow balconies, open shutters, flower boxes, laundry fluttering in the breeze; building colors are earthy but memorable—clay yellow, desert beige, the pink of a Mediterranean dawn; little shops sell cheese, pasta, coffee, bread, wine. Along one flank of Vieux Nice runs the Cours Saleya—a handsome tile-paved promenade lined with cafés, restaurants, and shops—and here, six mornings a week, one of the most famous flower and produce markets in France sets up. The particulars change with the seasons, of course, but the display is fragrant and colorful and evocative of the bounty of the Mediterranean and beyond. Wild mushrooms leach their damp perfume into the air in autumn; the first precocious fava beans and baby purple artichokes shine luminously in early spring; and all year long there are heaps of pungent olives, mounds of fresh-ground spices, rows of farm-made oils and cheeses, a panoply of breads. And always there is market fare: the famous chickpea flour crêpes called socca and the onion-topped tart known as pissaladière (see page 26)—which I've always thought of as the market itself arranged on a crust." —COLMAN ANDREWS

RECIPES

Anchovies and Onions

Because pissaladière is sometimes described as the Niçois pizza, it is tempting to think that the names of the two dishes are related. Not so. The term *pizza* is apparently Germanic in origin and has something to do with a word for piece or bit; *pissaladière*, on the other hand, derives from the Nissart words *pèi salat*, salted fish—and is named for the pissala, or fermented anchovy sauce, with which it was traditionally anointed. This ancient product, a relative of the garum of the Romans, is rarely found today, and a good-quality anchovy paste (like the superlative one from Jean-Gui, below) is a fine substitute. Anchovies aside, it is onions that define pissaladière, with the help of olives. The Niçois poet Victor Rocca, in fact, hailed pissaladière, in 1930, as "a sweet and proud synthesis / Which joins, beneath a triumphantly dry sky, / The white onion of the Berber and the olive of the Greek."

Pissaladière

(Niçois Onion Tart)

SERVES 6

THE TRADITIONAL formula for this classic Niçois specialty, most often eaten as street (and market) fare, calls for the layer of onions to be fully half as thick as the crust.

FOR DOUGH:
1 7-gram packet active dry yeast
Extra-virgin olive oil
3 cups flour
1 tbsp. salt
Cornmeal

FOR TOPPING:
¼ cup extra-virgin olive oil
2 ½–3 lbs. yellow onions, peeled and very thinly sliced
Salt and freshly ground black pepper
Bouquet garni (see sidebar, page 59) with 2 sprigs marjoram and 1 sprig rosemary added
Anchovy paste
⅓ cup niçoise olives
12 anchovy filets (optional)

1. For dough, dissolve yeast in 1 cup warm water in a small bowl, let stand for 5 minutes, then add ¼ cup oil. Combine flour and salt in a medium bowl, add yeast mixture, and stir with a wooden spoon, adding a bit more water if necessary, until ingredients are well mixed. Turn out dough on a lightly floured surface, dust hands with flour, and knead until dough is smooth, firm, and elastic, about 3 minutes. Form dough into a ball, then place in a lightly oiled medium bowl and cover with a damp cloth. Allow dough to rise in a warm spot for about 1 hour.

2. For topping, heat oil in a large pan over medium-low heat. Add onions and season generously with salt and pepper. Add bouquet garni and cover pan to let onions slowly simmer for 45 minutes, stirring occasionally. Uncover and continue cooking until the moisture has evaporated and the onions have cooked down to a very tender marmalade-like consistency, 30–40 minutes. Remove and discard bouquet garni, then set onions aside.

3. Place a pizza stone in oven and preheat to 450°. Roll dough out on a floured surface into a thin, flat rectangle. Transfer dough to a baker's peel, a cookie sheet or inverted baking sheet, dusted with cornmeal. Cover dough with a damp cloth and allow to rest for 30 minutes.

4. Remove cloth from dough and spread a thin layer of anchovy paste over top. Spread onion mixture evenly over anchovy paste. Arrange olives and anchovy filets (if using) over the onions, season lightly with pepper, then slide pissaladière onto hot pizza stone. Bake until crust has browned, 15–20 minutes. Serve warm or at room temperature, cut into squares.

Crudités

(Raw Vegetable Salads)

SERVES 6

AN ASSORTMENT of raw vegetables tossed in simple dressing—usually vinaigrette—is a staple of the old-style French bistro menu. Celery root and carrots are de rigueur.

CAROTTES RAPÉES
5–6 young carrots, peeled and julienned
2–3 tbsp. fresh lemon juice
Salt and freshly ground black pepper
2 tbsp. minced fresh parsley

CÉLERI RÉMOULADE
1 tbsp. dijon mustard
2 tbsp. fresh lemon juice
2 tbsp. peanut oil
Salt and freshly ground black pepper
1 bulb celery root, peeled and julienned

SALADE DE TOMATES
2 tsp. dijon mustard
2 tbsp. red wine vinegar
4 tbsp. peanut oil
Salt and freshly ground black pepper
6 small ripe tomatoes, sliced
1 clove garlic, peeled and minced
1 small red onion, peeled and finely chopped

SALADE DE CONCOMBRES
2 tsp. dijon mustard
2 tbsp. red wine vinegar
4 tbsp. peanut oil
Salt and freshly ground black pepper
2 cucumbers, peeled and thinly sliced

CAROTTES RAPÉES (Grated Carrot Salad): Put carrots and lemon juice in a small bowl and toss to mix well. Season to taste with salt and pepper. Arrange on a platter or divide evenly between 6 small plates, and garnish with parsley.

CÉLERI RÉMOULADE (Celery Root in Mustard Dressing): Whisk together mustard and lemon juice in a large mixing bowl. Drizzle in oil, continuing to whisk until dressing is smooth and emulsified. Season to taste with salt and pepper. Add celery root, toss to mix well, and adjust seasoning. Arrange on a platter or divide evenly between 6 small plates.

SALADE DE TOMATES (Tomato Salad): Whisk together mustard and vinegar in a small mixing bowl. Drizzle in oil, continuing to whisk until dressing is smooth and emulsified. Season to taste with salt and pepper. Fan out tomato slices on a platter or divide evenly between 6 small plates. Drizzle with vinaigrette, then scatter garlic and onion over tomatoes and season to taste with salt and pepper.

SALADE DE CONCOMBRES (Cucumber Salad): Whisk together mustard and vinegar in a small mixing bowl. Drizzle in oil, continuing to whisk until dressing is smooth and emulsified. Season to taste with salt and pepper. Arrange cucumbers on a platter or divide evenly between 6 small plates. Drizzle with vinaigrette and season to taste with salt and pepper.

A Grand-Mère's Trick

B ière d'Avallon, the beer of Avallon, was first made in the town of the same name, in northwestern Burgundy, in 1780. It was still being produced, and appreciated, in the early years of this century—until, in fact, World War II. "When the Germans came through," recalls Marcelle Gueneau (above), who then owned the brewery with her husband, Fernand, "they took all the copper. You can't make beer without copper, so after the war, we made lemonade instead." Today, she is retired and her husband is deceased—but she still cooks good old-fashioned meals in her roadside house, next door to where the brewery used to be. When she invited us to lunch not long ago, for instance, she offered us little pastries filled with cheese and blood sausage, hearts of palm in a luxuriant vinaigrette, and a definitive coq au vin. "I stir a little potato starch into my vinaigrette so that it doesn't separate," she told us proudly. "That's not a chef's trick. It's a grandmother's trick!"

Island Cooking

The Île de Porquerolles is a tiny, verdant piece of land just off the Provençal coast near Hyères, about a dozen miles east of Toulon and 50 southeast of Marseille. The island is an unexpected Eden of dirt roads and rock beaches, thick with stands of Aleppo pines, eucalyptus, live oak, plane trees, and palms, accented everywhere by purple pelargoniums, fuchsia-hued bougainvillea, fragrant bushes of mock orange. There are even vineyards (below). On one end of the island is Le Mas du Langoustier, a low-key but polished hotel-restaurant owned by Marie Caroline Le Ber and her husband,

Georges Richard, and put on the culinary map by the talent of their young chef, Joël Guillet (facing page, upper right). Guillet draws enthusiastically from the vocabulary of Provençal cooking— using garlic, olive oil, basil, rosemary, sage, licorice, saffron, tomatoes, eggplant, artichokes, fennel, and olives with calculated abandon. He also fills his menu with adaptations of such regional specialties as escabèche, panisses, mesclun, soupe de poisson, and tapenade. He surrounds classic brandade (see page 163) with sweet tiny clams in their own juices; he mixes flavors and textures with high-wire bravura by combining tender island octopus with puréed artichoke hearts, raw baby spinach leaves, and deep-fried periwinkles; he redefines steak au poivre by skewering pieces of filet on rosemary branches, grilling them, then serving them in black pepper sauce with crushed (not silkily puréed) potatoes. And his gâteau d'ail confit, which uses one of the world's most vivid flavors not for shock value but as an accent and an illumination, is as good a definition as any we can think of for contemporary Provençal cuisine.

Gâteau d'Ail Confit
(Garlic Custard with Chanterelles and Parsley Sauce)

SERVES 4

NO FLAVOR is more definitive of Provence than that of garlic, and chef Joël Guillet of Le Mas du Langoustier uses it freely. This recipe is for serious garlic lovers only.

4 large heads garlic
6 tbsp. olive oil
1 tsp. sugar
Salt and freshly ground
    black pepper
¾ cup half-and-half
⅓ cup heavy cream
2 eggs, lightly beaten
2 plum tomatoes, peeled,
    seeded, and coarsely
    chopped
4 cups coarsely chopped
    fresh parsley leaves and
    stems, plus additional
    sprigs for garnish
1 tbsp. butter
½ lb. chanterelles or other
    wild mushrooms,
    trimmed and sliced

1. Preheat oven to 350°. Halve 3 heads garlic crosswise, place on a large sheet of aluminum foil, drizzle with 1 tbsp. of the oil, sprinkle with sugar, season to taste with salt and pepper, and tightly wrap garlic in foil. Bake until soft, about 1½ hours. Remove from oven, unwrap, allow to cool, then squeeze garlic pulp from cloves into a small bowl; discard peels.

2. Separate remaining head of garlic into cloves, and peel and slice each clove lengthwise as thinly as possible. Heat 2 tbsp. of the oil in a small nonstick skillet over medium-low heat. Add garlic slices and cook, stirring, until soft, about 5 minutes. Drain on paper towels.

3. Reduce oven to 300°. Combine roasted garlic pulp, half-and-half, cream, and eggs in a food processor and purée until smooth. Lightly brush 4 ramekins, 3" wide and about 1½" high, with 1 tbsp. of the oil, then line the bottom of each with garlic slices. Spoon about 2 tbsp. garlic custard into each ramekin, evenly divide tomatoes between ramekins, then cover with about 3 more tbsp. custard.

4. Transfer ramekins to a roasting pan, place pan in oven, then add enough water to come 1" up the side of the pan. Bake custards until set, about 30 minutes, remove from pan, and allow to cool for about 20 minutes.

5. Meanwhile, blanch chopped parsley in a large pot of boiling salted water until bright green, 20–30 seconds. Drain, and transfer to a food processor. Add ¼ cup water and purée until smooth. Transfer pulp to the center of a clean thin kitchen towel and squeeze out juice into a small saucepan. Discard parsley. Warm over low heat, then whisk in butter.

6. Heat remaining 2 tbsp. oil in a medium skillet over medium-high heat. Add mushrooms and cook, stirring, until tender, 2–5 minutes. Adjust seasoning to taste with salt and pepper. To serve, turn each custard out onto a medium plate and garnish with parsley sauce, mushrooms, and parsley sprigs.

Terrine de Canard

(Duck Terrine)

SERVES 10–12

THIS LUXURIOUS terrine was inspired by a recipe from cookbook author Richard Olney, an American living in France, who regularly inspires the creation of good food.

2 1½-lb. muscovy ducks
Salt and freshly ground
   black pepper
¼ tsp. saltpeter (optional;
   see sidebar, page 38)
1 tbsp. olive oil
¼ cup cognac
4 sprigs fresh thyme
4 sprigs fresh parsley
1 medium yellow onion,
   peeled and halved
1 carrot, peeled and
   halved
1 clove garlic, peeled and
   minced
½ cup fresh bread crumbs
1 lb. fatback (ask butcher
   to slice into thin sheets
   to line a terrine)
¼ lb. ground veal
¼ lb. ground pork
1 egg
¼ tsp. ground nutmeg
1 tsp. juniper berries,
   coarsley ground
¾ cup shelled pistachios
¼ lb. foie gras, cut into
   3" pieces

1. Rinse ducks and pat dry. Remove skin, then remove meat, setting leg meat and bones aside. Cut breast meat into ½" strips, season to taste with salt and pepper, and sprinkle with saltpeter (if using). Put in a bowl with oil, cognac, and 2 sprigs each of thyme and parsley. Cover and marinate in refrigerator for 2 hours.

2. Put duck bones, onions, carrots, remaining 2 sprigs each of thyme and parsley, ½ tsp. salt, and 4 cups water in a saucepan. Bring to boil over high heat, then reduce heat to medium and simmer until broth is reduced to ½ cup, about 1¼ hours. Strain.

3. Preheat oven to 350°. Mix broth, garlic, and bread crumbs in a small bowl to make a paste. Finely chop reserved leg meat and place in a medium bowl. Chop enough fatback to make ⅓ cup, then add to leg meat with bread paste, veal, pork, egg, nutmeg, juniper berries, pistachios, and 1 tbsp. salt. Mix well with a wooden spoon.

4. Cut 1 sheet of fatback into 3 pieces, then use each to individually wrap foie gras pieces. Line a 1½-quart terrine with remaining fatback, allowing a 2" overhang. Spoon half the meat mixture into terrine. Lay half the strips of marinated breast meat (lengthwise) on top, then place wrapped foie gras down the center. Top with remaining breast meat, then with remaining meat mixture. Fold over fatback to enclose. Cover, place in a pan, and add enough hot water to come halfway up the side. Cook in oven until juices run clear, about 1¼ hours. Cool, then pour off juices.

5. Cut a piece of cardboard to fit into terrine. Wrap cardboard in aluminum foil, place in terrine, and weigh down with a few cans. Refrigerate for at least 2 hours. Remove cardboard lid, run a thin knife under warm water, slide around edge of terrine, and invert onto a platter. Serve chilled. The terrine may be stored in the refrigerator for up to 1 week.

Ducks Deluxe

F oie gras, confit de canard, free-range organic chickens and turkeys, capons and poussins, wild and farmed game birds and venison, buffalo, rabbit, nitrite-free bacon, demi-glace, and at least four kinds of ducks, just for starters. At SAVEUR, we'd be lost without D'Artagnan—our favorite one-stop source for countless culinary riches, most of them with a southwestern French accent. D'Artagnan, named for the celebrated fictional Gascon musketeer, was founded in 1985 by George Faison, a Texan with an MBA from Columbia University, and Ariane Daguin (the two are below), daughter of André Daguin, one of the preeminent chefs of southwestern France. Today, the company is the largest wholesaler of fresh foie gras and game meats in the country, and about the only place to get scores of other products on a consistent, dependable basis. We find ourselves calling 800/DARTAGN (or signing on to www.dartagnan.com) about as often as we phone home.

La Nouvelle Escoffier

F abienne Parra was born in Australia to French parents, and brought up outside Lyon. Her father is a chef/restaurateur, and she apprenticed in his kitchens. He still runs a restaurant, called Hermitage Corton, in the Burgundian wine capital of Beaune (home of the world-famous annual wine auction at the Hospices de Beaune, facing page)—and it was while working for her father as sommelier that she met and fell in love with another apprentice, Pierre Escoffier. The two were married in 1983, opened a wine shop in Beaune called Cave Ste-Hélène in 1989, and in 1996 turned the space next to the shop into a highly personal, absolutely wonderful little restaurant called Ma Cuisine. Fabienne wants her cooking to be simple and true, she says, and to have "heart"—and to make the wines she and Pierre have chosen shine. She succeeds on all counts.

Terrine de Foies de Volaille

(Chicken Liver Terrine)

SERVES 10–12

THE TINY Ma Cuisine in Beaune, a great favorite among local vintners, is literally a two-person show: Pierre Escoffier serves as maître d'hôtel, waiter, busboy, and sommelier; his wife is the entire kitchen staff—which is why she likes to serve dishes that can be made up in advance, like this one.

1 tbsp. butter
1 medium yellow onion,
   peeled and minced
12 oz. chicken livers
   (about 8)
1½ lbs. ground lean pork
2 cloves garlic, peeled
   and minced
1 tsp. minced fresh thyme
¼ tsp. ground cloves
¼ tsp. ground nutmeg
¼ cup cognac
2 eggs, lightly beaten
Salt and freshly ground
   black pepper
¼ tsp. saltpeter (optional;
   see sidebar, page 38)
1 lb. fatback (ask butcher
   to slice into thin sheets
   for a terrine)
2 bay leaves

1. Melt butter in a skillet over medium heat, and sauté onions until soft, about 15 minutes. Meanwhile, coarsely chop about ⅓ of the chicken livers, then combine with whole livers, pork, garlic, thyme, cloves, nutmeg, cognac, and eggs in a large mixing bowl. Add sautéed onions and use your hands to mix well, taking care to leave livers whole. Season to taste with salt and pepper. Sprinkle with saltpeter (if using), mix well, cover and refrigerate for about 2 hours.

2. Preheat oven to 325°. Line a 1½-quart terrine with sheets of fatback. Fill with pâté mixture, packing mixture well to release any air pockets. Place bay leaves on top, then cover with a single layer of fatback. Cover terrine with lid or several layers of foil and put it in a large baking pan filled with enough boiling water to come halfway up the sides of the terrine. Bake to an internal temperature of 180°, about 1½ hours.

3. Allow to cool, then cut a piece of cardboard to fit into terrine. Wrap cardboard in aluminum foil, place in terrine, and weigh down with a few cans. Refrigerate for at least 24 hours before serving, then remove cardboard lid, run a thin knife under warm water, slide around edge of terrine, and invert onto a platter. Serve chilled. The terrine may be stored in the refrigerator for up to 1 week.

Gâteau de Foies Blonds de Volaille

(*Chicken Liver Mousse*)

SERVES 4

AT THE POPULAR Café des Fédérations in Lyon (below), this mousse is served with a hearty tomato sauce. We like their recipe, but prefer a more traditional crayfish sauce.

10 oz. chicken livers
   (about 6)
2 tbsp. flour
2 whole eggs
2 egg yolks
½ cup milk
½ cup cream
Pinch ground nutmeg
Salt and freshly ground
   black pepper
1 tbsp. butter
4 sprigs fresh flat-leaf
   parsley
1 cup crayfish sauce
   (see page 190)

1. Preheat oven to 325°. Combine chicken livers, flour, whole eggs, egg yolks, milk, cream, and a pinch nutmeg in a food processor. Season to taste with salt and freshly ground black pepper and purée.

2. Divide liver mixture between 4 buttered 3" ramekins. Place ramekins in a baking pan, place pan in oven, then add enough hot water to come three-quarters of the way up sides of ramekins. Bake until mixture is firm, 25 minutes. Loosen sides with a paring knife, unmold, garnish with parsley, and serve with warm crayfish sauce.

Pâté? Cake?

The French love to eat rich appetizers of ground, shredded, or puréed meat, fish, or fowl, and they distinguish between several varieties: **MOUSSE** Light, soft preparations, sweet or savory, in which ingredients are blended and then folded together; mousses are often set in a mold (in this form they are also sometimes called gâteaux, literally cakes). **PÂTÉ** According to *Larousse Gastronomique*, the word meant a filled pastry shell baked in the oven and served hot—a kind of pie. In today's usage, *pâté* more commonly means a terrine (see below)—though pâté en croûte (see page 38) conforms to the original definition. **RILLETTES** Pork, rabbit, goose, poultry, or oily fish cooked in lard or its own fat with herbs, then pounded to a coarse paste in a mortar, potted, and served as a cold hors d'oeuvre. **TERRINE** Technically, any food cooked or served in a terrine dish (see page 256). Terrines are commonly of meat, but can also be made with fish, seafood, or vegetables. Meat terrines are usually served cold or at room temperature; their ingredients may be marinated in alcohol, and terrines are typically lined with caul fat or other pork fat, and covered with a layer of fat or gelée.

Pink Salt

B esides the obvious ingredients—pork, salt, spices—most French charcuterie contains a substance not exactly common in the average American home kitchen: potassium nitrate, or saltpeter. A trace mineral that used to be present in all salt (but is now usually refined out), saltpeter helps inhibit spoilage and lends an attractive pinkish-red color to meat even after it has been cooked. Already used to cure sausages as long ago as the 16th century, saltpeter—available in drugstores—is still employed by many charcutiers today. Some chefs, however, prefer a derivative called sel rose, or pink salt—a blend of saltpeter, salt, cochineal (a natural red dye) and other natural colorings, and various spices. Home cooks, who are less likely to mind if their terrines or sausages turn grayish during cooking, don't need either one—but those who wish to try it the professional way should follow this rule of thumb: When mixing the ingredients for a 1½-quart terrine, add about a ½ teaspoon of saltpeter to every 5 lbs. of meat in addition to the salt called for in the recipe. If you find sel rose, usually only available from restaurant-supply firms, follow the manufacturer's directions.

Pâté en Croûte
(Pâté in a Pastry Crust)

A SPECIALTY of the region of Berry in central France (lower left), this complexly flavored pâté is one of the glories of traditional French cooking. Serve the pâté either warm or cold, accompanied by a green salad. And unless you're a professional, don't make your own puff pastry; Dufour and other store-bought brands are excellent.

8 oz. smoked bacon
1 12-oz. duck breast, skin removed
2 6-oz. chicken breasts, skin removed
3 tbsp. olive oil
1 cup sancerre or other dry white wine
¼ tsp. saltpeter (optional; see sidebar, left)
1 tsp. crushed coriander seeds
½ tsp. ground nutmeg
2 tsp. fresh thyme leaves
¼ cup chopped fresh chervil
¼ cup chopped fresh chives
3 eggs
2 tbsp. crème fraîche
Salt and freshly ground black pepper
½ cup flour
1 lb. frozen puff pastry, defrosted but cold
3 hard-cooked eggs, peeled

1. Cut bacon, duck breast, and chicken into medium pieces. Put in a medium bowl, add olive oil, wine, and saltpeter (if using), mixing to coat pieces well. Cover and marinate for 1 hour in the refrigerator.

2. Preheat oven to 400°. Drain meat, discarding marinade. Put meat, coriander, nutmeg, herbs, 2 of the eggs, crème fraîche, and salt and pepper to taste in a food processor fitted with a metal blade. Pulse until finely chopped.

3. On a floured work surface, unfold cold puff pastry and cut into two rectangles. Roll both sheets of pastry into 8" x 11" shapes. Place one pastry rectangle on a nonstick baking sheet. Divide meat mixture in half and spread half down the center of pastry. Put hard-cooked eggs in a line down middle of meat. Pat remaining meat over eggs. Pull up the pastry on the sides, then completely cover with second rectangle of pastry. Cut off and reserve excess pastry, wet edges with water, and press together. Cut a small hole in center of pâté and place a small piece of rolled parchment in it to allow steam to escape during baking. Beat remaining egg with a little water and brush egg wash over pâté. Cut decorative shapes out of excess pastry and press onto pâté. Brush again with egg wash.

4. Bake for 20 minutes, then lower heat to 350° and bake for another 20 minutes. The pâté should rest for 30 minutes before serving so that it is firm enough to slice.

Ham in France

The French do love their ham. Annual per capita consumption of cooked ham (jambon cuit, also known as jambon blanc, or white ham) in France is over ten pounds. Some of it is eaten in dishes like the jambon persillé at right—but much more is consumed in the form of "jambon beurre" (ham and butter) sandwiches on split baguettes. The best-known French cooked ham is jambon de Paris, easily identified by its oblong shape. France also produces jambon sec, or cured ham, rubbed with salt and aged in the manner of Italy's prosciutto crudo or Spain's jamón serrano. Excellent jambon sec is made in the Savoie, the Vendée, the Massif Central, and the Ardennes, but most connoisseurs consider that of Bayonne, in the French Basque country, to be the best.

Jambon Persillé Maison

(Parsleyed Ham in Aspic)

SERVES 20

WE HAVE ALWAYS loved this Burgundian specialty and have eaten it all over France—but we have never found a better version than this one, made by Fabienne Escoffier at Ma Cuisine, her little jewel of a restaurant in Beaune.

---

1 6–7 lb. cured ham, bone in
2 2½–3 lb. calfs' feet, split
3 carrots, trimmed
1 large yellow onion, peeled
1 clove
1 leek, trimmed and washed
Bouquet garni (see sidebar, page 59)
1 bottle dry white wine
Salt and freshly ground black pepper
4 egg whites
2 cloves garlic, peeled and minced
2 shallots, peeled and minced
2 cups minced fresh parsley
¼ cup red wine vinegar
2 tbsp. vegetable oil

1. Put ham, calfs' feet, carrots, onion studded with the clove, leek, bouquet garni, and white wine in a stockpot, add water to cover, and bring to a simmer over high heat. Reduce heat to low, cover, and simmer until ham is fork tender, about 5 hours.

2. Remove ham and allow to cool. Strain stock through a cheesecloth-lined sieve, discarding all solids, then return to pot. Bring stock to a gentle boil over medium-high heat and cook until reduced to about 8 cups. Skim fat and season to taste with salt and pepper.

3. Beat 4 egg whites with a whisk in a clean metal bowl until they form stiff peaks. Spread egg whites onto surface of stock and simmer for 15 minutes, until solids get caught in the egg-white "raft" that forms and stock is clarified. Strain stock, pouring carefully to avoid disturbing raft, then discard raft.

4. Shred ham into long pieces, then coarsely chop. Combine ham, garlic, shallots, parsley, and vinegar in a bowl and use your hands to mix well. Season to taste with salt and pepper.

5. Pour about ½ cup stock into each of 2 oiled 1½-quart terrines, then divide and layer about ⅓ of the ham mixture into the terrines, pressing the mixture down to compact it. Pour about ¾ cup of stock over each layer of ham mixture. Repeat process twice more, ending with stock. Refrigerate for 24 hours. Unmold terrines and serve with cornichons and dijon mustard on the side, if you like.

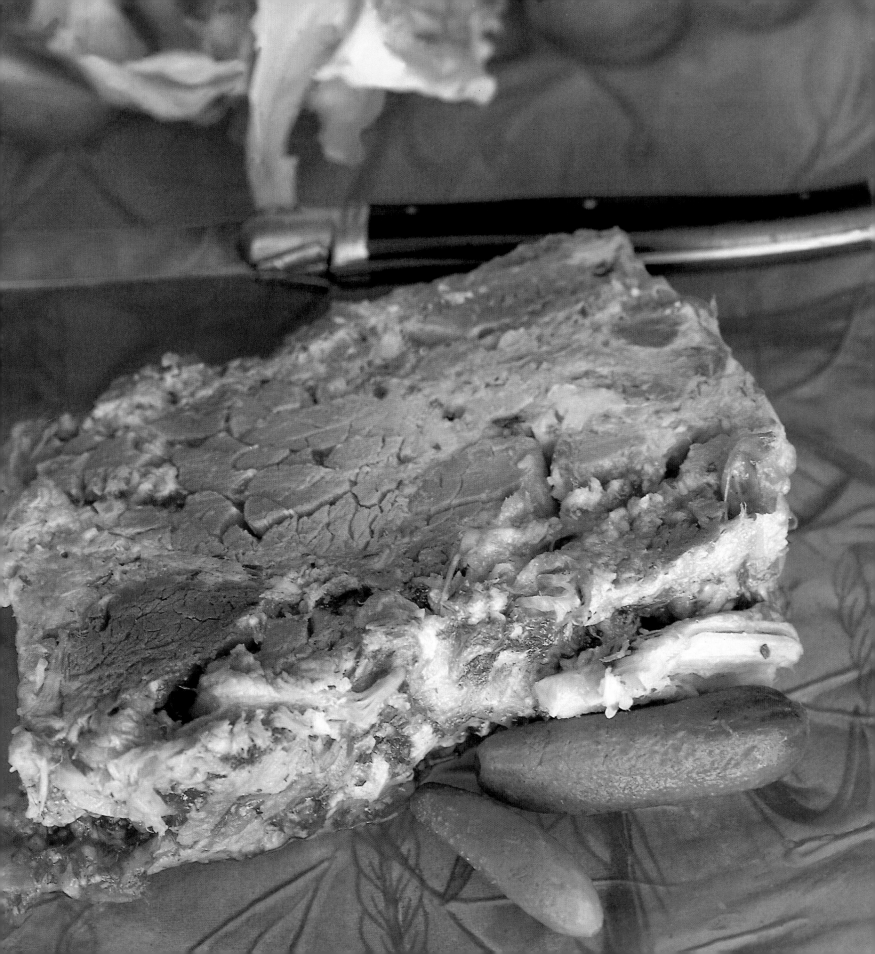

Pétoncles Farcis à la Provençale
(Stuffed Scallops Provençal-Style)

SERVES 6

WHEN HE MAKES this simple appetizer at his restaurant in Vence, Jacques Maximin (right) uses the small Mediterranean scallops known as pétoncles provençals and serves them in their own shells. It can also be made with shelled bay scallops and presented in separately purchased shells.

Home Cooking

Jacques Maximin is one of the most celebrated and notorious chefs in France—celebrated for his prodigious talents, notorious for his moods. Born in rainy northern France, he came of age professionally in the sunny south. As chef at Chantecler in Nice's Hôtel Negresco, and then in his own grand place, set in a 39,000-square-foot former theater in the center of Nice (where he installed the kitchen on the stage, behind a red velvet curtain that rose solemnly after dinner), he gained critical acclaim for his inventive, pure-flavored cooking. Alas, the theater closed—but in 1996, he opened a more modest restaurant, on the ground floor of his house in Vence, about a dozen miles from Nice. Sampling dishes here like a salad of crisp haricots verts tossed in a tomato-spiked cream dressing with fresh hazelnuts (see page 111), white beans with miniature squid in ink sauce, tiny scallops stuffed with dried mushrooms (above), and broiled baby pigeon with lentils—all simple, confident, and very good— it was clear to us that Maximin is at home in more ways than one.

2 oz. dried porcini mushrooms
8 tbsp. butter, slightly softened
2 shallots, peeled and minced
3 cloves garlic, peeled and minced
2 tbsp. cognac
¼ cup finely chopped fresh parsley
Salt and freshly ground black pepper
30 fresh bay scallops, in shell (or 30 shelled bay scallops and 30 scallop half-shells); ask your fishmonger
2 tbsp. freshly grated parmigiano-reggiano

1. Rinse mushrooms, then put in a medium bowl. Add very hot water to cover, top with a plate, and set aside to soften for about 20 minutes. Drain, rinse, then finely chop mushrooms.

2. Heat 2 tbsp. butter in a medium skillet over medium heat. Add shallots, garlic, and mushrooms and cook, stirring, until shallots are soft, about 5 minutes. Add cognac and simmer until almost completely evaporated, about 30 seconds. Remove from heat and set aside.

3. Place remaining 6 tbps. butter in a medium bowl. Add mushroom mixture and parsley. Season to taste with salt and pepper and mix thoroughly.

4. Preheat broiler. Gently pry open scallops by running a paring knife through scallop muscle to separate it from shell. Remove and discard dark stomach. Using your fingers, pull away and discard small muscle, which wraps partially around scallop. Set scallops aside. Thoroughly wash and dry half the shells. (Remaining shells can be cleaned and stored for future use.)

5. Place scallop shells in a single layer on a cookie sheet. Put a scallop in each shell and top with about 1 tbsp. of mushroom butter. Sprinkle with parmigiano-reggiano and broil until cheese is golden, 1–2 minutes. Serve warm. (Shells can be washed and reused.)

Huîtres Glacées en Sabayon

(Oysters in Champagne Sauce)

SERVES 4–6

RAW OYSTERS on the half shell are a tradition in France, of course, but the classical French repertoire includes cooked oyster dishes, too, like this one from À Sousceyrac in Paris.

¾ lb. fresh spinach, trimmed and washed
Salt
24 large oysters (about 3" in length) such as bluepoint
Rock salt
¾ cup French champagne
¾ cup fish stock (see page 62)
¾ cup heavy cream
3 egg yolks
Freshly ground white pepper

1. Plunge spinach in a pot of boiling salted water for about 30 seconds. Drain, squeeze dry, and set aside.

2. Shuck oysters, reserving liquor and half the shells and discarding the rest. Put oysters in a medium saucepan with oyster liquor, cover, and simmer over medium-low heat until oysters are opaque and slightly firm, 1–3 minutes (**A**). Remove oysters with a slotted spoon. Strain liquor through a fine sieve, return to pan, and set aside. Wash and dry oyster shells. Make a ½" bed of rock salt on 4 or 6 ovenproof plates and divide shells between plates, arranging them in a circle in the salt.

3. Bring champagne to a boil in a small saucepan over medium-high heat. Cook until reduced by half, about 5 minutes, then set aside to cool.

4. Add fish stock to reserved oyster liquor. Bring to a boil over medium-high heat and cook until almost syrupy, 12–15 minutes, then add cream and cook, stirring, until reduced by two-thirds, 10–12 minutes.

5. Transfer reduced champagne to the top of a double boiler over simmering water on medium-low heat. Whisk in egg yolks and cook until thick and shiny, about 5 minutes. Remove from heat and slowly whisk in fish stock mixture. Season to taste with salt and pepper.

6. Preheat broiler. Spread a thin layer of spinach in each shell and top with 1 oyster (**B**). Spoon 1–2 tbsp. sauce over each (**C**) and broil for 3–5 minutes. Serve hot.

Oyster Culture

Two species of oyster are grown in France today: huîtres plates, or flat oysters (*Ostrea edulis*) and huîtres creuses, or concave oysters (*Crassostrea gigas*). The belon, named for the Belon River in Brittany (but also grown elsewhere, including Maine and the Pacific Northwest), is the most highly prized of the flats. Raised in a combination of fresh- and saltwater, the belon has what the French describe as "un petit goût de noisette" or slight hazelnut flavor, and an iodine character. The most prominent creuses are fines de claires and spéciales de claires from the Marennes basin in the Charente-Maritime. Another well-regarded creuse is the bouzigue, a Mediterranean oyster from the Thau basin in the Hérault. The French classify oysters according to weight. Flats are numbered from 000 (the largest) down to n°6 (the smallest). Confusingly, fines, spéciales, and all other creuses are rated according to a different system, with n°1 being the largest and n°6 the smallest (n°2 and n°3 are the most common). Very small but meaty oysters are called huîtres papillons, or butterfly oysters.

45

Crêpes de Sarrasin

(Savory Buckwheat Crêpes)

MAKES 8 CRÊPES

BUCKWHEAT, called *sarrasin* or *blé noir* in French, is eaten in parts of France where wheat doesn't grow readily, and is often associated with the cuisine of poverty. In Breton tradition, the first crêpe in every batch, often considered to be substandard, was torn up and tossed into soup.

3 eggs
1 cup white buckwheat
    flour
¼ cup whole buckwheat
    flour
Salt and freshly ground
    black pepper
½ lb. gruyère, freshly
    grated
4 tbsp. butter

1. Whisk eggs and 1½ cups water together in a large mixing bowl. Sift together white buckwheat flour, whole buckwheat flour, salt and pepper to taste, then stir into egg mixture. Cover with plastic wrap and refrigerate overnight.

2. To cook, heat a large nonstick pan over medium-high heat. When pan is very hot, remove from heat and pour ¼ cup batter into the center. Tilt pan to distribute batter and return to heat. Cook crêpe until lightly browned, about 2 minutes, then flip with a spatula and cook for 1 more minute. Transfer to a plate and keep warm in a low oven while making remaining crêpes.

3. Return cooked crêpes to pan one at a time, sprinkle ¼ cup of the cheese in the middle, and fold to make a square. Cook until cheese melts, about 30 seconds. Serve immediately, seam side down, with a pat of butter.

Pancake Ceremony

T he crêpe symbolizes all that is Brittany," says chef Patrick Jeffroy (below), from the Breton town of Plounérin. More basic to the region's gastronomy than bread, crêpes come in two main varieties: sweet ones made with plain wheat flour mixed with eggs and milk and generally folded over a sweet filling of some kind, and salted ones, also called galettes, made with buckwheat flour, eggs, and water, and usually filled with savory ingredients. Crêperïes, which dot almost every street in Brittany, serve extensive all-crêpe menus, offering fillings ranging from a sprinkling of sugar or a bit of jam to layers of ham, vegetables, and cheese. Crêpes are eaten at any time of day, as a snack or as a full meal—and are almost always accompanied by a cup or bowl of locally pressed cold hard cider. "There is a whole ceremony based around making crêpes at home," says Jeffroy. "The entire house smells good and the whole family comes together."

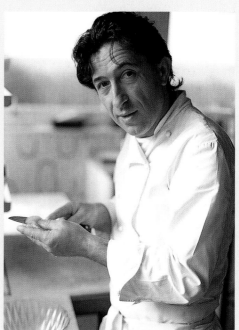

Queen of Crêpes

Millette Coquillon is famous for her coq au vin and her boeuf à la bourguignonne (see page 204), but she is known in the Morvan region— where she has run her La Petite Auberge (Chez Millette) for the last 36 years—most of all as "la reine de la grapiau", the queen of the Burgundian crêpe. Coquillon first worked in restaurants as a waitress, and claims to have learned to cook simply by watching what the chefs were doing. The daughter of Morvandelle *paysans*, she calls her cooking, which is based on fresh produce and on the region's excellent meats and charcuterie, *cuisine familiale*. Most of her clientele during the week, she says, is local—workers, generally. (We also saw a coterie of gendarmes enjoying a long lunch there one day.) On weekends, adds Coquillon, a few tourists are likely to be added to the mix. "But don't say too much about me," she cautions. "There isn't much to say anyway. What I really like is just simplicity."

Grapiaux
(*Burgundian Crêpes*)

MAKES 16 CRÊPES

THIS SAVORY appetizer pancake, which is heartier than its Breton cousins, was once eaten in some form all over Burgundy—but today it is found mostly only in the Morvan (see page 205), a region famous for its pork products, and for its simple cooking. Millette Coquillon of La Petite Auberge in Planchez, considered by local connoisseurs to be the master of the grapiau, shared her recipe with us.

2 cups flour
2½ cups milk
4 eggs
Salt and freshly ground
    black pepper
8 oz. salt pork, diced

1. Sift flour into a mixing bowl, then gradually add milk, whisking constantly until batter is smooth. Add eggs, one at a time, and continue whisking until they are incorporated into the batter. Season to taste with salt and pepper, cover, and set aside for 1 hour.

2. Scatter 5–6 cubes salt pork into an 8" seasoned crêpe pan or nonstick skillet and fry over medium-high heat until just crisp. Pour about ¼ cup batter into the pan and cook until the crêpe is crispy and richly browned on 1 side, about 1 minute. Flip crêpe over and fry for an additional 30 seconds. Repeat process to make 16 crêpes.

SOUPS

"THEY'D CROWD against the zinc bar, their heads bent over steaming bowls of soupe à l'oignon, their mouths connected to it by endless ribbons of golden cheese—

and as the clock struck midnight, they'd turn from soup to champagne, and cries of 'Bonne Année!' would ring out across the room…. Until 1969, when the immense Parisian wholesale market complex called Les Halles began closing, this was the typical New Year's Eve scene at Chez Clovis, one of the many market bistros. 'On New Year's Eve,' recalls Claude Cornut, second-generation proprietor of Chez Clovis (with his wife, Françoise, facing page, lower right), 'everybody had soupe à l'oignon. It was the tradition. People would come by after their parties, and between 2 and 8 in the morning, we'd serve 1,600 bowls of it.' But consumption of this rich onion-filled, cheese-topped broth, at places like Chez Clovis and the celebrated Au Pied de Cochon (whose chef ladles it up still, facing page, top left), was hardly restricted to the year's end.

Every night, Parisian swells on their way home from a night out would join workers from the market for bowls of this restorative tonic. 'Les Halles was a village unto itself in the very heart of Paris,' Cornut continues. 'We were so content and self-sufficient that we would forget that there was a world outside. Imagine the ambience of a place that is alive at least 20 hours of the day! It was extraordinary! There was never a void, never a dull moment. You'd see the pork butcher, spattered with blood, and the scale-covered fishmonger, laughing and drinking, right across from a party of elegant characters just arrived from an evening at the opera. There was this kind of colorful and hearty interaction at all hours of the night, any night of the year, with all the richness of the smells and sounds that accompanied it.'" —MEGAN WETHERALL

RECIPES

Soupe à l'Oignon Gratinée

(French Onion Soup)

SERVES 8

WE DEVELOPED this recipe based on the many early-morning onion soups we've enjoyed at Parisian bistros like Au Pied de Cochon (right) and Chez Clovis (pages 51-52).

6 tbsp. butter
1 tbsp. olive oil
3 lbs. medium yellow
 onions, peeled and
 thinly sliced
1 tsp. sugar
Salt
1 tbsp. flour
8 cups beef stock
 (see page 59)
2 cups dry white wine
Freshly ground black
 pepper
1 baguette
1 lb. gruyère, shredded

1. Melt 3 tbsp. of the butter and the oil in a large heavy pot over medium-low heat. Add onions, cover and cook, stirring occasionally, until soft and translucent, about 20 minutes. Increase heat to medium-high, uncover, and add the sugar and season to taste with salt. Sauté, stirring often until onions are very soft and a deep golden brown.

2. Reduce heat to medium, sprinkle in flour and cook, stirring constantly, for 2–3 minutes. Add about 2 cups of stock and stir to blend, then add remaining 6 cups of stock and the wine. Season to taste with salt and pepper and simmer for about 30 minutes. Adjust seasoning to taste.

3. Preheat oven to 425°. Meanwhile, slice the bread into at least 8 thick slices. Butter both sides of the bread with the remaining 3 tbsp. of butter, then toast until golden brown on both sides in the oven.

4. Place a slice of toast in each of 8 ovenproof bowls, then fill bowls with the onion soup. Spread a thick layer of cheese on top of soup. Set bowls in 2 baking pans, place in the oven and bake until cheese has browned.

A Sensible Soup

An oft-repeated culinary legend notwithstanding, it is extremely unlikely that soupe à l'oignon was invented by Louis XIV (who concocted it, according to one story, with champagne!). Nor did the soup necessarily originate in Lyon, despite the fact that the region is famous for its onions (and that dishes cooked à la lyonnaise inevitably contain them). According to Dr. Paul Henry, a respected Lyonnais historian, the origins of the soup are probably quite pedestrian. Until relatively recently in rural France, soup was a staple of every household, kept simmering on the stove and eaten daily, often for breakfast. It was made of anything that was cheap, or grew plentifully in the garden—and the onion certainly qualified. It also had the virtue of being available most of the year—and was one of the more flavorful of vegetables. "The addition of cheese to the soup and its evolution to a 'gratinée'," adds Henry, "would probably have come from the Savoie, where cheese is often used in cooking."

Stock Options

S tocks are the "fonds de cuisine" in a French kitchen—literally the very foundations of cooking. Butter and cream and wine may be vital to many classical French dishes, but it is stock that gives them texture, richness, and real depth of flavor. Making stock involves the slow cooking of meat, poultry, or fish—including their bones—in water, with vegetables and seasonings added. (Stock can also be made from vegetables alone.) If meat and bones are browned first with the vegetables, the result will be a fond brun, or brown stock—darker in color and even richer in flavor than a fond blanc, or white stock, made without browning. (Below, from left: demi-glace, made by reducing brown veal stock [see sidebar, page 61]; fish stock; chicken stock; brown veal stock.) Making stock is a great activity for a rainy day: It requires virtually no labor, but does benefit from occasional attention (skimming impurities off the surface)—and a simmering stockpot will both warm and perfume your house. There is no point making just a little stock, incidentally. Make plenty, use what you need, and freeze the rest. Every kitchen needs solid foundations.

Fond Blanc de Volaille

(Clear Chicken Stock)

MAKES ABOUT 2 QUARTS

FAR FROM LOSING its flavor, the chicken used to make stock by this method soaks up lots of flavor from the vegetables, and is delicious in salads, soups, and sandwiches.

1 3-lb. chicken
3 leeks, trimmed, washed, and chopped
2 carrots, peeled and chopped
2 stalks celery, chopped
Bouquet garni (see sidebar, page 59)
Black peppercorns
Salt

1. Put chicken, leeks, carrots, celery, bouquet garni, and a few peppercorns in a large heavy stockpot. Add 3 quarts water and 2 tsp. salt, then bring to a boil over high heat.

2. Reduce heat to low and gently simmer stock, partially covered, for 1 hour. (At this point, if you like, you may remove chicken from pot, pick the meat from the bones to reserve for another use, and return carcass to pot.) Uncover, and continue to simmer for another hour, occasionally skimming off any foam that rises to the surface.

3. Pour stock through a strainer lined with cheesecloth, discarding chicken carcass and vegetables. Transfer stock to a bowl, cover with plastic wrap, and refrigerate for at least 4 hours, or overnight. Remove and discard fat that has formed on surface. Stock may be stored in the refrigerator for up to 3 days, or in the freezer for up to 6 months.

Fond Brun de Boeuf

(Brown Beef Stock)

MAKES ABOUT 2 QUARTS

HEARTY beef stock, like this one, is a classic building block for many traditional French dishes. Besides the food-stuffs called for in the recipe below, the most important ingredient here is patience: Long, slow cooking is essential.

6 lbs. beef bones (shin, oxtail, and neck)
2 tbsp. vegetable oil
Salt and freshly ground black pepper
2 tbsp. tomato paste
2 carrots, scrubbed and coarsely chopped
4 stalks celery, coarsely chopped
2 medium yellow onions, halved
2 leeks, trimmed, washed, and coarsely chopped
2 cloves
8 cloves garlic, peeled and lightly crushed
1 cup red wine
Bouquet garni (see sidebar, right)

1. Preheat oven to 375°. Brush beef bones with 1 tbsp. oil, season generously with salt and pepper, put in a large roasting pan, and roast until just browned, about 30 minutes. Smear tomato paste over bones and roast for 20 minutes more. Toss carrots, celery, onions, leeks, cloves, and garlic with remaining oil, and add to pan with bones. Roast for 20 minutes more.

2. Transfer bones and vegetables to a large stockpot. Deglaze roasting pan on stovetop over medium heat with red wine, scraping up browned bits from bottom of pan, then pour juices into stockpot. Add bouquet garni and cover with 5 quarts water. Bring to a boil over high heat, then reduce heat to low and simmer, uncovered, until stock is reduced by two-thirds, about 4 hours, occasionally skimming off any foam that rises to the surface. Strain stock and discard solids. Transfer stock to a bowl, cover with plastic wrap, and refrigerate for at least 4 hours, or overnight. Remove and discard fat that has formed on surface. Stock may be stored in the refrigerator for up to 3 days, or in the freezer for up to 6 months.

Bouquet Garni

For a classic bouquet garni, (above) the basic French bundle of herbs that flavors so many stocks, soups, and sauces, lay 3 sprigs of parsley, 2 sprigs of thyme, 1 bay leaf, and 3–5 pepper-corns in the middle of a 6" square of washed cheesecloth, then gather up the edges and tie into a bundle with kitchen string. Or cut a 4" length of the light green part of a leek, split it in two length-wise, and lay herbs and peppercorns inside one of the leaves, reassemble leek, and tie with kitchen string (see photos, page 57). Some cooks leave a little extra string on both kinds of bouquet garni to tie it to the pot handle, for easy retrieval.

Fond Brun de Veau

(Brown Veal Stock)

MAKES ABOUT 3 QUARTS

THIS INTENSELY flavorful stock is widely used in French cooking, both on its own and in twice-reduced form, as the chefs' "secret ingredient" known as demi-glace.

8 lbs. cracked veal bones
3 carrots, peeled and
  chopped
3 yellow onions, peeled
  and chopped
3 stalks celery, chopped
2 tbsp. tomato paste
2 cups dry white wine
  (optional)
2 plum tomatoes, chopped
2 cloves garlic, peeled
2 bay leaves
10 black peppercorns
3 sprigs fresh parsley

1. Preheat oven to 400°. Put veal bones in a large roasting pan and roast until browned, about 1 hour. Add carrots, onions, celery, and tomato paste, mix well, and continue roasting until vegetables and bones are well browned, 30–40 minutes.

2. Transfer bones and vegetables to a large stockpot. Deglaze roasting pan on stovetop over medium heat with white wine (if using) or 2 cups water, scraping up browned bits from bottom of pan. Simmer for 1 minute, then pour juices into stockpot.

3. Add tomatoes, garlic, bay leaves, peppercorns, parsley, and about 4 quarts water to stockpot. Bring to a boil over high heat, then reduce heat and simmer, uncovered, over medium heat until stock is reduced by about one-quarter, about 2 hours, occasionally skimming off any foam that rises to the surface. Strain stock and discard solids. Transfer stock to a bowl, cover with plastic wrap, and refrigerate for at least 4 hours, or overnight. Remove and discard fat that has formed on surface. Stock can be stored in the refrigerator in a sealed container for up to 3 days or frozen for up to 6 months.

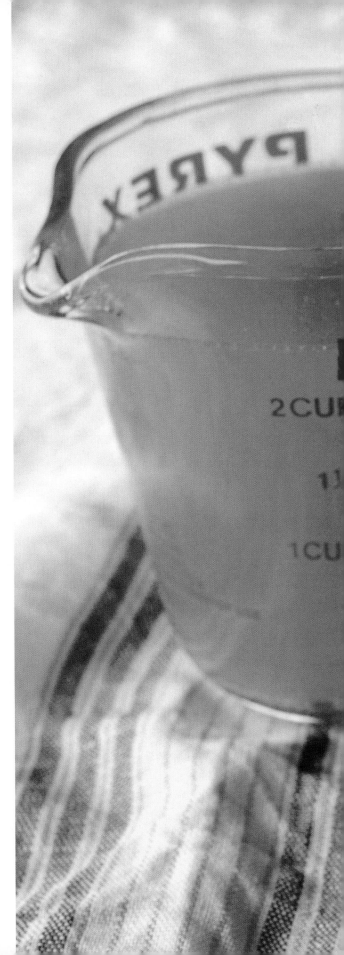

The Soul of Sauces

To make 2 cups of demi-glace, a rich, versatile brown "half-glaze", render fat from ¼ lb. finely chopped bacon in a large heavy pot over medium-low heat, cooking for about 15 minutes. Add 1 chopped, peeled yellow onion and 1 chopped, peeled carrot and cook, stirring occasionally, for 5 minutes. Sprinkle vegetables with ¼ cup flour and continue cooking, stirring occasionally, for 10 minutes. Add 2 tbsp. tomato paste, 10 sprigs fresh parsley, 2 bay leaves, 2 sprigs fresh thyme, and 2 quarts brown veal stock (see recipe, left). Simmer, skimming occasionally, over medium heat until sauce has reduced by three-quarters, about 2 hours. Strain sauce and return to pan. Add 2 more cups brown veal stock and simmer over medium-low heat until sauce has reduced by half, about 2½ hours, then strain. Store in refrigerator in a sealed container for up to 1 week or frozen for up to 6 months.

Fishmongers' Soup

Unsuspecting diners sometimes feel cheated in French restaurants when they order soupe de poisson and get something with no fish in it. That's because soup *with* fish is soupe aux poissons; soupe de poisson is an intense, orange-hued, long-reduced fish-flavored soup, traditionally served with croutons, spicy rouille (see recipe, page 146), and grated gruyère. Jars of this specialty (above) are sold in fish shops and markets all over France, and almost nobody bothers to make it at home. According to Dominique Pillet, a sixth-generation Trouville fishmonger, the soup must be made in large quantities in order to achieve the requisite concentration and intensity of flavor. He adds that in earlier times, fishmongers used to moonlight by cooking seafood specialties in for the Parisian vacationers who rented houses in the area. Soupe de poisson, perceived as a festive dish, ideal for serving at big family gatherings, was particularly popular among the holiday-makers. Not surprisingly, they took a taste for it back to Paris, and it soon became part of the standard French culinary repertoire.

Fumet de Poisson

(Fish Stock)

MAKES ABOUT 2½ QUARTS

IN BUYING fish carcasses for making fumet, avoid salmon and other freshwater varieties, and oily fish like mackerel and tuna. Monkfish and various kinds of rockfish are ideal.

3 tbsp. olive oil
3 small leeks, white part only, trimmed, washed, and diced
1 celery stalk, finely chopped
1 fennel bulb, finely chopped
2 medium carrots, peeled and finely chopped
Zest of ½ orange
3 cloves garlic, peeled
3 tomatoes, coarsely chopped
Bouquet garni (see sidebar, page 59)
6 lbs. fish carcasses (with heads)
1 bottle dry white wine

1. Heat oil in a large stockpot over medium-low heat. Add leeks, celery, fennel, carrots, and orange zest. Cook, stirring occasionally, until vegetables are soft, about 15 minutes. Add garlic, tomatoes, and bouqet garni. Continue to cook for 1–2 minutes.

2. Break fish carcasses into large pieces. Add to vegetables along with the wine and 4 quarts water. Increase heat to medium-high, bring stock to a boil, then reduce heat to medium and simmer, uncovered, for 1 hour, occasionally skimming off any foam that rises to the surface. Allow stock to cool slightly, then strain through a fine sieve, return to pot, and reduce by about half over medium-high heat for about 1 hour. Stock can be stored in the refrigerator in a sealed container for 3 days or frozen for up to 6 months.

Soupe d'Écrevisses

(Crayfish Soup)

SERVES 4–8

CRAYFISH were once so plentiful in Alsace that soups like this one, served by father-and-son chefs Jean and Michel Orth (right) at their L'Écrevisse in Brumath, were common. Today, most "Alsatian" crayfish is imported from the U.S.

3 ¾ lbs. live crayfish, rinsed
2 tbsp. peanut oil
½ cup cognac
2 stalks celery, chopped
1 medium carrot, peeled and chopped
6 cloves garlic, peeled and finely chopped
2 tbsp. tomato paste
7 cups fish stock (see page 62)
5 sprigs fresh thyme
3 bay leaves
1 ½ tsp. arrowroot
1 cup crème fraîche
Salt and freshly ground black pepper
2 tbsp. finely chopped fresh chives

1. Bring a large pot of water to a boil over high heat. Add crayfish, cook for 5 minutes, then drain and run under cold water. Remove meat from tails, reserving shells. Devein crayfish as you would shrimp: run a paring knife along back of tail and lift out and discard intestine. (This is easiest under running water.) Set meat aside.

2. Heat oil in a large pot over medium-high heat. Add shells and cook, stirring, for 3 minutes. Add cognac, then carefully ignite cognac with a long-handled match. (Keep lid handy so flame can be extinguished if necessary.) Allow alcohol to burn off, about 1 minute. When flame has died down, reduce heat to medium and add celery, carrots, and garlic. Cook, stirring often, until vegetables are soft, 10–15 minutes.

3. Reduce heat to medium-low, stir in tomato paste, and cook, stirring constantly, for 2 minutes. Add stock, thyme, bay leaves, and 1 cup water. Simmer for 30 minutes.

4. Strain soup through a fine sieve, discarding shells, herbs, and vegetables. Return soup to pot and simmer over medium heat for 15–20 minutes. Ladle ½ cup of soup into a small bowl, stir in arrowroot, mix until dissolved, then whisk mixture back into soup. Simmer for 1–2 minutes, reduce heat to medium-low, then whisk in crème fraîche. Season with salt and pepper, stir in crayfish meat, and simmer until heated through, about 2 minutes. Serve warm, garnished with chives.

Crayfish Tales

Écrevisses, or crayfish, are freshwater crustaceans of the superfamily Astacoidea, looking a bit like small lobsters and a bit like shrimp. Generally just the tail is eaten (it's the only portion of the creature that has much meat), but the claws and shells ooze wonderful flavor and can be pounded to make bisques or stocks. These are the crustaceans commonly eaten in France:

ÉCREVISSE À PATTES ROUGES: Red-clawed crayfish, large and flavorful. Almost decimated by water pollution and overfishing, they are extremely rare, and usually found today only at France's top restaurants.

ÉCREVISSE À PATTES BLANCHES: White-clawed crayfish, the most common variety in France today, found wild in mountainous areas and also successfully farmed.

LANGOUSTINE: Related to the Dublin Bay prawn and to the scampi of the Adriatic; in effect, a kind of saltwater crayfish.

LANGOUSTE: Spiny or rock lobster, similar to homard (see below), but with very long antennae and no claws. There are many different varities fished in the Atlantic and the Mediterranean (and also the Pacific).

HOMARD: Lobster, the real thing, found in Europe off the coast of Brittany and in the cold waters off Britain and Norway. It is the largest of crustaceans as well as the meatiest (because of its large claws).

Bisque de Homard

(Lobster Bisque)

SERVES 8

A BISQUE IS a rich cream soup. For classic lobster bisque, female lobsters are preferred, because their roe lends flavor and color to the soup. (Ask your fishmonger to select females for you.) This recipe comes from Gabriel Biscay (lower right, foreground), chef at Prunier (see sidebar, page 157), the celebrated Parisian seafood restaurant.

3 1½ lbs. live female
   lobsters
¾ cup peanut oil
6 tbsp. butter
2 carrots, peeled and
   finely diced
4 shallots, peeled and
   finely diced
2 cloves garlic, peeled
   and minced
1 6-oz. can tomato paste
¾ cup dry white wine
2½ quarts fish stock
   (see page 62)
1 small stalk celery,
   chopped
Bouquet garni (see sidebar,
   page 59) with 2 sprigs
   fresh tarragon and 12
   sprigs parsley added
Sea salt
Pinch cayenne
Freshly ground black pepper
4 tbsp. flour
1 tbsp. fresh tarragon,
   chopped, plus 8 sprigs
   reserved for garnish
4 tbsp. cognac
1 cup heavy cream

1. Set lobsters on a cutting board and, using a heavy knife, split lobsters in half through the heads lengthwise, taking care not to split the tail. Use the flat side of the knife to scoop up any juices from the lobster into a small bowl, and set aside. Discard the bitter, sandy interior of the head, but save tomalley and roe and add to bowl with reserved juices. Break or cut lobster into head, claws, and tail.

2. Heat oil in a large heavy pan over high heat. When the oil is hot, put lobster pieces in pan, flesh down, to sear. Use kitchen tongs to turn lobster pieces until shells are thoroughly red and almost blackened (add more oil if necessary), about 10 minutes. Transfer lobster to a large bowl and set aside.

3. Pour off leftover oil and return pan to stove. Melt 2 tbsp. of the butter in the pan over high heat then add carrots, shallots, and garlic and cook until soft and lightly browned. Add tomato paste and cook, stirring constantly, for 1–2 minutes. Add wine and cook for 3 minutes, then stir in fish stock. Return lobster to pan, add celery and bouquet garni, and bring to a boil. Skim off fat and any foam that rises to the surface with a large spoon. Reduce heat to medium-low, add 2 pinches of salt and the cayenne and season to taste with pepper. Gently simmer for 15 minutes, skimming regularly. Remove lobster from pan and set aside. Remove and discard bouquet garni and continue simmering stock for 15 minutes.

4. Meanwhile, melt remaining 4 tbsp. butter in a small saucepan over low heat. Whisk in flour, then add chopped tarragon and reserved tomalley, roe, and lobster juices and whisk until the mixture is smooth. Whisk in 1 tbsp. of the cognac and a little of the stock, then add butter mixture to bisque. Bring to a boil and continue whisking until smooth and thick. Reduce heat to medium, season to taste with salt and pepper, and simmer for another 15 minutes.

5. Remove meat from cooled lobster and discard shells. Cut meat into pieces and set aside, adding any juices to bisque. Pour bisque through a large, fine strainer into a large bowl, pressing solids with the back of a ladle, then return bisque to pan. Whisk in cream, adjust seasonings with salt and pepper, then add remaining 3 tbsps. of cognac.

6. Divide lobster between 8 bowls, then ladle bisque around it and serve garnished with tarragon sprigs.

Crème de la Crème

 lmost any vegetable can be turned into a simple cream soup—turnips, cabbage, cauliflower, potatoes, whatever. To serve 6, peel and trim vegetables as needed to yield 1½–2 lbs. Melt 2 tbsp. butter with 1 tsp. vegetable oil in a large, heavy pot over medium heat. Add 1 chopped onion and cook until soft, about 15 minutes. Cut vegetables into small pieces, add to pot, and cook for 10 minutes. Add 2 quarts chicken stock (see page 56) and season to taste with salt and freshly ground white pepper. Bring to a boil, then reduce heat to low and simmer, uncovered, until vegetables are soft, about 40 minutes. Stir in ½ cup heavy cream and cool slightly. Purée in a blender or food processor, and adjust seasoning. Reheat before serving.

Crème de Potiron
(Cream of Squash Soup)

SERVES 8

"MANY'S the bride who has tried to duplicate her French mother-in-law's famous *potage au potiron*," note Julia Child and Simone Beck in their *Mastering the Art of French Cooking*, vol. 2, "and finds that the secret ingredient…was squash rather than pumpkin." This recipe came to us not from a mother-in-law but from chef Patrick Jeffroy (see page 242).

4 lbs. butternut squash, or princess or cheese pumpkin
½ small cauliflower
2 tbsp. butter
3 medium yellow onions, peeled and diced
6 cups chicken stock (see page 56)
6 tbsp. heavy cream
Salt and freshly ground white pepper
Freshly grated nutmeg
8 fresh chervil sprigs

1. Cut squash in half, remove seeds, and peel. Cut about an eighth of the squash into a fine dice and set aside. Cut remaining squash into pieces about 2" square and set aside.

2. Cut off about half of cauliflower florets, the smallest ones from the crown of the cauliflower, and set aside. Break remaining cauliflower into larger florets and set aside. Blanch diced squash and small cauliflower florets in a large pot of boiling water for 60 seconds then drain, refresh in a bowl of ice water, and set aside.

3. Melt the butter in a large heavy pot over medium heat. Add onions, 2" squares of squash, and large cauliflower florets, cover tightly and cook until slightly soft, about 15 minutes, lifting the lid occasionally to stir. Increase heat to high, add chicken stock, and bring to a simmer, then reduce heat to medium-low and simmer, partially covered, until vegetables are very soft, about 15 minutes more.

4. Transfer vegetables and broth to a blender or food processor and purée. Strain the puréed soup back into pot, set over low heat, stir in cream, and season to taste with salt, pepper, and nutmeg. Divide reserved vegetables between 8 bowls, then ladle hot soup over vegetables and garnish each bowl with a chervil sprig.

Harold l'Américain

The expression 'joie de vivre' was invented for my Dad, Harold Wright [in checked shirt, below and facing page, upper right and lower left],who now lives part of the year in France," writes author Clifford A. Wright. "Curiously and refreshingly, his love of the country has no similarity with any of the affected Francophilia popular among the cosmopolitan cognoscenti in America today. He doesn't care about the art, the literature, the wine; as far as he knows, a Michelin three-star is a kind of tire. But in 1984 he bought an old ramshackle barn in the village of Frayssinet [facing page, upper left] in the southwestern French département of the Lot. Dad is an outgoing and charming man, who kisses the ladies and bounces the children, and is now a fixture in the village—where he is known as Harold l'Américain. Once the mayor came by reminding everyone of a community meal being held in the village meeting hall. Dad remarked, 'But I only live here part of the year.' The mayor replied, 'Yes, but you're a part of our community.' After that, Dad really felt welcome, and his life in the village evolved into the idyllic retirement we all hope for. Dad doesn't cook much, but he eats well, thanks to his neighbors—enjoying such earthy local preparations as a fava bean soup that is memorably cooked in duck fat. 'They like to eat duck and lamb around here,' Dad once informed us, sounding genuinely surprised."

Soupe de Fèves
(Fava Bean Soup)

SERVES 8

ODETTE COCULA sometimes cooks this rustic soup for her neighbor, Harold Wright, a well-liked part-time American resident of the village of Frayssinet in the Lot.

3 tbsp. duck fat
1 medium yellow onion, peeled and finely chopped
3 cloves garlic, peeled
2 leeks, white part only, split lengthwise, washed and sliced
1 tbsp. tomato paste or 1 ripe plum tomato, peeled and finely chopped
2 potatoes, peeled and diced
10 cups chicken stock (see page 56)
3 cups fresh fava beans, shelled, blanched, and peeled, or 3 cups frozen fava beans, blanched and peeled
Salt and freshly ground black pepper
8 slices country bread

1. Melt the duck fat in a large heavy pot over medium-high heat. Add onions, 2 cloves of the garlic, and the leeks and sauté until vegetables are soft, about 15 minutes.

2. Stir in tomato paste and cook for 1–2 minutes. Add potatoes and chicken stock and simmer for 1 hour. Use a potato masher to slightly crush vegetables. Add fava beans and cook for 5 minutes, then season to taste with salt and pepper.

3. Rub bread on both sides with remaining garlic clove, then toast the bread in a preheated broiler. Put a piece of toasted bread in each of 8 soup bowls, then ladle soup and vegetables over bread.

Soupe Corse

(Corsican Soup)

SERVES 8

WHEN THEY MAKE this hearty mountain soup, the Juillard sisters of Murato use the French beans called cocos roses. We found navy beans to be an excellent substitute.

½ lb. dried navy beans
3 tbsp. olive oil
3 large yellow onions, peeled and finely chopped
10 small potatoes, peeled and diced
2 medium leeks, trimmed, washed, and finely chopped
2 medium zucchini, trimmed and diced
½ small green cabbage, cored and finely chopped
½ lb. haricots verts, trimmed and finely chopped
1 medium carrot, peeled and diced
1 medium tomato, peeled, seeded, and chopped
4 sprigs fresh marjoram, chopped
1 ham bone with some meat attached (have butcher cut in half crosswise)
¼ lb. tagliatelle, broken in half
3 cloves garlic, peeled and minced
5 fresh basil leaves, minced
Salt and freshly ground black pepper

1. Put beans in a medium bowl, cover with cold water by 2", and set aside to soak for at least 4 hours or overnight. Drain and set aside.

2. Heat oil in a large stockpot over medium heat. Add onions, potatoes, leeks, zucchini, cabbage, haricots verts, carrots, tomatoes, marjoram, and soaked beans and cook, stirring often, until fresh vegetables are slightly soft, about 10 minutes. Add ham bones and 10 cups cold water, increase heat to medium-high, and bring to a boil. Reduce heat to medium and simmer, stirring often, until vegetables are very soft and soup is thick, about 2 hours.

3. About 20 minutes before soup is finished cooking, add tagliatelle, garlic, and basil and cook, stirring often, until pasta is tender. Remove ham bones and season soup to taste with salt and pepper. Soup will thicken as it sits, and may be thinned with a little water, if you like.

Universal Soup

 rom the village of Murato, high in the hills above the Corsican port city of Bastia," reports writer George Semler, "I could just make out the French mainland to the northwest, hovering cloudlike in the distance. 'You're in luck,' said Henri Thiers. 'You can see the continent from here only two or three days a year.' Murato is justly famous for its extraordinary 12th-century polychrome church, San Michele de Murato—but there is another, almost equally compelling reason to visit the town: the 15-year-old restaurant Ferme Campo di Monte, which Thiers owns with sisters Pauline and Josiane Juillard. Corsicans seldom agree about anything, but they all seem to admire the place. When I arrived there that afternoon, the sisters were busy in the kitchen preparing the night's dinner: On the stove were goat stew, storzapreti—gratinéed cheese dumplings with mint and egg—and soupe corse. 'We took the soup off the menu once,' Pauline confides, 'but we had an uprising. Our patrons protested. It's the most universal Corsican dish.'"

Soupe Paysanne
à Boire et à Manger

(Peasant Soup to Drink and Eat)

SERVES 12

IN BORDEAUX, when a few spoonfuls of soup are left in the bowl, locals pour in a few ounces of red wine, swirl it around, then drink the liquid directly from the bowl.

Love and Garlic

G arbure is a hearty farmers' dish of cabbage, meat (usually salted pork and/or duck or goose confit), and seasonal vegetables, native to southwestern France. Rural households always had a pot of it on the stove, so it thickened and grew ever more intense in flavor; connoisseurs of garbure say that it should be so dense that a ladle will stand up in it. As with many traditional dishes, the recipe changes from season to season, from village to village, and even from house to house. The most famous of all garbures are those from Oloron-Ste-Marie, a town about 20 miles southwest of Pau, which styles itself La Capitale de la Garbure. Oloron hosts an annual Garburade, or garbure festival, which includes a competition for the best version of the dish. Basic ingredients include potatoes, leeks, and "corn beans", which are beans that grow around the cornstalk in the field—but vegetables as diverse as pumpkin, sugar-snap peas, dried chiles, nettles, and Chinese artichokes (crosnes) are also considered acceptable. Garbure, adds Fernand Pon, president of the Garburade, should be made with "a lot of love and a little bit of garlic"—though in the southwest of France, a little bit of garlic can turn out to be quite a lot.

2 tbsp. duck fat
1 medium yellow onion, peeled and finely chopped
2 shallots, peeled and finely chopped
1 ham hock
1 head garlic, separated into cloves, then peeled and crushed
1 leek, trimmed, rinsed and thickly sliced
3 carrots, peeled and thickly sliced
2 large turnips, peeled and cut into large cubes
1 celery stalk, thickly sliced
1 small cabbage, cored and chopped into large pieces
1½ cups navy beans
Salt and freshly ground black pepper
1 large loaf rustic sourdough bread

1. Melt duck fat in a large heavy pot over medium heat. Add onions and shallots and cook until slightly softened, about 5 minutes. Add ham hock and brown, turning occasionally, for another 10 minutes.

2. Increase heat to high, add garlic, leeks, carrots, turnips, celery, cabbage, and beans, then add 5 quarts water and season to taste with salt and pepper. Once soup has come to a boil, reduce heat to low, partially cover, and simmer gently for 4 hours. Adjust seasoning, then serve with bread to soak up any leftover broth.

3

CHEESE AND EGGS

"THE ALPS are an emblematic range, romantic, imposing, operatic—mountains as metaphor. They inspire us to poetry and to heroic deeds. They also inspire, in those who traverse them, whether on foot, on skis, or by car, an enormous hunger—and, as a result, old-fashioned French mountain cooking is robust and satisfying. It thrives most vigorously today in the départements of Savoie and Haute-Savoie, in the heart of the French Alps. It is not sophisticated fare. Polenta and buckwheat pasta are common in traditional kitchens, as is the hearty one-pot meal called potée (see page 222). Though there are wild mushrooms and glorious apples, pears, plums, and cherries in summer and fall, and wild game well into the winter, many of the region's dishes are based on charcuterie, potatoes, and dairy products—above all cheese. One specialty combines all of these: reblochonnade (also called tartiflette), a dish of thinly sliced potatoes sautéed with bacon and onions, moistened with cream, baked, and finally topped with generous slices of creamy reblochon, the Haute-Savoie's most famous cheese—which is melted over it. Another variation of the cheese-and-potato theme is raclette (facing page, upper right), made by melting the cheese of that name over potatoes and cornichons. The region's most celebrated cheese dish, of course, is fondue savoyarde (see page 80)—gruyère-like beaufort (or French-made gruyère) melted with white wine and kirsch and scooped up with cubes of bread. Beaufort, like reblochon (and its larger relative, beaumont), is also much appreciated on its own. Another great cheese of the region is the medium-rich, slightly nutty-tasting tomme de Savoie, which cheese expert Steven Jenkins has called 'the most accessible cheese taste experience in the world.'" —GASTON PINARD

RECIPES

FONDUE SAVOYARDE, page 80; GOUGÈRES (*French Cheese Puffs*), page 83; PLATEAU DE FROMAGES (*Assorted Cheese Platter*), page 85; CRÈME D'ÉCHALOTES (*Shallot Custard*), page 86; SOUFFLÉ AUX ARTICHAUTS ET AUX CHAMPIGNONS (*Artichoke and Mushroom Soufflé*), page 89; QUICHE LORRAINE, page 90; OEUFS FARCIS À LA PÉRIGOURDINE (*Périgord-Style Stuffed Eggs*), page 93; OEUFS EN MEURETTE (*Poached Eggs in Red Wine Sauce*), page 94; OEUFS EN BOUILLON (*Eggs in Broth*), page 97.

Cheese Fight

I s gruyère, that most popular of Alpine cheeses, Swiss or French? It's hard to say. In 1115, the first count of Gruyère, in what is now Switzerland, accepted taxes from the Priory of Rougemount in the form of a cheese whose description matches that of modern-day gruyère. (The town, in turn, was named after the *grue*, or crane, that appears on the count's coat of arms.) The French, though, maintain that during the time of Charlemagne (A.D. 742–814), forestry authorities known as *agents gruyers* (from the Old German word *grüejen*, to grow, as in greenery) roamed what is now France, collecting taxes on firewood—and that they, too, were paid in cheese, eventually lending it their name. The issue of gruyère's paternity was officially, but inconclusively, contested at the International Cheese Conference in Rome in 1930 and at the 1951 Convention of Stresa. Finally, the French-Swiss Treaty of 1974 settled the matter: The glory of gruyère was to be shared by France and Switzerland.

Fondue Savoyarde

SERVES 4

FONDUE POTS, essential in any "gourmet" household of the 1960s, are back in the stores. The best ones, though, are the old models, which turn up sometimes at garage sales. According to fondue tradition, if your bread cube slips off your fork into the pot, you must buy the next round of drinks—or, some say, kiss the man or woman to your left.

1 clove garlic, peeled and crushed
1 ½ cups Savoyard white wine, such as chignin or crépy, or other light, dry white wine
1 lb. beaufort or gruyère cheese, grated or cubed
1 tsp. freshly grated nutmeg
Freshly ground black pepper
¼ cup kirsch
8 thick slices French country bread, cut into 1" cubes, each one with a piece of crust

1. Rub a medium-size heavy pot with garlic, then discard garlic. Add wine and bring to a boil over high heat. Reduce heat to medium and gradually add cheese, stirring constantly with a wooden spoon, until it has melted. Do not allow to boil. Continue to cook, stirring frequently, until mixture has thickened, about 20 minutes. Add nutmeg, pepper to taste, and kirsch. Transfer to a chafing dish or fondue pot.

2. To serve fondue, put the fondue pot in the middle of the table, with the bread cubes in a basket. Diners spear cubes with their fondue forks and dip them in the pot. Stir the pot frequently to prevent the cheese from coagulating. If fondue becomes too thick, stir in ¼ cup of dry white wine.

Gougères

(French Cheese Puffs)

MAKES 3 DOZEN

IN BURGUNDY, where they originated, gougères are considered the perfect hors d'oeuvre—complementary to wine and satisfying to the palate without being filling. According to Jean-Pierre Silva of Le Vieux Moulin in Bouilland, whose recipe this is, the secret of successful gougères is to add the flour all at once and the eggs one at a time.

8 tbsp. butter, cut into
    pieces
¾ cup milk
Salt and freshly ground
    white pepper
1 cup flour
4 large eggs, at room
    temperature
1½ cups grated comté or
    gruyère cheese

1. Preheat oven to 400°. Combine butter, ½ cup of the milk, and ½ cup water in a medium saucepan over high heat. Season generously with salt and pepper. Bring to a boil, and when butter has melted, remove pan from heat. Add flour all at once and stir vigorously with a wooden spoon until mixture forms a thick dough and pulls away from the sides of the pan, 1–2 minutes. Return pan to heat for 1 minute, stirring constantly. Remove from heat.

2. Let dough cool to room temperature, then beat in eggs, one at a time, making sure each egg is completely incorporated into mixture and dough is smooth after each addition. Dough should be thick, shiny, and smooth. Add 1 cup of the cheese and beat in until well combined.

3. Spoon tablespoon-size mounds of dough on nonstick baking sheets, leaving about 1" between each. Brush tops with remaining ¼ cup milk, then sprinkle with remaining ½ cup cheese. Bake one tray at a time in lower third of oven until gougères have doubled in size and are golden, 20–25 minutes. Serve warm or at room temperature.

Mastering the Puff

F rench grandmothers can make gougères in their sleep—but for the rest of us, despite the simplicity of the recipe, they can be a little tricky. These tips will help: Correct measurements are vital (**A**). For the flour, fill a dry measuring cup, then sweep it clean with the flat side of a knife. Always use a glass measuring cup for liquids so that you can see the level of the liquid. And be sure that the eggs are graded large, not extra-large or jumbo; this is one case where bigger is not better. Dump the flour into the hot milk and butter all at once, then begin beating mixture vigorously with a wooden spoon (**B**). The batter should almost seize up and pull away from the sides of the pan. Beat the eggs into the cooled batter one at a time (**C**). The batter will be slippery and a little hard to beat, but it will eventually absorb the eggs and become a smooth, shiny mass.

Plateau de Fromages

(Assorted Cheese Platter)

RESTAURANTS in France typically offer diners a choice of 20 or 30 cheeses (as at the three-star Arpège in Paris, left). At home, two or three of varying pungency (see below) is sufficient; half a dozen would be generous. The cheeses below are made in France, but available in the U.S.; feel free to make substitutions from America, Italy, Holland, Spain, Switzerland, or anywhere else that makes good cheese.

MILD CHEESES:
Brillat-savarin (cows'
  milk; triple cream)
Chaource (cows' milk)
Explorateur (cows' milk;
  triple cream)
Montrachet (goats' milk;
  usually wrapped
  in chestnut or grape
  leaves), fresh
Port-Salut (cows' milk;
  a brand name for cheese
  known generically as
  st-paulin)
Reblochon (cows' milk)
St-Marcellin (goats' or
  cows' milk), fresh
St-Nectaire (cows' milk;
  can grow stronger)
Vacherin (also called
  mont-d'or; cows' milk)

FULL-FLAVORED
CHEESES:
Bleu de Bresse (cows' milk;
  blue)
Brie de Meaux (cows' milk)
Brindamour (sheeps' milk;
  coated with rosemary
  and savory)
Camembert (cows' milk)
Cantal (cows' milk;
  reminiscent of English
  farmhouse cheddar)
Montrachet (goats' milk;
  usually wrapped
  in chestnut or grape
  leaves), aged
Rocamadour (sheeps' or
  goats' milk; the latter is
  somewhat stronger)
St-Marcellin (goats' or
  cows' milk), aged
Tomme de Savoie (cows'
  milk)

PUNGENT CHEESES:
Beaufort (cows' milk;
  sometimes sold as French
  gruyère)
Comté (cows' milk; also
  sometimes sold as French
  gruyère)
Crottin de Chavignol
  (goats' milk)
Époisses (cows' milk)
Fourme d'Ambert (cows'
  milk; blue)
Livarot (cows' milk)
Munster (cows' milk; not
  to be confused with mild
  deli-counter muenster)
Pont-l'Évêque (cows' milk)
Roquefort (sheeps' milk;
  blue)
Valençay (goats' milk),
  aged

Cheese Platter Tips

C heese deserves special treatment," the legendary Parisian *fromager* Pierre Androuët once wrote, so it should always be served on a platter, not a plate—even if you're only offering one or two examples. Here are some other things to remember when serving cheese at home: Choose a small number of the best available examples, allowing 3–4 oz. per person total; if possible, ask a knowledgeable cheese seller to help you pick out those at peak ripeness; serve them at room temperature; arrange them in ascending order of pungency (see lists at left); fruit is optional (grapes or sliced apples or pears are best), but good bread or neutral-flavored crackers are essential. Butter? This is disputed, but Androuët says yes—and we agree.

Unimposing Perfume

I n France," reports writer Claudia M. Caruana, "shallots are considered positively essential in the kitchen. The best thing about them is their flavor—onionlike, but without the onion's bite. The 19th-century French gourmet Charles Monselet observed that the shallot 'perfumes without imposing'. This is a distinction much appreciated by the French. Botanically speaking, the shallot is either *Allium cepa*, var. *Aggregatum* (a descendant of the wild onion native to Turkmenistan's Kopet-Dag mountains) or *Allium ascalonicum*, a name that is most likely a corruption of Ashkelon, an ancient port in Palestine. The Crusaders supposedly first introduced the 'Ascalonian onion' to Europe on their return from the Holy Land. There is quite a range in shallot flavor: The standard French red shallot, also known as the Brittany red, since the bulk of French production comes from that region, has a pronounced but muted flavor. The Dutch yellow (facing page), which has a higher sulfur content, is spicier. The gray shallot has the most complex and attractive flavor of all—but it's ugly and hard to peel, and not found very often in America anyway."

Crème d'Échalotes
(Shallot Custard)

SERVES 4

THE PRICE of shallots has come down noticeably in recent years, due at least partially to an increase in domestic production. They are also easy to grow, and most seed catalogues offer several varieties—even the ugly but tasty gray.

FOR SHALLOTS:
4 large shallots, peeled
1 tbsp. butter
1 tsp. sugar
Freshly grated nutmeg
Salt and freshly ground
  white pepper
¼ cup dry sherry

FOR CUSTARD:
2 eggs
1 ½ cups cream
½ tsp. salt
Freshly ground white pepper
Freshly grated nutmeg

1. For shallots, trim each bulb by removing any fibers from root end, leaving base intact. Using a paring knife, "fan" each shallot by thinly slicing from the tip to—but not through—the base. (Shallots should retain their original shape, but will open slightly during cooking.)

2. Melt butter in a medium skillet over medium-high heat. Add shallots, sprinkle with sugar, and season to taste with nutmeg and with salt and pepper. Turn shallots to coat with butter mixture, then cook until golden, 2–3 minutes per side. Add sherry, stir gently, then reduce heat to low. Cover and cook until shallots are tender and well browned, about 25 minutes. (If skillet becomes too dry during cooking, add 1–2 tbsp. water.) Drain shallots and cool on paper towels.

3. For custard, preheat oven to 275°. Put eggs, cream, and salt in a medium bowl. Add a pinch of pepper and nutmeg and whisk until mixture is just smooth; do not overbeat.

4. Arrange shallots in 4 ramekins (1" high and 4¾" across), gently fanning and separating slices. Ladle ½ cup custard into each dish, cover tightly with plastic wrap, then place in a large baking pan.

5. Place baking pan in oven. Add enough hot water to come about halfway up sides of custard dishes, then cook until custards are set, about 20 minutes. To check for doneness, carefully lift plastic wrap from one custard and insert a toothpick in the center. Custards are done if toothpick comes out clean. Remove remaining custards from baking pan, lift off plastic wrap, then set custards aside to cool. Serve warm or at room temperature.

Soufflé aux Artichauts et aux Champignons

(Artichoke and Mushroom Soufflé)

SERVES 4

THE PARCHMENT technique described below yields soufflés with dramatic golden crowns (left). As always with soufflés, the egg whites must be beaten in a *very* clean bowl.

4 globe artichokes
Salt
4 tbsp. butter
2 tbsp. olive oil
3 white mushrooms, finely chopped
Freshly ground black pepper
3 tbsp. flour
1 cup hot milk
¼ cup hot heavy cream
Freshly grated nutmeg
5 eggs, separated

1. Trim artichokes, then cook in boiling salted water until tender, about 30 minutes. Drain and set aside until cool enough to handle. Break off leaves, scrape off meat with a spoon (this should yeild about 1½ cups), discard leaves and set meat aside. Remove and discard choke from artichoke heart, then trim stem so heart that it sits flat.

2. Put each trimmed heart into a buttered, individual (1½ cups) soufflé dish. Use 2 tbsp. of the butter to grease 4 strips of parchment paper or foil, 12" x 4". Wrap and tie buttered parchment collars around soufflé dishes with kitchen string. Put dishes on a baking sheet.

3. Heat oil in a sauté pan and add mushrooms and reserved artichoke meat. Sauté until mushrooms have released and reabsorbed their juice. Season to taste with salt and pepper. Divide mushroom mixture evenly between artichoke hearts.

4. Preheat oven to 400°. Melt remaining 2 tbsp. butter in a heavy-bottomed pan and stir in flour. Cook over medium heat for 2 minutes, then remove pan from heat and slowly whisk in milk and cream. Return saucepan to heat and cook, whisking constantly, until smooth and very thick, about 2 minutes. Remove pan from heat and season with salt, pepper, and a pinch of nutmeg. Beat in egg yolks one at a time. Set aside.

5. In a very clean metal bowl, beat egg whites with a pinch of salt until stiff peaks form. Add a third of the egg whites into thickened milk mixture and gently fold together, then fold mixture into remaining egg whites. Divide mixture evenly between soufflé dishes, spooning it over filled artichoke bottoms. Bake until puffed and golden, about 15 minutes. Remove collars and serve immediately.

A Friend of Soufflé

J acqueline Margulis (above) learned to cook soufflés at a convent in the countryside near Bordeaux—where, she recalls, "We were taught to smell, touch, and feel all sorts of food." In 1958, at 22, she emigrated to New York. Later she moved west, and in 1979 opened Café Jacqueline in San Francisco—where she offers diners nothing but soufflés. Does she ever get bored? "Never," she replies, "for every soufflé is different and I am forever inventing new ones." You must be among friends to enjoy a soufflé, she adds— "both to share it fairly and to enjoy the wait as the eggs are being cracked!" One of her favorite soufflés, says Margulis, is made with roquefort. To serve 2 or 3 (friends), preheat oven to 400°. Melt 2 tbsp. butter in a heavy-bottomed medium saucepan over medium heat. Add 3 tbsp. flour and cook, stirring constantly with a wooden spoon, for 1½ minutes (do not brown). Remove from heat and whisk in 1 cup hot milk. Return saucepan to heat and cook, whisking constantly, until smooth and very thick. Season with a pinch of salt and freshly ground white pepper to taste. Whisk in 4 extra-large egg yolks, one at a time. Set aside. Beat whites of 5 extra-large eggs until stiff peaks form. Add a third of the egg whites to milk mixture and gently fold together. While folding in remaining egg whites, sprinkle in 4 oz. shaved roquefort. Do not overmix. Spoon into a buttered medium (6 cup) soufflé dish. Bake until soufflé stands tall and is golden brown, 25–30 minutes. Serve immediately.

Real Quiche

If you think
quiche lorraine
is a frou-frou
brunch dish, best accompanied by a healthy little
green salad, you might be
interested to learn that in
this specialty's homeland—
the Lorraine (above),
next door to Alsace in
northeastern France—it is
traditionally served on
May Day alongside roast
suckling pig in aspic. In
other words, it is serious
food in these parts.
Apparently invented in
the 16th century in
the city of Nancy, then
capital of Lorraine, it
derives its name from the
German *Küchen*, or cake.
Though quiche was
originally made with bread
dough, a short pastry crust
has become standard, and
the recipe rarely varies in
Lorraine itself. About the
only disagreements seem
to be whether or not to
add nutmeg (we do) and
whether or not to blanch
the bacon before sautéing
it (we do this, too).

Quiche Lorraine

SERVES 4–6

ADAPTED from *Mastering the Art of French Cooking*, vol. 1,
by Julia Child, Louisette Bertholle, and Simone Beck, this
is the real thing, with no cheese, no onions, no vegetables.

FOR CRUST:
2 cups flour
½ tsp. salt
Pinch sugar
*8 tbsp. cold butter, cut
  into small pieces*
*3 tbsp. cold vegetable
  shortening, cut into
  small pieces*
1 egg, lightly beaten

FOR FILLING:
6 oz. slab bacon, diced
2 eggs, lightly beaten
1 ½ cups heavy cream
½ tsp. salt
Freshly grated nutmeg
*Freshly ground black
  pepper*

1. For crust, sift together flour, salt, and sugar into a mixing bowl. Use a pastry cutter or 2 knives to work butter and
shortening into flour until it resembles coarse meal. Sprinkle in up to 6 tbsp. ice water, stirring the dough with a fork
until it just begins to hold together. Using your hands, press
the dough firmly into a rough ball, then transfer to a lightly
floured surface. Give the dough several quick kneads with
the heel of your hand to form a smooth dough, then shape
into a ball, flatten slightly to make a disk, and dust with
flour. Wrap disk in plastic and refrigerate for 2 hours.

2. Preheat oven to 400°. Allow dough to sit at room temperature to soften slightly before rolling out on a lightly
floured surface into a 14" round. Fit dough, without stretching it, into a buttered 10" bottomless metal flan ring, 1½"
deep, set on a parchment-lined cookie sheet with no rim.
Press overhanging dough down slightly into sides of ring
to make the sides of the crust a little thicker and sturdier.
Run the rolling pin over the top of the ring to remove any
overhanging dough. Using a fork, prick bottom lightly,
then make a decorative edge around the rim. Line dough
with buttered aluminum foil, then add pie weights or dried
beans. Bake until crust is set and edge just begins to
color, about 25 minutes. Remove foil and weights, brush
bottom and sides with egg, and continue baking until crust
is pale golden, another 2–5 minutes.

3. For filling, reduce heat to 375°. Put bacon in a medium
pan, cover with cold water, and bring to a boil over medium-
high heat. Boil for 5 minutes, then drain. Return bacon to
pan, and cook over medium heat until lightly browned,
about 3 minutes. Transfer bacon with a slotted spoon to a
paper towel to drain, then arrange in bottom of crust.

4. Beat together eggs, cream, and salt in a medium bowl
and season to taste with nutmeg and pepper; pour into crust.
Bake until custard is puffed and golden and just set in the
center, 30–35 minutes. Slide quiche off parchment paper
onto a serving platter and remove ring. Serve quiche warm
or at room temperature, sliced into wedges.

Oeufs Farcis à la Périgourdine

(Périgord-Style Stuffed Eggs)

SERVES 4

ONE OF THE dishes Lucian K. Truscott IV and his wife made in their kitchen in the Dordogne (the region historically known as the Périgord), these eggs may be served as an hors d'oeuvre or first course, or with a salad for lunch.

4 hard-cooked eggs, peeled
  and halved lengthwise
2 tbsp. coarsely chopped
  smoked ham
2 tbsp. walnut oil
1 tsp. finely chopped
  fresh thyme
1 tsp. finely chopped
  fresh rosemary
1 tsp. finely chopped
  fresh parsley
Salt and freshly ground
  black pepper
2 tbsp. goose or duck fat
  or vegetable oil
1 egg white, beaten
  until frothy

1. Remove yolks from hard-cooked eggs, put them in a small bowl, and mash them with a fork. When they're mashed, stir in ham, walnut oil, thyme, rosemary, and parsley, and season to taste with salt and pepper. Spoon mixture into hard-cooked whites, rounding and smoothing it as you go.

2. Heat fat or oil in a large nonstick skillet over medium-high heat. Dip stuffed eggs into beaten egg white, then place in pan, stuffed side down first, and fry for about 30 seconds on each side, until lightly browned. Drain on paper towels, arrange on a platter, and garnish with thyme, if you like.

Being There

"Three years ago," reports writer Lucian K. Truscott IV, "my wife, Carolyn, our 2-year-old daughter Lilly [above], and I rented a house for a week in a little village called St-Julien-de-Crempse, just north of Bergerac in the Dordogne. The house was part of a 17th-century farm compound atop a hill, overlooking fields of hay and corn and sunflowers. From our bedroom window, we could see into a coop of chickens, with a rabbit hutch just beyond. The yard in front of the house had a walled garden planted with roses, fragrant lavender, and lilies, and the kitchen was a delightfully serious cooking space. Every day, we'd shop at one of the region's farmers' markets [facing page], then come back here to cook ourselves dishes like pasta with a sauce of fresh peas, white asparagus, and melted chèvre; eggs stuffed in the Périgord style with ham and herbs; grilled duck breast with fresh cherry and apple sauce; and guinea hen stuffed with green onions and Toulouse sausage and wrapped in smoked pork. One day we bought plump, tiny mussels from the coast near Bordeaux that were so good they left us wondering, Why don't we just move here?"

French Locomotive

A rich, old-fashioned bistro dish, oeufs en meurette—its name is thought to derive from *muire*, an Old French term for brine—is hard to find these days. One place that still serves it (and makes it the right way, poaching the eggs in good red wine instead of acidulated water as other establishments apparently do) is a sophisticated Parisian restaurant called Le Récamier (facing page). Opened in 1969 by a dedicated amateur named Martin Cantegrit, it specializes in the cooking of Burgundy, and has proven remarkably consistent in quality over the years. Cantegrit is a culinary chauvinist, who maintains that "The French are gastronomic because only in France do you find such a concentration of products in one small hexagon"— and that "France must teach the rest of the world about fine food; it must be the locomotive by which each country rediscovers its own culinary traditions." Sampling chef Robert Chassat's snail and wild mushroom fricassée, stuffed cabbage, truffled pork sausage with puréed split peas, or, well, oeufs en meurette, it is easy to agree with him.

Oeufs en Meurette
(Poached Eggs in Red Wine Sauce)

SERVES 4

USE EGGS that come straight from the refrigerator for this dish, counsels Robert Chassat, chef at Le Récamier in Paris, who gave us this recipe; cold eggs hold their shape better while poaching. At the restaurant, he allots two eggs per serving, but at home, you may find one to be sufficient.

4 tbsp. butter, softened
¼ lb. slab bacon, coarsely chopped
½ lb. small white mushrooms, sliced
1 large shallot, peeled and minced
1 medium carrot, peeled and coarsely chopped
1 sprig fresh thyme
1 bay leaf
5 ¼ cups French red burgundy or other dry red wine
1 cup demi-glace (see sidebar, page 61)
1 ¾ cups beef stock (see page 59)
2 tbsp. flour
4–8 eggs
Salt and freshly ground black pepper
4 slices bread, preferably pain brioche, lightly toasted, crusts removed
4 sprigs fresh chervil

1. Melt 1 tbsp. of the butter in a medium skillet over medium heat. Add bacon and cook until crisp, 7–10 minutes. Remove bacon with a slotted spoon, drain on a paper towel, and set aside. Add mushrooms to skillet and cook, stirring occasionally, until golden, about 10 minutes. Transfer to a bowl and set aside.

2. In the same skillet, melt 1 tbsp. of the butter, add shallots, and cook, stirring, until fragrant, about 1 minute. Stir in carrots, thyme, and bay leaf and cook until carrots begin to brown, about 7 minutes.

3. Increase heat to medium-high, add 2 cups wine, and cook until reduced by three-quarters, about 25 minutes. Add demi-glace and stock and cook, skimming frequently, for 10 minutes. Remove skillet from heat and strain sauce through a fine sieve into a small saucepan. Combine flour and remaining 2 tbsp. butter in a small bowl, forming a paste. Whisk paste into sauce a little at a time, then simmer over medium-low heat for 2 minutes. Reduce heat to low and keep sauce warm.

4. Place remaining 3¼ cups wine in a small saucepan and bring to a simmer over medium heat. Poach eggs two at a time by cracking each egg into a saucer, then carefully slipping into wine. Poach until whites are firm and yolks just set, 5–7 minutes. Using a slotted spoon, transfer eggs to a plate and cover with foil. Repeat process with remaining eggs.

5. Add reserved bacon and mushrooms to sauce and season to taste with salt and pepper. Divide bread between 4 plates, place one or two eggs on each piece, spoon sauce over them, and serve garnished with chervil.

Oeufs en Bouillon

(Eggs in Broth)

SERVES 4

AT HER CHEZ MILLETTE in Planchez (below), in the Morvan, Millette Coquillon sometimes serves guests these hard-cooked eggs in a rich meat stock before the plat du jour.

8 eggs
4–6 cups beef stock
  (see page 59)
¼ cup fresh parsley,
  chopped
Salt and freshly ground
  black pepper

1. Put eggs in a medium saucepan, cover with cold water, and bring just to a boil over medium heat. Reduce heat to low and simmer very slowly for 10 minutes. Drain, then run cold water over eggs until they are cool. Peel eggs and return them to pan.

2. Add enough stock to completely cover eggs, then bring to a simmer over medium heat and cook for 2 minutes. Remove from heat, cover, and set aside to marinate for 1 hour before serving. Serve eggs in stock, at room temperature, garnished with fresh chopped parsley. Serve salt and pepper on the side.

Ubiquitous Herb

The French, it is said, used to be wary of parsley, believing that it had magical powers. In a way, as it turns out, it does: It is impossible to imagine French cuisine without parsley today. It is an essential ingredient of the bouquet garni, that bundle of herbs that flavors so many French soups and sauces (see sidebar, page 59); it clings to meats in marinades; it is a special friend to garlic, often fried alongside it. And of course it garnishes plates and platters in bistros and at banquets alike, adding decorative accents with equal flair to modest, homey dishes like oeufs en bouillon (facing page) and elegant preparations of whole fish or roast meat (among many other things). It even shows up in idioms: *Avoir du persil*, to have some parsley, means to be witty or piquant. (On the other hand, *avoir du persil dans les oreilles*, to have parsley in one's ears, means to be unwashed.) *Faire son persil*, to do one's parsley, is to strut or preen. And not surprisingly, considering parsley's culinary ubiquity, a person who keeps turning up is said to be *partout, comme le persil*—everywhere, like you know what frilly green herb.

SALADS

"IN THE département of the Lot in south-

western France, feudal castles and bastides

loom high above strategic limestone cliffs,

and rivers flow gently through fertile val-

leys connecting medieval market towns,

hamlets, and farms. The Lot is famous for foie gras, truffles, and other delicacies—among them exquisite handmade walnut oil, which has been produced in the region since the 11th century, and which many connoisseurs consider the ultimate condiment for salads. (Because it has a low smoke point, it is rarely used for cooking.) The only artisan still making the oil in the Lot is André Castagné (facing page, lower left), proprietor of Huilerie Familiale du Lac de Diane near the town of Martel. I was led to my first taste of his superlative product by a modest roadside sign—one of the many that fill the local landscape, advertising culinary specialties. When I arrived at Castagné's mill, I found the man himself feeding a fire with walnut shells. The rich aroma of roasting walnuts filled the air as he bounced back and forth between the three pieces of equipment that make up his entire operation: an ancient granite mill to grind the walnut meat to paste; a cast-iron basin in which the paste is roasted; and a hydraulic press layered with steel plates, to extract the rich, golden oil. Castagné bought his mill in 1985 and rebuilt it to its original form. Now he presses oil almost daily most of the year. He offered me a taste. The flavor of the roasted nuts was immediate, followed by a delicate hint of maple; it was a marvel. Before World War II, Castagné told me, virtually every village in the Lot had its own mill, but these died out. Today, walnut oil and other walnut products (including apéritifs, digestifs, and preserves) are becoming popular again, and it seems possible that more old mills might reopen in the future. 'Working at the mill,' Castagné added with a smile, 'is good for families. It keeps the children at home.'" —ELAINE STERLING

RECIPES

Mushrooms under the Trees

T he Germans call it Eierschwamm (egg mushroom) or Gelbhahnel (yellow chick); to the Italians, it's capo gallo (cock crest) or orecina (little ear). The French identify it as the girolle, from the Old French word *girer*, to twist (a reference to its shape), or the chanterelle—a word derived from the Greek *kantharos*, meaning a kind of drinking vessel. Under whatever name, *Cantharellus cibarius* and other chanterelle species have apparently been plentiful throughout Europe since the beginning of recorded time; the first illustration of one supposedly appeared in Holland in 1581. Chanterelles grow only in the presence of living trees, with which they form a symbiotic relationship. The fungi draw nourishing sugar from the trees' younger roots, in turn providing them with phosphorus and other minerals. Thus, despite the best efforts of mycologists, all available chanterelles are still hand-gathered in the woods.

Salade de Chanterelles
(Chanterelle Salad)

SERVES 4

BECAUSE THEIR appearance is so distinctive and because they grow in such profusion when conditions are right, chanterelles are among the safest and easiest wild mushrooms to gather—which is fortunate, because they're expensive. Writer Lucian K. Truscott IV improvised this salad at a house he and his family rented in the Dordogne (see page 93).

¼ cup shelled walnut halves
5 tbsp. walnut oil
2 large cloves garlic, peeled and minced
½ lb. chanterelles, cleaned and trimmed
Salt and freshly ground black pepper
1 medium tomato, seeded and diced
2 oz. thinly sliced smoked ham, diced
1 tbsp. finely chopped fresh parsley
¼ lb. mixed baby greens

1. Place walnuts in a single layer in a large skillet. Toast over medium heat, turning once, for 10 minutes. Coarsely chop and set aside.

2. Heat 3 tbsp. of the oil in a large skillet over medium heat. Add garlic and cook, stirring until fragrant, for about 2 minutes. Increase heat to medium-high, add mushrooms, season to taste with salt and pepper, and cook, stirring, until mushrooms soften, about 5 minutes.

3. Reduce heat to low, add tomatoes, ham, and parsley, and cook, stirring, for 1 minute. Remove from heat and set aside.

4. Put greens in a small bowl and dress with remaining 2 tbsp. oil. Season to taste with salt and pepper, then divide between 4 small plates. Arrange mushroom mixture over lettuce, garnish with toasted walnuts, and serve.

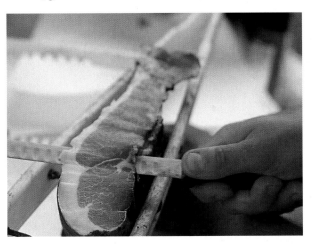

Salade Niçoise

SERVES 4

THE TRADITIONAL version of Nice's classic salad uses no lettuce, no cooked vegetables, no vinegar. And remember that the Niçois would never dream of making their salad with fresh tuna: This is a dish based on preserved fish.

4 ripe tomatoes, sliced
1 green bell pepper, stemmed, seeded, and finely chopped
8 radishes, thinly sliced
2 6⅛-oz. cans good-quality tuna packed in olive oil, well drained
4 hard-cooked eggs, peeled and quartered
8 oil-packed anchovies
4 fresh chives, chopped
Salt and freshly ground black pepper
½ cup niçoise olives
Extra-virgin olive oil, preferably French (see page 115)

1. Divide tomatoes, bell pepper, radishes, tuna, and eggs equally between 4 plates, arranging them attractively, working from the outside in.

2. Garnish each plate with 2 anchovy filets. Sprinkle with chives, and season to taste with salt and freshly ground black pepper. Scatter olives evenly over the salads, and drizzle with olive oil just before serving.

Nissa la Bella

At Barale, her restaurant near Nice's Vieux Port, Catherine-Hélène Barale (above) serves diners a nightly fixed-price encyclopedia of local cooking in an antiques-filled dining room. The procession begins with a wedge of crisp-crusted pissaladière (see page 26) and proceeds with a piece of socca (chickpea flour crêpe); a real salade niçoise; a healthy helping of ravioli, filled with swiss chard—the defining vegetable of Nice—and, moistened with meat juices; a main course of (usually) braised veal shoulder with mushrooms and sweet red peppers; and for dessert, a thick slab of tourte de blettes, a sweet swiss chard torte (see page 288). Then comes a big bowl of fruit, and finally a tiny glass of marc or cherry liquor. After dinner, Barale passes out little folders bearing the words to a patriotic Niçois anthem, "Nissa la Bella". Then she cranks up an old 78 on an ancient gramophone, and one and all—if they know what's good for them—bellow out "E toujou criderai / En la miéu ritournella, / Viva, viva Nissa la Bella" (And always I'll proclaim / Upon my return, / Viva, viva, Nice the Beautiful). After a meal like this—which is a revelation, a largesse, and a casually but shrewdly guided tour of the local gastronomic landscape, with all its simplicity and salt and savory intensity—it's hard to imagine anyone not wanting to join in.

Burgundy's Cheese

Burgundy's most famous cheese, and almost certainly its most distinctive, is époisses (above)—soft, politely pungent, pleasantly sharp on the palate, and a perfect foil for the region's famed red wines. Made from cows' milk in various parts of northwestern Burgundy—there is only one producer of the cheese in the pretty little town of Époisses itself, Fromagerie Berthaut—it is aged for three months by law, and traditionally has its rind rinsed two to three times a week for about a month with marc de bourgogne, the local version of grappa. (A law passed in early 1998 also awards recognition to a variation that is washed in chablis instead.) Époisses is one of only 40 French cheeses to have been granted an appellation d'origine contrôlée. The other famous cheese in this part of Burgundy is the not dissimilar, but milder, monastery-style cîteaux—named for the Cistercian monks who make it—which is aged two months and not marc-washed.

Salade des Moines

(*Green Salad with Cîteaux Cheese Croutons*)

SERVES 4

AT HOME at the family wine estate in Vosne-Romanée, Marielle Grivot mixes vinaigrette in the bottom of her salad bowl, puts greens on top of it, and tosses the salad at the table. To dress up a green salad, she adds croutons topped with melted cîteaux cheese (Canada's oka may be substituted). Her daughter Mathilde (right) often helps serve.

1 tbsp. sherry vinegar
2 tbsp. walnut oil
½ tsp. dijon mustard
Salt and freshly ground
  pepper
1 head butter lettuce,
  washed, dried, and torn
  into pieces
1 baguette
8 oz. cîteaux or oka

1. Place an oven rack in top third of oven and preheat broiler. Meanwhile, in a large salad bowl, whisk together the vinegar, oil, and mustard, and season to taste with salt and pepper. Add lettuce, toss with the vinaigrette, then divide between 4 plates.

2. Make croutons by cutting 12 thin round slices from the baguette, then place a slice of cîteaux cheese on top of each. Place slices on a baking sheet and broil until cheese is melted, 30–45 seconds. Garnish each salad with three croutons.

Salade de Lentilles du Puy

(Lentil Salad with Roasted Carrots and Beets)

SERVES 6

THIS RECIPE was developed for the esteemed lentils of Le Puy, but green lentils grown in America's best lentil country—an area, called the Palouse, stretching between Idaho, Oregon, and Washington—are similar, and work just as well.

3 small beets, peeled
    and diced
1 large carrot, peeled
    and diced
4 shallots, peeled and
    halved
½ cup extra-virgin olive
    oil, preferably French
    (see page 115)
2 sprigs fresh parsley
2 sprigs fresh thyme
Salt and freshly ground
    black pepper
¾ lb. lentilles du Puy, or
    other tiny French-style
    green lentils, picked over
    and rinsed
3 tbsp. sherry vinegar
¼ cup chopped fresh
    parsley

1. Preheat oven to 350°. Put beets, carrots, shallots, and ¼ cup oil in a medium roasting pan. Stir to coat vegetables evenly with oil. Add parsley and thyme, season to taste with salt and pepper, and cook, stirring once, until vegetables begin to brown, about 20 minutes. Add lentils and 3 cups of water, stir, then cover pan with foil. Continue roasting until lentils are tender and all water is absorbed, about 1 hour.

2. Remove pan from oven. Remove and discard herb sprigs. Whisk vinegar and remaining ¼ cup oil together in a small bowl, then pour over lentils. Allow lentils to cool slightly, then stir in chopped parsley. Adjust seasoning and serve.

Celebrated Legume

 entilles du Puy, tiny gray-green earthy ones from Le Puy, a town in the mountainous French region of Haute-Loire, are arguably the best in the world. They even have their own appellation contrôlée. Agriculturalists credit the local climate—dewy mornings, temperate days, cool nights—and volcanic soil with producing the distinct flavor of this legume. At Le Puy's annual Fête de la Lentille, more than 800 farmers compare their lentils, and chefs create new dishes, like sweet lentil preserves and lentil-flour tuile cookies.

Salade de Haricots Verts aux Noisettes Fraîches

(Salad of Haricots Verts and Green Hazelnuts)

SERVES 4

JACQUES MAXIMIN makes this salad with haricots verts grown near his restaurant in Vence (left), in the hills above Nice, and with green hazelnuts gathered from a tree in his own backyard. In the absence of these ingredients, good, fresh green beans and mature hazelnuts will do nicely.

Salt
1 lb. haricots verts or
   green beans, trimmed
½ cup green hazelnuts,
   skins removed, or mature
   blanched hazelnuts
¾ cup crème fraîche
1 tbsp. red wine vinegar
Freshly ground black
   pepper
2 medium tomatoes, seeded
   and diced
4 cups mixed baby greens
4 sprigs fresh basil

1. Bring a medium pot of salted water to a boil over high heat. Add haricots verts and cook until tender, 5–8 minutes. Drain, refresh in ice water, then drain, wrap in a dish towel and set aside.

2. If using green hazelnuts, coarsely chop and set aside. If using mature hazelnuts, heat a medium skillet over medium-high heat. Add hazelnuts to the dry skillet, and toast, turning, until nuts are golden, 5–7 minutes. Remove, coarsely chop, and set aside.

3. Put crème fraîche in a medium bowl. Whisk in vinegar and season to taste with salt and pepper. Add tomatoes, stir gently, then set aside for 10 minutes, allowing tomatoes to flavor and color dressing.

4. To assemble, toss greens in a medium mixing bowl with about 2 tbsp. dressing, then evenly divide between 4 plates. Put haricots verts in the same bowl, add about ½ cup dressing, and toss to coat. Arrange haricots verts on top of greens. Spoon remaining dressing over salads, taking care that a few diced tomatoes are on top of each one. Sprinkle with hazelnuts and garnish with basil leaves.

Well-Regarded Nuts

Hazelnuts, also called filberts, are among the most aristocratic of nuts, with an inimitably sweet, mild flavor cherished in candies, cookies, tortes, and other confections (see page 307) all over Europe. They're grown commercially on a large scale in four countries: Turkey, Italy, Spain, and the United States. The majority of the world's crop comes from Turkey, where the nuts are picked by hand from unpruned bushes. A mere 3 percent of the annual production comes from America, all from the Pacific Northwest—but the hazelnuts from this region are generally larger than those from other countries, and are widely considered to be tastier as well. In France, small quantities are grown in Corsica, the département of Pyrénées-Orientales, and the southwest. Hazelnuts are also used in savory dishes like terrines, salads, and fish dishes—and in the Catalan regions of France and Spain, they are ground along with other ingredients and stirred into soups and sauces for thickening and flavor.

Salade d'Artichauts à la Ventrèche

(Artichoke and Pork Belly Salad)

<small>SERVES 4</small>

VENTRÈCHE (pork belly), a specialty of southwestern France, is often cured for months in salt and pepper. A version of cured ventrèche is made in America—or pancetta may be substituted. This unusual salad is served by Jean-Pierre Xiradakis at La Tupiña in Bordeaux (see page 273).

Delicious Thistle

The artichoke, which most likely originated in the Middle East or North Africa as the descendant of a wild thistle, is one of the many culinary treasures popularly thought to have been introduced to France by the 14-year-old Catherine de Médicis when she crossed the Alps to marry the future French king Henri II in 1533. Catherine was a native of Tuscany, where artichokes were popular, and she was very fond of the vegetable. It took the French a while to succumb to its thorny charms, however; at first it was eaten more for its supposed medicinal value than for its flavor. It was also reputed to be an aphrodisiac. In France nowadays, artichokes are mainly grown in Brittany and throughout the South (from Provence to the Pyrenees)—and the French, besides eating the thing abundantly, describe somebody with a fickle heart as having "un coeur d'artichaut"—implying that they fall in love with one person one day and another the next, with the ease and confidence of someone peeling off yet another artichoke leaf, knowing that the heart is still safely cushioned beneath many more layers.

4 large globe artichokes
1 lemon, halved
2 tbsp. duck fat
24 thin slices ventrèche or pancetta, cut into 2" strips
8 scallions, trimmed and finely chopped
8 red radishes, trimmed and halved lengthwise
½ cup fresh shelled and peeled fava beans (optional)
2 tbsp. balsamic vinegar
½ lb. mixed baby greens
2 tbsp. peanut oil
Salt and freshly ground black pepper
½ bunch fresh parsley
½ bunch fresh chervil
1 bunch fresh chives
2 tbsp. finely diced, peeled carrot

1. Bend back short lower leaves of artichokes until they snap, leaving the meaty bottom parts of the leaves. Then cut off the stems and slice off remaining cone of leaves, right above the heart. Scrape out and discard the hairy choke with a sharp spoon or melon baller. Cut artichokes into thick slices, transfer to a bowl, squeeze lemon juice over them to prevent discoloration. Melt duck fat in a large nonstick skillet over medium-low heat, add artichokes and sauté until soft and golden, 8–10 minutes. Transfer to a large bowl and set aside.

2. Arrange ventrèche in the same skillet and cook until brown and crisp, about 10 minutes. Remove ventrèche from skillet and drain on paper towels. Pour off all but 1 tbsp. of fat, then add scallions, radishes, and fava beans and sauté for about 2 minutes. Transfer to the bowl with the artichokes, add ventrèche and toss together. Drain fat from pan, then return pan to heat, add vinegar and deglaze, stirring with a wooden spoon for about 1 minute. Remove from heat and set aside.

3. Put greens in a large bowl, drizzle with oil, season to taste with salt and pepper, and toss together. Divide greens between 4 plates, then arrange artichoke mixture on top of greens. Drizzle vinegar over salads, then, with a pair of sharp scissors, snip parsley, chervil, and chives evenly over salads. Scatter carrots on top for color.

Salade Tiède de Rougets aux Artichauts

(Warm Red Mullet and Artichoke Salad)

SERVES 4

RED MULLET, one of the Mediterranean's tastiest fish, is occasionally sold in the U.S.; red snapper makes a more than adequate substitute in this salad from Jacques Maximin.

Salt
2 cups penne rigate (ribbed penne pasta)
1 tsp. balsamic vinegar
8 tbsp. extra-virgin olive oil, preferably French (see sidebar, facing page)
Freshly ground black pepper
6 baby artichokes, trimmed
8 cloves garlic, unpeeled
½ lb. cleaned squid, body sliced into rings, tentacles quartered
4 5-oz. red mullets, cleaned, deboned, head and tail left on (or 2 10-oz. boneless red snapper filets, halved crosswise)
½ cup flour
¼ lb. parmigiano-reggiano in 1 piece
12 fresh basil leaves
8 fresh chives
8 sprigs fresh chervil
¼ cup niçoise olives

1. Bring a pot of salted water to a boil over high heat. Add penne. Cook 7–10 minutes. Drain, then dress with vinegar and 1 tbsp. of the oil, season to taste with salt and pepper, and set aside.

2. Halve artichokes lengthwise, then heat 2 tbsp. of the oil in a skillet over medium heat. Add artichokes and garlic and brown on all sides, 5–7 minutes. Remove and set aside.

3. Add 1 tbsp. of the oil to the same skillet, add squid, and cook, stirring until squid is firm, about 1 minute. Season to taste with salt and pepper, then immediately remove from skillet and set aside.

4. Wipe out skillet. Dredge fish in flour. Shake off excess, then season to taste with salt and pepper. Heat remaining 4 tbsp. oil in skillet over medium heat. Add fish and fry, turning once, 2–4 minutes per side. Drain on paper towels.

5. To assemble, divide penne, artichokes, and squid evenly between 4 plates. Arrange fish on top and thinly shave parmigiano-reggiano over it. Garnish with basil, chives, chervil, and olives. Serve drizzled with additional olive oil if you like.

Huile d'Olive

French olive oil consumption has doubled in the past 20 years—to one whole liter per person per year. The Greeks, in comparison, manage 25 liters, and the Italians a respectable 13 (Americans barely manage half a liter). The French, in other words, don't live and breathe olive oil as much as their Mediterranean neighbors do. Peanut or colza (canola) oil is more likely to be used for cooking. Still, olives are grown and oil is made in some 13 départements throughout the south of France and in Corsica. From a recent tasting of French oils, we found the recurring notes to be buttery, nutty, and grassy—not peppery like Tuscan oils or strongly flavored like many of those from Greece or Spain. French olive oils found in the U.S. tend to be expensive, and frankly aren't always worth the price. (One that retails for about $70 per 750 ml bottle seemed heavy and disconcertingly tropical to us.) The European Union has approved a five-year plan to improve the quality of French olive oils. In the meantime, among the examples now sold here, we like the pale fresh Plagniol and the soft, opaque green Le Vieux Moulin, both from Provence, and the rich, complex, golden-hued Soulas from the Gard.

FOIE GRAS, FROGS' LEGS, SNAILS, AND TRUFFLES

"THE 19TH-CENTURY English cleric

Sydney Smith once proposed that heaven

was 'eating…foie gras to the sound of

trumpets'. For me, you could hold the trumpets. Foie gras is the extravagance I crave most. It's my madeleine. Along with Romanesque cathedrals, foie gras was my first big discovery when I went to France as a kid. I never take a single silken bite without thinking back to the early 1950s, when I was so memorably disabused of my belief that all liver came from calves and all cathedrals were Gothic. Foie gras makes me feel young again, in other words. And it makes me feel, in the immortal words of Bob Strauss, the Texas politico, like 'a rich sumbitch'. People have been nuts about foie gras (it's pronounced 'fwah grah' and literally means 'fat liver') since antiquity. Egyptian paintings from 2500 B.C. show farmers holding geese by the neck and force-feeding them balls of grain. The Romans fed their geese figs, to obtain what they called *iecur ficatum*, or liver with figs; so closely was this fruit identified with this organ, in fact, that the modern Italian word for liver, *fegato*, derives from the Latin word for fig. Even the French don't argue that foie gras is the most easily digestible thing in the world. Don't eat too much of it, I'd advise, and certainly don't eat it too late at night. On the other hand, it is said that Bismarck used to drink a glass of milk and eat a slice of foie gras to cure his insomnia. No wonder they called him the Iron Chancellor." —R.W. APPLE JR.

RECIPES

TERRINE DE FOIE GRAS (*Foie Gras Terrine*), page 120; FOIE GRAS DE CANARD POÊLÉ AUX RAISINS BLANCS (*Seared Foie Gras with Green Grapes*), page 122; BAECKEOFFE DE FOIE GRAS (*Potted Foie Gras and Vegetables*), page 125; CUISSES DE GRENOUILLES AU BEURRE PERSILLADE (*Frogs' Legs in Parsley Butter*), page 126; MILLE-FEUILLES DE GRENOUILLES (*Frogs' Leg "Napoleons" with White Bean Sauce*), page 129; ESCARGOTS À LA BOURGUIGNONNE (*Snails in Parsley Butter*), page 130; FRICASSÉE D'ESCARGOTS AU COULIS DE PERSIL (*Fricassée of Snails with Parsley and Roasted Garlic Cream*), page 133; FRICASSÉE DE CÈPES AUX TRUFFES (*Cèpe Fricassée with Truffles*), page 134; POMMES À LA SARLADAISE AUX TRUFFES (*Sarladais-Style Potatoes with Truffles*), page 137; OEUFS BROUILLÉS AUX TRUFFES (*Scrambled Eggs with Truffles*), page 138; POULET DEMI-DEUIL (*Truffled Chicken*), page 141.

Terrine de Foie Gras

(Foie Gras Terrine)

SERVES 10

THIS OPULENT terrine, whose secrets we learned from chef Christian Guillut of Le Cordon Bleu in Paris, is one of the simplest but most memorable classics of French cuisine.

1 fresh duck foie gras (about 1 ½ lbs.), room temperature
⅓ cup good-quality sauternes
Salt and freshly ground black pepper
1 fresh black truffle, wiped clean and finely chopped (optional)

1. Starting with whole lobes of foie gras (**A**), pull any bits of translucent membrane from the surface of the foie gras and separate the two lobes, using a knife to sever any connecting veins (**B**). Probe for the main vein and its branches with your fingers, pulling it out as you follow its length. Inspect the folds for patches of bitter green bile and, if found, extract them with a knife. Slice off any bruises. Put foie gras in a nonreactive bowl with water to cover and plenty of ice cubes (**C**). Soak overnight in the refrigerator.

2. Drain foie gras and pat dry with paper towels, then break into even pieces. Put into a medium bowl or baking dish and drizzle sauternes over top. Season with salt and pepper and allow to marinate for 2 hours.

3. Preheat oven to 200°. Remove foie gras from marinade and press into a 2½-cup terrine, leaving a bit of space at top. Place terrine on 3 folded-over paper towels in the bottom of a deep ovenproof skillet (to steady terrine), and fill pan with hot water to reach halfway up sides of terrine. Place in the oven and cook until internal temperature of foie gras reaches 115° on a meat thermometer, about 30 minutes. Pour off and reserve fat. Set terrine aside to cool.

4. Cut a piece of cardboard to fit inside top of terrine and wrap it in plastic. Gently press cardboard onto foie gras and weight with a small can for 1 hour. Remove can and cardboard, return reserved fat to terrine, cover, and refrigerate 1–2 days.

5. To unmold, dip terrine in a bowl of warm water for 30 seconds, run a knife along edges, and invert onto a plate. (Reserve fat in terrine.) Serve sliced, garnished with truffle, if you like. If covered in reserved fat, foie gras will keep, refrigerated, for 1 week.

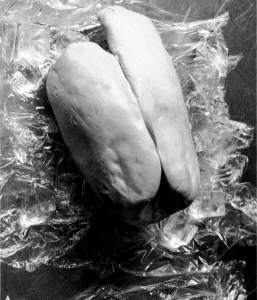

A

B

C

Liver Lore

T he French grade and classify foie gras, whether of duck or goose, with a manic fervor that defies comprehension by foreign infidels. Here are brief definitions of a few of the more important terms for the foie-gras buyer to understand:

FOIE GRAS FRAIS: Fresh raw liver. You buy it, take it home, and cook it right away. This is what the chefs of the great restaurants start with, and what you will need for the terrine recipe on the facing page.

FOIE GRAS ENTIER: This is the same as a terrine made with an entire lobe. At home, serve this as an appetizer with toasted brioche (for a little sweetness) or rustic sourdough and a glass of sauternes or port or other sweet wine.

BLOC OR MOUSSE DE FOIE GRAS: Reconstituted from smaller pieces or trimmings of foie gras (or lower-grade foie gras) and puréed. Serve on toasted bread to accompany an apéritif of sweet wine.

PÂTÉ DE FOIE GRAS: Often includes pork or chicken livers, pork fat, and/or puréed pork or ham, as well as scraps of duck or goose livers. Great in a baguette sandwich with a glass of red wine, but it's more pâté than foie gras.

Foie Gras de Canard Poêlé aux Raisins Blancs

(Seared Foie Gras with Green Grapes)

Serves 8

THE FRESHNESS of green grapes offsets the richness of the foie gras in this dish from Alain Dutournier's Au Trou Gascon in Paris—perhaps the most consistently satisfying outpost of southwestern French cooking in the capital.

Foie Gras as Talisman

I admit it," dancer and writer Marie-Pascale Lescot told us not long ago, "I smuggled a small, round, golden can of foie gras—my mother's homemade duck foie gras—into the United States. I couldn't help it. In the early 1970s, my parents settled into a sturdy 13th-century house in the middle of a cornfield in Bas Mauco, a 242-soul village in southwestern France. Before long, the local farmers had taught my mother an important local art: how to make duck foie gras. She became very good at it, and every November, she'd be flooded with orders from neighbors, friends, and relatives alike. But this was more than a small, homespun, under-the-table business. It became to us an autumn paean, a celebration of the richness, the generosity, the savor of the southwestern terroir. That's why I had to bring one of these cans with me to America when I left my French hometown—not as a gastronomic delicacy, but as an edible bond with a family, a region, a way of life. Passing through the airport in Boston, it did occur to me that I'd have no idea how to explain this rather Proustian concept to a U.S. customs official. Fortunately, I didn't have to—and when I finally got it to my new lodgings, I felt more than relief. I felt safe."

1 fresh duck foie gras
 (about 1 ½ lbs.), room
 temperature
Salt and freshly ground
 black pepper
¼ tsp. ground nutmeg
2 cups good-quality
 sauternes
1 clove garlic, crushed
 and peeled
1 tbsp. ruby port
¼ cup chicken stock
 (see page 56)
1 ½ tsp. sugar
1 tbsp. fine bread crumbs
2 cups large green grapes,
 halved and seeded

1. Starting with whole lobes of foie gras, pull any bits of translucent membrane from the surface of the foie gras and separate the two lobes, using a knife to sever any connecting veins. Probe for the main vein and its branches with your fingers, pulling it out as you follow its length. Inspect the folds for patches of bitter green bile and, if found, extract them with a knife. Slice off any bruises. Rinse foie gras under cold water, then pat dry with paper towels. Season to taste with salt, pepper, and nutmeg.

2. Reduce sauternes in a medium saucepan over medium heat for about 20 minutes, to about ½ cup, then set aside.

3. Preheat oven to 400°. Rub a large cast-iron skillet with garlic clove, then sear foie gras over high heat until nicely browned and crisp on the outside, about 2 minutes on each side. Remove foie gras and set aside. Pour off fat and reserve for another use.

4. Deglaze skillet with port, stock, and reduced sauternes. Add sugar, bread crumbs, grapes, and salt and pepper to taste. Cook over high heat 3 minutes. Return foie gras to skillet and place in oven 10–12 minutes, until interior is pinkish beige or reaches 120° on a meat thermometer. Serve thinly sliced, with sauce and grapes.

Baeckeoffe de Foie Gras

(Potted Foie Gras and Vegetables)

SERVES 4

ALSATIAN HOUSEWIVES used to fill crocks with meats and vegetables and take them to local bakers to be cooked; the resulting dish was called a baeckeoffe, literally a baker's oven. In Strasbourg (lower right), chef Émile Jung of the three-star Au Crocodile still seals his luxurious update of baeckeoffe with dough, lest we forget its humble origins.

*3 large red bliss potatoes,
   peeled and sliced*
*1 leek, white part only,
   washed and sliced*
*1 small yellow onion,
   peeled and sliced*
*5 small carrots, peeled
   and sliced*
*3 small turnips, peeled
   and sliced*
*1⅓ cups Alsatian riesling
   or other dry but fruity
   white wine*
*4 cups chicken stock
   (see page 56)*
3 bay leaves
3 sprigs fresh thyme
1 tbsp. duck or goose fat
*Salt and freshly ground
   black pepper*
*1 lobe of fresh duck foie
   gras (about ¾ lbs.),
   room temperature*
½ cup flour
*1 fresh black truffle,
   wiped clean and finely
   chopped (optional)*
*½ small head savoy
   cabbage, julienned*

1. Put potatoes, leeks, onions, carrots, turnips, wine, stock, bay leaves, thyme, and fat in a large pot. Season to taste with salt and pepper. Bring to a boil over high heat. Reduce heat to medium, cover, and simmer until vegetables are tender, about 25 minutes. Drain, reserving broth, and set vegetables aside.

2. Pull any bits of translucent membrane from surface of foie gras and use a knife to remove any of the connecting veins. Probe for the main vein and its branches with your fingers, pulling it out as you follow its length. Inspect the folds for patches of bitter green bile and, if found, extract them with a knife. Slice off any bruises. Season generously with salt and pepper.

3. Preheat oven to 400°. Mix flour with 5 tbsp. water in a bowl. Roll dough on a floured surface into the shape of a rope, about 24" long. Spoon half of the vegetables into a 2-quart terrine (with lid). Add foie gras, then truffles (if using) and remaining vegetables. Top with cabbage and reserved broth. Cover terrine, and wrap dough around rim to seal. Bake for 30 minutes. Remove baeckeoffe from oven, break seal, and remove lid. Transfer vegetables to a platter. Slice foie gras, then arrange over vegetables. Ladle broth from terrine over foie gras and vegetables before serving.

From Home to Haute

Alsace can boast 28 Michelin-starred establishments, including three that bear three stars, making it indisputably one of the gastronomic strongholds of France. The cuisine in the region, like the rest of local culture, shows vivid influences from both sides of the Rhine Valley—German and French—and can be both hearty and refined. There is an old Alsatian saying that "Meat is the best vegetable", and this is borne out by the continued popularity of such traditional dishes as choucroute garnie (with its veritable anthology of pork products; see page 226), baeckeoffe (lamb, beef, and pork layered with potatoes and baked slowly in a casserole), and stewed tripe, as well as a wide range of charcuterie and foie gras in several forms. Other definitive Alsatian specialties include crayfish soup (see recipe, page 65), coq au riesling (chicken cooked in white wine), flammekueche (a pizzalike tart), and numerous preparations of frogs' legs and snails. It is one of the reassuring glories of regional cookery here that these specialties seem to be able to exist as happily in homey and sophisticated versions.

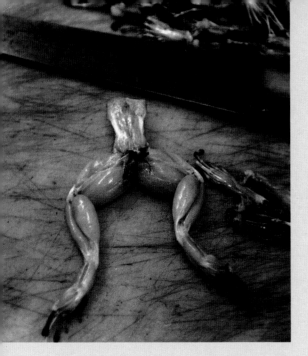

Frog Facts

Frogs apparently weren't eaten in Europe until the 16th century—before that time, they were associated with sorcery or thought to be poisonous (which in fact is true of some South American varieties)—and didn't become a gastronomic staple in France until the 1800s. Once the French nobility discovered the amphibians' culinary charms, however, they began devouring them at an alarming rate. By the end of World War II, the country's frog population was waning—helped towards oblivion by chemical pesticides polluting the ponds and marshes and by overfishing. In the 1960s, France began to import frogs from Yugoslavia and Albania, but those countries' stocks were quickly exhausted, too, and today the majority of the fresh frogs' legs imported by the French—some 600–700 tons of live creatures a year—come from Turkey and Egypt. France also imports, we are sorry to have to report, some 3,000–4,000 tons of frozen frogs' legs annually from Indonesia and China. Why is it only the legs of the frog that are consumed? Because the French prefer tiny frogs, whose muscular legs provide their only appreciable meat. However, many varieties of Asian frogs are bigger, and have bodies big enough to, well, suck on if not exactly chew.

Cuisses de Grenouilles au Beurre Persillade

(Frogs' Legs in Parsley Butter)

SERVES 4

SAUTÉING frogs' legs in butter with garlic and parsley is a classic Burgundian method of preparing this emblematic delicacy. We learned this simple procedure from chef Jean-Pierre Silva, whose Le Vieux Moulin in Bouilland, near Beaune (see sidebar, page 186), is one of Burgundy's best restaurants.

1½ lb. frogs' legs (about 8 large pairs), separated
½ cup flour
6 tbsp. butter
2 tsp. vegetable oil
Salt and freshly ground black pepper
4 cloves garlic, peeled and minced
½ cup minced fresh parsley

1. Rinse frogs' legs, drain, and thoroughly pat dry with paper towels. Dredge in flour and shake off excess.

2. Melt 4 tbsp. of the butter with the oil in a large nonstick skillet over medium-high heat. Add frogs' legs, season to taste with salt and pepper, and sauté until golden on all sides, about 4 minutes. Add garlic, parsley, and remaining 2 tbsp. butter and sauté 1 minute more. Divide frogs' legs between 4 warm plates, then drizzle with garlic parsley butter.

Mille-Feuilles de Grenouilles

(Frogs' Leg "Napoleons" with White Bean Sauce)

SERVES 4

THIS IMPROVISATION on a Burgundian theme was created by chef Jacques Lameloise at his three-star restaurant in Chagny. Look for fresh frogs' legs at Asian markets.

½ cup great northern
   beans
4 cloves garlic, peeled,
   1 whole and 3 minced
1 small yellow onion,
   peeled and finely
   chopped
1 oz. salt pork, finely
   chopped
1 bay leaf
5 sprigs fresh parsley
2 sprigs fresh thyme
2 medium carrots, peeled
   and finely chopped
1 cup strong chicken stock
   (see page 56)
2 cups heavy cream
Salt and freshly ground
   black pepper
6 tomatoes, peeled,
   quartered, and seeded
1 small stalk celery,
   minced
1 small zucchini, minced
3 tbsp. butter
2 lbs. frogs' legs (about
   12 pairs), separated
2 tsp. vegetable oil
4–8 sprigs chervil

1. Put beans, whole clove of garlic, half the onions, salt pork, bay leaf, parsley, thyme, and all but ⅓ cup of the carrots in a heavy pot. Add chicken stock and heavy cream. Bring to a boil over high heat, reduce heat to low, cover, and simmer until beans are very tender, about 2 hours. Season to taste with salt and pepper and cook 30 minutes more. Remove and discard bay leaf. Transfer beans and cooking liquid to a food processor and purée until smooth. Strain through a fine sieve back into the same pot. Cover to keep warm. Gently flatten tomato quarters, then season with salt and pepper and set aside.

2. Put remaining ⅓ cup carrots and 1 cup salted water in a saucepan, bring to a boil over high heat, reduce heat to medium, cover, and simmer for 3 minutes. Add celery and remaining onions and simmer, covered, for 3 minutes more. Add zucchini and simmer, covered, for another 4 minutes. Drain vegetables and return to pan. Add 1 tbsp. butter, and season to taste with salt and pepper. Cover and set aside.

3. Cut 8–12 of the frogs' legs into drumsticks and thighs. Melt remaining 2 tbsp. butter with oil in a nonstick skillet over medium heat, add minced garlic, and stir for 1 minute. Add all frogs' legs and sauté until golden on each side, about 3 minutes total, depending on size. Remove from heat and set aside 8–12 drumsticks. Remove and reserve meat from remaining frogs' legs, discarding bones.

4. Put a tart ring, 3" in diameter and 1½" deep, in the center of each of 4 plates. Arrange 2 tomato quarters, slightly overlapping, at bottom of each ring, then spread each evenly with ¼ cup reserved frogs' leg meat, then 2 tbsp. vegetables. Repeat layers, ending with tomatoes. Repeat process to make four "napoleons". Press down to help mold each one, then carefully slide off rings. Drizzle bean sauce around napoleons and garnish each plate with drumsticks and chervil.

L ameloise in Chagny is one of the surprisingly few French three-star restaurants that looks the part: Its marble floors are warmed with Persian carpets, its vaulted ceilings crossed with massive dark wooden beams, its white-washed stone walls hung with much better paintings than most elevated French restaurateurs seem to buy.

It is a comfortable monument to good taste. Under the direction of third-generation chef-proprietor Jacques Lameloise (above), it is also a monument to good flavors—both delicately contemporary and, best of all, heartily Burgundian; the great chefs of Burgundy are rarely better than when they stay close to home.

Snails have been a part of the human diet since prehistoric times, according to the evidence of heaps of shells found in archaeological digs. Today, the French are the world's leading consumers of the little gastropod by far, managing about 30,000 tons of them each year. The best French snails—and in fact the only ones that the official French snail-growers organization, Maîtres Escargotiers de France, recognize as escargots—are of the genus *Helix*. These include the celebrated and now endangered

escargots de Bourgogne (which come from the Franche-Comté, Savoie, and Champagne regions as well as Burgundy itself) and the petits-gris (little grays) of Provence and the Languedoc—as well as plain old escargots from other parts of the country. French snail lovers differentiate between *coureurs*, or runners, available in spring and fall; the *voilés*, or veiled ones, of summer (so called because the snails seal their apertures with a thin veil of mucus so that they don't dry out in the heat); and *operculés*, the operculated or covered ones, which seal themselves with a less permeable calcareous veil before hibernating for the winter. Connoisseurs collecting snails in the wild prefer voilés and operculés to coureurs; the latter have a higher moisture content.

Escargots à la Bourguignonne

(Snails in Parsley Butter)

SERVES 4

THE PLUMP, succulent snails of Burgundy (left), traditionally plucked from the vineyards, where they feed on vine leaves, were once among the region's gastronomic treasures—but like so many delicacies, they are disappearing. Fortunately, good-quality canned snails are fine in this dish.

½ lb. unsalted butter, softened
3 cloves garlic, peeled and minced
¼ cup minced fresh parsley
1 small shallot, peeled and minced
2 tsp. salt
½ tsp. freshly ground black pepper
Pinch freshly grated nutmeg
1 tbsp. dry white wine
1 tsp. cognac
2 dozen snail shells, cleaned
2 dozen canned giant snails (Burgundian if possible)
Rock salt

1. Beat together butter, garlic, parsley, shallots, salt, pepper, nutmeg, wine, and cognac in a medium mixing bowl. Cover and refrigerate for at least 4 hours, or overnight.

2. Preheat oven to 400°. Using a butter knife, fill each snail shell with about ½ tsp. butter mixture. Push a snail into each shell, then use remaining parsley butter to fill shells to the rim. Cover the bottom of a baking pan with rock salt and arrange escargots with butter side up. Bake until butter sizzles, about 10 minutes. Serve with good country bread, if you like, to soak up the butter.

Fricassée d'Escargots au Coulis de Persil

(Fricassée of Snails with Parsley and Roasted Garlic Cream)

SERVES 8

LIVE SNAILS (left) are preferred by most Burgundian chefs in preparing escargots. This elegant variation on the traditional local recipe (see page 130) is served at the Hostellerie des Clos in Chablis—an excellent restaurant noted both for its food and its encyclopedic local wine list.

3 small heads garlic
¼ cup olive oil
1 bunch flat-leaf parsley, trimmed
Salt
½ cup heavy cream
1 cup French chablis
Freshly ground black pepper
½ cup escargot brine (juice from canned snails, below)
6 tbsp. butter
4 dozen canned giant snails (Burgundian if possible)

1. Preheat oven to 250°. Slice off the top of each head of garlic, exposing cloves, and slightly spread cloves apart. Place garlic in a small baking dish, drizzle with oil, then cover dish with aluminum foil. Bake until cloves have softened, about 2 hours.

2. Reserve 8 parsley sprigs for garnish, and blanch the rest in a pot of boiling salted water over high heat for about 30 seconds. Drain and dry on paper towels, then finely chop and set aside.

3. Reserve 8 cloves roasted garlic in their skins for garnish, peel remaining cloves, and transfer to a blender or food processor. Add cream and 2 tbsp. of the chablis and purée until smooth. Season to taste with salt and pepper, transfer to a small saucepan, cover, and warm gently over low heat.

4. Combine escargot brine and remaining chablis in a small saucepan and bring to a simmer over medium heat. Season to taste with salt and pepper and cook for 5 minutes. Add 2 tbsp. of the butter, stirring until melted, then remove from heat. Stir in chopped parsley, and cover pan to keep warm.

5. Melt remaining 4 tbsp. butter in a large nonstick skillet over medium heat and sauté snails until hot, 3–5 minutes. Divide parsley sauce between 8 plates, then swirl garlic cream into each serving. Spoon snails in center of each plate and garnish with parsley sprigs and garlic cloves.

Chablis vs. Chablis

To Americans, chablis—much of it produced in California's hot, dry central valley—is cheap generic white jug wine; to the French, chablis—made only in and around the pretty little town of Chablis in the northwestern corner of Burgundy—is one of the world's great white wines. It all depends, of course, on whose "chablis" you're drinking; but under no circumstances confuse the two. The real thing, the original, is made entirely from chardonnay, and is sometimes said to embody that grape's flavor and aroma more purely and truly than any other wine. Some producers in the region have phased out the oak barrels traditionally employed for fermentation and/or aging in favor of stainless steel vats—on the theory that chablis is a wine whose unique character (it is famous for its minerally *goût de pierre à fusil* or gunflint flavor) is best left uncomplicated by the vanilla-scented richness of oak. Other makers of the wine—including some of the best, like René and Vincent Dauvissat and François and Jean-Marie Raveneau—maintain that judicious use of oak fills out the chablis, complementing its acidity and flint. Chablis is usually consumed young, but the best examples—especially those from the grands crus vineyards of Les Clos, Blanchots, Bougros, Vaudésir, Valmur, Les Preuses, and Grenouilles—can grow positively stunning with 10 or 20 years of age.

Buried Treasure

The "black" wine of Cahors, in the Quercy region, has been famous for centuries. Another black treasure drawn from local earth, even more sought after, has earned its celebrity a bit more recently—only in the past 150 years or so: This is the black truffle, *Tuber melanosporum*, one of the greatest of all gastronomic delicacies. Though the truffles of the Périgord region, immediately northwest of Quercy, are better known, the precious tubers have been harvested on Quercy's *causses*, or arid plains, since at least the late 19th century, and are an integral part of the local cuisine. Ironically, it was the destruction of the region's vineyards by phylloxera around 1880 that gave impetus to the truffle industry here: Recognizing that the thin soil and porous limestone earth of the causses offered ideal growing conditions for truffles, many local farmers replaced their ravaged vines with truffle oaks—whose root systems provide nutrients for the soil, encouraging the tubers to form (even as the truffles feed the trees). Though no one has yet cultivated truffles consistently, these farmers were largely successful in their efforts. In the winter months today, many Quercy towns have truffle markets offering the black jewels to wholesale and retail customers alike.

Fricassée de Cèpes aux Truffes

(Cèpe Fricassée with Truffles)

SERVES 6

CÈPES (*Boletus edulis*)—the wild mushrooms known in Italy as funghi porcini—"little pig mushrooms", for their size and succulence—are greatly appreciated in southwestern France, where they are sometimes combined with that other noble fungus, the truffle, as in this recipe from Cahors.

2 lbs. fresh cèpes
4 tbsp. olive oil
7 cloves garlic, peeled
1½ cups chicken stock
    (see page 56)
10 sprigs fresh thyme
Salt and freshly ground
    black pepper
3 oz. fresh black truffles,
    wiped clean
4 tbsp. butter, cut into
    small pieces

1. Separate cèpe stems from caps with a paring knife and remove and discard spongy underpart of caps if soft. Peel stems and cut into ¼"-thick slices. Cut caps into quarters or sixths depending upon size.

2. Heat 2 tbsp. oil in a large skillet over medium heat. Add 5 cloves of garlic and cook, stirring frequently, for 2 minutes. Add cèpe stems and cook until tender, about 5 minutes.

3. Transfer garlic and stems to a food processor, add stock, and purée until smooth. Strain through a fine sieve into a small saucepan. Simmer over medium-high heat until reduced by half, 7–10 minutes. Cover and keep warm over low heat.

4. Wipe out large skillet and heat remaining 2 tbsp. oil over medium-high heat. Add cèpe caps and remaining 2 cloves garlic and sauté for 3 minutes, then add 4 sprigs of the thyme, season to taste with salt and pepper, and cook, stirring occasionally, until caps are golden, about 3 minutes.

5. Using a truffle slicer or vegetable peeler, thinly shave truffles into skillet, toss with cèpes, and cook just until heated through, about 1 minute. Whisk butter into sauce, and season to taste with salt and pepper. Remove and discard sautéed garlic and thyme, evenly divide cèpe and truffles between 6 plates, surround with sauce, and garnish with remaining thyme.

Pommes à la Sarladaise aux Truffes

(Sarladais-Style Potatoes with Truffles)

SERVES 6

THIS RECIPE is from Pierre-Jean Duribreux, chef at Le Vieux Logis in Trémolat; *à la sarladaise* means in the style of nearby Sarlat—which now implies truffles and goose fat.

2 lbs. russet potatoes, peeled and chopped into ½" pieces
Salt
5 tbsp. goose fat
1 clove garlic, peeled and minced
2 tbsp. finely chopped fresh parsley
1 3–4 oz. fresh black truffle, wiped clean and cut into matchsticks
Freshly ground black pepper

1. Blanch potatoes in a large pot of boiling salted water for 3 minutes. Drain and pat dry with paper towels.

2. Heat a large cast-iron or heavy skillet over medium-high heat for 1–2 minutes. Add 2 tbsp. of the fat and all the potatoes; be careful of spattering fat. Cook, stirring occasionally, until a crisp golden crust forms, about 10 minutes. Add 1 tbsp. fat and continue to cook, scraping crust off the bottom of the skillet and turning the potatoes to brown on all sides, for another 10 minutes. Crush potatoes slightly with a large fork, taking care not to turn them into a purée. Reduce heat to medium, then add garlic, parsley, and remaining 2 tbsp. fat. Cook, stirring often, for 2 minutes. Add truffles, continue stirring, and cook for another 2 minutes. Season to taste with salt and pepper.

The event of the season each January in the portion of Provence called the Vaucluse—where 70 percent of France's annual truffle production originates—is the Messe de la Truffe, or truffle mass, held on the third Sunday of the month at the little church in the village of Richerenches, one of the local truffle capitals. The villagers, many of whom are truffle gatherers, and their families (facing page), come here to thank Saint Anthony, patron saint of the village, and to ask for a good truffle harvest. (Saint Anthony, remember, blesses the search for things lost.) In return, they contribute truffles instead of money when the alms basket is passed; the truffles are to be auctioned off later, for the greater good of the parish. The sermon intermingles religious considerations with the spirit of the hunt: Search for faith with as much passion as you search for truffles, the pastor might say; truffles are a gift from God's earth, so return a fair share for His glory; and remember that faith gives flavor to your life, as the truffle gives flavor to an omelette.

The Pig or the Dog?

Historically, France has been divided into regions that prefer the pig for truffle-hunting (the Dordogne, Quercy, and Provence) and those that swear by the dog (Burgundy, Champagne, and the Haut-Dauphiné). No one dog breed stands out for hunting truffles; spaniels, griffons, sheepdogs, and mongrels seem equally adept. Proponents of porcine truffle hunters point out that young female pigs have a very sharp, well-developed sense of smell—and that a well-trained sow will actually unearth the truffle with its snout, whereas dogs will only indicate its location. Why are dogs used more often than pigs today, then? The main reason, say experts, is the unfortunate extinction of most of France's indigenous porcine breeds. Dogs have more stamina and are more intelligent and obedient than the modern pig breeds, it is said, though the old breeds would have run them ragged. In the Dordogne and Quercy, truffle hunters who prefer the pig have high hopes for a newly imported breed, the Large White Yorkshire—said to be a natural.

Oeufs Brouillés aux Truffes

(Scrambled Eggs with Truffles)

IN HER 1960 CLASSIC *French Provincial Cooking*, Elizabeth David shares a secret she learned from a French truffle hunter: Before cooking eggs with truffles, as in this recipe, mix the two ingredients together and let them sit for a while, so that the truffle flavor permeates the eggs.

6 eggs
½ oz. fresh black truffle, wiped clean and very thinly sliced
1 ½ tbsp. cold butter
2 tbsp. heavy cream
Salt and freshly ground black pepper

1. Beat eggs in a bowl, add truffle slices, cover, and refrigerate for 3–4 hours. Melt butter in a large heavy-bottomed skillet over medium heat just until it stops foaming, about 1 minute. Mix cream into eggs, then pour into skillet. Wait for 5 seconds, then using a wooden spoon pull eggs in towards center of skillet allowing uncooked eggs to flow into the empty part of pan. Do not stir. Cook until eggs are set but still moist, 2–3 minutes. Season to taste with salt and pepper.

Poulet Demi-Deuil

(*Truffled Chicken*)

SERVES 4

THOUGH CHICKEN is the foodstuff most often prepared "demi-deuil" (in half-mourning), the term is also applied to truffled eggs, potato salad, and spiny lobster (langouste)— all "white" foods darkened with the black of la truffe. Chef and cookbook author James Peterson developed this simplification of the classic chicken version of the dish.

1 3½-lb. chicken, rinsed
  and dried
¾ oz. fresh black truffle,
  wiped clean and sliced
  into thin rounds
Salt and freshly ground
  black pepper
2 tbsp. butter, softened
1 clove garlic, peeled and
  halved lengthwise
1 tbsp. rainwater madeira
1 tsp. cognac

1. Working from the neck opening, use your fingers to gently pry chicken skin away from as much of the breast and legs as you can without tearing it. Slip truffle slices under skin in a single layer, covering as much flesh as possible. Truss chicken with kitchen string by tying legs together and binding the bird into a compact package. Wrap loosely in plastic, and refrigerate overnight.

2. Preheat oven to 400°. Rub chicken with salt and pepper and a little of the butter. Rub the inside of a small heavy casserole with garlic and remaining butter. (The casserole should have a tight-fitting lid and be just a little bigger than the chicken.) Pour madeira and cognac around chicken in casserole. Tightly cover and bake for 1 hour. Lift cover at the table to allow everyone to enjoy the fragrant steam. Serve with buttered egg noodles and good crusty bread, if you like.

Delicious Mourning

Mère Fillioux, one of the famous "mothers" of Lyonnais gastronomy, was famous for her poulet en demi-deuil, literally chicken in half-mourning—so called because of the black robe of truffles under its skin. Eugénie Brazier, another Lyonnais Mère, worked for Fillioux for three years at her restaurant, then went on to open her own place—where she became the first, and thus far only, female chef to earn the ultimate three-star rating in the Guide Michelin. In her honor, Paul Bocuse (who had worked in her kitchen as a young man) renamed the dish, which is traditionally made with the famous chickens of Bresse (see page 185), "poularde de Bresse truffée Mère Brazier". Today, Eugénie's granddaughter, Jacotte Brazier, runs the restaurant Eugénie founded, and still serves the classic chicken dish to which her ancestor's name has been attached.

CHAPTER

6

SEAFOOD

"IN THE FALL OF 1991, I moved to the pretty port town of Sanary-sur-Mer, just west of Toulon on the Mediterranean coast of France, to live for a time with a close-knit group of professional fishermen. For the better part of a year, I'd meet them at the dock in the predawn darkness, beneath a silvery moon, boarding one of their tiny fishing boats and heading out to sea. I learned a lot about these fishermen, and developed lasting friendships with them. Lucien Vitiello (facing page, lower left, in white shirt), the weathered leader of the group, spent the most time with me, and taught me about the passion that drives these men to devotedly pursue such a harsh existence. One beautiful spring afternoon, Vitiello invited me to his home in the hills above Sanary to share a bouillabaisse. I arrived to find him cleaning a large accumulation of fish, most of which he had netted the day before—a combination of soft-fleshed varieties like wrasse and forkbeard, which would disintegrate during cooking and enrich the soup, and firmer ones like john dory, conger eel, and of course rascasse, or scorpion fish [see page 147]. 'Of course,' he explained, 'you use what you're lucky enough to catch.' After cleaning the fish, Vitiello poured some fruity olive oil into an enormous pot, scattered onions and garlic into it, then added some fennel tops and herbs. Tomatoes and sliced potatoes went in next, then the fish, which were topped with a few more tomatoes. He doused everything with richly scented fish stock, tossed in a handful of tiny Mediterranean crabs and another of mussels, then gave the entire dish a spritz of pastis and a big pinch of saffron. His bouillabaisse was now ready for the fire. Less than an hour later, Vitiello's wife, Loulou, called out 'À table!'" —RICHARD GOODMAN

RECIPES

Bouillabaisse

LUCIEN VITIELLO (facing page) makes bouillabaisse this way, using a wide variety of fish. Rouille is the traditional accompanying red-pepper mayonnaise (*rouille* means rust).

1 24" baguette, cut into
½"-thick slices
2 cloves garlic, peeled

FOR ROUILLE:
4 cloves garlic, peeled
2 tbsp. fish stock
(see page 62)
½ tsp. saffron threads
1 cup mayonnaise
½ tsp. sweet paprika
Pinch cayenne
Salt

FOR BOUILLABAISSE:
½ cup olive oil
2 medium yellow onions,
peeled and sliced
5 cloves garlic, peeled and
crushed
3 sprigs fresh parsley
3 sprigs fresh thyme
1 bay leaf
¼ cup fennel tops
2 lbs. new potatoes, peeled
and sliced
1½ lbs. tomatoes, peeled,
seeded, and chopped
6 lbs. assorted cleaned fish
(see sidebar, facing page)
16 mussels, scrubbed and
debearded
2½ quarts warm fish
stock (see page 62)
1 tsp. saffron threads
½ cup pastis
Salt and freshly ground
black pepper

1. Preheat oven to 350°. Place bread on a cookie sheet and toast until golden, turning once, about 10 minutes per side. Rub toast on both sides with garlic, then discard them. Set bread aside.

2. For rouille, mince garlic and set aside. Put fish stock in a mortar, crumble in saffron, add minced garlic, and grind mixture with a pestle until smooth. Transfer to a bowl and stir in mayonnaise, paprika, and cayenne. Season to taste with salt and set aside. (Rouille should be made the day it is to be used; it does not keep well.)

3. For bouillabaisse, heat ¼ cup of the oil in a 10–12 quart pot over low heat. Add onions, garlic, parsley, thyme, bay leaf, and fennel tops. Add potatoes, then tomatoes. Add large, whole, firm fish first, then smaller, more delicate fish, and finally mussels.

4. Pour in stock and remaining ¼ cup of oil. Crumble in saffron and add pastis. Season to taste with salt and pepper and raise heat to high. Ingredients will cook as bouillabaisse comes to a boil; start checking after about 5 minutes and carefully transfer seafood to a platter as it cooks. (Discard any mussels that do not open.) When potatoes have cooked (this can take up to 25 minutes, depending on age of potatoes), transfer them to same platter, then strain broth and set aside.

5. To serve, for the first course, spread rouille on toast, put 3 or more pieces in each of 8 warmed soup bowls, and add broth. For the second course, serve a platter of fish and potatoes at room temperature. Moisten with additional broth and add a dollop of rouille, if you like.

B ouillabaisse without rascasse," asserts Lucien Vitiello, "is like paella without rice." Unfortunately for Americans, this common flavorful Mediterranean poisson, called scorpion fish in English, is rarely available here. The good news is that an excellent bouillabaisse can indeed be made without it. The important thing, French and American chefs alike agree, is to use the freshest, tastiest seafood available. Red snapper, sea bass, tilefish, grouper, striped bass, monkfish, halibut, john dory, even squid or cuttlefish are among the possibilities. Paul Bertolli, chef and part-owner of Oliveto in Oakland, California, recommends a selection of the small, inexpensive rockfish found in Asian markets. Most experts agree, though, that the American bouillabaisse-maker would do well to avoid freshwater fish like trout and catfish; mild fish, like swordfish or salmon; flaky fish, like cod; and strong, oily fish, like mackerel.

147

Cotriade

(Breton Seafood in Broth)

SERVES 6

THE FLAVOR of this Breton fisherman's dish is subtler than that of bouillabaisse. At his restaurant in Plounérin, Patrick Jeffroy sometimes dresses up cotriade with saffron and shellfish. Here is his version of this classic "soup".

4 tbsp. butter
2 small carrots, peeled and finely diced
2 medium yellow onions, peeled and finely chopped
2 leeks, white part only, washed and finely chopped
4 cloves garlic, peeled and minced
3 tomatoes, peeled, seeded, and diced
1 lb. white potatoes, peeled and diced
3 lbs. assorted fish, such as cod, halibut, red snapper, or monkfish, cut into pieces about 2" square
2 sprigs fresh thyme
1 sprig fresh dill
¼ tsp. saffron threads
1 tbsp. grated orange zest
1 tbsp. grated lemon zest
6 cups fish stock (see page 62)
Salt and freshly ground black pepper
2 cups dry white wine
2 medium shallots, peeled and finely chopped
2 dozen mussels, scrubbed and debearded
½ lb. jumbo shrimp, peeled and deveined
6 small crabs, cleaned (optional)

1. Melt butter in a large pot over medium-low heat. Cook carrots, onions, leeks, and garlic until soft, about 15 minutes. Add tomatoes and potatoes, and cook until potatoes are slightly tender, about 8 minutes.

2. Place fish on top of vegetables, thicker pieces on bottom, thinner pieces on top. Add thyme, dill, saffron, orange zest, lemon zest, and fish stock. Season with salt and pepper, increase heat to medium-high, bring to a simmer, then cover, and cook for 10 minutes. Remove fish and vegetables and set aside, reserving broth.

3. Meanwhile, add white wine and shallots to a large pot. Bring to a boil over medium-high heat and add mussels, shrimp, and crabs (if using). Cover and cook, shaking pan occasionally, until mussels open, shrimp turn pink, and crabs turn red, about 4 minutes. Remove shellfish with a slotted spoon, reserving liquid. Discard any mussels that don't open and set pan aside for about 10 minutes so that any sand in the liquid will settle to the bottom.

4. Ladle shellfish broth into fish broth, then strain through a fine sieve lined with cheesecloth, discarding solids. Season broth to taste with salt and pepper. Divide fish, vegetables, and shellfish between 6 warmed soup bowls and ladle broth on top. Serve with additional broth on the side.

Cauldrons of Seafood

The word *cotriade* is thought by some to derive from the Breton *kaoter* (cauldron) and *iad* (contents): Breton contract fishermen used to be paid in fish—the lesser varieties—and their wives would toss whatever they brought home into the pot. Since at least the beginning of the 18th century, when large fishing boats began setting out from ports along the coast of Brittany on expeditions that could last for weeks, even months, fishermen have been making cotriade themselves on shipboard. It was an ideal dish under the circumstances, based on easily stored, long-lived ingredients like garlic, onions, and potatoes (with leeks and carrots added when possible) and whatever lesser seafood was caught—for instance, mackerel, conger eel, and sometimes red mullet. Saffron may seem like an atypically luxurious ingredient under the circumstances, but in fact this costly spice has been cultivated in France since the 16th century, and has been used in Brittany as early as the 19th century—when it may well have been incorporated into cotriade.

I n French culinary terminology, à la marinière (or just "marinière") means seaman's style, and usually refers to shellfish cooked with onions or shallots, white wine, and herbs. Here are some other nautically inspired food terms:

À LA BATALIÈRE: In the style of a boatman or ferryman; a garnish of mushrooms, onions, fried eggs, and crayfish, or pastry boats filled with seafood in a white sauce.

À LA CANOTIÈRE: Also "boatman's style" (a *canot* is a small open boat), in this case meaning freshwater fish poached in white wine.

À LA CORSAIRE: Literally corsair- or pirate-style—not a fish dish at all, but an ancient chicken dish from St-Malo in Brittany, probably using assorted spices.

MATELOTE: "Sailor style", a term usually associated, gastronomically, with the Loire region, where it means a stew of mixed freshwater fish, especially eel, carp, pike, perch, or barbal, cooked in wine (sometimes red) with onions, mushrooms, and perhaps crayfish tails and fried bread.

À LA NAGE: Literally "swimming", and meaning shellfish that is poached in an aromatic broth of white wine, herbs, shallots, and usually cream.

Moules Marinière

(Mussels with White Wine)

SERVES 4–6

ON THE PROMENADE in the seaside town of Trouville, in Normandy, the bistro called Le Central is famous for its moules marinière (right), and this is their recipe. Local fishmongers will tell you that salt isn't necessary (the seawater-drunk mussels are salty enough) and that pepper "tue le goût"—kills the flavor—of these delicious bivalves.

½ lb. unsalted butter
4 medium yellow onions, peeled and chopped
¾ bottle dry, acidic white wine, preferably muscadet
8–9 lbs. mussels, scrubbed and debearded
1 bunch fresh parsley, finely chopped
Freshly ground black pepper (optional)
1 baguette (optional)

1. Melt butter in a large, deep skillet with a lid over medium heat. Add onions and sauté until soft and golden, about 15 minutes. Add wine and mussels and cover. Shake the skillet regularly, holding the lid down firmly, and continue to cook until mussels open, about 10 minutes. (Discard any mussels that don't open.)

2. Divide mussels and their broth between 6 warmed soup bowls. Sprinkle generously with parsley and, if using, with pepper. Serve with fresh crusty bread, if you like, to soak up the broth.

Homard à l'Armoricaine

(Lobster in Tomato Sauce)

SERVES 4

EVERY CHEF in Brittany has a favored version of this controversially named—and possibly Parisian-born—lobster specialty (see sidebar, right). We learned this interpretation from Breton chef Patrick Jeffroy (see page 242).

2 3-lb. live lobsters
¼ cup olive oil
1 medium yellow onion, peeled and finely chopped
3 medium shallots, peeled and minced
1 clove garlic, peeled and minced
2 carrots, peeled, trimmed, and finely diced
2 tomatoes, chopped
2 tbsp. tomato paste
2 cups dry white wine
3 tbsp. butter, softened
½ tsp. cayenne
2 tbsp. crème fraîche
2 tbsp. minced fresh parsley

1. Cook lobster in a large pot of boiling water for 10 minutes. When cool, split open, remove meat, and cut into large pieces. Reserve tomalley, coral, and shells.

2. Heat oil in a large skillet over medium-low heat. Add onions, shallots, and garlic and cook for 15 minutes. Add carrots, tomatoes, tomato paste, wine, and 1 cup water. Reduce heat to low, and simmer for 8 minutes.

3. Wrap shells in a dish towel and crush with a rolling pin. Add to sauce and cook until sauce is reduced by half. Strain through a fine sieve, and return to heat. Mix together tomalley, coral, and butter in a small bowl, then stir into sauce. Add lobster, season to taste with cayenne, and cook 2 minutes. Stir in crème fraîche. Serve over rice. Garnish with parsley.

Lobster à la What?

The most famous Breton seafood dish of all—made with cut-up lobster sautéed with shallots, tomatoes, and cayenne, sometimes with white wine, cognac, and/or a dash of cream added—is homard à l'armoricaine, the name derived from Armor, the ancient Celtic word for Brittany's coastal region. Or is it homard à l'américaine? *Larousse Gastronomique* says so, proposing that the dish was invented in Paris in the 1860s by a French chef named Pierre Fraisse, who had worked for a time in Chicago and, supposedly improvising it for last-minute customers one night, named it in honor of his American experience. Other sources suggest that "à l'américaine" was simply a menu misprint for à l'armoricaine, or even that the dish came from Minorca (known for its spiny lobster and its tomatoes), and was originally "à la minorcaine". We like to think, as the Bretons do, that it belongs to Brittany, to Armor.

Dorade Farcie Grillée

(Grilled Stuffed Sea Bream)

SERVES 4

SEA BREAM is one of the Mediterranean's tastiest fish. Striped bass may be substituted in this recipe from Joël Guillet of Le Mas du Langoustier on the Île de Porquerolles.

1 large red bell pepper
4 plum tomatoes, halved lengthwise and seeded
6 tbsp. olive oil
Salt and freshly ground black pepper
2 large shallots, peeled and minced
12 niçoise olives, pitted and coarsely chopped
2 anchovies, finely chopped
4 1-lb. sea bream, porgy, or striped bass, deboned, with heads removed and reserved for stock
6 small leeks, trimmed, washed and thinly sliced lengthwise
¼ cup fresh lemon juice
½ cup dry white wine
¼ tsp. saffron threads
8 tbsp. chilled butter, cut into small pieces

1. Preheat broiler. Place pepper and tomatoes on a baking sheet, drizzle with about 2 tbsp. of the oil, and broil, turning the pepper 3–4 times, until pepper is charred and tomatoes are soft, 12–15 minutes. Remove from broiler, set tomatoes aside, and transfer pepper to a small bowl. Cover bowl with plastic and set aside. When pepper is cool, halve, remove and discard seeds and veins, then peel, coarsely chop, season to taste with salt and pepper, and set aside.

2. Coarsely chop tomatoes, season to taste with salt and pepper, and set aside separately from peppers. Heat 2 tbsp. of the oil in a large skillet over medium-high heat. Add half of the shallots and cook, stirring, until fragrant, about 2 minutes. Add olives, anchovies, and peppers and cook, stirring, for 30 seconds. Add tomatoes, cook for 30 seconds more, season to taste with salt and pepper, then set aside to cool.

3. Preheat oven to 400°. Heat a grill pan over high heat. Lay fish out flat, butterfly fashion, then brush skin with oil, season to taste with salt and pepper, and fold closed into original shape. Grill fish in pan, turning once, about 1 minute per side, then transfer fish to a clean surface. Open fish, then spoon a quarter of the tomato mixture into each one. Fold each fish closed and transfer to a large baking dish. Bake until fish flake easily, about 7 minutes, then remove from oven, cover with foil, and keep warm.

4. Meanwhile, heat remaining 2 tbsp. oil in large skillet over medium heat. Add leeks and 2 tbsp. water. Cook, stirring frequently, until leeks are soft and pan almost dry, 5–8 minutes. Season leeks to taste with salt and pepper and set aside.

5. Combine lemon juice, wine, and remaining shallots in a medium saucepan. Bring to a boil over high heat and reduce liquid by three-quarters, about 5 minutes. Lower heat to medium-low, crumble in saffron, gradually whisk in butter, and season to taste with salt and pepper. Divide leeks between 4 plates. Arrange fish over leeks, then spoon sauce around it.

The Real Thing

The Romans admired the daurade royale, or gilthead bream, so much that they farmed it in Lake Lucrino, near Naples, fattening the fish on a diet of oysters—which were opened fresh for them day and night. The modern French agree. There are said to be as many as 22 varieties of bream in the Mediterranean alone, as well as a dozen or so close relatives, known as porgies, in North American waters (and more still in the Caribbean), but the gilthead is widely regarded to be the regal head of the family. Fished from May to October, and weighing as much as seven pounds, it bears a golden crescent on its forehead, and has firm, white, delicately flavored flesh. The French sometimes call it la vraie daurade, the real one, and even give it the honor of its own spelling: Lesser varieties of the fish are commonly called dorade instead. Another very good fish is the pagre, or couch's sea bream, which is the only Mediterranean

bream also found on the American side of the Atlantic (it is sometimes sold as red porgy in the U.S); it is this variety that chef Joël Guillet at Le Mas du Langoustier on the Île de Porquerolles (proprietors Georges Richard and Marie Caroline Le Ber, above) likes to use for the dish [facing page, right]. Other bream consumed in France include the denté, or dentex (literally "toothy"; its prominent lower jaw boasts as many as six canine teeth); the sar doré, or two-banded bream; the dorade rose, or red sea bream (also known as fausse daurade, or false daurade, and as gros yeux, or big eyes); and the dorade grise, or black sea bream. All of these can be quite delicious, and all are less expensive than the daurade royale.

Sole Meunière

(Sole Sautéed in Butter)

SERVES 4

GABRIEL BISCAY, the chef at Prunier in Paris, whose recipe we've adapted here, doesn't use flour in his sole meunière; we do, because it's traditional, and helps brown the fish. To filet sole, trace backbone with a knife, cutting through to bone, then lift flesh off. Gently lift out bone.

FOR CLARIFIED
  BUTTER:
1 lb. unsalted butter

FOR SOLE:
4 14-oz. whole dover sole
Salt and freshly ground
  black pepper
Flour
1 cup clarified butter;
  see step 1
1 large russet potato,
  peeled and thickly sliced
16 tbsp. (2 sticks) butter
Juice of 2 lemons

1. For clarified butter, put butter in a small heavy saucepan over very low heat. Do not stir or allow to come to a boil. When butter has melted, completely skim off foam and carefully pour yellow fat into a clean container, discarding milky sediment on the bottom of the pan. Keep refrigerated.

2. For sole, cut off head and fins with sharp kitchen scissors. Scrape scales from the white-skinned side (bottom) of the fish with a large wide knife. On dark side of fish, score skin just above the tail with a sharp knife, then, holding the fish by the tail with one hand, use the other to peel off the dark skin all at once. If the skin catches, use a sharp knife to free it from the flesh. (There is no need to skin the other side.) Wipe fish thoroughly with a damp kitchen towel, taking care to wipe away any blood. (To save these steps, ask your fishmonger to give the fish to you pan-ready.) Pat dry, season to taste with salt and pepper, and dredge in flour, shaking off any excess.

3. Pour ½ cup clarified butter in each of 2 large skillets set over medium-high heat. When butter is just smoking, about 3 minutes, place 2 fish, white side down, into each pan. Immediately place a slice of raw potato under tail of each fish to raise thin end of sole up from the heat and help prevent overcooking. Brown fish, about 3–4 minutes on each side, pressing down on fish with a spatula and basting continually with butter. Add 2 tbsp. of the regular butter to each pan, season to taste with salt and pepper and baste for 1 more minute. Transfer to serving platter and keep warm.

4. Melt remaining 12 tbsp. butter in a small skillet over high heat. Swirl pan over heat until butter foams and turns light golden. Whisk in lemon juice and pour over sole, coating them completely. Serve fish on a platter garnished with lemon and fresh herbs, if you like.

Mosaics and Oyster Shells

P runier, on the corner of the rue Traktir and the avenue Victor Hugo in Paris, is an excellent seafood restaurant and also an extraordinary testament to the glories of the Art Deco era in France. The establishment was opened by Émile Prunier in 1925, the year of the capital's famous Art Deco salon and exhibition, and some of the style's most celebrated architects and designers contributed to the design: Auguste Labouret undertook the mosaic façade; Louis-Hippolyte Boileau created the dining room, with its blue-black marble-encrusted walls; Gaston Le Bourgeois sculpted the area behind the bar to evoke the world beneath the sea. Sadly, Prunier, whose father had run the original Prunier in Paris, died the year his new restaurant opened—but his daughter Simone took the place over and made it a success, known especially for its oysters and other shellfish, including a definitive version of lobster thermidor. Today, Prunier is under the management of Jean-Claude Vrinat, proprietor of the three-star Taillevent (see page 221)—and remains one of the best seafood restaurants in Europe.

Cigars and Sea Sows

The French tend to give their fish and shellfish imaginative nicknames—which can color one's perception of the seafood in question. Here are some of the more colorful monikers:

◆ Bécasse de mer (woodcock of the sea): red mullet, so named because, like the famous game bird, it can be cooked ungutted ◆ Cigare (cigar): grey mullet, so named for its shape ◆ Cochon de mer (pig of the sea): triggerfish, a brightly colored Mediterranean species ◆ Coq de mer (sea rooster): box crab ◆ Crapaud (toad), diable de mer (sea devil), or truie de mer (sea sow): the notoriously ugly scorpion fish (above), which goes by the more dignified name of rascasse at the fishmonger's ◆ Estrangle belle-mère (mother-in-law strangler): a Provençal term for scad or horse mackerel, different from ordinary mackerel and not as good ◆ Ivrogne de mer (sea drunkard): a small fish with red scales ◆ Langue d'avocat (lawyer's tongue): a Bordelais name for small sole ◆ Sauterelle de mer (sea grasshopper): mantis shrimp ◆ Tomate de mer (sea tomato): red sea anemone.

Loup de Mer Rôti aux Herbes

(Whole Sea Bass Roasted with Herbs)

SERVES 4

FARM-RAISED striped bass, increasingly available in America, makes a good substitute for the loup de mer, or sea bass, used in Corsica (below) for this exquisitely simple dish.

4 1½-lb. farm-raised
    striped bass, cleaned
    and scaled
Salt and freshly ground
    black pepper
3 medium tomatoes, cored
    and sliced into rounds
2 medium lemons, sliced
    into rounds
3 cloves garlic, peeled and
    sliced
½ bunch fresh rosemary
½ bunch fresh thyme
½ bunch fresh mint
3–5 bay leaves
Extra-virgin olive oil

1. Preheat oven to 450°. Arrange fish on a large baking sheet. Season fish cavities with salt and pepper to taste, then divide the tomatoes, half the lemon slices, and a little of the garlic, rosemary, thyme, and mint between them, stuffing the cavities loosely. Scatter bay leaves and remaining lemons, garlic, rosemary, thyme, and mint over fish. Drizzle with olive oil and season to taste with salt and pepper.

2. Roast fish until skin is crisp and flesh is just cooked through, about 20 minutes. Allow fish to rest 5 minutes before serving.

Raie Raide
au Beurre Clarifié

(Skate in Clarified Butter)

SERVES 4

AT APICIUS, a highly original Parisian two-star, chef Jean-Pierre Vigato is famous for unlikely combinations of ingredients and the inspired use of modest ones, as in this recipe.

1 tbsp. extra-virgin olive oil
¼ tsp. fresh lemon juice
Salt and freshly ground black pepper
2 cups baby spinach leaves, trimmed and washed
6 tbsp. butter
3 ½ tbsp. aged sherry vinegar
1 tbsp. ketchup
¼ cup finely diced peeled granny smith apple
2 tbsp. finely diced peeled red bell pepper
2 tbsp. finely diced peeled celery, blanched
1 tbsp. finely diced peeled pithed lemon flesh
1 tbsp. capers
2 tbsp. minced fresh parsley
4 6-oz. skate filets
3 tbsp. clarified butter (see page 156, step 1)

1. Pour oil and lemon juice into a mixing bowl and whisk together. Season to taste with salt and pepper. Toss spinach in vinaigrette and set aside.

2. Melt butter in a small skillet over medium heat, then cook until it turns deep brown, about 4 minutes. Meanwhile, heat sherry vinegar in a medium skillet over medium heat until skillet is almost dry, about 2 minutes. Stir in browned butter and ketchup. Add apples, peppers, celery, lemon, capers, and parsley, and cook, stirring continually, until just heated through, about 10 seconds. Season to taste with salt and pepper and set aside.

3. Season skate on both sides with salt and pepper to taste. Heat clarified butter in a large skillet over medium-high heat, add fish, and cook until crisp and golden, about 2 minutes per side.

4. To serve, divide spinach between 4 plates, arranging in little piles. Place a skate filet on top of each pile of spinach, then spoon some of the fruit and vegetables with their sauce over skate.

Mouth Music

The seafood pavilions at Rungis, the immense wholesale food market outside Paris," reports writer Thomas McNamee (facing page, upper right, tasting sauce), "cover indoor acres, and are full of glistening rascasses, john dories, conger eels, spiny lobsters, and about a thousand other things. Everything looks fresher than anything I have ever seen, but the fish brokers prod, sniff, argue, reject. The pickiest of them will bring his haul to the likes of Jean-Pierre Vigato [facing page, upper right, at right], chef at the two-star Apicius in Paris. In his kitchen, I watch as Vigato's fish chef scrapes meat from tiny frogs' legs one by one. The pastry chef brings silky sheets of pasta to a young guy who scores them into squares, centers clumps of raw lobster and chopped vegetables in each, and ties them with threads of leek green into a pouch for steaming. For me, the American, Vigato wants to make his "ketchup dish". A thick chunk of skate wing sizzles in clarified butter while he reduces old sherry vinegar to almost nothing, then adds butter. Into that goes the spoonful of Heinz. Vigato grins. In go minutely diced red peppers, apple, lemon, celery, capers, parsley. Vigato slides the fish on top of a little spinach salad, drizzles the chunky sweet-and-sour sauce over and around it. Oh, Lord! The intensity of that super-reduced vinegar, the vivid sweetness of pepper—this is a Bach counterpoint."

Of Cod and Man

A s fish go, cod doesn't get much respect; it isn't sexy like salmon, trendy like tuna, handsome like striped bass. But historically, cod is the most important sea creature in the world: Because it lends itself superbly to preservation, through salting or drying, it became a nonpareil article of commerce as long ago as the 10th century, linking northern and southern Europe financially, spurring and provisioning sea journeys of exploration (Basque sailors who may have reached the shores of Canada were looking for new cod grounds), aiding the spread of Catholicism (it provided fast-day fare), and making it possible for protein-starved communities all over Europe, and later Africa, Asia, and the Caribbean, to survive. It is a tribute to the sheer gustatory value of both salted and dried cod that even today, when fresh fish is widely available around the world, these preserved varieties are still greatly appreciated—especially in parts of Spain, Portugal, Italy, and the south of France.

Brandade de Nîmes

(Puréed Salt Cod)

SERVES 6–8

THE ANCIENT Provençal capital of Nîmes was on the trade route between Scandinavia and southern Europe, and thus knew salt cod well. Its claim to have invented this simple preparation of the fish puréed with olive oil—eaten in similar form all over the Mediterranean—seems credible.

1 lb. salt cod
1 cup plus 2 tbsp.
*   extra-virgin olive oil*
¾ cup milk
Salt and freshly ground
*   white pepper*
1 loaf country bread,
*   sliced and toasted*

1. Put cod in a large bowl, cover with cold water, and refrigerate for 5 hours, changing the water 2–3 times.

2. Put soaked cod in a large pot with 6 cups cold water and bring to a simmer over high heat, about 12 minutes. Remove from heat and drain.

3. Heat 6 tbsp. of the oil in a heavy-bottomed skillet, add cod, and sauté, breaking up the fish with the back of a wooden spoon, for 2–3 minutes. Transfer to the bowl of a food processor fitted with a metal blade.

4. Heat milk and remaining ¾ cup oil in a heavy saucepan over medium-high heat until it just comes to a simmer. Drizzle milk and oil mixture into salt cod as you process for 1 minute. Season to taste with salt and pepper, then transfer cod to a gratin dish, spreading it to fill the dish but leaving surface uneven. Broil in a preheated broiler until golden brown on top, 5–10 minutes. Serve with toasted bread.

Saumon Sauvage Juste Tiède

(Warm Wild Salmon Filets)

SERVES 4

W ILD SALMON (i.e., not farm-raised) from the Pacific Northwest is sometimes available at premium fish markets in this country. It's well worth the search. Frédy Girardet won't make this dish, or any other, with farmed salmon.

The Master

H e may be Swiss, but Frédy Girardet (facing page) is widely considered to be the greatest French (-style) chef in the world—the master, the Pope of cuisine. Unfortunately for the world's diners, he sold his three-star establishment in Crissier, near Lausanne, in 1997, and retired with his family to his roomy, art-filled villa above the wine-producing village of Féchy. It was here that Girardet cooked dinner for us one post-retirement evening, offering us a dazzling repast that included sesame seed–coated fried langoustines with curry sauce; wild Scottish salmon filets roasted in butter in a very slow oven, then served warm over an emulsion of fennel (see recipe, right); young pigeon stuffed with foie gras and truffles and encased in a crust of parsley and more truffles; and a local traditional specialty, a very thin tarte à la crème vaudoise. After such a meal, we couldn't help but regret his retirement. Girardet seemed to regret it, too. "I was a chef for 45 years," he said as we finished. "To stop, after so long, has not been easy."

1 tomato, peeled, halved, and seeded
2 tbsp. extra-virgin olive oil, preferably Provençal
6 loosely packed cups fennel tops
1 ¼ cup fish stock (see page 62)
3 tbsp. heavy cream
1 tsp. pastis (optional)
8 tbsp. butter, softened
4 6-oz. skinless center-cut salmon filets
2 tbsp. lemon juice
1 tsp. Chinese chili oil
Salt and freshly ground black pepper
1 tbsp. peeled and minced red bell pepper
3 tbsp. minced fresh dill
Coarse sea salt

1. Preheat oven to 275°. Place tomato halves on a baking sheet, drizzle with 1 tbsp. of the oil, and bake for 3½–4 hours. Finely dice and set aside.

2. Reduce oven heat to 225°. Place fennel in a pot with salted water to cover and boil over high heat for about 10 minutes. Drain well, transfer to a blender, add ¼ cup fish stock, and blend until smooth. Pass through a fine sieve set over a bowl. Whisk in heavy cream and pastis (if using) and set aside.

3. Spread 1 tbsp. butter over each salmon filet, and put salmon, rounded side up, in an ovenproof dish. Cover dish with aluminum foil and bake for about 20 minutes. (Salmon should be barely cooked, just warm but still translucent.)

4. Meanwhile, in a small saucepan, reduce remaining cup of the fish stock by half over medium heat. Whisk in lemon juice, remaining 1 tbsp. olive oil, and chili oil and season to taste with salt and pepper. Whisk in remaining 4 tbsp. butter, 1 tbsp. at a time, until sauce thickens a bit. Stir in tomato, bell pepper, and dill.

5. Divide fennel sauce between 4 plates, leaving a 1½" border all around. Place a salmon filet, rounded side up, in the middle of each plate, on top of fennel sauce, and spoon dill sauce around the edges. Sprinkle coarse sea salt and pepper over salmon.

Sandre au Pinot Noir

(Pike Perch Braised in Pinot Noir)

IN ALSACE, rich, aromatic white wines like riesling and gewürztraminer are often served with hearty game dishes—and the region's light, fragrant pinot noir might end up in sauce for delicate pike perch (related to America's northern pike), as in this recipe from the Husser family's Le Cerf.

1 5½-lb. whole northern pike or walleye, cleaned
Salt and freshly ground black pepper
5 tbsp. butter
3 small carrots, peeled and thinly sliced
3 stalks celery, chopped
2 small yellow onions, peeled and chopped
3 small leeks, white parts only, washed and sliced
1 lb. white mushrooms, trimmed and quartered
1 bottle of Alsatian pinot noir or other light red wine
1 tsp. tomato paste
5 bay leaves
4 sprigs fresh thyme
½ cup heavy cream

1. Rinse fish, pat dry, and season generously inside and out with salt and pepper.

2. Preheat oven to 350°. Place a metal roasting pan large enough to hold fish (about 18" x 14") spanning two burners. Melt butter over medium-low heat, add carrots, celery, onions, and leeks, and cook, stirring occasionally, until vegetables are soft, about 20 minutes. Add mushrooms and cook, stirring often, for 5 minutes more.

3. Stir wine, tomato paste, bay leaves, thyme, and 1 cup water into roasting pan. Spread out vegetable mixture evenly, then put fish on top of vegetables. Cover pan with aluminum foil, and braise fish in oven, without turning, until fish flakes easily, about 30 minutes.

4. Remove pan from oven. Using two spatulas, carefully transfer fish to a large serving platter and cover with aluminum foil to keep warm while you finish sauce.

5. Place pan spanning two burners. Bring vegetable mixture to a simmer over medium-high heat, and cook, stirring often to prevent vegetables from scorching, until liquid is reduced by half, about 15 minutes. Reduce heat to medium, stir in cream, and simmer, stirring, until sauce thickens enough to coat the back of a spoon, about 2 minutes. Remove bay leaves. Season to taste with salt and pepper, then spoon vegetables and sauce over fish.

Family Continuity

I n Alsace," reports writer David Downie, "family ties are strong—and Alsatian restaurants, from the simplest to the most exalted, tend to be family-run and rich in family tradition. Three generations of the Husser family, for instance, run the acclaimed Le Cerf in Marlenheim [below, from left, Marcelle and Robert; Robert's mother, Irmgard; and Marcelle and Robert's daughter-in-law, Cathy, and son, Michel]. Michel Orth is the sixth-generation chef at the venerable Hostellerie à L'Écrevisse in Brumath; the family's sprawling, cluttered restaurant has occupied the same spot since the 1840s. Vintner Martin Gaertner opened a country auberge called Aux Armes de France in the wine-growing village of Ammerschwihr, just outside Colmar, in 1920. Philippe Gaertner, Martin's grandson, is the chef today. Émile Jung serves adaptations of his chef-father's recipes at his elegant three-star Au Crocodile in Strasbourg. He might be speaking for most Alsatian restaurants when he says 'Our heritage is never lost. The soul of the family is passed down with the generations.'"

POULTRY

"ONE EVENING, I was guest of honor

at a dinner attended by a large contingent

of the Grande Confrérie du Cassoulet de

Castelnaudary, a gastronomic brother-

hood devoted to that epic French dish, at

a restaurant called Hostellerie Étienne in the village of Labastide-d'Anjou, about five miles west of Castelnaudary. Connoisseurs distinguish between the cassoulets of Carcassonne, Toulouse, and Castelnaudary—but generally acknowledge that the dish was born in the last of these. Celebrated turn-of-the-century chef Prosper Montagné wrote that cassoulet was the God of southern French cuisine, with three incarnations, of which Castelnaudary's was God the Father. Anatole France, in his *Histoire comique*, spoke with great warmth of a restaurant in Paris where a Castelnaudary-style cassoulet had been simmering in the same pot for 20 years—but added, this 'must not be confused with cassoulet in the style of Carcassonne, a simple leg of mutton with beans'. When I arrived at the Hostellerie Étienne, many of the Confrérie were already there, dressed in flowing brown robes with yellow trim and sporting large hats shaped like a *cassole*—the dark brown earthenware bowl, resembling a squashed flowerpot, for which cassoulet is named. In the kitchen, I could see a short man with white hair and glasses. 'That's Étienne Rousselot,' one of the brothers told me. 'He's the champion.' As I shoveled forkfuls of sumptuous, perfectly cooked beans, crispy duck confit, and spicy sausage into my mouth, I was more than happy to agree. After the meal, I asked the 71-year-old chef when he planned to retire. 'Never,' he said. 'My dream is to die with an oven full of cassoulet.'" —MICHAEL BALTER

Cassoulet

SERVES 8–10

THOUGH IT CONTAINS pork and sometimes lamb, cassoulet is usually defined by the presence of duck or goose confit. Beyond that, disputes abound, about what kind of beans to use, how long to cook the dish—and how often the cassoulet's top crust should be broken and pushed down. Étienne Rousselot, whose recipe we adapted here, recommends doing it often enough to keep the beans moist—at least four times; others counsel breaking the crust hourly.

4 cups dried great
    northern or other small
    white beans
4 fresh ham hocks (about
    1 lb. each)
3 large yellow onions,
    peeled and quartered
5 sprigs fresh thyme
Salt and freshly ground
    black pepper
⅓ lb. fresh pork rind,
    cubed
1 ham bone
1 tbsp. duck fat
1 lb. unseasoned fresh pork
    sausage (about 4 links),
    cut into 2" pieces
1 large head garlic,
    separated into cloves
    and peeled
Confit of 1 quartered
    duck or 4 whole legs
    (see page 175)
¼ tsp. ground nutmeg

1. Rinse beans thoroughly, pick through and discard stones. Set beans aside.

2. Put ham hocks in a large pot. Add 1 onion, thyme, and season to taste with salt and pepper. Cover with water and bring to a boil over high heat. Reduce heat to low and simmer, partially covered, for 2 hours. Remove from heat, allow to cool for 15 minutes, then drain ham hocks, discarding onion and thyme. Cut meat from each hock into 2 pieces. Discard bones and set meat aside.

3. Meanwhile, put pork rind and 1 onion in a large heavy-bottomed pot. Cook over medium heat, stirring frequently, until pork rind is rendered, about 20 minutes. Add beans, ham bone, and 4 quarts of water. Bring to a simmer, then reduce heat to low, and cook until beans are tender, about 1½ hours. Season to taste with salt, then set beans aside to cool. Remove and discard ham bone and onion from beans with a slotted spoon (it's all right if some pieces of onion remain).

4. Heat duck fat in a large skillet over medium-high heat. Add sausages and cook, turning to brown on all sides, for about 10 minutes. Put garlic, remaining 1 onion, and ½ cup water in a blender and purée until smooth. Add garlic paste to sausages and reduce heat to medium-low. Cook, turning sausages occasionally, for 10 minutes more.

5. Preheat oven to 350°. Assemble cassoulet in layers: Using a slotted spoon, transfer about half the beans with pork rind to a heavy wide-mouthed 5–6-qt. cast-iron, clay, or earthenware pot. Place the meat from the ham hocks on top of the beans and cover with sausages and garlic paste. Divide duck confit into 8 pieces, then arrange duck on sausages. Spoon in remaining beans with pork rind. Season with nutmeg and add just enough reserved bean cooking liquid to cover the beans (about 3 cups), reserving remaining liquid. Bake, uncovered, until cassoulet comes to a simmer and a crust begins to form, about 1 hour.

6. Reduce heat to 250° and cook for 3 hours, checking every hour or so to make sure cassoulet is barely simmering (a little liquid should be bubbling around edges). If cassoulet appears dry, break crust by gently pushing it down with the back of a spoon, allowing a new layer of beans to rise to the surface. Add just enough reserved bean cooking liquid (or water) to moisten beans.

7. Remove cassoulet from oven. Allow to cool completely, then cover with a lid or aluminum foil and refrigerate overnight.

8. Remove cassoulet from refrigerator and allow to warm to room temperature for at least 45 minutes. Meanwhile, preheat oven to 350°. Bake for 1 hour. When cassoulet begins to simmer, break crust and add enough warm water to just cover beans (about 1 cup). Reduce heat to 250° and bake, breaking crust and adding water as needed, for 3 hours. Remove cassoulet from oven and allow to rest for 15–20 minutes. Serve cassoulet from the pot, breaking the crust at the table.

Confit de Canard

(Duck Confit)

I N A M E R I C A, the duck most often eaten is the long island (or white pekin), which is mild in flavor and inexpensive—but not very highly regarded by French chefs. For confit, they (and we) prefer the fatty moulard, a cross between pekin hen and muscovy drake bred for foie gras, often available from specialty butchers (or see page 33).

1 8-lb. moulard duck
  (see page 33)
4 tbsp. coarse sea salt

1. Preheat oven to 350°. Remove skin and all fat from duck and set duck aside. Cut skin and fat into 1½" x 4" strips. Put in a baking pan and bake until skin is golden and crisp, about 3½ hours. Drain skin on paper towels and use to garnish salads. Strain fat through fine sieve. (Rendered fat can be stored in the freezer for up to 6 months.)

2. Meanwhile, cut duck into 2 legs with thighs attached, 2 wings with tips removed, and 2 breasts. Put duck pieces in a nonreactive pan and sprinkle salt on all sides of the bird. Cover with plastic wrap and refrigerate overnight.

3. The next day, brush away as much salt as possible with a paper towel (some will have dissolved). Melt rendered duck fat in a tall heavy pot over low heat. When fat reaches 200° on a kitchen thermometer, barely simmering, add duck and simmer, completely submerged, until very tender, about 2 hours. Remove pan from heat. Transfer duck and fat to a container, and cover. Make sure that the duck is completely submerged in the fat. Refrigerate; the flavor will improve for a week. Confit will keep for at least a month.

Goodness Preserved

T he French culinary term *confit* can apply to foods preserved in different ways—by coating them in sugar syrup (as with, for instance, candied fruit), by bottling them in alcohol (commonly done with cherries and grapes, among other things), by curing them in vinegar (various pickles), and, as in the case of duck and goose (and also pork), by cooking them and then storing them in their own fat. The confit process was known to the ancient Greeks and Romans, and the latter probably introduced it to southwestern France—along with the production of foie gras, which it parallels: When birds are force-fed to fatten their livers, they simultaneously develop an ample layer of subcutaneous fat—and when they are slaughtered for their livers, that same fat is the perfect medium in which to preserve their meat. There's more to the notion of confit than mere preservation, though. Marinating the meat in salt and sometimes other spices (cloves are typical) and then simmering it in its own fat turns it rich and succulent without—believe it or not—making it fatty. Though it is commonly used in cassoulet, incidentally, confit is also eaten by itself as a meat course, often with a salad on the side.

Canard en Croûte d'Herbes et de Sel

(Duck Baked in a Crust of Herbs and Salt)

ROBERT LALLEMAN, chef at his family's acclaimed Auberge de Noves near Avignon, makes this dish with the famous ducks from the town of Challans, in the Vendée, in western France; muscovy ducks make a good substitute.

3 cups flour
1½ cups kosher salt
10 egg whites
Freshly ground black
  pepper
2 tbsp. finely chopped fresh
  rosemary
2 tbsp. finely chopped fresh
  thyme
¼ cup finely chopped fresh
  cilantro
1 5-lb. muscovy duck
  (see page 33)
Salt
1 tbsp. olive oil
2 tbsp. white wine vinegar
½ cup dry white wine
1 shallot, peeled and
  minced
Bouquet garni (see sidebar,
  page 59) with ½ tsp.
  coriander seeds added
1 tbsp. acacia honey
½ cup chicken stock
  (see page 56)
½ cup veal stock
  (see page 60)

1. Combine flour, salt, egg whites, 2 tbsp. pepper, rosemary, thyme, and cilantro in a large bowl and mix until dough holds together. Turn dough out onto a lightly floured surface and knead until smooth and elastic, about 2 minutes. Form dough into a ball, wrap in plastic, and refrigerate for 30 minutes.

2. Preheat oven to 450°. Prick duck skin all over with a fork. Season inside and out with salt and pepper. Heat oil in a large ovenproof skillet over medium-high heat. Add duck and brown on all sides, turning as it browns, about 15 minutes in all. Put the skillet with the duck in the oven for 15 minutes. Remove duck from pan and set aside to cool.

3. Turn dough out onto a lightly floured surface and roll into a 10" x 14" rectangle. Place cooled duck in center of dough, breast side down, then wrap dough around duck, pinching to seal. Place duck, seam side down, on a baking sheet and bake for 30 minutes. Remove from oven, leaving oven on.

4. Meanwhile, put vinegar, wine, shallots, and bouquet garni into a sauté pan and cook over medium-high heat until reduced by three-quarters, about 7 minutes. Add honey, chicken stock, and veal stock. Cook until sauce is slightly thickened, about 5 minutes more, then strain, season with salt and pepper, and keep warm.

5. To serve, use a sharp knife to cut through dough crust, then peel away and discard. Thinly slice breast meat and arrange on 4 plates. Spoon warm sauce over meat. Cut legs (with thighs) from duck and return them to oven, until skin is crisp, 15–30 minutes. Serve legs as second course.

Cooking for Provence

Robert and Suzanne Lalleman opened the Auberge de Noves, about nine miles southeast of Avignon, in 1955. Their son André, today a charming gentleman with a thick white mustache and a ready smile, took over management of the place in 1972, and now runs it with his wife, Jacqueline. Their son, another Robert, a good-looking, rangy young man who worked at Pic, Troisgros, and Chapel, among other temples of French gastronomy, is now in charge of the kitchen, and the food is confident, sophisticated, and unmistakably Provençal. "All the things I learned in other restaurants," says Robert, "I transformed when I came back here, to use local products and develop stronger flavors. When people eat in Provence, they expect strong flavors. This is not Paris."

177

Wine from Apples

To anyone who thinks cider is just apple juice, the handcrafted ciders Eric Bordelet makes at Château de Hauteville, his family's farm in the département of Mayenne, about 150 miles southwest of Paris, are a revelation. (His deluxe cuvée is sold in the U.S. under the name Sydre Argelette.) Cidermaking is thought to have been introduced here from Spain in the 13th century. By the 16th century, orchards had replaced grapevines in the region, and cider began appearing on the best local tables. Louis XIV sometimes even served it instead of champagne. By the 19th century, it had become France's second most popular alcoholic beverage—after wine but ahead of beer. Today, notes Bordelet—who left his job as sommelier at the trendsetting Arpège restaurant in Paris in 1991 to move back to the farm and make cider of his own—"Cider is underestimated because most of it is mass-produced or poorly made. Wine has continued to evolve but cider has stagnated, if not regressed. It will take ten years to restore its nobility." Bordelet may well be the first farmhouse cider producer to have studied winemaking before returning to the farm to make cider. "I'm not there yet," he admits, "but when my ciders are offered at auction at Christie's, I will have arrived."

Canard Rôti au Cidre avec Navets

(Roast Duck with Cider and Turnips)

SERVES 4

CIDERMAKER Eric Bordelet's family (his father and mother, Roger and Claudine Bordelet, are at far right) cooks duck with sweet potatoes in cider sauce, and serves it with more cider. We adapted the recipe to use turnips and a shot of that other great French apple product, calvados.

1 5-lb. muscovy or long island duck (see page 33), fat trimmed
Salt and freshly ground black pepper
5 shallots, peeled
5 cloves garlic, crushed and peeled
1 tbsp. butter, softened
2 tbsp. calvados
2 lbs. turnips, peeled and quartered
1¼ cups Sydre Argelette or other good-quality French hard cider
1 cup chicken stock (see page 56)

1. Preheat oven to 400°. Season cavity of duck with salt and pepper. Stuff duck with shallots and garlic and truss with kitchen string. Rub with butter, season with salt and pepper, and place duck, breast side down, on a rack in a medium roasting pan.

2. Pour calvados over duck and put turnips in pan around it. Roast duck, basting frequently, for 20 minutes, then turn duck breast side up and continue roasting until juices run clear, about 30 minutes more. Remove duck from oven, transfer to a serving platter and set aside to rest for 15 minutes. Return pan to oven and continue cooking turnips until tender, about 10 minutes more.

3. Arrange turnips around duck. Pour any accumulated juices from duck's cavity into roasting pan and bring to a boil over medium-high heat on top of the stove. Skim fat from pan juices, add cider, and simmer, stirring constantly until pan is almost dry, about 10 minutes. Reduce heat to medium, add stock, season with salt and pepper, and cook for 3–5 minutes more. Carve duck, and serve with turnips and pan juices.

Magret de Canard à la Cheminée

(Duck Breast Cooked on the Coals)

SERVES 4

IT IS NOT UNCOMMON to find Jean-Pierre Xiradakis (see page 273) cooking magret in the hearth—the oversize fireplace—at his La Tupiña in Bordeaux. "For centuries," he explains, "the hearth was the heart of the home." A magret is the lean breast of a fat duck, which in France is usually a moulard or muscovy that has been fattened for foie gras.

2 1-lb. moulard
    duck breast halves
    (see page 33)
Sel de Guérande (see
    sidebar, right)
Freshly ground black
    pepper

1. Light wood or charcoal in a barbecue and wait until the fire dies down and the coals are uniformly glowing and hot. Trim skin (with fat attached) from duck breasts, leaving a lengthwise strip about ½" wide across the middle of each.

2. Put duck breasts on grill, skin side down, and grill until brown, about 3 minutes. Turn and cook on the other side until brown, about 2 minutes. (Duck breasts should be crisp on the outside and rare in the middle, like a steak.)

3. Transfer duck breasts to a cutting board and set aside to rest for 5 minutes, then slice thinly, and arrange on a warm serving platter. Season generously with sel de Guérande and pepper.

Salient Thoughts

Sel de Guérande, one of the most respected of French condiments, is nothing more than gray sea salt from a small peninsula on the Brittany coast. It is swept by the movement of the tides into a series of natural pools, stretching across 5,000 acres, and then harvested manually, from mid-June to mid-September, by *paludiers*, or salt-marsh farmers (facing page). They gather two types of salt: coarse, darkish gros sel, detached from pool bottoms with long wooden rakes; and fleur de sel, or flower of salt, snowy flakes that float to the water's surface. The latter is the caviar of salt, usually sprinkled over finished dishes, not used for cooking. Both kinds are high in magnesium and potassium—but contain less sodium than other salts—and are available here in the U.S.

Poussin Vallée d'Auge

(Baby Chicken with Calvados and Cream)

SERVES 6

FROM THE VALLÉE D'AUGE in Normandy comes the famed apple brandy called calvados (see page 225). This simple, classic, calvados-flavored Norman preparation can be adapted to larger chickens, other fowl, and pork.

6 *poussins or cornish hens*
Salt and freshly ground
   black pepper
4 *tbsp. unsalted butter,*
   softened
2 *cups pearl onions*
½ *cup calvados*
¾ *cup heavy cream*

1. Preheat oven to 400°. Rub poussins inside and out, generously, with salt and pepper.

2. To truss poussins, fold wing tips back beneath shoulders (drumsticks should fit snugly against the tip of breastbone) and hold in place by tying legs together with kitchen string.

3. Rub birds with butter and arrange in a roasting pan so they do not touch. Scatter unpeeled onions around birds, then place pan in lower third of oven and cook for at least 45 minutes, basting several times. Prick fat part of drumstick on 1 bird after 45 minutes; if juice runs clear the birds are done.

4. Transfer poussins and onions to a serving platter. Place the roasting pan on top of the stove and bring the pan drippings to a boil over medium-high heat, scraping with a wooden spoon to loosen any browned bits stuck to the bottom of the pan. Warm calvados in a small pot, then add to pan juices, and carefully ignite with a kitchen match, keeping a large pan lid nearby to extinguish flames if necessary. When flames die out, stir in cream, and continue to reduce sauce until thickened, about 5 minutes. Adjust seasonings as needed. Untie string and discard. Pour sauce over and around poussins.

Bird Talk

I n France, where chickens are classified according to weight, method of rearing, and age at slaughter, a poussin is a chicken that is killed at an age of about four weeks, and weighs about a pound. It has delicately flavored flesh and is ideal for broiling, grilling, or roasting. (Longer cooking methods, like stewing, tend to turn poussins dry and stringy.) Poussins are now available in the U.S., but if you can't find them, the best substitute would be the small North American rock Cornish game hen—bred from the Plymouth rock hen and the white Cornish game cock. It is killed slightly later than the poussin, and is larger than that bird, both because of its age and because of its accelerated feeding program. It can weigh up to two pounds, and cooking time must be adjusted accordingly.

Coq au Vin

(Rooster in Red Wine Sauce)

SERVES 6

COQ AU VIN isn't chicken cooked in cheap red wine; it's rooster cooked in something good enough to drink. But it is hard to find even in France today, and all but impossible in the U.S. (unless you know a poultry farmer); a roasting chicken or a large capon is the best substitute.

Patriotic Chicken

The squawks are varied, loud, and constant at the Monday poultry market in Louhans, in southern Burgundy (above)—where fowl of every sort, from gawky geese to tiny pigeons, are offered for sale. The stars of the market are the famed poulets de Bresse, a unique breed of chicken, grain-fattened in the region. Acclaimed by gastronomes since the mid-19th century, these birds are considered a quintessential symbol of la cuisine française—not least because their blue feet, white feathers, and red wattles echo the colors of the French flag.

1 6-lb. roasting chicken, capon, or rooster, cut into 10 pieces
2 large yellow onions, peeled and chopped
3 shallots, peeled and chopped
2 large carrots, peeled and chopped
3 large cloves garlic, peeled
Bouquet garni (see sidebar, page 59)
1½ bottles good, rich red burgundy or California pinot noir
Salt and freshly ground black pepper
¼ cup vegetable oil
2 tbsp. flour
¼ cup good cognac
1½ tbsp. unsweetened cocoa powder
6 oz. salt pork, diced
¾ lb. small white mushrooms, stems trimmed and caps peeled

1. Put chicken, onions, shallots, carrots, garlic, and bouquet garni in a large bowl and add wine. Mix all the ingredients together with your hands, then cover bowl with plastic wrap and refrigerate for 24 hours.

2. Remove chicken from marinade, reserving marinade, and dry well on paper towels. Season to taste with salt and pepper. Heat oil in a large heavy pan over medium-high heat. Working in batches to avoid crowding pan, add chicken and brown on all sides, turning as pieces brown, about 15 minutes in all. Remove pieces as done and set aside. Add flour to the pan and cook, stirring constantly for 2 minutes. Return chicken to pan and add cognac. Remove pan from heat and carefully ignite cognac with a kitchen match, keeping pan lid nearby to extinguish flames if necessary. Return pan to stove top, add marinade, and bring to a boil over high heat, scraping up browned bits from bottom of pan. Reduce heat to low and simmer, partially covered, until chicken is tender, about 1½ hours.

3. Remove chicken from pan and set aside. Strain sauce through a sieve, discard solids, and return sauce to pan. Put cocoa in a small mixing bowl and whisk in ½ cup of strained sauce, whisking until smooth. Stir cocoa mixture into pan, then reduce sauce over medium heat to about 4 cups, 15–20 minutes. Reduce heat to low and return chicken to pan.

4. Meanwhile, sauté salt pork in a skillet over medium heat until crisp, about 10 minutes, then remove from skillet with a slotted spoon and add to chicken. Add mushrooms to the same skillet and sauté in salt pork fat until golden, about 10 minutes. Drain and add mushrooms to chicken, stirring them in gently. Serve finished dish with croutons (rounds of lightly toasted French bread) if you like.

Celestial Carrots

O ne afternoon not long ago in Burgundy, I bit into a carrot. It was tiny and neatly beveled, lightly steamed and glazed in butter...[and] I thought for a moment that it was perhaps the most perfect thing I had ever tasted...." SAVEUR editor Colman Andrews wrote those words 16 years ago, in an article about an unassuming country inn called l'Hostellerie du Vieux Moulin, in the hamlet of Bouilland, near the Burgundian wine capital of Beaune. The proprietors were Jean-Pierre and Isabelle Silva, a young couple then in the process of developing a style of food and service (and a wine list) that would eventually make their establishment an essential stop on any gastronomic tour of Burgundy. At the time, Jean-Pierre (facing page, at the market in Chalon-sur-Saône, and above, left foreground, enjoying a market breakfast with friends and colleagues, including three-star chef Jacques Lameloise, in red sweater) cooked in a relatively straightforward, then-inescapably "nouvelle" way. Over the years, his style grew both more sophisticated and more demonstrably expressive of the region—even when it took off on such flights of fancy as cannelloni stuffed with shredded coq au vin; sweetwater pike perch in vinegar sauce with lentils cooked in veal reduction (a particularly successful example of Burgundian-rustic lily-gilding); and roast lamb from a nearby farm with a bouquet of exquisite, simply cooked local vegetables— perfect carrots assuredly among them.

Pâtes Farcies de Coq au Vin

(Coq au Vin "Cannelloni")

SERVES 4

THIS ITALIAN-accented specialty of Bouilland's Hostellerie du Vieux Moulin is a delicious illustration of the way chef Jean-Pierre Silva reinterprets Burgundian traditions.

4 cups leftover coq au vin (see recipe, previous page) with sauce, meat shredded and bones removed and discarded
4 carrots, peeled and finely chopped
1 large yellow onion, peeled and finely chopped
12 pasta sheets, 4" square
Salt
1 cup shelled fresh peas
2 cups chicken stock (see page 56)
2 tbsp. heavy cream
6 tbsp. butter, cut into pieces
1 tsp. minced fresh rosemary
Fresh rosemary sprigs for garnish

1. Combine coq au vin (with sauce), carrots, onions, and 1 cup water in a heavy pot. Cook over medium heat until sauce has reduced and thickened, about 30 minutes.

2. Cook pasta in a large pot of boiling salted water over high heat until tender, about 8 minutes. Drain on a kitchen towel. Divide coq au vin mixture between pasta sheets, roll up, arrange on a platter, cover, and keep warm.

3. Meanwhile, cook peas in a medium pot of boiling salted water until just cooked, about 4 minutes. Drain and set aside.

4. Combine stock, cream, butter, and minced rosemary in a small pot and bring to a boil over medium heat. Cook, whisking constantly, until slightly thickened. Pour over pasta. Garnish with rosemary sprigs and peas.

Volaille Fermière au Vinaigre

(Farmhouse Chicken in Vinegar Sauce)

SERVES 4

PHILIPPE GAERTNER, chef—like his father and grandfather before him—at the respected Aux Armes de France in the Alsatian town of Ammerschwihr, prefers to make this classic dish with the local honey-perfumed melfor vinegar. In the absence of this strictly regional product, he recommends using cider vinegar sweetened with a bit of honey.

1 3½-lb. chicken, cut into 8 pieces
Salt and freshly ground black pepper
2 tbsp. olive oil
6 tbsp. butter
8 cloves garlic, peeled and minced
4 shallots, peeled and minced
½ cup cider vinegar
1 cup Alsatian riesling or other dry but fruity white wine
1 tbsp. honey
1 tbsp. tomato paste
1 cup chicken stock (see page 56)
1 tbsp. finely chopped fresh parsley

1. Rinse chicken, pat dry, and season to taste with salt and pepper. Heat oil and 2 tbsp. of the butter in a large skillet over medium-high heat. Working in batches to avoid crowding pan, add chicken and brown on all sides, turning as pieces brown, for about 15 minutes in all. Remove pieces as done and set aside. When all chicken has browned, pour off most of the fat from the skillet, leaving just enough to thinly coat it.

2. Reduce heat to medium, add garlic and shallots, and cook, stirring frequently, until slightly soft, about 5 minutes. Deglaze skillet with vinegar and wine, add honey and scrape browned bits off bottom with a wooden spoon. Reduce by about one-third, 3–5 minutes, then stir in tomato paste. Return chicken to skillet, pour in stock, and simmer for 10–15 minutes. Turn chicken and continue cooking until juices from chicken run clear, about 15 minutes.

3. Remove chicken from skillet and set aside. Increase heat to medium-high, and continue cooking until sauce is thick and glossy, about 5 minutes. Cut remaining 4 tbsp. butter into small pieces. Remove skillet from heat and whisk butter into sauce. Adjust seasonings. (Sauce should be smooth but tart; add additional vinegar if you like.) Return chicken to skillet, turning to coat evenly with sauce and serve, sprinkled with parsley.

Vins d'Alsace

The hilly vineyards of Alsace (facing page) produce some of France's best white wine—fragrant, flavorful dry riesling and gewürztraminer most notably, but also muscat, pinot gris, sylvaner, and pinot blanc (as well as a bit of light red wine from pinot noir). Very good sweeter wines, labeled vendange tardive or sélection de grains nobles, are also made. Granted appellation contrôlée status only in 1962, Alsatian wines are labeled not according to subregion, but by grape variety—which made them immediately attractive to American consumers, used to the varietal labeling of California wines. Look for the wines of Trimbach and Hugel or, for a real treat, those of Domaine Weinbach, Zind-Humbrecht, or Gustave Lorentz.

189

Mixed Metaphors

S tudents of the American psyche might well speculate on the impulse behind the creation of that much- (and justly) maligned American/Continental restaurant classic called surf and turf—which is usually steak and lobster on the same plate. Was it an expression of plenty? A way of showing off? A misguided attempt to make a really great dish by combining a couple of very good ones? The underlying principle behind poulet aux écrevisses, a specialty of the French département of the Rhône-Alpes, is clearer: The best chickens in France come from the nearby plains of Bresse (see page 185), and crayfish thrive in the Alpine streams to the east of Lyon, and especially around the town of Nantua. What could be more logical than to marry these two regional treasures? It is a French tradition, after all, to let local ingredients inspire the creation of local dishes.

Poulet aux Écrevisses
(Chicken with Crayfish)

SERVES 4

LIVE CRAYFISH (see page 65), sometimes available from specialty seafood markets, are best for this dish. If you can't find them, use frozen precooked whole crayfish instead.

FOR SAUCE:
3 tbsp. olive oil
1 ¼ lbs. live or defrosted
   frozen crayfish, rinsed
2 tbsp. cognac
2 yellow onions, peeled
   and chopped
3 shallots, peeled and
   minced
2 carrots, peeled and
   chopped
4 medium tomatoes, peeled
1 tbsp. tomato paste
3 sprigs fresh thyme
1 sprig fresh tarragon
3 bay leaves
2 cups dry white wine
¾ cup heavy cream
Salt and freshly ground
   black pepper
Fresh parsley sprigs for
   garnish

FOR CHICKEN:
1 4-lb. chicken, cut into
   8 pieces
Salt and freshly ground
   black pepper
3 tbsp. olive oil

1. For sauce, heat oil in a large skillet over medium-high heat. Add crayfish and cook, stirring, for 5 minutes (2 minutes if using precooked crayfish). Remove skillet from heat, add cognac, and carefully ignite with a kitchen match, keeping skillet lid nearby to extinguish flames if necessary. Return pan to heat and cook until flames die out.

2. For chicken, preheat oven to 350°. While sauce cooks, season chicken with salt and pepper. Heat oil in a large ovenproof skillet over medium heat. Working in batches to avoid crowding pan, add chicken and brown on all sides, turning as pieces brown, about 15 minutes in all. Remove pieces as done and set aside. Return chicken pieces to skillet and put in oven. Cook until juices run clear, about 20 minutes more. Turn off oven, transfer chicken to a large platter and cover with aluminum foil. Return chicken to oven to keep warm.

3. Remove one-third of crayfish from skillet and set aside. Reduce heat to medium, add onions, shallots, and carrots, and cook until soft, 20 minutes. Add tomatoes, tomato paste, thyme, tarragon, bay leaves, and wine. Cook for 10 minutes, then add cream and simmer, stirring occasionally, until sauce thickens, about 30 minutes. Strain through a fine sieve, season sauce with salt and pepper to taste, then spoon over chicken. Add reserved crayfish and garnish with parsley.

Chapon Farci Rôti

(Roast Capon with Stuffing)

WHEN MEATY force-fed capons aren't in season—they're a year-end specialty in France—Jean-Pierre Xiradakis uses chicken instead for this dish at his La Tupiña in Bordeaux.

1 6–7-lb. capon
Olive oil
Salt and freshly ground black pepper
1 loaf country-style white bread
1 head garlic, cloves separated, peeled and slightly crushed
1 tbsp. butter
1 medium yellow onion, peeled and chopped
2 shallots, peeled and chopped
6 oz. mushrooms, trimmed and chopped
1½ lbs. pork sausages, removed from casings
1 carrot, peeled and chopped
1 turnip, peeled and chopped

1. Preheat oven to 400°. Rinse capon, pat dry with paper towels inside and out, rub all over with 1–2 tbsp. oil, then generously season with salt and pepper and set aside. Slice bread into thick slices. Rub both sides of one of the crusty heels of the bread with 1 garlic clove, then discard garlic. Brush bread generously with oil, then stuff into the bird's cavity. Arrange the rest of the bread in a shallow roasting pan and scatter remaining cloves of garlic on top of bread.

2. Put capon, breast side down, directly on an oven rack set in the middle of the oven. Set the roasting pan with the bread on a rack under the capon so that the fat and juices will drip onto the bread. After 15 minutes pour 2 cups of water over bread. Add another 2 cups water after 15 minutes more. After 40 minutes turn capon breast side up. Roast until the skin turns crisp and golden, about 35 minutes more.

3. Meanwhile, melt butter in a large skillet over medium-high heat. Add onions and shallots and cook for 2 minutes. Add mushrooms and cook until they release their juices, about 5 minutes. Stir in sausage meat, carrots, and turnips and reduce heat to medium-low. Stir occasionally with a wooden spoon, breaking up and crumbling sausage meat. Reduce heat to low and cook until vegetables caramelize slightly, about 30 minutes.

4. When capon is done, remove from oven and allow to rest for 10–15 minutes. Spoon about ¼ cup of the pan juices into the meat and vegetables. Carve the capon and serve with the stuffing and the roasted bread.

An Edible Heritage

J ean-Pierre Xiradakis, chef–owner of the celebrated La Tupiña restaurant in Bordeaux, was brought up in the southwest of France, eating and loving its exceptional culinary raw materials. But as long ago as the 1960s, he began to worry that they were disappearing. Local farmers were increasingly mass producing for agro-industry, trucking their goods to warehouses instead of to the open-air markets of Xiradakis's childhood. Game animals were getting crowded out of their environment; migrant herdsmen, whose flocks once fertilized and weeded the fields, were becoming an endangered species. "Restaurateurs have an obligation to defend the traditions of their region," declares Xiradakis—which is why, for 30 years, he has combed the region, talking, tasting, and encouraging. In the 1970s, when France fell in love with nouvelle cuisine, Xiradakis's quest for authentic regional ingredients grew into a genuine fear for the culinary heritage. "When nouvelle cuisine took off," he says, "my God, I thought no one was going to care anymore about the real cuisine." Xiradakis started looking for products that had vanished, like the beef of Bazas, the capon of Landes, and the lamb of Pauillac, all of which he claims credit for rejuvenating. "It's imperative," he proclaims, "that we don't forget our heritage!"

Under Pressure

Every French housewife, it has been said, owns a *cocotte-minute*—a pressure cooker. Widely (and unfairly) distrusted in America, this kitchen appliance, in fact, was invented in France. It traces its origins to Denis Papin, a physicist from Blois, who, in 1675, built a machine "for softening bones and cooking meat". For some time afterward, small-scale manufacturers in France and elsewhere produced various models of the contraption (like the 19th-century example, probably French, on the facing page)—all of which had one flaw in common: Their pressure valves tended to stick, which caused the pot to explode. It was not until 1953 that the Burgundy-based Société d'Emboutissage de Bourgogne was able to solve this problem by installing a stirrup-shaped handle on the lid, which slotted under two ear-shaped side pieces. The handle was turned to seal the pot—but if the valve stuck, pressure inside the vessel would force the handle to turn, allowing steam to escape through the sides. Today, SEB is one of the world leaders in home cooking equipment, selling its wares under the SEB, Tefal, Calor, and Rowenta brands.

Pintade au Chou

(Guinea Hen with Cabbage)

SERVES 4

WHEN **M**ARIELLE **G**RIVOT prepares this dish for her husband, Étienne, and their children (he helps run the family's wine estates, one of Burgundy's best), she often serves it with potatoes freshly dug from the garden.

1 2½–3-lb. guinea hen
Salt and freshly ground
  black pepper
2 tbsp. vegetable oil
8 oz. lean salt pork, diced
2 medium yellow onions,
  peeled and finely
  chopped
2 tbsp. butter
2 carrots, peeled and sliced
  into thin rounds
12 new potatoes
1 medium savoy cabbage,
  quartered, cored, and
  cut into ¼"-wide strips
1 12-oz. bottle of lager-
  style beer

1. Rub guinea hen inside and out with salt and pepper, then tie legs together with kitchen string.

2. Heat 1 tbsp. of the oil in the bottom of a pressure cooker over medium heat, add salt pork, and sauté until brown and crisp, about 10 minutes. Remove salt pork with a slotted spoon and set aside. Sauté onions in salt pork fat until soft, about 20 minutes. Remove with slotted spoon and set aside.

3. Add butter and remaining 1 tbsp. oil to pressure cooker. Add hen and brown all over, turning several times, for about 20 minutes. Season to taste with salt and pepper, then add salt pork, onions, carrots, potatoes, and cabbage. Pour beer over hen and vegetables. Place lid on pressure cooker, close tightly, and process according to manufacturer's instructions at a pressure of 10 lbs. or on high for 20 minutes. Remove from heat, let stand for 5 minutes, and carefully open cover.

Monsieur Mustard

T here's probably not a brasserie or bistro in France that doesn't have a jar of mustard on the table—and chances are that it comes from the Burgundian capital of Dijon. The Romans brought mustard seeds to the region, and by the Middle Ages, the bright yellow blossoms of mustard plants (right) could be seen covering local hills each spring. As early as the 14th century, local ordinances in Dijon laid out rules for the manufacture of mustard, more or less as we know it; one specified the use of only "good mustard seed soaked in good vinegar". By 1634, an official alliance had been formed in Dijon to regulate the profession of the moutardier. Dijon mustard is creamy and spicier than the old-style, coarse-grained mild mustard often referred to in French as *à l'ancienne*. Like the wines of Burgundy, it is protected by an appellation con-trôlée, granted in 1937— and like the wines of Burgundy, it is both definitive of the region and appreciated the world around.

Lapin à la Moutarde

(Rabbit with Mustard Sauce)

SERVES 4–6

RABBIT COOKED with mustard is a classic French grandmother's dish. This version is from Parisian-born grandmother Viviane Lago, long a resident of Rouen, who learned it from her own *grandmère*. Like her, she adds, "I cook with my heart, not my hands." (Rabbit isn't poultry, strictly speaking, but is sold in poultry shops in France and cooked similarly.)

1 large rabbit (3–4 lbs.), cut into 6–8 serving pieces
½ cup dijon mustard
Salt and freshly ground black pepper
2 tbsp. unsalted butter
1 small yellow onion, peeled and finely chopped
½ cup French chablis or other dry white wine
Bouquet garni (see sidebar, page 59)
⅓ cup crème fraîche
2 tbsp. finely chopped fresh parsley

1. Smear rabbit pieces all over with mustard, and season generously with salt and pepper.

2. Heat butter in a large skillet over medium-high heat. Add onions and cook until soft, about 10 minutes. Add rabbit pieces and cook, turning frequently, until rabbit is golden brown, about 15 minutes. Transfer to a platter.

3. Add wine to skillet and scrape up any browned bits from the bottom of the pan with a wooden spoon. Reduce heat to medium and return rabbit pieces to the skillet, along with bouquet garni. Cover and cook until rabbit is tender, about 35 minutes.

4. Remove skillet from heat. Discard bouquet garni and stir in crème fraîche. Garnish with parsley.

The Red and the Black

The Romans introduced winemaking to the region of Cahors—a handsome medieval walled town on the Lot River in Quercy, in southwestern France—and Caesar reportedly exported its "black" red wine to Rome. In medieval times, the reputation of cahors spread across Europe; its biggest promoter was Pope John XXII, the former bishop of Cahors, who made it the communion wine when he became the second Avignon pope during the 14th-century schism with the Vatican. Cahors gets its intensity and dark color mostly from the sturdy malbec grape (though some tannat and an increasing measure of merlot is also used), and from the dry limestone soils that predominate in the region's vineyards—which encourage the retention of heat and moisture. In the Middle Ages, when the wines of Bordeaux were a literally paler version of their current selves, cahors was often blended in to lend body and color. By the 18th century, though, bordeaux's fame had eclipsed that of cahors—and around 1880, the vine pest phylloxera wiped out the region's vineyards. Cahors began rebuilding its wine industry after World War II (the fact that the town doctor, Bernard Pons, was appointed minister of agriculture in the early '70s—and promptly got Cahors its own appellation contrôlée—didn't hurt), and today cahors has become something approaching fine wine.

Civet de Lapin

(Rich Rabbit Stew)

SERVES 6

JEAN-LOUIS PALLADIN, chef at Napa in the Rio Hotel Las Vegas and at his own new Palladin in New York City, grew up and began cooking not far from Cahors. He created this variation on a classic dish for SAVEUR.

4 tbsp. butter
3 tbsp. olive oil
2 2½-lb. rabbits, each cut into 6 pieces, with hearts, kidneys, and livers reserved
Salt and freshly ground black pepper
1 medium yellow onion, peeled and finely chopped
4 cloves garlic, peeled and minced
1 leek (white part only), washed and chopped
2 carrots, peeled and chopped
1 turnip, peeled and chopped
2 celery stalks, chopped
3 sprigs fresh rosemary
6 sprigs fresh thyme
1 bay leaf
3⅓ cups cahors or other rich, dry red wine
4 cups chicken stock (see page 56)
1 lb. pearl onions, blanched and peeled
1 tbsp. sugar
¼ lb. pancetta, julienned
1 lb. small white mushrooms

1. Melt 2 tbsp. butter and 2 tbsp. oil in a large, deep skillet over medium-high heat. Season rabbit with salt and pepper, then, working in batches to avoid crowding pan, add to skillet and brown for about 3 minutes on each side. Remove pieces and set aside. Reduce heat to medium, add chopped onions and garlic, and cook until slightly softened, about 5 minutes.

2. Add leeks, carrots, turnips, celery, rosemary, thyme, and bay leaf to pan. Cook, stirring occasionally until vegetables begin to brown, 7–10 minutes. Add wine and cook until reduced by two-thirds, about 30 minutes. Add stock and rabbit, reduce heat to medium-low, cover, and cook for 25 minutes more.

3. Remove rabbit from skillet with a slotted spoon and set aside. Increase heat to medium-high and simmer, skimming occasionally, until liquid is reduced by half, about 15 minutes. Add hearts, kidneys, and livers. Simmer until firm to the touch, about 5 minutes, then transfer to a food processor with a slotted spoon. Strain cooking liquid into food processor (discard vegetables and herbs) and purée until smooth. Season sauce with salt and pepper and set aside.

4. Wipe out skillet, then add pearl onions, sugar, remaining 2 tbsp. butter, and 1 cup water. Bring to a boil over high heat, reduce heat to medium, and simmer until most of the liquid evaporates, about 15 minutes. Stir to coat onions in syrup, and continue to cook, stirring, until onions begin to caramelize, 3–5 minutes. Heat remaining 1 tbsp. oil in another skillet over medium heat, add pancetta, and cook until crisp, about 8 minutes. Remove with a slotted spoon and drain on paper towels. Increase heat to medium-high, add mushrooms, and sauté until golden, about 5 minutes.

5. To assemble, pour sauce through a fine sieve into large skillet. Add rabbit and warm over medium heat. Add pearl onions, pancetta, and mushrooms and heat through.

MEATS

"YOU SEE THEM all over Burgundy—

sturdy, impassive, off-white cattle, brows-

ing in the fields and pastures. These are

the charolais, which yield the finest beef

in France. The breed is thought to have pre-historic origins, but in its present form was probably developed in the 18th century, around the town of Charolles, not far from Mâcon in southeastern Burgundy. The full-flavored, well-marbled, famously tender meat of the charolais was first shipped to the markets of Paris in 1747, and by the late 19th century it had earned its reputation as the most prized of all meats sold in Parisian boucheries. Though charolais cattle are now seen all over France—and, increasingly, in other countries as well (even the U.S.; the rangeland of Texas, and the Midwest, is crowded with them)—they remain emblematic of Burgundy. As much as the region's immense plantings of sunflowers and rapeseed, its fecund orchards, its patchwork grids of market gardens full of vegetables and herbs, its lush meadows accented with trees (said to be the model for the formal gardens of the region's great estates)—as much even as its world-famous vineyards—the charolais are an integral part of the Burgundian landscape. They are mythic animals, edible symbols of a way of life. Anyone who seeks to understand why Burgundy produces so much hearty, honest cooking, and why that cooking is linked so intimately to the earth, would do well to stop and appreciate, visually as well as gastronomically, these mighty beasts." —COLMAN ANDREWS

Boeuf à la Bourguignonne

(Beef Stew Burgundy-Style)

SERVES 4–6

W HEN WE ASKED Burgundian chef Marc Meneau, of the estimable l'Espérance in St-Père-sous-Vézelay, where we could find simple, classic Burgundian cooking, he sent us down to the little town of Planchez, in the southwestern reaches of the Morvan, Burgundy's most rural region, to sample boeuf à la bourguignonne as made by Millette Coquillon at her popular Chez Millette. This is her recipe.

3 lbs. beef chuck, cut into large pieces
1 large yellow onion, peeled and finely chopped
2 carrots, peeled and finely chopped
2 cloves garlic, peeled
Bouquet garni (see sidebar, page 59)
1 bottle good, rich red burgundy or California pinot noir
6 oz. lean salt pork, diced
Salt and freshly ground black pepper
⅓ cup flour
1 lb. small white mushrooms, stems trimmed and caps peeled

1. Put beef, onions, carrots, garlic, and bouquet garni into a large bowl and add wine. Using your hands, mix all the ingredients together, then cover bowl with plastic wrap and refrigerate for 24 hours.

2. Remove beef from marinade, reserving marinade, and dry meat well on paper towels. Fry salt pork in a large pot over medium heat until crisp, about 7 minutes. Season beef with salt and pepper to taste. Add to pot and brown on all sides, about 7 minutes. Sprinkle in flour, and cook, stirring constantly, for 3 minutes. Add marinade and 2 cups water and bring to a boil over high heat, scraping up browned bits from bottom of pan with a wooden spoon. Reduce heat to low, cover, and cook until meat is tender, about 3 hours. Add mushrooms and cook for 30 minutes more. Remove bouquet garni before serving.

Rural Soul

The Morvan is a mountainous region defined by a distinct topography—an ecology, if you will. It isn't one of the four départements that compose Burgundy, but occupies corners of all of them—lying mostly in the Nièvre, spilling over into the Yonne, the Côte-d'Or, and the Saône-et-Loire. The Morvan is wild Burgundy, repository of the region's rural soul. The terrain can be mountainous, and the Morvan is recognizable even from a distance, as the Michelin guide notes, "by its vast and sombre forests". Much of the region, in fact, is designated as a nature park by the French government. There are no vineyards to speak of; the autoroute seems a world away, and roads run past not vast panoramas of open farmland, but small fields divided by hedgerows. The physical characteristics of the Morvan have shaped the personality of its inhabitants, who are known for being tough and self-reliant. They have also shaped local eating habits: This is the domain of pork, wild mushrooms, snails, and honey. It is also the place to eat big, hearty, winter-beating dishes like boeuf à la bourguignonne—as prepared, for instance, by Millette Coquillon and her daughter Giselle Morin (below, from left) at their Chez Millette in the Morvan village of Planchez.

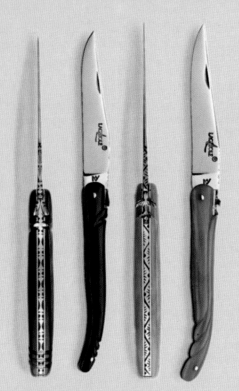

Pointed Elegance

T he small French mountain town of Laguiole (pronounced "lie-yole"), about 350 miles south of Paris, is famous for its cattle, its cheese, and above all its cutlery. The Laguiole knife exists in numerous forms. The original, dating from the early 19th century, was a farmer's tool, sometimes with a corkscrew and an awl set into the handle. A refinement is the Laguiole steak knife (above)—common today, among other places, on the tables at French three-star restaurants, where it is the meat-cutting tool of choice. The knife's form is elegance itself, with a gently curving blade, an elongated pistol-grip handle, and a small stylized bee or fly (no one is quite sure which, or why) set into the bolster. Put them together and you've got a knife that bears as much resemblance to the usual chophouse slicer as a Baccarat goblet to a souvenir-shop coffee mug.

Filet de Boeuf au Vin de Marcillac

(Filet of Beef with Marcillac Wine Sauce)

SERVES 4

MARCILLAC IS A SMALL, isolated wine region in France's Massif Central, producing spicy, aromatic reds (and a few rosés) based on a grape called mansois. Other full-bodied French red wines may be substituted. This recipe comes from the Grand Hôtel Auguy, on Laguiole's main square.

Olive oil
2 medium carrots, peeled and chopped
2 stalks celery, chopped
1 small yellow onion, peeled and chopped
3 tbsp. cognac
1 cup red wine vinegar
3 cups marcillac, cahors, or other hearty red wine
3 cups veal stock (see page 60)
Cracked black pepper
4 6-oz. beef filets, each about 1½" thick
Coarse salt
2 tbsp. cold butter, cubed

1. Heat 1 tbsp. oil in a heavy pot over medium heat. Add carrots, celery, and onions, and sauté until browned, about 5 minutes. Add cognac and carefully ignite with a kitchen match, keeping pot lid nearby to extinguish flames if necessary. When flames die out, add vinegar, wine, veal stock, and 1 tbsp. pepper. Reduce heat to low and cook until sauce is reduced by three-quarters, about 1½ hours. Strain, discard solids, and set sauce aside.

2. Season filets to taste with salt. Heat 1 tbsp. oil in a heavy skillet over high heat until hot but not smoking. Add filets and cook for 7 minutes on each side, then transfer to 4 plates. Reduce heat to medium, add sauce to skillet, whisk in butter, then spoon sauce over filets.

Daube de Boeuf

(Beef Braised in Red Wine)

SERVES 4

DAUBE MIGHT be called a more rustic cousin of boeuf à la bourguignonne, typically made with heartier red wine and perfumed with earthy dried cèpes (porcini mushrooms). In Nice, it is usually served with plain buttered noodles or polenta. This is an adaptation of Franck Cerutti's recipe.

½ oz. dried porcini mushrooms
2 lbs. beef chuck, cut into 2" pieces
Salt
1 tbsp. butter
1 tbsp. olive oil
1 medium yellow onion, peeled and diced
2 medium carrots, peeled and diced
2 cloves garlic, peeled and chopped
2 large plum tomatoes, peeled, seeded, and roughly chopped
1 stalk celery, diced
Bouquet garni (see sidebar, page 59)
1 tbsp. flour
2 cups red côtes-de-provence or other dry, hearty red wine
Freshly ground black pepper

1. Put mushrooms in a bowl, cover with boiling water, and set aside. Generously season beef with salt.

2. Heat butter and oil in a large, heavy pot over medium-high heat. Working in batches to avoid crowding pan (pieces shouldn't touch), add beef to pot and brown on all sides, turning pieces as they brown, for about 15 minutes in all. Remove pieces as done and set aside.

3. Lower heat to medium-low and pour off all but a small amount of oil and butter. Add onions, carrots, garlic, tomatoes, and celery and cook for about 5 minutes, stirring with a wooden spoon to scrape browned bits from the bottom of the pot and coat vegetables with oil.

4. Return meat to pot and add bouquet garni. Mix together flour and half the wine with a fork in a small bowl, making sure there are no lumps. Stir into pot, then add remaining wine. Cover and simmer over low heat for 2 hours.

5. Drain mushrooms, reserving soaking water, then rinse and roughly chop mushrooms. Strain mushroom water through a coffee filter, then add mushrooms and strained soaking water to pot. Simmer for 1 hour more, then remove bouquet garni and season to taste with salt and pepper.

Elusive Perfection

I n many ways, Don Camillo—a small family-owned establishment just off the Promenade des Anglais in Nice—was the perfect French restaurant: With young Franck and Véronique Cerutti (below) in the kitchen and dining room, respectively, and with her parents helping out, it ignored fads and trends and dug deep into regional culinary tradition—but with a contemporary sensibility and a top chef's regard for the integrity of raw materials. Every town in France ought to have had a place like this. In 1996, though, with business at the restaurant increasingly erratic, Cerutti left his sous-chef in charge of the kitchen and went back to work for an old boss—celebrity chef Alain Ducasse—at the three-star Le Louis XV, in the Hôtel de Paris in Monte Carlo. Don Camillo stayed as good as ever for a couple of years...until the Ceruttis sold it to new proprietors, who have kept the name, but not the wonderful food.

Dining with Claude

"I met Claude Caspar-Jordan," recalls SAVEUR editor Colman Andrews, "in 1966, on my first night in Paris. Claude [above, with wife, Pepita, and facing page, lower right, getting fed at a reception] was 60 at the time, and I was 21. When he'd been about 21 himself, he'd worked in America for a year on the *Chicago Daily News*, where my father was an editor. The two became fast friends, but lost touch after Claude returned to Paris; in 1963, by chance, they rediscovered each other, and when I headed off to discover Europe, it seemed natural that I'd look Claude up. He and I got along pretty well—I suppose I was the son he'd never had, and he provided an amiable personal entree into the heart of a culture I loved—and over the next 28 years, we must have shared hundreds of meals. We dined at his house (Pepita was a great cook), at Parisian bistros like Aux Amis du Beaujolais and Allard, in three-star restaurants from Alsace to Burgundy, in rural Provençal cafés. We talked, we enjoyed our food and drink, we learned (I think) from each other. The last time I saw him, in his hospital bed, we talked about the next meal we were going to have together."

Boeuf à la Mode aux Carottes

(Braised Beef with Carrots)

SERVES 6

BERNARD PICOLET of Aux Amis du Beaujolais in Paris still delights his regular customers (like those pictured at near right) with old-fashioned bistro classics like this one.

1 ½ lb. veal knuckle, cracked
2 ½–3 lbs. chuck roast, larded and tied by butcher
Salt and freshly ground black pepper
3 tbsp. lard or vegetable oil
1 medium yellow onion, peeled and roughly chopped
1 head garlic, halved
8 carrots, peeled, 4 roughly chopped, 4 cut into 1" pieces
2 stalks celery, roughly chopped
¼ lb. pork rind
3 cups dry white wine
3 cups beef stock (see page 59)
1 tbsp. white wine vinegar
Bouquet garni (see sidebar, page 59)
1 tbsp. butter
1 tbsp. sugar
1 tsp. arrowroot (optional)
Fresh parsley for garnish

1. Preheat oven to 400°. Put veal knuckle in a roasting pan and roast, turning to brown on all sides, for about 1½ hours.

2. Season beef liberally with salt and pepper. Melt lard in a large pot (with a cover) over medium heat. Add beef and brown on all sides, turning as it browns, for about 15 minutes in all, then remove beef from pot, reduce heat to medium, and add onions, garlic, the 4 roughly chopped carrots, and celery. Cook, stirring occasionally, until vegetables caramelize, 12–15 minutes.

3. Meanwhile, put pork rind in a medium saucepan with enough water to cover. Bring just to a boil over high heat, then drain. Return beef to pot with vegetables, add veal knuckle, pork rind, wine, beef stock, vinegar, and bouquet garni. Bring to a boil over medium-high heat, then reduce heat to low, cover, and simmer, turning beef occasionally, until meat is easily pierced with a kitchen fork, 2½–3 hours.

4. Remove beef and set aside. Increase heat to medium and simmer broth to concentrate flavor for 15 minutes. Remove and discard veal knuckle, pork rind, and bouquet garni. Strain broth through a fine sieve, pressing vegetables with the back of a spoon, then return liquid to pot and skim fat.

5. Add remaining 4 carrots to broth, cover, and cook over low heat until tender, 15–20 minutes. Melt butter in a medium saucepan over medium heat and stir in sugar. Transfer carrots from pot to saucepan with a slotted spoon. Cook, stirring occasionally, until carrots are caramelized, about 10 minutes. Taste sauce, season to taste with salt and pepper, and, if necessary, thicken with arrowroot. Remove string from beef, cut beef into thick pieces, and return to sauce to heat through. Serve with carrots and, if you like, boiled potatoes. Garnish with parsley.

Pot-au-Feu

(French Boiled Beef Dinner)

SERVES 8

FRENCH-BORN Alice Tunks, whose recipe is adapted here, offers this pot-au-feu advice: Use both lean and fatty meats; cook potatoes separately so the broth doesn't cloud; and make enough so that there's some left for the next day.

---

11 medium leeks, trimmed and washed

12 carrots, peeled and halved crosswise

12 celery stalks, trimmed and halved crosswise

1 large yellow onion studded with 3 cloves

Bouquet garni (see sidebar, page 59) with 1 clove peeled garlic added

1 4-lb. rump roast, tied by butcher

2 1-lb. beef shanks, about 1½" thick

2 1-lb. beef short ribs

Coarse sea salt

1 2-lb. beef marrow bone, cut into 2" pieces (ask your butcher)

4 medium turnips, peeled, trimmed, and cut into quarters

16 baby new potatoes, scrubbed

Freshly ground black pepper

8 slices toasted country bread

1. Put 3 leeks, 6 carrot pieces, 6 celery pieces, onion, and bouquet garni in a large stockpot. Place rump roast, beef shanks, and short ribs on top of vegetables. Press about ½ tsp. salt into each end of 2 marrow bone pieces and add to pot, tucking them between meats. Add enough cold water to cover meats (about 7 quarts), and bring to a boil over high heat. Reduce heat to medium and simmer for 3 hours, skimming foam. Press about ½ tsp. salt into each end of remaining bones and place in pot along with turnips and remaining leeks, carrots, and celery. Cook, partially covered, until vegetables are very tender, about 1 hour more.

2. Meanwhile, put potatoes in a medium pot and cover with cold water. Add a generous pinch of salt and bring to a boil over medium-high heat. Lower heat to medium and simmer until potatoes are easily pierced with a knife, about 20 minutes. Drain water from pot and set aside, covering pot to keep potatoes warm.

3. Carefully remove top layer of vegetables from stockpot and arrange on a large, warm serving platter. Remove bones from pot and set aside. Remove meats, cut off and discard strings from rump roast, carve meats, and arrange on serving platter with vegetables and potatoes. Cover to keep warm. Strain broth through a colander, discarding remaining vegetables and bouquet garni. Return broth to pot and skim off fat. Season to taste with salt and pepper and keep warm over medium-low heat.

4. To serve: For the first course, ladle about 1 cup broth into each of 8 large soup bowls. Pass marrow bones at the table and serve with toasted country bread for spreading with marrow scooped from bones. For the second course, ladle some of the remaining stock over the meat and vegetables, and serve with additional sea salt, cornichons, and mustard, if you like.

The Eternal Pot

My mother's pot-au-feu," SAVEUR research editor Marina Tunks Ganter tells us, "was more than just a rustic meal; it was an ode to joy. Unlike chicken soup meant to soothe a variety of ills, pot-au-feu turned a meal into a rich and glorious feast, representing qualities the French have held dear throughout their turbulent history: resourcefulness, common sense, resilience, boldness, and most of all, joie de vivre." Literally "pot on the fire", pot-au-feu dates back to the Middle Ages and is now unarguably the national dish of France. And though adaptations abound from household to household and region to region, it has remained basically unchanged since its creation. "My mother likes to point out," Ganter continues, "that the oldest French cookbooks didn't even bother including a recipe for pot-au-feu; it was simply assumed that it was inscribed in our genes. So it must be. The pot-au-feu I grew up with is the same one my great grandmother Hélène (below center, with daughter Caroline, left, and grandaughter Alice, right) enjoyed as a child."

C'est Fini

Jean and Christiane Giusti were the owners of La Merenda—a tiny, one-of-a-kind restaurant on the edge of Vieux Nice—and, respectively, its chef and its waitress/hostess/manager. A blackboard in the window of the place spelled out the house rules to prospective customers: pas de chèques, pas de cartes de crédit, pas de téléphone. It was open only Tuesday through Friday, reservations were not (officially) accepted, and when all the seats were taken, Christiane hung a sign on the door—with a certain satisfaction, one suspects—reading C'EST FINI. The Giustis (right, standing in center) who sold the restaurant several years ago to Dominique Le Stanc, former chef at the elegant Chantecler in Nice's first-class Hôtel Négresco (it remains La Merenda, but not quite the Giustis' La Merenda)—were famous for their uncompromising Niçois specialties: the defining local classic called estocaficada (a kind of ragoût of stockfish, or dried cod), squash-blossom beignets (which were called the best in France), a classic daube, unctuous pâtes au pistou—and tripes à la niçoise so succulent that even tripe haters were converted.

Tripes à la Niçoise

(Nice-Style Tripe)

SERVES 4

T RIPE MUST be cooked long and very slowly to tenderize it properly. At La Merenda in Nice, the Giustis always served this dish with the savory chickpea-flour "fries" called panisses, but polenta goes well with it, too.

2 lbs. beef tripe, cut into
    2" x ½" strips
¼ cup white vinegar
¼ cup extra-virgin
    olive oil
2 cups dry white wine
4 tomatoes, peeled, seeded,
    and roughly chopped
4 cloves garlic, peeled and
    finely chopped
2 medium yellow onions,
    peeled and sliced
Bouquet garni (see sidebar,
    page 59)
1 small dried red chile
    (optional)
Salt and freshly ground
    black pepper
Freshly grated
    parmigiano-reggiano

1. Rinse tripe very well in several changes of cold water. Bring a large pot of water to a boil over high heat and add vinegar. Blanch tripe for 20 seconds in boiling water, then drain.

2. Heat oil in a medium pot over medium heat and add tripe. Cook for about 2 minutes, stirring frequently. Stir in wine, tomatoes, garlic, onions, bouquet garni, chile (if using), and salt and pepper to taste.

3. Cover, reduce heat to very low, and simmer for at least 8 hours. Adjust seasoning and serve with grated parmigiano-reggiano and panisses, if you like.

"Blanquette" de Veau

(Veal Stew)

SERVES 4

BY DEFINITION, the meat in a blanquette is simmered but never browned. Arlette Hugon (behind bar, left), however—who runs the wonderful Lyonnais bouchon called Chez Hugon with her husband, Henri (seated, left) and son Éric (in chef's whites)—redefines the dish on her own terms: She likes the heartier flavor browning lends—so she browns.

2 ½ lbs. boneless veal shoulder, trimmed and cut into 2"–3" pieces
Salt and freshly ground black pepper
1 tbsp. flour
2 tbsp. vegetable oil
1 yellow onion, peeled and chopped
2 cloves garlic, peeled and minced
2 ½ cups dry white wine
1 small leek, white part only, washed and chopped
3 sprigs fresh thyme
3 bay leaves
1 cup beef stock (see page 59)
1 lemon, halved
1 cup heavy cream
2 tbsp. capers, drained

1. Season veal with salt and pepper, then dust with flour. Heat oil in a large pot over medium-high heat. Working in batches to avoid crowding pan, add veal and brown on all sides, turning pieces as they brown, for about 5 minutes in all. Remove pieces as done and set aside. When all veal is browned, return to pot, add onions and garlic, and cook, stirring frequently, until vegetables are golden, about 10 minutes.

2. Add wine, leeks, thyme, and bay leaves to pot. Reduce heat to medium-low and simmer for 10 minutes, then add stock. Cover pot and continue simmering until veal is tender, about 1½ hours.

3. Remove veal from pot with a slotted spoon and set aside. Squeeze juice from both lemon halves into sauce, then add squeezed-out shells. Stir in cream and simmer, stirring occasionally, until sauce thickens, about 30 minutes. Remove and discard lemon halves, bay leaves, and thyme. Transfer sauce to a food processor and purée until smooth. Strain through a fine sieve and return to pot. Season sauce to taste with salt and pepper, then return veal to pot and heat through for about 10 minutes. Serve garnished with capers.

Corking Good

B ouchons, the informal, usually family-run little eating places native to Lyon," reports political and gastronomic analyst R.W. Apple, Jr., "are bistros of a sort, but with even more limited menus. Their decor tends to be modest to the point of austerity. Some have paper tablecloths, and some don't change the cutlery between courses—but the food and ambience of any good bouchon will warm the coldest heart. The food is almost always based on humble ingredients—not foie gras, lobster, and truffles, but things like cocks' combs, calves' feet, cardoons, lentils, and swiss chard. The first bouchons were 19th-century Lyonnais equivalents of our truck stops—taverns where grooms and coachmen paused for a glass and a bite after brushing down their horses. Since bouchon means 'cork', I had always assumed these places took their name from the many bottles that were uncorked inside. But a bouchon is also the handful of straw used for rubbing down horses, and a more likely explanation is that taverns with facilities for horses hung bundles of straw over their doors as insignia, the way bakeries hung out pretzels."

Liver is one of the many *abats de boucherie*, or variety meats, with which the French create culinary masterpieces. (In English these are known as *offal*, from "off-fall", meaning the parts that virtually fall out when the butcher opens an animal's carcass.) The most famous liver in French kitchens, of course, is the fattened kind from ducks and

geese—foie gras. Bresse chicken liver, called foie blond, is also highly regarded, and used often in terrines. The next most appreciated liver is certainly that of the calf—like the one displayed on the facing page by Jean-Pierre Mouton (!) at his Triperie Mouton in Paris. In traditional Chinese medicine, liver is thought to engender strength and courage. In French gastronomy, it engenders pleased palates.

Foie de Veau Poêlé

(Sautéed Calf's Liver)

SERVES 4

IN FRANCE, where offal of every kind is appreciated, calf's liver is often served in thick, rosy-pink slabs instead of the thinner, crisper scallops Americans seem to prefer. For mild flavor and tender texture, look for young calf's liver—and soak the meat in milk for at least an hour before cooking.

½ cup flour
4 6-oz. slices calf's liver
Salt and freshly ground
    black pepper
3 tbsp. vegetable oil
⅔ cup butter
4 shallots, peeled and
    thinly sliced
½ cup cognac
¾ cup minced fresh chives

1. Pour flour into a shallow dish. Dredge slices of calf's liver in flour, coating well on both sides. Shake off excess and season with salt and freshly ground black pepper. Warm oil in a skillet over medium heat until hot but not smoking. Add liver and cook, turning once, until medium rare, about 3 minutes per side. Remove liver and cover loosely with aluminum foil to keep warm.

2. Pour off and discard oil from skillet, then wipe out skillet with paper towels. Melt butter in skillet over medium heat. Add shallots and cook until golden, about 5 minutes. Add cognac, cook for 1 minute, then stir in chives and adjust seasoning. To serve, spoon sauce over liver.

Ris de Veau
à l'Ancienne

(Veal Sweetbreads in the Old Style)

SERVES 8

SWEETBREADS are the thymus or the pancreas gland of (usually) calves or lambs. Thymus glands are long and irregular in shape; pancreas glands may be larger and rounder.

4 9-oz. pieces veal sweet-breads, halved
Salt
Juice of half a lemon
24 asparagus tips, trimmed
½ cup fresh peas
¼ lb. haricots verts, trimmed
16 pearl onions, peeled
¼ lb. baby carrots, peeled and trimmed
¼ cup peanut oil
8 tbsp. butter
Freshly ground black pepper
¼ cup dry vermouth
1 cup veal stock (see page 60)
2 tbsp. minced fresh flat-leaf parsley

1. Wash sweetbreads in cold water, then put them in a large bowl, cover with ice water, and refrigerate for 2 hours, changing the water several times. Next, put sweetbreads in a saucepan, cover with cold salted water, add lemon juice, and bring to a boil over medium heat. Boil for 1 minute. Drain, then transfer sweetbreads to a bowl of ice water to cool them. When cool, clean sweetbreads by removing and discarding all fat and sinew. Blot dry with a kitchen towel, wrap in plastic, and refrigerate overnight.

2. Preheat oven to 325°. Bring a large pot of salted water to a boil over medium-high heat. Cook asparagus, peas, and haricots verts separately for 3–4 minutes each, removing each from water when done with a slotted spoon, and setting aside. Cook onions and carrots separately for 6–8 minutes each, removing from water and setting aside as above.

3. Heat oil and 4 tbsp. butter in a large ovenproof skillet over medium heat until butter begins to sizzle. Generously season sweetbreads with salt and pepper, then sauté until just browned, about 5 minutes per side. Add 3 tbsp. butter and transfer skillet to oven for 20 minutes. Remove skillet from oven, transfer sweetbreads to a heated platter, cover loosely with foil, and set aside. Pour off and discard fat, then add vermouth to same skillet. Cook for 1 minute over high heat, stirring with a wooden spoon to loosen any browned bits stuck to the bottom of the pan. Add stock and reduce by half, about 5 minutes.

4. Melt remaining 1 tbsp. butter in a large sauté pan over medium heat, pour in ¼ cup of reduced stock, then add vegetables, season to taste with salt and pepper, and cook until heated through. Arrange vegetables around sweetbreads on platter. Spoon remaining reduced stock over sweetbreads and sprinkle with parsley.

Easy to Love

THE gougères and champagne arrive almost immediately, fueling the diner as he tackles the pleasantly difficult task of deciding between the snails braised with sorrel and the crabmeat cannelloni in sauce ravigote, and then perhaps between the truffled pig's foot sausage, the sautéed foie gras in gingerbread crumbs, and the sweetbreads à l'ancienne (see recipe, left). The wine list, conveniently printed right on the menu itself, offers a similarly vexing embarrassment of riches. But never mind. The attentiveness of the staff—which goes beyond mere "service"—is so remarkable and reassuring, and the elegantly paneled dining room is so calmly attractive that the whole experience is absolutely unintimidating, a veritable breeze. And that's why Taillevent in Paris (above) really is quite possibly the best, most perfect restaurant in the world.

Potluck Dinner

Potée, according to *Larousse Gastronomique*, is any dish cooked in an earthenware pot, but the term usually applies to a mixture of meat (mainly pork) and vegetables—especially cabbage and potatoes—cooked in stock and served as a single course. Potée is a very old dish and is found throughout rural France, often under other names—among them hochepot, garbure, and oille. Recipes vary with region: Potée alsacienne, for instance, is made with smoked bacon fat, white cabbage, celery, carrots, and haricots verts—the vegetables sweated in goose fat before liquid is added; potée auvergnate includes fresh or salt pork, sausages, half a pig's head, cabbage, carrots, and turnips; potée bourguignonne uses bacon, pork shoulder, ham hocks, cabbage, carrots, turnips, leeks, and potatoes (plus peas and haricots verts in spring); potée bretonne's ingredients include lamb shoulder, duck, sausages, and various vegetables (an eel potée is also made in Brittany); potée lorraine contains lean bacon, filet or shoulder of pork, cabbage, carrots, haricots verts, dried or fresh white haricot beans, peas, turnips, leeks, celery, potatoes, and sometimes lentils; and potée champenoise, or grape pickers' potée, is a mix of unsmoked bacon, salt pork, cabbage, turnips, celeriac, potatoes, sometimes sausages or smoked ham, and perhaps chicken.

Potée
(Savoyard Pork and Vegetable Stew)

SERVES 10

THIS VERSION of potée, from the mountains of the Savoie region of southeastern France, is considered one of the most traditional of all. You'll need a 24-quart stockpot.

1 3-lb. pork shoulder, rolled and tied
2 smoked ham hocks
3 lbs. smoked kielbasa
6 medium yellow onions, peeled, each studded with 1 clove
4 cloves garlic, peeled
Coarse salt
5 black peppercorns
3 bay leaves
6 leeks, trimmed and washed
10 whole carrots, peeled
10 small turnips, scrubbed
10 small potatoes, scrubbed
1 head savoy cabbage, cored and quartered
Freshly ground black pepper

1. Put pork, ham hocks, kielbasa, 1 onion, garlic, 1 tsp. salt, peppercorns, and bay leaves in a 24-quart stockpot with water to cover. Bring to a boil over medium-high heat. Reduce heat to low and gently simmer for 2 hours, skimming fat and foam.

2. Add leeks, carrots, turnips, potatoes, and remaining 5 onions, increase heat to medium, and bring back to a simmer. Cook until vegetables are almost tender, about 30 minutes. Add cabbage and cook for 10 minutes more.

3. Transfer meat and vegetables from pot to a large platter and keep warm in a low oven. Increase heat under stockpot to high and reduce stock by one-quarter, about 15 minutes. Season to taste with salt and pepper.

4. Slice meat and sausages and place in the center of a deep platter; surround with vegetables. Ladle some broth over the dish and sprinkle with salt and pepper. Serve with remaining broth in bowls with toasted bread, if you like.

Rôti de Porc aux Pommes

(Pork Loin with Apples, Cider, and Calvados)

SERVES 8–10

INSPIRED BY the celebrated apples of Normandy, we developed this recipe to use apples in three forms, two of them liquid. Though pork has been eaten by the French since the time of the Gauls, it was long regarded as the meat of the common people; this preparation ennobles it.

1 4½-lb. pork loin roast
1 tbsp. flour
Salt and freshly ground black pepper
2 tsp. finely chopped fresh rosemary
4 tbsp. butter
3 medium yellow onions, peeled and chopped
2 cloves garlic, peeled and chopped
4 stalks rosemary (optional)
5 baking apples, cored and quartered
½ cup Sydre Argelette (see sidebar, page 178) or other good-quality French hard cider
¼ cup good-quality calvados

1. Preheat oven to 325°. Tie pork loin every 2" with kitchen string so that it holds a cylindrical shape. Mix together flour, salt and pepper to taste, and chopped rosemary in a small bowl. Rub the flour mixture all over the pork loin, coating evenly and well.

2. Heat 2 tbsp. butter in a large heavy skillet and sear meat over high heat, turning often, until browned on all sides, about 15 minutes. Transfer meat with pan juices to a large baking pan and scatter onions and garlic around it. Cut up remaining butter and distribute evenly over onions. Add rosemary stalks (if using) to pan. Cover pan with foil.

3. Put in oven and cook for 45 minutes, then add apples and hard cider to pan. Baste pork and apples with pan juices. Re-cover and cook for 30 minutes more. Raise oven temperature to 400°, remove foil, baste, and cook for another 15 minutes.

4. Transfer roast to a cutting board, remove string, and allow to rest for 10 minutes before slicing. Meanwhile, transfer onions and apples to a platter. Put pan on top of the stove over medium-high heat and reduce pan juices by half, about 5 minutes. Warm calvados in a small pan, add to the pan juices, and carefully ignite with a kitchen match, keeping pan lid nearby to extinguish flames if necessary. Simmer sauce while you slice the pork loin. Arrange meat over apples and onions and serve with the sauce.

Apple Spirits

There is no secret to making good calvados, says Claude Camut. "All you need is the *bonne fortune* of being in the right place, on the right farm, with the right apples, for 800 years." Calvados, of course, is Normandy's famed apple brandy, distilled from cider just as cognac is from wine. At the turn of the century, 90 percent of all calvados was made by farmers. Today, it's a mere 2 percent, with the rest turned out by large companies. Farmer Camut grows all his own apples, makes and distills his own cider, and ages it himself. Each of the 25 traditional apple varieties he grows, says Camut, contributes something distinctive to his calvados. "In Paris," he says, laughing, "they think it is very funny we can make such a marvelous spirit with such horrible-looking apples."

T he word *choucroute* has also come to mean the show-stopping dish, definitive of Alsatian cuisine, of sauerkraut topped with copious portions of pork in myriad

forms—but it translates simply as fermented cabbage. The earliest reference to sauerkraut in Alsace dates from the 15th century. For hundreds of years, until the early 1900s, Sürkrüt-schniders, or sour-cabbage cutters, toured the countryside, shredding cabbage to order. Today, the process is left to professionals. "You could make it at home," says Xavier Schaal, managing director of the Choucroutal cooperative in Geispolsheim, "but you'd need at least a hundred kilos of raw cabbage at a time."

Choucroute Garnie à l'Alsacienne

(Sauerkraut Garnished with Smoked, Cured, and Fresh Pork)

SERVES 6–8

NO OTHER dish shows off the richly varied charcuterie of Alsace quite like choucroute. This recipe was adapted from one of eight varieties served at Maison Kammerzell, Guy-Pierre Baumann's legendary choucroute institution in Strasbourg.

1½ lbs. fresh ham hocks
¼ cup goose fat
3 small yellow onions, peeled and finely chopped
4½ lbs. sauerkraut, drained and rinsed
3¼ cups Alsatian riesling or other dry but fruity white wine
1½ lbs. boneless pork loin
1 lb. smoked ham
½ lb. slab bacon
Bouquet garni (see sidebar, page 59) with 1 head garlic, 3 whole cloves, 6 juniper berries, and 5 coriander seeds added
Salt and freshly ground black pepper
12 medium red bliss potatoes, peeled
6 fresh pork sausages, such as saucisses de Strasbourg
3 blood sausages (optional)
1 tbsp. peanut oil
6 smoked pork sausages

1. Place ham hocks in a large pot. Cover with water and simmer over medium heat for 1½ hours. Drain and set aside.

2. Preheat oven to 350°. Melt goose fat in a dutch oven, or a large heavy pot with a lid, over medium heat. Add onions, cook until soft, 10–15 minutes, then add sauerkraut, wine, ham hocks, pork loin, ham, bacon, and bouquet garni. Season with salt and pepper, cover, and cook in oven until meats are tender, about 1½ hours.

3. About 35 minutes before serving, place potatoes in a pot of salted water over medium-high heat and cook until tender, 20–25 minutes. Drain and keep warm.

4. Prick fresh and blood sausages, if using, with a fork, then place in a skillet, cover with water, and simmer over medium heat for 10 minutes. Drain. Dry skillet, add oil, and heat over medium heat. Brown fresh and blood sausages (if using), turning occasionally, then remove. In the same oil, adding more if necessary, brown smoked sausages, turning occasionally, then remove. To serve, spoon sauerkraut onto a large platter, discarding bouquet garni. Slice pork loin, ham, and bacon, and arrange on platter with ham hocks, potatoes, and all sausages.

Rôti de Porc aux Pommes

(Pork Loin with Apples, Cider, and Calvados)

SERVES 8–10

INSPIRED BY the celebrated apples of Normandy, we developed this recipe to use apples in three forms, two of them liquid. Though pork has been eaten by the French since the time of the Gauls, it was long regarded as the meat of the common people; this preparation ennobles it.

1 4½-lb. pork loin roast
1 tbsp. flour
Salt and freshly ground black pepper
2 tsp. finely chopped fresh rosemary
4 tbsp. butter
3 medium yellow onions, peeled and chopped
2 cloves garlic, peeled and chopped
4 stalks rosemary (optional)
5 baking apples, cored and quartered
½ cup Sydre Argelette (see sidebar, page 178) or other good-quality French hard cider
¼ cup good-quality calvados

1. Preheat oven to 325°. Tie pork loin every 2" with kitchen string so that it holds a cylindrical shape. Mix together flour, salt and pepper to taste, and chopped rosemary in a small bowl. Rub the flour mixture all over the pork loin, coating evenly and well.

2. Heat 2 tbsp. butter in a large heavy skillet and sear meat over high heat, turning often, until browned on all sides, about 15 minutes. Transfer meat with pan juices to a large baking pan and scatter onions and garlic around it. Cut up remaining butter and distribute evenly over onions. Add rosemary stalks (if using) to pan. Cover pan with foil.

3. Put in oven and cook for 45 minutes, then add apples and hard cider to pan. Baste pork and apples with pan juices. Re-cover and cook for 30 minutes more. Raise oven temperature to 400°, remove foil, baste, and cook for another 15 minutes.

4. Transfer roast to a cutting board, remove string, and allow to rest for 10 minutes before slicing. Meanwhile, transfer onions and apples to a platter. Put pan on top of the stove over medium-high heat and reduce pan juices by half, about 5 minutes. Warm calvados in a small pan, add to the pan juices, and carefully ignite with a kitchen match, keeping pan lid nearby to extinguish flames if necessary. Simmer sauce while you slice the pork loin. Arrange meat over apples and onions and serve with the sauce.

Apple Spirits

There is no secret to making good calvados, says Claude Camut. "All you need is the *bonne fortune* of being in the right place, on the right farm, with the right apples, for 800 years." Calvados, of course, is Normandy's famed apple brandy, distilled from cider just as cognac is from wine. At the turn of the century, 90 percent of all calvados was made by farmers. Today, it's a mere 2 percent, with the rest turned out by large companies. Farmer Camut grows all his own apples, makes and distills his own cider, and ages it himself. Each of the 25 traditional apple varieties he grows, says Camut, contributes something distinctive to his calvados. "In Paris," he says, laughing, "they think it is very funny we can make such a marvelous spirit with such horrible-looking apples."

Choucroute Garnie à l'Alsacienne

(Sauerkraut Garnished with Smoked, Cured, and Fresh Pork)

SERVES 6–8

NO OTHER dish shows off the richly varied charcuterie of Alsace quite like choucroute. This recipe was adapted from one of eight varieties served at Maison Kammerzell, Guy-Pierre Baumann's legendary choucroute institution in Strasbourg.

1 ½ lbs. fresh ham hocks
¼ cup goose fat
3 small yellow onions, peeled and finely chopped
4 ½ lbs. sauerkraut, drained and rinsed
3 ¼ cups Alsatian riesling or other dry but fruity white wine
1 ½ lbs. boneless pork loin
1 lb. smoked ham
½ lb. slab bacon
Bouquet garni (see sidebar, page 59) with 1 head garlic, 3 whole cloves, 6 juniper berries, and 5 coriander seeds added
Salt and freshly ground black pepper
12 medium red bliss potatoes, peeled
6 fresh pork sausages, such as saucisses de Strasbourg
3 blood sausages (optional)
1 tbsp. peanut oil
6 smoked pork sausages

1. Place ham hocks in a large pot. Cover with water and simmer over medium heat for 1½ hours. Drain and set aside.

2. Preheat oven to 350°. Melt goose fat in a dutch oven, or a large heavy pot with a lid, over medium heat. Add onions, cook until soft, 10–15 minutes, then add sauerkraut, wine, ham hocks, pork loin, ham, bacon, and bouquet garni. Season with salt and pepper, cover, and cook in oven until meats are tender, about 1½ hours.

3. About 35 minutes before serving, place potatoes in a pot of salted water over medium-high heat and cook until tender, 20–25 minutes. Drain and keep warm.

4. Prick fresh and blood sausages, if using, with a fork, then place in a skillet, cover with water, and simmer over medium heat for 10 minutes. Drain. Dry skillet, add oil, and heat over medium heat. Brown fresh and blood sausages (if using), turning occasionally, then remove. In the same oil, adding more if necessary, brown smoked sausages, turning occasionally, then remove. To serve, spoon sauerkraut onto a large platter, discarding bouquet garni. Slice pork loin, ham, and bacon, and arrange on platter with ham hocks, potatoes, and all sausages.

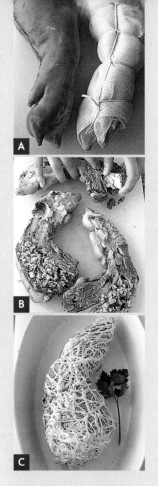

A

B

C

Good Food Afoot

Americans eat about 16 billion pounds of pork annually—but pork "parts" like pigs' feet remain largely unappreciated. Making the Lyonnais classic (facing page, bottom) is a good way to get acquainted with this delicacy. Ask your butcher to halve pigs' feet lengthwise, then reassemble them, wrap tightly in cheesecloth, and tie with kitchen string (**A**). After cooking, unwrap, remove any bones, and fill with stuffing (**B**), then wrap in caul fat (**C**) before roasting.

Pieds de Cochon Farcis

(Stuffed Pigs' Feet)

CAUL FAT is a lacy, netlike pork membrane, often used in France as casing for homemade sausages and other ground meat dishes. Though not readily available in the U.S., it can usually be special-ordered from your butcher.

⅓ cup red wine vinegar
3 sprigs fresh thyme
3 bay leaves
1 tsp. black peppercorns
4 pigs' feet, split in half lengthwise (ask your butcher)
2 cups finely chopped soft white bread
⅔ lb. boiled ham, finely chopped
2 large shallots, peeled and minced
½ cup finely chopped fresh parsley
¼ cup milk
1 egg yolk, lightly beaten
½ cup dry white wine
Salt
1 lb. caul fat, rinsed

1. Combine vinegar, thyme, bay leaves, and peppercorns in a pot large enough to accommodate 4 whole pigs' feet. Reassemble split pigs' feet, wrapping each foot in cheesecloth, then tying with kitchen string. Add enough water just to cover, weight with a heavy plate, then cover and slowly simmer over medium-low heat for 4 hours. Cool, then refrigerate pigs' feet in cooking liquid overnight.

2. Preheat oven to 375°. Combine bread, ham, shallots, parsley, milk, egg yolk, and ¼ cup of the wine in a medium bowl. Mix well and season with salt. Unwrap and separate pigs' feet. Using your fingers, remove and discard leg bone down to ankle joint and discard (foot bones should remain in place). Divide stuffing between feet, spooning about ¼ cup into each cavity. Rinse caul fat and cut into four pieces, each about 12" x 12". Reassemble pigs' feet, wrap each in caul fat, then fit snugly in a roasting pan in a single layer. Add remaining ¼ cup wine and roast until golden, about 45 minutes. Separate halves again and serve warm.

Informal Gourmand

Gérard Oberlé (above)—a rare-book dealer born in Alsace but Burgundian by choice—is a kind of profane cherub of a man with a generously beaming face and an unapologetic gourmand's lust for good food. When he invited us to lunch one day at his house in Montigny-sur-Canne, a hamlet near Château-Chinon, the Morvan's main town, he promised us an informal meal. As we arrived, he introduced us to "a colleague"—Marc Meneau, chef-proprietor of l'Espérance in St-Père-sous-Vézelay, arguably the best restaurant in Burgundy—who had collaborated with him on the informality. Our main course was the definitive coq au vin, and there were wonderful cheeses and homemade apple and rhubarb tarts for dessert—but the most memorable dish was our first course, a veritable culinary monument composed of potatoes and the sweet meat of pigs' snouts encased in perfect pastry. Was it unexpected? Yes. Daunting? No, surprisingly. Delicious? *Absolument!*

Tourte de Groins de Porc
(Torte of Pigs' Snout)

SERVES 8

IF PIGS' SNOUTS are unavailable from your butcher, says Marc Meneau—who gave us the recipe for this uncompromising Burgundian specialty—substitute pigs' feet.

2 lbs. pigs' snouts, soaked in water overnight, or 3 pigs' feet (5–6 lbs. total)
Salt
1 cup dry white wine
2 tbsp. flour
1 medium yellow onion, peeled
2 cloves
1 carrot, trimmed and halved
1 leek, trimmed, halved and washed
1 celery stalk, trimmed and halved
Bouquet garni (see sidebar, page 59)
5 waxy potatoes
3 tbsp. butter
1 shallot, peeled and minced
4 cloves garlic, peeled and minced
2 tbsp. minced fresh tarragon leaves
2 tbsp. minced fresh chervil leaves
2 tbsp. minced fresh parsley leaves
1½ tbsp. dijon mustard
¼ cup white wine vinegar
Freshly ground black pepper
2 sheets Dufour or other good-quality prepared puff pastry
1 egg, lightly beaten

1. Put meat into a large pot, cover with cold salted water, and bring to a boil over high heat. When foam rises to the top, drain, rinse meat and pot, then return meat to pot. Add wine to flour in a small bowl, whisking until smooth, pour over meat, then add salted water to cover. Stud onion with cloves and add to pot with carrots, leeks, celery, and bouquet garni. Bring to a boil over high heat, reduce heat to low, and simmer, partially covered, until meat is tender, 4–5 hours. Remove meat from pot and allow to cool. Discard vegetables and stock from pot. When meat has cooled, finely chop. (Debone pigs' feet if using them.)

2. Preheat oven to 400°. Put potatoes in a large pot of cold salted water, then bring to a boil over high heat. Cook until tender, about 25 minutes. Allow to cool, then peel and thinly slice. Set aside.

3. Melt 2 tbsp. butter in a sauté pan over medium heat. Add shallots and garlic and cook until soft, about 5 minutes, then combine with meat, tarragon, chervil, parsley, mustard, and vinegar in a large bowl. Season to taste with salt and pepper.

4. Roll out pastry sheets on a lightly floured surface into 2 16" rounds. Set a buttered and floured 8" x 2½" vacherin mold on a parchment-lined baking sheet. Fit 1 pastry sheet into ring, leaving 1" overhanging edge. Layer in a third of potatoes, then add half the meat mixture (**A**). Repeat layers, finishing with potatoes. Fold pastry over potatoes (**B**) and place second pastry sheet over it. Trim pastry, leaving 1" overlap, then tuck overlap inside ring with a dinner knife. Insert a 2" parchment tube in center of torte as a steam vent and cut decorative slits in the center of the pastry (**C**). Mix together egg and 1 tbsp. water, then brush over top of torte. Bake for 40 minutes. Let rest for 20 minutes before slicing (**D**).

A B
C D

Haricot d'Agneau

(Lamb Stew with White Beans)

SERVES 6–8

DESPITE THE WHITE BEANS (haricots blancs) in this dish from À Sousceyrac in Paris, the name *haricot* probably derives from the verb *halicoter*, "to cut into small pieces".

1 lb. dry emergo or other
   large white beans
½ cup goose or duck fat
3 lbs. stewing lamb,
   trimmed and cut into
   2 ½" pieces
Salt and freshly ground
   black pepper
3 medium yellow onions,
   peeled
4 medium carrots, peeled
2 whole heads of garlic,
   halved
2 sprigs fresh thyme
1 bay leaf
3 medium tomatoes, seeded
   and diced
5 cloves
¾ cup dry bread crumbs
¼ cup melted butter

1. Soak beans overnight in the refrigerator in a large bowl with cold water to cover.

2. Heat 3 tbsp. of fat in a large dutch oven over medium heat. Season lamb with salt and pepper. Working in batches to avoid crowding pan, add lamb and brown on all sides, turning as pieces brown, for about 10 minutes in all per batch. Remove pieces with a slotted spoon as done and set aside.

3. Coarsely chop 2 onions and 3 carrots, then add to dutch oven with 1 head garlic, 1 sprig thyme, and bay leaf. Cook, stirring occasionally, over medium heat for 12–15 minutes. Add tomatoes and cook, stirring, for 1 minute, then add lamb and enough water to cover (about 6 cups). Bring to a boil, then reduce heat to low, cover, and simmer, skimming fat, until lamb is tender, about 2 hours. Liquid should not fall below half the height of lamb; add more water if necessary.

4. Meanwhile, drain beans. Heat remaining 5 tbsp. fat in large saucepan over medium heat, add beans, and cook, stirring frequently, for 7–10 minutes. Stud remaining onion with cloves, halve remaining carrot, and add both to beans with remaining garlic and thyme and enough water to cover (about 8 cups). Reduce heat to low, and simmer until beans are tender, about 45 minutes. Remove onion, carrots, garlic, and thyme from beans and discard.

5. When lamb is done, remove meat from liquid with a slotted spoon and set aside. Discard bay leaf and thyme sprig. Purée vegetables and lamb broth together in a blender or food processor. Strain through a fine sieve and adjust seasoning.

6. Preheat broiler. Drain beans, reserving cooking liquid. Transfer beans to dutch oven, layer lamb on top, then pour in strained sauce and, if necessary, enough reserved bean cooking liquid to come up just to the level of the lamb. Combine bread crumbs and butter in a bowl, spread evenly over lamb, and broil until brown, about 5 minutes.

Serious Eaters

y friends Claude and Pepita Caspar-Jordan," SAVEUR editor Colman Andrews recalls (see sidebar, page 210), "took me to À Sousceyrac, one Christmas Eve in the early 1970s, for the first of many visits. I shocked them a bit, I think, by arriving with an Older Woman, about a dozen years my senior, whom I had brought to Paris for the holidays. But Pepita was always *très correcte*, and Claude, as usual when addressing my foibles, displayed something closer to avuncular bemusement than to parental disapproval—so the evening went well, full of chatter and champagne. My companion might even have impressed Claude a bit by the way she held her own at a table fairly heaped with foie gras, grilled boneless pigs' feet, whole braised sweetbreads, and the restaurant's famous lièvre à la royale—an elaborately old-fashioned dish of hare stuffed with foie gras, truffles, and its own innards and stewed in wine. À Sousceyrac—under the direction of brothers Patrick and Luc Asfaux, who run the kitchen and the dining room, respectively [their father, Gabriel, facing page, still cooks at lunchtime], is a restaurant for serious eaters only."

Border Food

Meitat França, meitat Espanya,
no hi ha altra terra com la Cerdanya,"
goes the refrain in the Catalan
language—half France, half Spain, there is
no other country like the Cerdanya. This wide
and luminous valley in the eastern Pyrenees—
solomonically sliced in two in the 17th
century by the Treaty of the Pyrenees—
straddles the border about 75 miles north of
Barcelona and 95 south of Toulouse. In the
end, food and language (i.e., Catalan) seem to
be the ties that bind. One of the region's best
cooks is unquestionably Françoise Massot.
For her hearty, memorable meals, she grows or
buys the best meat, fowl, and produce
she can procure high in the Pyrenees between
France and Spain. But she also forages daily in
the woods around Cal Pai, her bucolic inn
overlooking the 6,000-foot-high Pic Carlit,
highest in the Pyrénées-Orientales. Locals
call her "Framboise"—and indeed she seems to
know the whereabouts and quality of every
wild framboise (raspberry) in her part of the
mountains—as well as every strawberry, blue-
berry, églantine (wild rose hip), chanterelle,
morel, asparagus, plum, pear, and apple.
All of these seem to end up on her table.

Épaule d'Agneau à la Catalane

(Catalan-Style Shoulder of Lamb)

SERVES 8–10

AT HER INN in the Pyrenees, Françoise Massot makes this dish with banyuls, a fortified wine from the town of the same name on the French Catalan coast, on the Spanish border. If you can't find it, substitute a good ruby port.

3 lemons
1 7–8 lb. boneless lamb
    shoulder, trimmed
Salt and freshly ground
    black pepper
10 cloves garlic, peeled
2 sticks cinnamon
1 lb. ripe tomatoes,
    peeled and seeded, or 1
    28-oz. can whole peeled
    tomatoes with their juice
1 bottle sweet banyuls or
    ruby port
2 sprigs fresh thyme
2–3 bay leaves

1. Bring a medium pot of water to a boil over high heat, then add lemons and blanch for 2 minutes. Drain, then cut each lemon into 8 pieces lengthwise and set aside.

2. Season lamb generously with salt and pepper. Set a large, heavy roasting pan over 2 burners on top of the stove. Add lamb and cook, without additional fat, over medium-high heat, turning once, until well browned on both sides, about 20 minutes in all. Remove lamb and set aside, then pour off and discard excess fat and return pan to stove.

3. Add lemons to roasting pan and cook over medium heat, stirring and crushing lemons with a wooden spoon and scraping up any browned bits stuck to the bottom of the pan, about 2 minutes. Add garlic and cinnamon and cook for about 3 minutes. Add tomatoes, wine, thyme, and bay leaves and cook for 1 minute longer. Season to taste with salt and pepper, then return lamb to the pan. Reduce heat to low, cover pan tightly with foil, and slowly braise until lamb is tender, about 1¾ hour. Remove cinnamon, thyme, and bay leaves before serving.

Cabri à la Corse

(Corsican-Style Kid)

SERVES 6

GOAT MEAT is little appreciated in mainstream American cooking, but its sweet, flavorful, pork-plus-lamb-like meat is widely available in Hispanic and Greek markets.

6 lbs. boneless shoulder of kid (baby goat), cut into medium-size pieces (ask your butcher)
Salt and freshly ground black pepper
Olive oil
4 small yellow onions, peeled, halved, and thinly sliced
3 cloves garlic, peeled and minced
3 medium tomatoes, peeled, seeded, and diced
3 tbsp. tomato paste
2 cups red wine
½ bunch fresh parsley, minced
6 sprigs fresh thyme, minced
1 tbsp. flour
1 bay leaf

1. Generously season kid with salt and pepper. Heat 3 tbsp. oil in a large heavy pot over medium-high heat. Working in batches to avoid crowding pan, add meat and brown on all sides, about 10 minutes per batch. Transfer meat to a bowl and set aside.

2. Reduce heat to medium-low, add more oil if needed, and cook onions and garlic, stirring constantly, until soft, about 5 minutes. Increase heat to medium and add tomatoes, tomato paste, wine, parsley, and thyme, scraping with a wooden spoon to loosen any browned bits stuck to bottom of the pot. Cook until alcohol has evaporated, about 5 minutes.

3. Return meat with accumulated juices to pot. Sprinkle in flour, season to taste with salt and pepper, and cook, stirring often, for 5 minutes. Add 3 cups water and bay leaf, bring to a simmer, and cook until meat is tender and sauce has thickened, about 1 hour, basting and turning the meat as it cooks. Remove bay leaf and adjust seasonings before serving.

Flavor in the Air

Corsica's maquis, or scrub—a dense, fragrant underbrush of oak, juniper, thorn, heather, and wild herbs and flowers that covers much of the island—yields up a bittersweet lemon-pepper aroma; Napoleon Bonaparte, the island's most famous son, was so enamored of it that he dreamed of the maquis during his days on Elba. In addition to its perfume, the scrub provides ideal grazing for wild game and for free-range pigs, cows, sheep, and goats. This means especially flavorful meats—which Corsica's industrious cooks utilize to the fullest—usually in simple, sturdy preparations.

The Deer Farmer

U nless you're a hunter or a hunter's friend, the venison you eat in America today is likely to be farm-bred (put out to pasture to feed on planted grasses) or ranched (allowed to range free over large expanses of land). About 80 percent of the venison sold here comes from New Zealand; another 15 percent is domestic, raised or harvested primarily in New York and Texas. The remainder comes mostly from Scotland. Whatever their origin, these deer are usually the Eurasian species—most commonly red, fallow, and sika—as America's native white-tailed deer do not breed well in captivity. The animals' managed diet also gives their meat (everything from chops to the shoulder meat and sausage at right) a slightly milder flavor than that of their wild cousins.

Civet de Chevreuil
(Rich Venison Stew)

SERVES 6

A HEARTY GAME STEW, civet is traditionally thickened with the blood of the animal used; our venison stew substitutes flour, for a lighter, more easily accomplished version.

3 lbs. boneless venison
  shoulder, cut into
  large pieces
1 medium carrot, peeled
  and diced
1 medium yellow onion,
  peeled and diced
3 cloves garlic, peeled
12 sprigs fresh parsley
2 sprigs fresh thyme
2 bay leaves
15 black peppercorns
1 bottle côtes-du-rhône
  or other dry, hearty
  red wine
¼ lb. bacon slices,
  julienned
Salt and freshly ground
  black pepper
2 tbsp. olive oil
2 tbsp. flour
12 small boiling onions,
  peeled
1 tsp. sugar
4 tbsp. butter
½ lb. white mushrooms,
  trimmed and sliced
2 tbsp. cognac

1. Combine venison, carrots, diced onions, garlic, 2 sprigs of the parsley, thyme, bay leaves, peppercorns, and wine in a large bowl. Cover and refrigerate for 24 hours to tenderize venison.

2. Fry bacon in a heavy pot or dutch oven over medium heat until crisp, 8–10 minutes. Remove with a slotted spoon and drain on paper towels, leaving fat in pot.

3. Remove venison from marinade and blot dry with paper towel. Strain liquid into a bowl, discarding herbs and vegetables. Generously season meat with salt and pepper. Add oil to bacon fat in pot and increase heat to medium-high. Working in batches to avoid crowding pan, add venison and brown on all sides, turning as pieces brown, for about 10 minutes in all per batch. Remove pieces with a slotted spoon as done and set aside. When all meat is browned, return to pot, sprinkle flour over meat, then add bacon. Cook, stirring, until flour turns a nut-brown color, about 1 minute. Add marinade, bring to a simmer, then reduce heat to medium-low, cover, and cook until venison is tender, 2–2½ hours.

4. Meanwhile bring a medium pot of salted water to a boil. Add small whole onions and sugar and simmer over medium heat until tender, 25–30 minutes. Drain and set aside. Heat 2 tbsp. butter in a medium skillet over medium-high heat. Add mushrooms and cook, stirring, until golden, about 3 minutes.

5. Remove venison from pot to finish sauce. Increase heat to medium-high, add cognac, and cook for 5 minutes. Remove pot from heat and whisk in remaining butter. Return venison to sauce, add onions and mushrooms, and mix thoroughly. Chop remaining 10 sprigs of parsley and sprinkle on top. Garnish with slices of toasted country bread, if you like.

VEGETABLES

"THE BOUNTY of Brittany—which is

the westernmost portion of France—is

displayed every Saturday in the bustling

open-air market in Morlaix, a river port

in the département of Finistère. Though

Finistère means 'end of the earth', there is no feeling of desolation or privation here. Fish of many varieties, just pulled from the neighboring sea, are laid out on ice; also on view is pork and pork sausage, as well as succulent lamb raised on nearby salt marshes. Dairy farmers sell fresh milk and the region's famous butter. But the most glorious stalls of all are those brimming with produce grown in the golden belt of rich farmland that curves around the coastline—leeks, cauliflower, onions, peas, cabbages, the especially plump and tasty local artichokes, apples from orchards in the Argoat (as the Breton interior is called), strawberries from Plougastel, tiny new potatoes from the sandy flats just inland from the sea…. And in the middle of the market, most Saturday mornings, you're liable to see chef Patrick Jeffroy (facing page, lower left)—perhaps plucking a couple of leaves from an artichoke and rubbing them together near his ear. Jeffroy, proprietor of an acclaimed hotel-restaurant (called simply Patrick Jeffroy) in nearby Plounérin, grew up just a few steps from the marketplace, and has been coming here since he was a boy. He remembers vividly and with great affection the days he spent on his grandmother's farm not far away. And he recalls her tricks: 'My grandmother, who shopped at this market before I was born, taught me how to "hear" if an artichoke was really fresh. When you rub the leaves together, they should sing.'"—JUDY FAYARD

Poireaux Tièdes en Vinaigrette

(Warm Leeks with Vinaigrette)

SERVES 4

"THERE ISN'T a day of the year that we don't use leeks in one form or another," says Claude Cornut of the venerable Paris bistro Chez Clovis (see page 51). In spring, the leeks are always dressed with vinaigrette—for one of the simplest, most delicious of all French vegetable dishes.

4 *large winter leeks*
6 *cups chicken stock (see page 56)*
2 *large shallots, peeled and sliced*
2 *tsp. dijon mustard*
1 *tbsp. red wine vinegar*
3 *tbsp. peanut oil*
Salt and freshly ground *pepper*
Pinch freshly grated *nutmeg*
8 *sprigs fresh flat-leaf parsley*

1. Remove roots and outer leaves from leeks. Trim off greens to 2" above the white part. Slice leeks in half lengthwise, not quite all the way through so that you can open the leek like a book. Wash leeks under cold running water to remove all sand and dirt, and set aside.

2. Bring chicken stock to a simmer over medium heat in a large skillet. Lay leeks, all facing in the same direction, in the simmering stock. Reduce heat to medium-low, cover and cook until leeks are soft but not mushy, 10–15 minutes. Transfer leeks to a rack to drain. Add shallots to the simmering stock and cook until soft, about 3 minutes, then remove shallots from stock with a slotted spoon and set aside. Reserve stock for another use.

3. Whisk together mustard and vinegar in a small bowl and gradually drizzle in peanut oil. Season to taste with salt and pepper, then continue whisking until vinaigrette is smooth and creamy.

4. Arrange leeks in circles on a platter or on individual plates and scatter shallots on top. Drizzle vinaigrette over leeks, season with nutmeg, and garnish with parsley.

Cuisine or Not?

There are those who will tell you that Brittany has no real cuisine of its own. Even Patrick Jeffroy, one of the region's best chefs, admits that "Old-fashioned Breton cooking is simple. It's not belabored or particularly polished. We don't want to cover up the flavor of the ingredients." Indeed, in Brittany, the quality of the ingredients that go into a dish has always been more important than any complicated techniques or fancy sauces that might be applied to them. So maybe it's not a cuisine. Maybe it's just a panoply of fresh, unpretentious, full-flavored things to eat.

The Essential Olive

T he département of the Alpes-de-Haute-Provence, northeast of Marseille and northwest of Nice, is unknown Provence—a rugged land of steeply terraced mountains and vast rocky plains softened here and there by water (like the Lac de Ste Croix, facing page). The soil is poor, and if those ancient Provençal crops, the vine and the olive tree, endure, it is only because their roots are deep. The olive tree, though, is the ideal metaphor for Haute Provence: It is as thrifty, modest, and hardworking as the people whose needs it serves. It doesn't ask for much—just meager earth and a little rain—yet it generously provides a great deal in return. It shelters the land with a delicate year-round shade that protects plants growing beneath its foliage. Its twigs and branches are carved into useful implements or burned for cooking fuel. An herbal tea is made from olive sprouts, and olives themselves are splendid food. And as for olive oil, well, it's impossible to imagine Provençal cuisine without it (see page 115).

Tartare de Légumes
(Marinated Vegetable and Herb Salad)

SERVES 6

AS CHEF AT the Hostellerie de la Fuste in Manosque, in Haute Provence, Dominique Bucaille served this salad to show off the region's wealth of fresh summer vegetables.

FOR SALAD:
Salt
Hearts of 2 small
  artichokes, diced
1 small bulb fennel, diced
2 small carrots, peeled
  and diced
2 small turnips, peeled
  and diced
1 small zucchini, diced
1 small acorn squash,
  peeled, seeded, and diced
6 small asparagus stalks,
  trimmed and diced
1 cup fresh shelled peas
½ cup shelled fava beans
2 ripe tomatoes, seeded
  and diced
½ cup total of the following finely chopped fresh
  herbs: basil, parsley,
  chives, chervil, tarragon,
  and/or sage

FOR VINAIGRETTE:
1 tbsp. dijon mustard
2 tbsp. balsamic vinegar
⅔ cup extra-virgin
  olive oil
Salt and freshly ground
  black pepper

Additional fresh herbs
  for garnish
Extra-virgin olive oil

1. For salad, bring a large pot of salted water to a boil over medium-high heat. Cook artichokes, fennel, carrots, and turnips separately for 2 minutes each, removing each from water when done with a slotted spoon and plunging into a large bowl of ice water. Cook zucchini, squash, asparagus, and peas for 30 seconds each, removing each from water with a slotted spoon as before and adding to the bowl of ice water. Cook fava beans for 30 seconds, removing them from water as above, then slip them out of their tough outer skins before adding to bowl of ice water. Drain vegetables first in a colander, then on paper towels, so that they are as dry as possible. Set aside.

2. For vinaigrette, whisk mustard and vinegar together in a large salad bowl, adding olive oil in a thin stream. Season to taste with salt and pepper. Add cooked vegetables, tomatoes, and chopped herbs. Mix together gently but thoroughly. Cover bowl and refrigerate overnight.

3. To serve, garnish with fresh herbs and a drizzle of olive oil.

Asperges Blanches au Sabayon à l'Huile d'Olive

(White Asparagus with Olive Oil Sabayon)

SERVES 4

THE COOKING TIME for white asparagus depends on the age and thickness of its stalks, but is always considerably longer than for the green variety—particularly since, unlike its green cousin, white asparagus is never eaten crisp.

1 cup dry white wine
⅓ cup white wine vinegar
2 egg yolks, lightly beaten
⅓ cup extra-virgin
   olive oil
Salt and freshly ground
   white pepper
1 lb. white asparagus,
   peeled

1. Combine wine and vinegar in a saucepan and bring to just below the boiling point over medium-high heat. Continue cooking until liquid is reduced by three-quarters, about 15 minutes, then allow to cool and transfer to the top of a double boiler.

2. Whisk egg yolks into wine reduction. Set over simmering water over medium heat and cook, whisking constantly, until yolks thicken enough to fall into thin ribbons when whisk is lifted from pan. Remove top of double boiler from bottom and, off heat, gradually whisk in olive oil. Thin, if necessary, with 1–2 tbsp. water. Season to taste with salt and pepper and set aside.

3. Tie asparagus together in a bundle with kitchen string and stand upright in an asparagus cooker or a deep, narrow saucepan. Add about 4" water and bring to a simmer over medium-high heat. Reduce heat to medium, cover pan with a lid or aluminum foil, and cook until asparagus is tender, 15–30 minutes. Untie bundle, transfer to a platter, and spoon sauce over asparagus.

Underground Delicacy

G reatly prized in Germany, Holland, Italy, France, and just about everywhere else in Europe, white asparagus is grown under mounds of earth to protect its pale stalks from the sunlight-inspired chlorophyll that would otherwise turn them green. Underground, the asparagus cores often grow fibrous and woody, so they need a long cooking time; and their skins tend to toughen—which is why white asparagus is virtually always peeled before cooking. Lay the brittle spears flat on a clean dish towel to peel and drain them, suggests Robert Lalleman (facing page, standing, with his father, André)—who serves flawless white stalks from a neighbor's farm with an olive oil sabayon at the family's Auberge de Noves near Avignon.

Ratatouille

SERVES 8

WITH ALL DUE respect to Jacques Médecin, Mamé Clairette, and other experts on Niçois cuisine (see sidebar), we've found that sautéing ratatouille vegetables separately and then cooking them together yields superior results. Mamé Clairette recommends making more ratatouille than you need, so there'll be some to eat later, hot or cold.

3 medium eggplants, cut into 2" cubes
4 medium zucchini, quartered lengthwise, then cut into 2" pieces
Coarse kosher salt
½ cup extra-virgin olive oil
6 medium yellow onions, peeled and thinly sliced
4 medium green or red bell peppers, cored, seeded, and cut into 1" x 2" strips
6 small tomatoes, peeled, seeded, and quartered
8 cloves garlic, peeled and minced
20 leaves fresh basil
1 bunch fresh parsley, stems trimmed
8 sprigs fresh thyme
Freshly ground black pepper

1. Put eggplant and zucchini in 2 separate strainers and toss each with 1 tbsp. salt. Allow to drain for 30 minutes. Blot dry with paper towels.

2. Heat 2 tbsp. oil over medium-low heat in a large skillet. Add onions and sauté until translucent, about 15 minutes, then transfer to a bowl and set aside. Add 2 tbsp. oil to same skillet, increase heat to medium-high, add eggplant, and sauté until golden, about 20 minutes. Transfer eggplant to a large heavy pot with a cover and spoon a thin layer of onions on top. Add 2 tbsp. oil to skillet, then add zucchini and sauté until golden, about 10 minutes. Transfer to pot and cover with a thin layer of onions. Add 1 tbsp. oil to skillet, then add peppers and sauté until edges turn brown, about 15 minutes. Transfer to pot and cover with a thin layer of onions.

3. Add remaining 1 tbsp. oil to skillet, add tomatoes, garlic, and basil, lightly crushing tomatoes with the back of a fork, and cook until slightly thickened, about 15 minutes. Transfer to pot, add remaining onions, parsley, and thyme, and season to taste with salt and pepper.

4. Simmer, partially covered, over low heat, gently stirring occasionally, for 1½ hours. Adjust seasoning, then cook about 30 minutes more.

From the Experts

C ontrary to what is generally believed," writes Jacques Médecin, the late mayor of Nice and an expert on Niçois cuisine, in his *La Cuisine du comté de Nice* (Juillard, 1972), "ratatouille is a dish requiring a particularly long and difficult preparation". That's because, he insists, the ingredients of this mix of (mostly post-Columbian) Mediterranean vegetables should be cooked individually, then married together in one pot just before serving. Mamé Clairette, the Niçois grandmother interviewed by Bernard Duplessy in his *Cuisine traditionnelle en pays niçois* (Édisud, 1995), agrees, proposing that little touches like salting the eggplant and the zucchini before cooking and then using separate pots for the vegetables are "what makes the difference between the ratatouille of Nice and the mishmashes of the incompetent".

Beignets de Fleurs de Courgettes

(Deep-Fried Zucchini Blossoms)

SERVES 6

AT LA MERENDA, on the edge of Vieux Nice, former owner Jean Giusti made the most extraordinary deep-fried zucchini blossoms, using large pale green flowers delicately veined in egg-yolk yellow. This is our version of his recipe.

1 ½ cups flour
1 tsp. salt
1 tbsp. extra-virgin
  olive oil
1 egg, lightly beaten
18 large or 36 small
  zucchini or other
  squash blossoms
Vegetable oil
1 clove garlic, peeled
  and finely chopped
2 tbsp. finely chopped
  fresh flat-leaf parsley
Salt

1. Sift flour and salt together into a medium bowl. Whisk in oil, egg, and 2 cups water.

2. Remove center and discard stamens from the squash blossoms, then carefully wash and pat dry. Pour vegetable oil into a heavy skillet to a depth of 2". Heat oil over medium-high heat to 375° or until it sizzles when you drop in a little batter. (If oil isn't hot enough, squash blossoms will absorb too much of it.) Just before frying, add garlic and parsley to batter, stirring well. Dip flowers in batter, coating them inside and out. Drop into oil—working in batches and not crowding the pan—and fry until lightly golden, 1–3 minutes, turning frequently. Use a slotted spoon to transfer to paper towels, drain, and sprinkle with salt.

Flower Power

A lthough the flowers from any variety of squash can be eaten, those of the zucchini are the most popular in the south of France—where it sometimes seems as if the flowers are more genuinely appreciated than the fruit itself. The blossoms sold for frying purposes in Provence and along the Côte d'Azur are usually male—i.e., blossoms that will never yield an actual zucchini. It's easy to tell the difference between the male and female flowers on the vine: Male ones grow on long stems; female ones extend from the zucchini itself.

Farcis à la Niçoise

(Nice-Style Stuffed Vegetables)

SERVES 6

JACQUES MÉDECIN, that most authoritative of authorities on the subject of Niçois cooking, maintains that each vegetable in this classic assortment should be stuffed with a different filling. In reality, most Niçois restaurants and home cooks alike use one all-purpose stuffing recipe like this one.

---

3 small eggplants
6 small green or red
    bell peppers
½ cup extra-virgin
    olive oil
Salt
3 small yellow onions,
    peeled
3 small zucchini
3 medium tomatoes
¼ lb. lean salt pork, diced
½ lb. ground lamb
¾ cup cooked rice
1 cup finely chopped
    fresh flat-leaf parsley
2 cloves garlic, peeled
    and minced
Freshly ground black
    pepper
2 eggs, lightly beaten
½ cup finely grated
    parmigiano-reggiano
½ cup fresh bread crumbs
1 bunch fresh thyme

1. Preheat oven to 350°. Cut eggplants in half lengthwise. Cut tops from peppers, then core and seed them. Place eggplants and peppers on an oiled baking sheet and brush lightly with oil. Bake for 30 minutes, then remove from oven and set aside to cool. When eggplants are cool enough to handle, scoop out pulp, leaving about ½"-thick shell. Chop pulp finely and set aside in a large bowl.

2. Heat a large pot of salted water over medium heat. Add onions and zucchini and simmer for about 10 minutes. Drain and set aside to cool.

3. Halve onions crosswise and remove centers, leaving a shell of about 3 outer layers. Halve zucchini lengthwise and scoop out pulp, leaving about ½"-thick shell. Halve tomatoes crosswise, then squeeze out and discard seeds and juice. Scoop pulp from tomatoes, finely chop, and add to eggplant pulp. Finely chop onion centers and zucchini pulp and add them to eggplant mixture as well.

4. Increase oven temperature to 375°. Heat 2 tbsp. oil in a large pan over low heat. Stir in vegetable mixture, salt pork, lamb, rice, parsley, and garlic. Season to taste with salt and pepper. Cook for about 15 minutes, stirring occasionally. Remove from heat, cool slightly, then stir in eggs.

5. Fill vegetable shells (don't pack too tightly), top with parmigiano-reggiano and bread crumbs, drizzle with remaining olive oil, and bake for 30 minutes on an oiled baking sheet. Serve garnished with fresh thyme sprigs.

Clever Cooking

Stuffed vegetables are eaten all along the French Riviera, and perhaps no genre of dishes more dramatically characterizes the region's legendary frugality and ingenuity. Faced with the challenge of feeding a whole family with the meager daily output of a kitchen garden, housewives along this portion of the Mediterranean coast figured out that by scooping out the flesh of vegetables they grew, mixing it with wild herbs, crumbs of hardened bread, leftover rice, and maybe a bit of meat and/or a few wild mushrooms, then packing it back into the shells, they could virtually double the volume of their produce. This kind of inventiveness is common to the region's kitchens. A little flour can be stretched into tourte dough, filled with wild greens and a bit of cheese, and served to half a dozen people; the lowly chickpea can be turned into flour and the flour into the crêpe-like socca or the fried-polenta-like panisse; a hint of dried mushrooms or dried or salted fish can perfume a huge pot of soup. Abundance sometimes yields great food, but so can impoverishment.

Name That Dish

The tian is not just something to eat, but also the shallow earthenware vessel in which it is traditionally cooked. A number of other French dishes derive their names from the vessels that contain them. **COCOTTE:** A round dish, usually ceramic or cast-iron, used for casseroles (e.g. poulet en cocotte) or, in smaller form, for dishes like oeufs (eggs) en cocotte. **DAUBE:** From *daubière*, an earthenware pot; a daube is meat, poultry, game, or fish braised in wine and stock with vegetables, etc. Used without qualification, daube means beef in red wine. **MARMITE:** A tall stew pot, and the (usually) fish and shellfish stew cooked in one. **RAMEQUIN:** An individual baking dish, or the little treat (e.g. ramequin au fromage, cheese tartlet) that fills it. **TERRINE:** A dish, usually rectangular (like those above) and traditionally made of earthenware (the name comes from the Latin *terra*, or earth), in which pâtés are cooked (see page 37)—thus becoming, at least in traditional terminology, terrines. **TIMBALE:** A round high-sided mold, originally designed to imitate pastry crust; today, timbales are usually fish or vegetable purées or small mousses, unmolded and served with a sauce.

Tian de Légumes

(Mediterranean Vegetable Casserole)

SERVES 6

THE VEGETABLE dishes (sometimes bound with eggs) called tians are popular in traditional kitchens all over the south of France. Originally, it is said, tians were constructed so that their cooking time corresponded to the time it took to bake bread in a communal oven, because housewives would make them up at home, then bring them to these once-common public facilities to share the baker's fire.

1 medium eggplant, peeled
Salt
2 medium yellow onions, peeled and chopped
3 cloves garlic, peeled and minced
½ cup extra-virgin olive oil
Freshly ground black pepper
2 medium zucchini, sliced diagonally
6 medium ripe tomatoes, sliced
Leaves from 3–4 sprigs fresh herbs, such as thyme, rosemary, or oregano
½ cup grated parmigiano-reggiano

1. Cut eggplant into 1" cubes, sprinkle with 1 tsp. salt, and place in a colander. Drain for 30 minutes, then pat dry with paper towels.

2. Cook onions and garlic in 3 tbsp. olive oil in a large skillet over medium heat until lightly browned, about 10 minutes. Transfer to a medium baking dish. Add 2–3 tbsp. olive oil to the same skillet, then add eggplant and cook until tender and slightly browned, about 10 minutes. Season to taste with salt and pepper, and stir into onion mixture.

3. Preheat oven to 400°. Arrange zucchini and tomatoes in alternating layers over eggplant mixture. Top with herbs, drizzle with remaining 2–3 tbsp. oil, season to taste with salt and pepper, and bake 30–40 minutes. Sprinkle with cheese just before serving.

Grand Aïoli

(Vegetables and Salt Cod with Garlic Sauce)

SERVES 6–8

AÏOLI IS BOTH a garlic mayonnaise and a dish of salt cod (or cold meats) and vegetables with which the sauce is served. This recipe comes from the Relais Notre-Dame (right), a family-run hotel-restaurant surrounded by wheat and lavender fields in Quinson, in the southern part of Haute Provence.

FOR SALT COD
AND VEGETABLES:
2 lbs. salt cod
2 bay leaves
4 black peppercorns
9 whole small yellow
    onions, peeled
2 cloves garlic, peeled
Salt
Hearts of 8 small
    artichokes
1 whole cauliflower,
    separated into florets
8 whole carrots, peeled
1 lb. green beans, trimmed
8 medium potatoes, peeled
8 medium beets, trimmed,
    peeled, and halved
8 hard-cooked eggs

FOR AÏOLI:
6 cloves garlic, crushed
    and peeled
Coarse salt
2 egg yolks
2 cups extra-virgin
    olive oil
Juice of 1 lemon (optional)

1. For salt cod, put fish in a large bowl with cold water to cover completely and soak for 24 hours in the refrigerator, changing the water 3 or 4 times.

2. Combine bay leaves, peppercorns, 1 of the onions, and garlic in a medium pot with 4 cups water. Bring to a boil over medium-high heat, then reduce heat to low and simmer for 20 minutes. Allow to cool, then add salt cod and return to a simmer for 20 minutes. Drain fish, set aside to cool, and remove and discard any skin or bones.

3. For vegetables, bring a large pot of salted water to a boil over medium-high heat. Cook artichokes, cauliflower, and carrots separately, until tender but not overcooked, about 10 minutes each, removing each from water when done with a slotted spoon and setting aside. Cook green beans until tender but not overcooked, about 5 minutes, then remove from water and set aside as before. Cook potatoes and beets separately (making sure to cook beets last) until tender but not overdone, about 20 minutes each, then remove from water and set aside as before.

4. For aïoli, using a large mortar and pestle, pound garlic and a good pinch of salt together into a smooth paste. Work egg yolks into garlic paste with pestle or a whisk until mixture is thick and pale yellow. Drizzle in oil a few drops at a time, whisking continuously. When sauce begins to emulsify, increase flow of oil to a fine stream, continuing to whisk in until all the oil is used up. Whisk in lemon juice 1 tsp. at a time to thin, if you like. Season to taste with salt. To serve, arrange salt cod, vegetables, and eggs on platters and serve with aïoli on the side.

Divine Aïoli

E ssentially a garlic mayonnaise (it takes its name from the Provençal words for oil and garlic), aïoli may have been invented by the Roman emperor Nero, who is said to have been a great connoisseur of garlic. The Byzantines favored an eggless version of the sauce, roasting garlic whole, then crushing it with olive oil and salt. Writer Léon Daudet (son of writer Alphonse, and one of the epic gastronomes of the late 19th century), considered aïoli

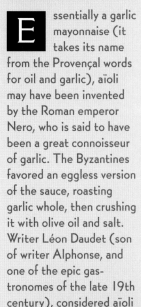

the finest culinary use to which garlic could be put. Mistral, the great Provençal poet, imbued it with almost spiritual power, writing "When they are seated around the divine aïoli, fragrant aïoli, deep in color as a golden thread, where, tell me where are those men who do not recognize that they are brothers."

Raviolis de Bourrache

(Borage Ravioli)

SERVES 4–6

BORAGE IS a mild Mediterranean herb that remains something of a rarity in America, though found in some specialty markets and easy to grow. Dandelion leaves may be substituted in this recipe from Le Cagnard in Cagnes.

FOR PASTA:
4 eggs, lightly beaten
2 tbsp. extra-virgin olive oil
2 tbsp. white vinegar
4 cups flour

FOR FILLING:
4 tbsp. extra-virgin olive oil
2 small yellow onions, peeled and finely chopped
1 ½ lbs. borage, cleaned and chopped
6 cloves garlic, peeled and minced
1 tbsp. minced fresh basil
1 tbsp. minced fresh sage
½ cup minced fresh parsley
2 tbsp. minced fresh thyme
Salt and freshly ground black pepper
2 oz. mild chèvre

FOR SAUCE:
2 cups chicken stock (see page 56)
2 tsp. demi-glace (see sidebar, page 61)
3 tbsp. butter
4 fresh sage leaves, julienned

1. For pasta, whisk together eggs, oil, and vinegar in a small bowl. Put flour in a large mixing bowl or food processor. Gradually work egg mixture into flour, then turn out onto a lightly floured surface and knead for about 5 minutes, until smooth and elastic. Form dough into a ball, wrap in plastic, and refrigerate for 1 hour.

2. For filling, heat oil in a large skillet over medium heat. Add onions and cook, stirring often, until they begin to soften, about 7 minutes. Add borage, garlic, basil, sage, parsley, and thyme, season to taste with salt and pepper, then cook, stirring frequently, until greens wilt, about 5 minutes. Drain and set aside to cool, then put greens in a clean kitchen towel and squeeze dry. Transfer to a large bowl. Mix in chèvre and adjust seasoning with salt and pepper.

3. Divide dough into 4 parts. Using a pasta machine, roll out dough as thin as possible, then transfer to a lightly floured surface. Cut out about 60 rounds using a 2" cutter. To assemble ravioli, spoon about 1 tsp. of filling in the center of a dough round, brush edge with water, then top with another round, pinching to seal. Repeat process, using up all pasta rounds and filling.

4. For sauce, bring stock and demi-glace to a simmer in a medium saucepan over medium heat. Reduce by three-quarters, 20–30 minutes, then whisk in butter.

5. Meanwhile, cook ravioli in batches in a large pot of boiling salted water until they rise to the surface, 3–4 minutes. Drain and divide between 4–6 small plates. Top with sauce and garnish with julienned sage.

Culinary Heights

Rising above the seaside town of Cagnes-sur-Mer, just west of Nice, is the medieval hillside village of Haut-de-Cagnes (left)—once the haunt of Renoir, Modigliani, and Soutine, among other artists, and today the home of a charming hotel hideaway called Le Cagnard. Here, Jean-Yves Johanny—who must be one of the best unknown chefs in France— prepares light, pure-flavored, elegant (but not fussy) food—dishes like mushroom-stuffed squid with lobster sauce, poached veal loin with an herb and olive vinaigrette, and a remarkable borage-filled ravioli in a chicken-stock reduction. "More than anything," Johanny declares, "I look for simplicity in my cooking. I believe that cuisine *must* be simple. But it is very difficult to be simple in cuisine."

261

Cold Cabbage

L lívia is "in" France, but it *isn't* France: The Treaty of the Pyrenees, which established the mountain border between France and Spain over 300 years ago, gave to France all "villages" north of a certain line—but the citizens of Llívia came up with proof that they were officially a town and not a village; therefore, they still belonged to Spain. Food lovers from both sides of the frontier visit the place today for foie gras, local trout, or beef cooked on Pyrenean slate—or for reassuringly simple fare at places like the cheese shop turned restaurant called La Formatgeria de Llívia. One specialty here is trinxat, an age-old, prototypical mountain dish made of winter cabbage, potatoes, and salt pork. The cabbage, say local epicures, is best after it has semi-frozen—or at least been thoroughly frostbitten—in the fields.

Trinxat

(Catalan Cabbage and Potatoes)

SERVES 6

TRADITIONAL COOKING in the Catalan Pyrenees, on both sides of the border, is straightforward, hearty, and based on modest mountain ingredients. Trinxat (the name means "chopped" in Catalan) is a typical example. This recipe comes from Marta Pous of La Formatgeria de Llívia.

1 2-lb. savoy cabbage
Salt
2 lbs. russet potatoes, peeled
Cumin seeds (optional)
12 thick slices of salt pork or bacon
3 tbsp. extra-virgin olive oil
1 clove garlic, peeled and minced
2½ oz. fatback, rind removed, thinly sliced
Freshly ground black pepper

1. Pull off and discard tough outer leaves of cabbage. Bring two pots of generously salted water to a boil over medium-high heat. Put cabbage in one and potatoes in the other and cook both until very tender, about 30 minutes for the potatoes and 60 minutes for the cabbage.

2. Drain potatoes in a colander, then transfer to a large bowl. Drain cabbage in a colander and allow to cool slightly, then pull out and discard core and drain well, pressing cabbage to release water. Transfer cabbage to bowl with potatoes and mash together with a potato masher. Season to taste with salt, and with cumin if using.

3. Lightly brown salt pork strips on both sides in a 10" skillet over medium heat, working in batches to avoid crowding pan. Remove from skillet as done, drain on paper towels, and set aside. Pour off fat and wipe pan clean with paper towel.

4. Heat oil in same skillet over medium heat. Add garlic and cook until soft, 2–3 minutes. Stir oil and garlic into cabbage mixture.

5. In the same pan, heat half the fatback, until fat is rendered. Add half of the cabbage mixture and flatten into a ¾"-thick pancake. Cook over high heat until bottom crust has formed and pancake slides easily in the skillet, 5–10 minutes. Invert a large plate over pan and carefully flip trinxat over onto plate, then slide it back into pan, browned side up. Season to taste with salt and pepper and cook until bottom is crisp and brown. Slide pancake onto a platter and arrange 6 salt pork strips on top. Repeat process with remaining fatback and cabbage mixture to make second pancake.

Cardons à la "Bagna Cauda"

(Cardoons with Anchovy-Garlic Sauce)

SERVES 6

EUROPEAN CARDOONS can be eaten raw in preparations like this one—but the American variety needs to be cooked thoroughly to leach out its extreme bitterness.

2 lemons, 1 halved,
   1 thinly sliced
3 lbs. cardoons, washed
Salt
¼ cup extra-virgin
   olive oil
2 tbsp. butter
1 clove garlic, peeled and
   minced
12 oil-packed anchovy
   filets, chopped

1. Squeeze juice from the halved lemon into a large pot filled with cold water, then add halves and lemon slices to the pot. Remove and discard outer stalks of cardoons, then trim off thorns (**A**) and peel off stringy fibers with a vegetable peeler (**B**). Cut into 2" pieces, and put them in the pot of lemon water as soon as they're cut to prevent discoloration (**C**).

2. Add salt to taste, and bring to a simmer over medium-high heat. Cook until cardoons are tender, about 30 minutes, then drain and dry on paper towels.

3. Heat olive oil and butter in a small saucepan over low heat. When butter is melted, add garlic and cook until fragrant, 1–2 minutes. Stir in anchovy filets, mash with a spoon, and cook, stirring occasionally, until flavors blend, about 10 minutes. Meanwhile, divide cardoons with a few lemon slices (discard halves) between 6 plates. Spoon anchovy-garlic sauce over cardoons.

Soothing Cardoons

As a child in Provence," writes Nice-born Mireille Johnston, "I viewed our big holiday meals as fraught with danger. Too many opinionated, theatrical relatives, all with nostalgic regrets—all waiting, it seemed, for lightning to strike. But at our annual *souper maigre*, the meatless meal served before midnight Mass on Christmas Eve, something interesting happened every year: The minute a basket of crisp, raw cardoon pieces was served as part of the first-course *bagna cauda*—literally 'hot bath', a Piedmontese vegetable dish adopted in Provence, featuring raw vegetables and a warm anchovy-garlic-and-olive-oil dip—conversations would shift from familial scandals to the food at hand. The process of preparing cardoons is long and messy, but they might help encourage the relatives to behave."

The Novelty of Petits Pois

P eas were eaten in France as long ago as the seventh century B.C., in the Languedoc, where archaeologists have found them fossilized in the debris left by early inhabitants. They don't seem to have entered serious French gastronomy, though, until around 1600, when the pois mange-tout, or sugar pea, arrived from Holland. And the green pea, or petit pois, as we know it today dates only from 1660 in France. In January of that year, one Sieur Audiger, sent to Italy on a confidential mission by Louis XIV, returned from Genoa to present his monarch with a hamper of them. Audiger recorded the response of the courtiers who "all declared with one voice that nothing could be more of a novelty, and that nothing like it, in that season, had ever been seen in France before". The peas were shelled and prepared for the Court—whose delight was such that the pea became the most fashionable of vegetables.

Petits Pois aux Morilles

(Ragoût of Peas and Morels)

SERVES 4

CANNED PEAS? The French actually prefer them for the traditional preparation of petit pois with lettuce; three-quarters of the French pea crop, in fact, ends up in cans. For this springtime ragoût, however, only fresh peas will do.

12 small dried morels
12 pearl onions
2 tbsp. butter
8 whole small carrots, peeled and trimmed
½ tsp. sugar
1 cup shelled fresh peas
Salt and freshly ground black pepper

1. Wash morels under running water and trim root ends from onions. Bring 4 cups water to a boil in a medium saucepan. Add morels and onions, cover, and remove from heat. After 1 minute, remove onions with a slotted spoon. Replace cover and soak morels until soft, about 10 minutes. Peel onions.

2. Remove morels from water with a slotted spoon and rinse well, reserving soaking liquid. Pour soaking liquid through a sieve lined with a coffee filter and return to saucepan. Bring to a boil over medium-high heat and cook until liquid is reduced to 1 cup, about 20 minutes.

3. Melt butter in a skillet over medium-high heat. Add carrots and cook until lightly browned, about 3 minutes. Reduce heat to medium-low, add onions, sugar, and ½ cup water, and simmer until liquid evaporates, about 15 minutes. Add morels and morel stock, cover, and cook for 7 minutes more. Add peas and cook for 5 minutes more. Season to taste with salt and pepper.

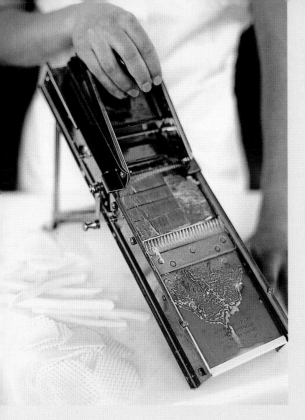

Kitchen Music

G ourmet shops are filled with work- and time-saving gizmos," notes SAVEUR executive editor Christopher Hirsheimer, "and heaven knows I've bought my fair share over the years. Most of them have ended up as drawer food. But when I decided to make pommes soufflées recently, I dug around and pulled out an old friend: my sturdy, nickel-plated stainless steel French mandoline. This super-efficient cutting tool, with its adjustable and interchangeable blades, cuts piles of potatoes in minutes. I thought it was wildly expensive when I bought it 20 years ago (it cost over a hundred bucks even then!), but it turned out to be well worth the investment. I can't imagine making pommes soufflées, or plenty of other things, without it."

Pommes Soufflées

(French Potato Puffs)

IT'S TRICKY to make these elegant cousins of the french fry. They must be cut evenly and to precisely the right thickness, and the (two) temperatures of the oil must be exact.

6–8 *large russet potatoes*
 (5–6 lbs.), peeled
Peanut oil
Salt

1. Shape whole potatoes into rectangles or cylinders about 2½" long and about 1½" wide, then slice potatoes evenly with a mandoline or a very sharp knife (a mandoline is better; see facing page) to a thickness of ⅛". Place slices in a nonreactive bowl and cover with water.

2. Heat about 4" oil in a cast-iron pot over medium heat. Drain potatoes, then dry very thoroughly with paper towels. Check oil temperature with a kitchen thermometer. When oil reaches 250°, cook potatoes, without browning, in small batches, turning occasionally, until they are tender and slightly blistered and their edges are slightly crisp, about 4 minutes. Drain potatoes on paper towels and allow to cool for about 20 minutes. (Potatoes may be cooked to this point several hours in advance of serving and kept in refrigerator until ready for second frying.)

3. Reheat oil. When temperature reaches 400°, fry potatoes in small batches until they puff up, which should be immediate. Continue frying until potatoes are crisp, about 1–2 minutes per batch. Serve immediately, generously salted, or recrisp for 20 seconds in 400° oil before serving and salting.

Gratin Dauphinois

(Potatoes Baked in Milk and Cream)

SERVES 6

A GRATIN IS SIMPLY a dish whose top is browned in the oven. In the Dauphiné, the best-known version is made with sliced potatoes—but it may also be prepared with macaroni, ground meat, pumpkin, beets, cardoons, wild mushrooms of various kinds, or crayfish tails.

2 lbs. large russet potatoes, peeled and thinly sliced
1½ cups whole milk
1½ cups heavy cream
Salt and freshly ground black pepper
Freshly grated nutmeg

1. Preheat oven to 275°. Arrange layers of slightly overlapping potato slices in an 8-cup gratin or baking dish. Mix together milk and cream in a bowl, then pour over potatoes to cover completely (use a little more cream or milk if necessary). Bake for 1½ hours.

2. Increase heat to 400°. Remove pan from oven and generously season top of potatoes with salt, pepper, and nutmeg. Return pan to oven and cook until brown and bubbling, about 30 minutes more.

Potatoes and Cream

The Dauphiné, which stretches from Savoie to Provence—and is sometimes called "the country of the four mountains" (these being the peaks of Lans-en-Vercors, Villard-de-Lans, Autrans, and Sassenage)—is renowned for, among other things, the quality and abundance of its milk and cream. Local legend has it that around 1900, one Mère Revollet of the Hôtel Revollet in the village of St-Nizier devised a way to cook potatoes, another well-regarded specialty, that made good use of these dairy products. Later adaptations of the gratin dauphinois added garlic, butter, cheese, and/or eggs—and even, in gastronomic Lyon, slices of black truffle. Another regional variation, the gratin savoyard, uses stock in place of milk and cream, and alternates layers of potatoes and beaufort cheese, with knobs of butter throughout.

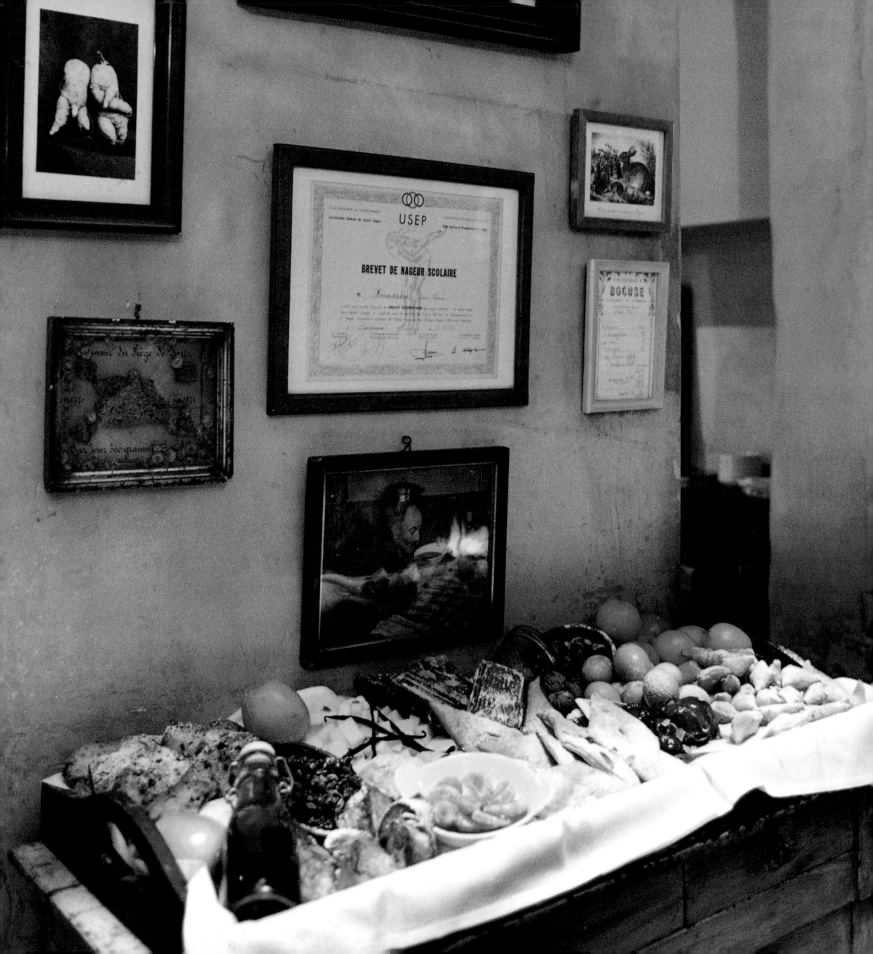

DESSERTS

"AS WE STEP from a cobbled street in

Bordeaux's old quarter through the thick

stone doorway of the restaurant called La

Tupiña, we see Jean-Pierre Xiradakis cook-

ing before an open hearth. Wide-eyed with

enthusiasm, his shirt damp from the heat, he cranks a pulley that rotates a chicken roasting on an iron spit. Xiradakis (facing page, upper left and lower right) steps back and surveys his cast-iron skillets, griddles, and caldrons. 'I started La Tupiña [itself named for a kind of cooking pot],' he tells us, 'to offer the food my mother and grandmother cooked when I was a child.' A surprising number of the old Bordelais dishes he's talking about utilize one of the great gastronomic treasures of southwestern France: the flavorful purplish plum called prune d'ente when fresh and pruneau d'Agen when dried. This modest fruit, versatile and bountiful, gets added to red wine sauces (like rabbit with dried prunes, and even the local version of coq au vin), and to all manner of confections. Xiradakis admits, however, that plums were not his favorite childhood food; his mother made her children eat them more for good health than for sheer enjoyment. Nonetheless, he uses them freely in desserts today—in, for instance, an homage to his grandmother's plum tart (see page 277); in an opulent prune ice cream; and in his remarkable pruneaux à l'armagnac, in which the prunes have spent three woozy weeks steeped in that great brandy until they have puffed up to look almost like fresh plums again. There is a saying in the region to the effect that 'The aroma of the countryside is found in a plum.' Creations like these make that easy to believe." —DAVID CASE AND MEGAN WETHERALL

RECIPES

Tarte aux Prunes Façon Grand-Mère

(Grandmother's Plum Tart)

SERVES 8

FRANCE'S CELEBRATED prune d'ente was originally called the *prune datte*, or date plum, and later dubbed the *robe de sergent*, or sergeant's cloak—in reference to its purplish hue, which evoked the color of civil guards' uniforms.

FOR PASTRY:
1½ cups flour
¼ cup confectioners' sugar
10 tbsp. butter, cut into
 small pieces
1 whole egg
1 egg yolk
½ tsp. vanilla extract

FOR FILLING:
1 lb. dried pitted prunes
1 cup armagnac
½ cup sugar
2 tbsp. butter, cut into
 small pieces
2 egg yolks
⅔ cup heavy cream

1. For pastry, sift together flour and sugar in a mixing bowl. Add butter, and using a pastry cutter, 2 knives, or the tips of your fingers, blend butter into flour mixture until it resembles coarse meal. Beat together egg, 1 egg yolk, and vanilla in a small bowl. Add to flour mixture and mix with your hands until dough holds together. Turn dough out on a lightly floured surface and work dough by "smearing" it with the heel of your hand until it is smooth. Form into a ball, cover with plastic wrap, and refrigerate for at least 2 hours, or overnight.

2. For filling, soak prunes in armagnac and 1–2 cups hot water in a covered container for at least 2 hours or overnight.

3. Preheat oven to 400°. Roll out dough on a lightly floured surface into a 13" round. Ease dough into an 11" flan ring set on a parchment-lined baking sheet and roll the rolling pin across top to cut off excess dough. Line shell with parchment, fill with weights or dried beans, and bake for 30 minutes. Remove from oven and lift out weight-filled parchment.

4. Drain prunes, then arrange in pastry shell, sprinkle with sugar, and dot with butter pieces. Return to oven for 10 minutes to allow butter and sugar to melt into a syrup. Meanwhile, whisk together 2 egg yolks and cream in a small bowl until just mixed. Remove tart from oven and pour custard over prunes. Return to oven for another 10 minutes until custard just sets. Remove tart from oven and set aside to cool completely. Transfer tart to a serving platter by removing flan ring and lifting parchment and tart onto the platter, then gently slip parchment out from under tart.

Spirit of the Plum

Although the plum called prune d'ente is delicious to eat by itself, delicious when cooked into pastries and other desserts, and legendary in its dried form (as the pruneau d'Agen), it is appreciated in still another form by connoisseurs of southwestern French gastronomy: as vieille prune, or old plum—which is to say brandy made from the fruit. Among the best vieille prune is that produced about 90 miles south of Bordeaux, in the Pays Basque, under the Etienne Brana label. Martine Brana, daughter of the late Etienne, ferments plum juice—mostly from prunes d'ente with a soupçon of another variety, the greengage, added—in stainless steel vats, then transfers it to airtight tanks before distilling it in copper pot stills. The resulting brandy is then diluted to a strength of 100 proof and blended with older brandies. The result is a remarkable spirit, suggesting both calvados and armagnac but with an identity very much its own—characterized by an elegant bouquet and a fresh plum flavor that deepens and grows more complex as it lingers on your palate.

Upper Crusts

The French don't make "pie crust"; they make pastry dough, and in five main varieties: **PÂTE BRISÉE** is shortcrust or basic tart dough, composed of just flour, butter, salt, and water, with an egg or a bit of sugar as optional additions; it is used for savory tarts, quiches, and pâtés en croûte. **PÂTE SUCRÉE**, sweet shortcrust pastry, is the sweet, more sugary version of pâte brisée. It is the classic base for dessert tarts. **PÂTE SABLÉE** is a close relative of pâte sucrée, even sweeter; although it is delicate and thus difficult to work with, it forms a delicious base for fresh fruit tarts and for petits fours. **PÂTE À CHOUX**, which is easier to make than one might imagine, is formed from a dense white panade, or sauce, of flour, water, and butter, seasoned with salt, into which eggs are beaten; it is essential for savory delights like gougères (see page 83) and for such pastries as éclairs, profiteroles, and croquembouche (see page 308). Finally there is the revered **PÂTE FEUILLETÉE**, so difficult to make that even French housewives buy it ready-made. Fashioned from equal quantities of butter and flour plus water and salt, it is turned, rolled out, and folded back upon itself as many as eight times; when it bakes, the butter melts and steam pushes up the dough layers into the famous mille-feuille or thousand-leaf effect.

Tarte aux Pommes
(Apple Tart)

SERVES 8

AFTER LUNCH at bookseller and gastronome Gérard Oberlé's house in Burgundy (see page 230), out came thin-crust apple and rhubarb tarts made by Giles Brezol, Oberlé's friend and business partner. Oberlé's housekeeper, Lucette Malinouski, demonstrates the apple tart basics at right.

FOR PASTRY:
2 cups flour
Pinch salt
1 tbsp. sugar
9 tbsp. butter, cut into
*   small pieces*

FOR FILLING:
3–4 granny smith apples
¼ cup sugar

1. For pastry, sift flour, salt, and sugar together into a mixing bowl. Add butter, and using a pastry cutter, 2 knives, or the tips of your fingers, blend butter into flour mixture until it resembles coarse meal. Add up to 6 tbsp. ice water, 1 tbsp. at a time, mixing with a fork until dough just holds together. Cover with plastic wrap and refrigerate for 30 minutes.

2. Preheat oven to 425°. Roll out dough on a lightly floured surface into a 14" round (**A & B**). Fit pastry into a buttered 10" false-bottomed tart pan, taking care not to stretch dough (**C & D**). Roll the rolling pin across top of tart pan to cut off excess pastry. Prick the bottom of the pastry all over with a fork (**E**).

3. For filling, peel (**F**), core, and thinly slice apples. Sprinkle 1 tbsp. sugar across surface of pastry. Working from outer edge towards the center, overlap apple slices in concentric circles (**G & H**), then evenly sprinkle with remaining 3 tbsp. sugar (**I**). Bake until edge of tart is golden, about 40 minutes. Allow to cool before serving.

Tarte aux Fraises

(*Strawberry Tart*)

SERVES 6

TO AVOID the flavorless-strawberry problem, buy fresh strawberries only in season, look for the best local varieties—and make this tart only when you can find those tasty fruits.

FOR STRAWBERRIES:
4 cups fresh strawberries,
*   washed and hulled*
¼ cup sugar

FOR PASTRY:
1 ½ cups flour
½ tsp. salt
1 tbsp. sugar
9 tbsp. butter, cut into
*   small pieces*

FOR PASTRY CREAM:
1 cup milk
½ vanilla bean, split
*   lengthwise*
3 egg yolks
¼ cup sugar
1 tbsp. flour

1. For strawberries, put strawberries in a bowl and sprinkle with sugar. Set aside to macerate for at least 30 minutes at room temperature.

2. For pastry, preheat oven to 400°. Sift flour, salt, and sugar into a bowl. Rub butter into flour mixture with your fingers until it resembles coarse crumbs. Sprinkle in 3 tbsp. ice water. Work dough on a floured surface until it just holds together. Form into a ball, wrap in plastic, and refrigerate for 30 minutes.

3. For pastry cream, put milk and vanilla bean in a medium heavy saucepan. Bring milk just to a boil over medium heat. Cool slightly, remove vanilla bean, scrape seeds into milk, then discard the pod. Whisk egg yolks and sugar together in a bowl until blended, then sprinkle in flour, continuing to whisk the mixture. Gradually whisk in milk, then return mixture to saucepan. Cook over low heat, stirring, until thickened, about 10 minutes. Remove from heat and set aside to cool.

4. Roll out pastry dough on a floured surface into a 12" round then fit into a 9" tart pan, taking care not to stretch the dough. Roll the rolling pin across top of tart pan to cut off excess pastry. Prick the bottom of the pastry all over with a fork. Cover dough with foil and fill with dried beans. Bake for 15 minutes, then remove foil and beans and continue baking until shell is golden, 10–15 minutes. Allow to cool.

5. Stir juice from berries into pastry cream, then spread mixture evenly in tart shell. Arrange strawberries upright atop mixture. Serve at once.

Drunken Strawberries

Appealing though a homemade strawberry tart may be, there's an even easier and no less delicious way to present good berries: as fraises au vin rouge, strawberries in red wine. To serve 4, wash and hull 4 cups fresh, ripe strawberries, then halve them lengthwise. Sprinkle berries with 2–3 tbsp. sugar, mix gently, then set aside to macerate for about 1 hour. Divide berries between 4 large wine goblets, then pour in enough red wine—preferably a fruity young pinot noir or beaujolais—to cover berries. (Certain elegant Parisian restaurants used to offer fraises au Lafite, made with guess what wine—but that may be overdoing things a bit.) Serve topped with a dollop of crème fraîche, if you like.

281

Tarte Tatin
(Upside-Down Apple Tart)

SERVES 8

IN HONOR of the role played by Maxim's in popularizing this classic tart, we asked Jean-Yves de Charme (right), the restaurant's present-day chef-pâtissier, for this recipe.

FOR APPLES:
2½ sticks (20 tbsp.)
   butter, cut into small
   pieces
1½ cups sugar
9 golden delicious apples,
   peeled, cored, and
   halved

FOR PASTRY:
1 cup flour
½ tsp. salt
1 tbsp. sugar
6 tbsp. butter, cut into
   small pieces

1. For apples, preheat oven to 400°. Scatter butter pieces and sprinkle sugar evenly in a 9–10" copper tatin pan or a heavy baking pan. Tightly pack 14 apple halves around inside edge of pan, standing upright, nestled against one another, with round side tilted down. Place 4 remaining halves in similar position in center of pan. (Apples will shrink as they cook and slip round side down into pan.) Bake for about 2 hours.

2. Transfer pan from oven to stove top and cook over medium-high heat until butter and sugar caramelize to a rich brown, 15–20 minutes. Remove from heat, and gently ease sticky apples away from the side of pan with a knife. Refrigerate overnight so that apples firm up and "confit" further.

3. For pastry, preheat oven to 350° about 1 hour before serving tart. Sift flour, salt, and sugar into a bowl. Rub butter into flour mixture with your fingers until it resembles coarse crumbs. Sprinkle in 3 tbsp. ice water and work dough until it just holds together. Form into a ball, wrap in plastic, and refrigerate for 30 minutes. Roll out dough on a floured surface into a 12" circle.

4. Drape pastry over apples and pan. Roll the rolling pin across top of pan to cut off excess pastry and allow pastry to fall over apples against inside edge of pan. Bake in oven (still at 350°) until pastry is flaky and golden, about 20 minutes.

5. Remove from oven, place a flat ovenproof platter on top of tatin pan and invert quickly and carefully. Do not unmold yet. Reduce heat to 300° and return platter and pan to oven for 10 minutes. Remove tatin pan and serve warm.

VARIATION: *Puff Pastry Tarte Tatin*—Follow steps 1 and 2 above. Preheat oven to 350°. Roll out 1 puff pastry sheet on a floured surface and use a sharp knife to cut it into a 12" circle. Bake on a parchment-lined baking sheet for 15 minutes. Pastry will puff, turn golden, and shrink to fit pan. Put on top of apples and bake for 20 minutes. Proceed with step 5 above.

Delicious Accident

J ean Tatin was a baker and pastry chef in the village of Lamotte-Beuvron, in the Sologne, 110 miles north of Paris, and his daughters, Caroline and Stéphanie, opened the Hôtel Tatin there in 1860. In the hotel kitchen one day, Stéphanie, who had learned her father's craft, apparently either accidentally or deliberately upturned an apple tart onto a baking tray and put it in the oven. The results were good, and the tart became a specialty of the hotel. The story goes that news of the new dessert reached the ears of one Monsieur Gaillard, a frequent visitor to the Sologne (where he hunted wild game) and owner of the legendary Maxim's in Paris. He is said to have become a regular customer at the Tatins' table, and he eventually introduced Stéphanie's creation to his own customers—who happened to be the crème de la crème of Parisian society. The rest is dessert history.

Lemon Fest

France's most famous lemon-producing region is the *arrière-pays*, or back-country, around Menton, abutting the Italian border on the Mediterranean coast. So vividly are the lemons identified with the town, in fact, that its annual version of carnival is called the Fête du Citron, or lemon festival. Every year, just before Lent, local enterprises, neighboring towns, and even foreign participants (the German spa town of Baden-Baden, for instance) construct elaborate, massive set pieces out of lemons, oranges, and other citrus fruit, to be put on display in the public garden called Jardins Biovès (below). In a sort of puckery variation on the Rose Parade, floats similarly decked out roll down the city streets on Shrove Tuesday evening, and there are concerts, fireworks shows, art exhibitions, and special dinners, too. Shortly after Ash Wednesday everything stops, and any fruit still in edible condition gets sold off at bargain prices, for use in such local specialties as vin d'orange and vin de citron—wine macerated with spices and oranges or lemons, respectively.

Tarte au Citron

(Lemon Tart)

SERVES 6

AT ONE OF our favorite Lyon bouchons (see page 217), À Ma Vigne, proprietors Patrick and Joséphine Giraud and Francine Ballay (facing page, top right, from left) offer this flaky-crust tart as a specialty. If you have dough left over after rolling out the shell, make a pastry lattice for the top.

FOR PASTRY:
2 cups flour
2 tbsp. sugar
½ tsp. salt
12 tbsp. cold unsalted
  butter, cut into pieces

FOR FILLING:
1 ¼ cups sugar
2 eggs
10 tbsp. butter, melted
  and cooled
Juice and minced zest of
  2 lemons

1. For pastry, combine flour, sugar, and salt in a large bowl. Cut in butter with a pastry cutter or 2 knives (mixture should resemble coarse cornmeal). Sprinkle with up to 3 tbsp. ice water so that dough holds together, then form into a ball, wrap in plastic, and refrigerate for at least 1 hour.

2. Preheat oven to 375°. Transfer dough to a lightly floured surface, then flatten and roll into a 9" round. Ease dough into an 8" false-bottomed tart pan. Prick the bottom of the pastry all over with a fork. Cover dough with foil and chill for at least 20 minutes, then fill with pie weights or dried beans and bake for 15 minutes. Remove foil and beans and continue baking for 5 minutes more. Remove from oven and set aside to cool.

3. For filling, beat sugar and eggs together in a bowl with an electric mixer until mixture is pale yellow. Continue beating as you gradually add melted butter. Then stir in lemon juice and zest. Spoon filling into tart shell and bake until crust is golden and filling is set and lightly browned, about 25 minutes. Cool completely before serving.

Clafoutis

(Black Cherry Batter Cake)

SERVES 8

THIS OLD-STYLE recipe, given to us by Auvergnat grandmother Jeanne Barbet, calls for unpitted cherries. This is the tradition in the region, not as a labor-saving shortcut, but because the pits are believed to add flavor to the cake. If the idea unsettles you, use pitted cherries instead.

1 tbsp. butter
1 tbsp. vanilla extract
6 eggs
6 tbsp. sugar
1 ¼ cups milk
2 tbsp. kirsch
Pinch salt
¾ cup flour
3 cups black cherries,
   pitted or unpitted
Confectioners' sugar
   (optional)

1. Preheat oven to 425°. Generously butter a 9" cast-iron skillet or a baking dish. Combine vanilla extract, eggs, sugar, milk, kirsch, and salt in a blender. Blend for a few seconds to mix ingredients, then add flour and blend until smooth, about 1 minute.

2. Pour batter into buttered skillet, then distribute cherries evenly over top. Bake until a skewer inserted into batter comes out clean and a golden brown crust has formed on top and bottom of clafoutis, about 30 minutes. Dust with confectioners' sugar, if you like.

VARIATION: *Prune Clafoutis*—Marinate 2 cups pitted prunes in 2 cups armagnac overnight or longer. Drain prunes, reserving armagnac marinade, and proceed with step 1 above, substituting 2 tbsp. of armagnac marinade for kirsch, then proceed with step 2 above, substituting prunes for cherries.

Cherries of Controversy

When the Académie Française defined clafoutis as a "sort of fruit flan" some years ago, inhabitants of Limoges—capital of the Limousin region, where the confection was born—protested, forcing the venerable institution to change the definition to the more precise "cake with black cherries". Black cherries are the meatiest, juiciest, and sweetest of varieties, and if you mix plenty of them into what may best be described as a slightly thickened crêpe batter, you'll have the makings of a traditional clafoutis limousin. The recipe is old but not ancient, probably dating from around the 1860s. The unusual name (sometimes spelled clafouti) comes from *clafir*, a dialect word meaning "to fill". Next door to the Limousin, in the Auvergne, the same sort of cake is known as *milliard*, and is made not only with cherries but also with red currants or with prunes soaked in armagnac.

Versatile Chard

Swiss chard (*Beta vulgaris cicla*) is a kind of beet grown for its leaves instead of its root. These leaves have a quilted texture and thick striated ribs typically either bright red or ivory-hued (though there are also varieties with ribs in yellow, pink, and various shades of green). Chard (below, foreground) grows easily and has a mild but pronounced flavor, and perhaps for these reasons is the most appreciated of all greens in Nice and vicinity and in the neighboring Italian region of Liguria. In these areas, it is widely used in soups and stews, as a filling for ravioli and various savory tourtes and torte, and as a coloring and flavoring agent for pasta. In Nice, for some reason, chard has scatological associations: Gnocchi made with potatoes and swiss chard (typically served with a meat sauce or just tossed with olive oil and parmigiano-reggiano) are known as *merda de can*—dog turds—for their murky green color. And the people of Nice themselves are sometimes jocularly referred to in the region as *caga-bléa*, meaning (to put it politely) that they eat so much chard they positively excrete it.

Tourte de Blettes
(*Swiss Chard Torte*)

SERVES 8

ALL OVER the Mediterranean, greens of various kinds are cooked with pine nuts and raisins; in Nice, this savory combination is turned into dessert. Our version of this specialty is adapted from a recipe given by SAVEUR consulting editor Mireille Johnston in her *Cuisine of the Sun: Classical French Cooking from Nice and Provence* (Fireside, 1990).

FOR PASTRY:
3 cups flour
½ cup sugar
½ lb. butter, softened
2 eggs, beaten

FOR FILLING:
2 lbs. swiss chard,
    washed, ribs removed
¼ cup golden raisins
2 tbsp. dark rum
⅓ cup pine nuts
½ cup confectioners' sugar
2 eggs, beaten
Grated rind of 1 lemon
2 large golden delicious
    apples, peeled, cored,
    and thinly sliced
1 egg yolk, beaten

1. For pastry, sift flour and sugar into a large bowl. Mix in butter and eggs with a fork; mixture will look crumbly. Turn out onto a floured work surface and knead briefly. Shape into a ball, wrap in plastic and refrigerate for 2 hours.

2. For filling, bring a large pot of water to a boil, add chard, and cook for 15 minutes. Drain in a colander, then cool under running cold water. Squeeze out moisture, finely chop, and set aside.

3. Preheat oven to 375°. Cook raisins and rum in a small saucepan over medium-low heat until raisins absorb most of the rum, about 1 minute. Cool, then mix with chard, pine nuts, sugar, eggs, and lemon rind in a large bowl.

4. Lightly butter an 11" x 13" baking dish. Divide dough into 2 uneven balls, ⅓ for the top and ⅔ for the bottom. Roll out both pieces to ⅛"-thick rectangles. Line bottom and sides of pan with the larger piece. Prick all over with a fork and add chard mixture. Arrange apples in a single layer over chard. Cover with smaller piece of dough. Crimp edges, trim excess dough, and prick top with fork. Brush top with egg yolk. Bake until crust is golden, about 30 minutes. Sprinkle with additional confectioners' sugar, if you like, before serving.

Gâteau aux Noix

(Walnut Cake)

SERVES 8

THE CASTAGNÉ FAMILY produces superb artisanal walnut oil at its Huilerie Familiale du Lac de Diane near Martel, in the Lot (see page 100), and makes a cake similar to this one with oil and nuts from their own orchards (like those displayed by Marie-Louise Castagné, left). Walnut liquor is often used to moisten the cake or is served on the side.

½ cup chopped walnuts
3 eggs
1 cup sugar
⅓ cup walnut oil
⅓ cup dry white wine
1 ½ cups flour
2 tsp. baking powder
⅛ tsp. salt

1. Preheat oven to 350°. Place walnuts in a small dry saucepan and cook over medium heat, shaking pan, until nuts are lightly toasted, 5–10 minutes. Set aside.

2. Beat eggs in a medium bowl with an electric mixer. Gradually add sugar and beat until mixture is light and fluffy. Add walnut oil and wine and mix well. Batter will be quite thick.

3. Generously grease a 9" cake pan. Sift together flour, baking powder, and salt into a large bowl. Add egg mixture to flour mixture and mix with a wooden spoon until just combined. Gently fold in nuts, then spoon batter into pan.

4. Bake cake until a toothpick can be inserted and pulled out clean, about 40 minutes. Remove cake from oven, cool for 10 minutes, and then turn out onto a cooling rack. Allow to cool completely, then serve in wedges drizzled with walnut liqueur or accompanied by vanilla ice cream, if you like.

The Nut Party

I n southwestern France, walnuts are mostly harvested in October, when whole families head for the orchards to fill burlap sacks with the fruit. The walnuts—franquette, mayette, marbot, and corne are the varieties most often grown—are quite damp when fresh, and must be dried over a gas stove. Most of the shelling is done by hand— and the occasional *soirée dénoisillage*, or nut-cracking party, still takes place. At these get-togethers, veterans whack the nuts with a wooden hammer; skilled practitioners of this art can shatter the shell while leaving the meat intact. This is desirable, since whole walnuts bring a higher price than the cracked ones— called *les invalides*—which are sent to mills to be crushed for oil. Though walnut is now a pricey specialty oil, it was once commonly used by the agrarian poor. Until at least the end of the 18th century, in fact, walnuts were sustenance in the Southwest. Walnut shells were used to make bread in times of famine, and the meat was pressed into a kind of milk.

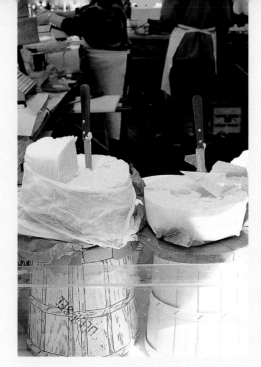

A Butter Culture

Butter, *amann* in the Breton language (the word also means "ointment"), has a symbolic importance in Brittany that must seem all but incomprehensible to the cholesterol-phobic American. In recent memory, older Bretons still placed a slab of butter near somebody suffering from cancer in the belief that it would absorb the disease; even today, mothers often rub a butter pomade on their childrens' bruised elbows. Butter was also used by women to slick their hair back under their starched Breton headdresses. And of course, Bretons *eat* butter. Since the Middle Ages, they've been renowned for their formidable butter consumption, putting it on virtually everything—even fish, which was contrary to the religious and dietary principles of medieval times. The main difference between butter from Brittany and those from other French regions is that Breton butter is almost always salted, with a sea salt content ranging from .5 to 5 percent. The salt allows it to be conserved longer, to have a lower water content and, according to the Bretons, to have far more flavor and character than unsalted butter.

Kouign Amann
(Breton Butter Cake)

SERVES 8

PASTRY CHEFS in Brittany warn that making a perfect kouign amann (pronounced kween ah-MAN) isn't easy, but we've found that this simple recipe yields delicious results.

2 7-gram packets active dry yeast
1 tsp. salt
2 cups flour
12 tbsp. butter (keep 8 tbsp. or 1 stick in refrigerator until ready to use)
1 ¼ cups sugar

1. Dissolve yeast in ⅓ cup lukewarm water in a large bowl. Set aside until yeast begins to activate (it will foam a little), about 10 minutes.

2. Add salt and 1 cup of the flour to yeast mixture, stirring with a wooden spoon. Add ⅓ cup water, and when well blended, add remaining 1 cup flour and another ⅔ cup water. Stir until dough forms into a ball, then transfer to a lightly floured surface and knead with the heels of your palms until smooth and elastic, about 10 minutes. Coat the inside of a large bowl with 2 tbsp. butter, place dough in bowl, and cover with a damp cloth or plastic wrap. Set aside to rise until doubled in bulk, about 1 hour.

3. Preheat oven to 450°. Grease a 9" pie pan with 1 tbsp. butter and dust with flour. Roll out dough on a lightly floured surface into a large rectangle, about 12" x 18", with the shorter side nearest you.

4. Cut chilled stick of butter into 10–12 pieces. Dot middle portion of dough with butter pieces and sprinkle with ½ cup of the sugar. Working quickly, fold short sides towards the center, over the butter and sugar. Edges should slightly overlap. Sprinkle dough with ¼ cup of the sugar and roll over seams to seal. Turn dough again so that the shorter side is nearest you and fold into thirds, as you would a letter. Let dough rest 15 minutes in refrigerator.

5. Roll out dough on a sugar sprinkled surface, dusting with ¼ cup sugar as you go, into a large rectangle. Fold into thirds again and let dough rest another 15 minutes in refrigerator.

6. Roll out dough on a sugar-sprinkled surface into a square slightly larger than the pie pan. Dust with remaining ¼ cup sugar, and ease dough into pan, loosely folding edges towards the center. Melt remaining 1 tbsp. butter, and drizzle over dough. Bake until golden brown, 35–40 minutes. Remove from pan while hot and serve warm.

Gâteau de Riz

(Rice Pudding)

SERVES 8–10

BERNARD PICOLET uses his grandmother's recipe to makes this creamy but cakelike rice pudding at Aux Amis du Beaujolais in Paris. She cooked it for hours near an open fire. Picolet bakes it in the oven, in a caramelized pan, dresses it up with crème anglaise, and calls it a gâteau.

⅓ cup raisins
¼ cup dark rum
6 cups milk
1 cup short-grain white rice (such as Italian arborio)
1½ cups plus 1 tbsp. sugar
1 vanilla bean, split lengthwise
4 eggs, separated
Crème anglaise (optional; see sidebar, page 304)

1. Soak raisins in rum in a bowl for 1 hour. Combine milk, rice, ½ cup of the sugar, and vanilla bean in a medium saucepan. Bring to a boil over medium heat, reduce heat to medium-low, cover, and cook, stirring occasionally, until rice absorbs all liquid, about 1 hour. Remove from heat, scrape seeds from vanilla bean into rice, and discard pod. Set rice aside to cool to room temperature.

2. Pour 1 cup of the sugar into a skillet, shaking the skillet so that sugar spreads evenly, and place over medium-high heat. Cook, without stirring, until sugar begins to melt, about 2 minutes, then stir with a wooden spoon until golden and just beginning to foam, about 3 minutes. Remove from heat and carefully pour into a 9" baking pan, then, working quickly before caramel hardens, tilt to coat bottom and sides.

3. Preheat oven to 375°. Stir egg yolks and raisins (discarding rum) into rice. Beat egg whites until foamy. Sprinkle in remaining 1 tbsp. sugar, continue to beat until soft peaks form, then fold into rice mixture. Transfer to caramelized pan, set pan in a shallow pan of water, and bake until a knife inserted into the middle comes out clean, about 1 hour. Cool slightly in pan, then turn out onto a platter. Serve with crème anglaise, if you like.

Friends and Family

y friend Claude and I [see page 210]," recalls SAVEUR editor Colman Andrews, "went to Aux Amis du Beaujolais, on the corner of the rue de Berri and the rue d'Artois, a few blocks off the Champs-Élysées, all the time. It was Claude's canteen, his hangout. Aux Amis du Beaujolais (With the Friends of Beaujolais) was opened in 1921 by Philibert Bléton, a young man from Fleurie, one of the Beaujolais villages that lend their names to that region's grand cru wines. His brother Georges went to work for him in the late '30s, eventually buying the place from him in 1949. Georges's brother-in-law, Maurice, was in charge when Claude first brought me there—but he is now long since deceased, and the current proprietor is Maurice's son, Bernard. I remember meeting him in 1980, a year before he took over—a nice young man in a stylish suit. 'The next time I come here,' I said to Claude, 'there'll be raw tuna with pineapple beurre blanc on the menu instead of boeuf à la bourguignonne.' I was wrong. The decor has changed (it looks almost Californian in its light-hued stylishness), and there is more fish on the menu than there used to be because that's what people eat these days. But all the old bistro specialties remain, and Picolet cooks them just as well as his predecessors did. His son Christian helps him in the kitchen, and is learning the old ways, too."

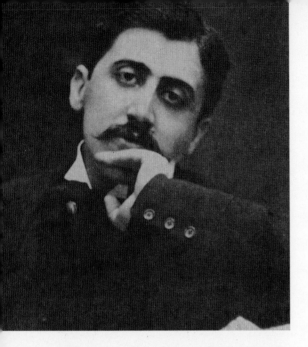

Proust on Madeleines

Madeleines

MAKES 16 LARGE MADELEINES

THE MOST famous of literary confections, the madeleine—which was perhaps named in honor of Madeleine Paumier, a 19th-century French pastry cook—inspired the narrator of Marcel Proust's *Remembrance of Things Past* to embark on his epic exploration of time, memory, and love. This version of the classic recipe was given to us by Michel Richard, whose restaurants include Citronelle in Washington, D.C.

3 eggs
1 cup sugar
1 cup butter (2 sticks), softened
1 cup flour
1 tsp. baking powder
Zest of 1 lemon

1. Preheat oven to 375°. Beat eggs and sugar together with an electric mixer until pale yellow and a little frothy, about 3 minutes. Scrape down sides of the bowl. Continuing to beat, add butter 1 tsp. at a time until all the butter is incorporated, about 5 minutes. (Batter may appear slightly curdled.)

2. Sift together flour and baking powder, then gradually add to the batter, beating on low speed. Add lemon zest and mix until batter is smooth, about 1 minute more.

3. Spoon the batter into a well-buttered and floured madeleine mold. Bake until golden, about 20 minutes. Remove from oven, and allow to cool before unmolding.

Tomates Confites Farcies aux Douze Saveurs

(Sweet Tomatoes Filled with a Dozen Flavors)

SERVES 4

AT HIS THREE-STAR Arpège in Paris (right), Alain Passard serves this unusual dessert exclusively in the summertime—because only small, sweet, perfectly sun-ripened tomatoes will produce a successful interpretation of this dish.

4 small, very ripe and
  sweet tomatoes, blanched,
  stemmed, and peeled
12 tbsp. sugar
1 medium golden delicious
  apple, peeled, cored, and
  finely diced
1 ripe comice pear, peeled,
  cored, and finely diced
¼ cup finely diced fresh
  pineapple
1 tbsp. raisins
Pinch freshly grated
  orange zest
1 tsp. freshly grated
  lemon zest
½ tsp. minced fresh ginger
Pinch ground cloves
Pinch aniseed
Pinch ground cinnamon
3 walnuts, chopped
5 almonds, chopped
10 pistachios, chopped
1 sprig fresh mint, finely
  chopped
2 vanilla beans, split
  lengthwise
Juice of 1 small orange,
  strained
Vanilla ice cream (optional)

1. Slice ⅓ of the blossom end off tomatoes and reserve caps. Hull and seed tomatoes, discarding solids. Set tomatoes upside down on a rack to drain.

2. Preheat oven to 400°. Sprinkle 2 tbsp. sugar evenly into a medium ovenproof skillet over medium heat. Cook sugar until it melts and turns golden, about 5 minutes. Add apples, pears, and pineapple, increase heat to high, and cook, stirring, until fruit is coated in caramel juices and just tender, about 2 minutes. Remove pan from heat, then add raisins, orange and lemon zest, ginger, cloves, aniseed, cinnamon, walnuts, almonds, pistachios, mint, and vanilla beans. Mix well, then transfer to a medium bowl and set aside to cool.

3. Remove and reserve vanilla beans from fruit mixture. Stuff each tomato with fruit mixture, then replace tops. Sprinkle remaining 10 tbsp. sugar evenly into same skillet over medium-high heat. Cook sugar until it melts and turns golden, about 7 minutes. Add orange juice and reserved vanilla beans, and cook, stirring, until smooth, about 1 minute. Arrange tomatoes in pan and baste with pan syrup, then transfer to oven and bake, basting often, until tomatoes are soft and filling is hot, 10–12 minutes. To serve, place 1 tomato on each plate, then spoon pan syrup over tomatoes. Serve with vanilla ice cream, if you like.

Give Me Arpège

At the Parisian three-star restaurant called Arpège," reports writer Thomas McNamee, "the dinner tasting menu costs 1,200 francs per person. That's 200 dollars to you, pilgrim. Service and taxes are included; wine is extra. Surely, no meal, even a ten-course lollapalooza, could be worth maybe 300 bucks a head. At least that's what I thought. Then I sat down for a meal at Arpège, and four hours later, when I floated past the undulating pearwood paneling of the dining room and out into the street, I had begun to understand. I was not drunk. I was not stuffed. Every tiny bite had been...the only word is sublime. This one meal proved to me, beyond the slightest doubt, that food can be a work of art. The food at Arpège appears at first to have been born in a realm of pure abstraction. The owner-chef, Alain Passard, is slight, elegant, contemplative, and unabashedly artistic. His cooking fits precisely the definition of Apollonian: characterized by clarity, harmony, and restraint. Great art is always expensive, always rare, always oblivious to the injustices that make it possible. And his is great art."

Soufflé au Chocolat

(Chocolate Soufflé)

SERVES 3–4

THE FIRST SOUFFLÉS (the name comes from the French verb *souffler*, to blow or whisper) were savory, not sweet like this one. We prefer this more delicate flourless version of the dish to the more traditional flour-stabilized version.

3 tbsp. milk
5½ tbsp. sugar, plus
    additional for dusting
    soufflé dish
4 oz. semisweet chocolate,
    coarsely chopped
2 egg yolks
3 egg whites
Confectioners' sugar

1. Preheat oven to 375°. Place milk and 4 tbsp. of the sugar in a small saucepan and stir over medium-low heat until sugar dissolves, about 45 seconds. Stir in chocolate and cook until melted, 1–2 minutes. Transfer to a large mixing bowl, cool for 5 minutes, then beat in egg yolks.

2. Beat egg whites in a clean glass or stainless-steel mixing bowl until foamy, then sprinkle in remaining 1½ tbsp. sugar, beating until stiff peaks form.

3. Butter a small (3 cup) soufflé dish (2½" deep and 6" diameter; soufflé will not rise in a larger dish), then lightly dust with sugar. Gently mix one-third of the egg whites into chocolate mixture, then fold in remaining whites, one-third at a time. Do not overmix. Spoon batter into dish.

4. Make sure oven rack is low enough to allow soufflé room to rise as much as 2" above the dish. Bake until puffed, about 25 minutes. Dust with confectioners' sugar and serve immediately. (Soufflé will begin to deflate after about 2 minutes.)

Surmounting the Uneven Rise

I 'd only been at the Cordon Bleu in Paris for a few weeks," reports SAVEUR associate editor Catherine Whalen, "when chef Michel Cliche announced that our next lesson would be on soufflé au chocolat. The thought of tackling this regal dessert brought on an instant surge of what-am-I-doing-in-cooking-school anxiety. Sure enough, my first attempt emerged at a jaunty but unsoufflé-like angle. 'Uneven rise,' Chef flatly diagnosed. My second try was a feeble, sticky pancake. 'Overwhisked whites,' Chef accused, arching a disapproving eyebrow. My next several efforts were all tasty but, in varying degrees, fluffy failures. Then Chef let us in on the secret: Perfectly whisked whites, he said, start with a perfectly clean bowl; even the smallest speck of grease can deflate the volume. The bowl, therefore, should be cleaned with lemon juice, carefully rinsed, and thoroughly dried. I tried it his way, and pulled from the oven what I took to be a masterpiece. I beamed as I showed it to Chef. He just shrugged. 'Pas mal,' he said."

Crème Brûlée

SERVES 4

WHEN HE WAS the pastry chef at Le Cirque in New York City in the early '80s, Dieter Schorner developed his own version of crème brûlée; it became a sensation and introduced New Yorkers to the dessert. This is our adaptation of his recipe. Though there are numerous methods of caramelizing the sugar on top of the crème brûlée, we've found a small kitchen blowtorch to be best for the purpose.

2 cups heavy cream
5 tbsp. sugar
½ vanilla bean, split
    lengthwise
Small pinch salt
4 egg yolks

1. Preheat oven to 275°. In a small pan, bring cream, 2 tbsp. sugar, vanilla bean, and salt just to a boil over medium heat. Remove from heat and set aside to cool. Scrape seeds from vanilla into cream then discard vanilla pod.

2. In another bowl, whisk egg yolks with 1 tbsp. of the sugar until sugar dissolves. Slowly whisk in cooled cream (if it is not cool, yolks will scramble), then strain through a fine sieve.

3. Divide custard between 4 shallow baking dishes, each about ½ cup in capacity. Place dishes in a baking pan, then place pan in oven. Pour enough cold water into pan to come about halfway up sides of dishes. Bake until custards set, 30–35 minutes.

4. Cover cooled custards with plastic wrap. Chill in refrigerator for at least 4 hours or overnight. Before serving, sprinkle 1½ tsp. sugar on each custard and use a kitchen blowtorch to caramelize tops, holding torch at an angle (flame should barely touch surface) to brown sugar. (You can also brown the sugar in a preheated broiler, taking care to turn the gratin dishes to avoid hot spots.)

A Burning Question

A t his Willi's Wine Bar in Paris, Mark Williamson (above) offers a dessert he describes on the menu as "Spécialité du Collège de Cambridge". When his French customers encounter that description, he reports with delight, they unfailingly and innocently inquire, "Excusez-moi, monsieur, but what is this?" Williamson pauses, smiles, and replies, "Why, it's crème brûlée, bien sûr"—and steps swiftly away from their inevitable splutters of indignation. The French, the Catalans, and the English all claim to have created this unique dessert—whose name literally means "burnt cream"—and as an Englishman abroad, Williamson naturally supports the English theory. It was introduced to Trinity College, Cambridge, he says, in the 1850s, by a young scholar whose nanny had made it. It soon became a permanent item on the refectory menu. Unfortunately, university archives supposedly documenting the birth of this dish have never been made available to the public.

Crème Anglaise

To make this delicate custard sauce, put 2 cups milk and 1 split vanilla bean in a heavy-bottomed saucepan and bring just to a simmer over medium heat. Meanwhile, whisk together 6 egg yolks and ¼ cup sugar in a mixing bowl. Reduce heat to low and slowly whisk ½ cup hot milk into egg mixture, then whisk egg mixture into remaining hot milk. Cook, stirring constantly with a wooden spoon, until mixture is thick enough to coat the back of the spoon, about 15 minutes. Remove from heat, strain through a fine sieve, and transfer to a mixing bowl. Stop custard from overcooking by placing bowl immediately into a larger bowl of ice water. Scrape seeds from vanilla bean into custard and discard pod. Cool to room temperature, then refrigerate until cold. Makes 2 cups.

Oeufs à la Neige
(Floating Islands)

SERVES 6

AMONG THE MOST ingenious of classical French desserts, oeufs à la neige (the name literally means eggs in the snow) has become an American dessert tradition, too.

4 cups milk
1 vanilla bean, split
    lengthwise
6 egg yolks
1 ⅓ cups sugar
4 egg whites

1. Bring 2 cups of milk to a boil in a large heavy saucepan over medium heat. Remove from heat, add vanilla bean, cover, and steep for about 15 minutes.

2. Beat egg yolks in a mixing bowl, slowly sprinkling in ⅓ cup sugar. Continue beating until thick and pale yellow in color.

3. Remove vanilla bean from milk, scrape seeds from bean into milk, then discard pod. Pour milk in a fine stream into egg yolks, beating continuously, then return the mixture to saucepan and cook over low heat, stirring constantly until it forms a custard thick enough to coat the back of a spoon, about 15 minutes; don't rush the process or eggs may scramble. Pour custard through a strainer into a shallow serving bowl. Cool to room temperature, then refrigerate.

4. Beat egg whites until foamy, then gradually add ⅓ cup sugar. Continue to beat until whites are shiny and stiff but not dry.

5. Put remaining 2 cups milk in a large shallow pan and bring to a low simmer. Using a large slotted spoon, form 6 large egg shapes out of whites and poach in the milk for 30 seconds on each side. Do not overcook. Drain "eggs" on a clean towel. Discard poaching liquid.

6. Combine ⅔ cup sugar and ⅓ cup water in a small heavy saucepan. Cook over medium-high heat until sugar caramelizes. To avoid burning caramel, which can happen very quickly, remove pan from heat just before sugar darkens; it will continue to caramelize off heat. Cool caramel for 5 minutes or until it forms into threads when drizzled from the tines of a fork.

7. Using a slotted spoon, carefully arrange "eggs" on top of custard. Working quickly, dip a fork into the slightly cooled caramel and wave it over the dessert to form threads of caramel that crisscross and tangle. Serve immediately.

Dacquoise

SERVES 6

THIS CONFECTION was born in the southwestern French town of Dax. Our recipe was adapted with the help of Andrew Shotts, pastry chef at La Côte Basque in Manhattan.

FOR MERINGUES:
2 cups confectioners' sugar
1⅓ cups finely ground roasted hazelnuts (see sidebar)
1¼ cups finely ground blanched, sliced almonds (see sidebar)
9 egg whites, room temperature
½ cup granulated sugar

FOR GANACHE:
1 cup heavy cream
5 oz. bittersweet chocolate, chopped
3 oz. milk chocolate, chopped

FOR BUTTERCREAM:
2 cups granulated sugar
5 egg whites, room temperature
1 lb. unsalted butter, cut into pieces and softened
3 tbsp. coffee extract

2 cups sliced almonds, toasted
Confectioners' sugar (optional)

1. For meringues, preheat oven to 250°. Line 2 baking sheets with parchment and draw three 8" circles on paper. Sift together confectioners' sugar, hazelnuts, and almonds into a bowl, working any lumps through sieve with your fingers, then set aside. Put egg whites in the clean bowl of a standing mixer and whisk on medium-low speed for 2 minutes. Increase speed to medium and whisk whites to soft peaks, about 2½ minutes. Gradually add granulated sugar while whisking, increase speed to medium-high and whisk until whites form medium-stiff peaks, about 1½ minutes. Transfer whites to a large bowl and carefully fold in ⅓ of nut mixture at a time with a rubber spatula. Divide meringue between parchment circles and gently spread out evenly. Bake in middle of oven, rotating positions hourly until lightly golden and hollow sounding when tapped, for 2–4 hours. Allow to cool.

2. For ganache, heat cream in a medium saucepan and bring to a boil over medium heat. Remove from heat, add bittersweet and milk chocolates, and let sit for 1 minute. Whisk until smooth and set aside until thick enough to spread.

3. For buttercream, combine ⅓ cup water and 1½ cups of the sugar in a small saucepan and cook over medium heat until mixture reaches 250° on a candy thermometer. Put egg whites in the clean bowl of a standing mixer and whisk on medium-low speed for 2 minutes. Increase speed to medium and whisk whites to soft peaks, about 1½ minutes. Gradually add remaining ½ cup sugar while whisking, then increase speed to medium-high and whisk until whites form stiff peaks, about 2 minutes. Slowly pour sugar syrup into whites, whisking until cool, about 10 minutes. Add butter, bit by bit, whisking until shiny and fluffy, about 8 minutes (it may curdle, but will come together). Add coffee extract and set aside.

4. To assemble: Spread ⅓ of buttercream over each of 2 meringues (**A**). Spread ganache over remaining meringue. Layer meringues, placing the one with ganache in the middle (**B**). Spread remaining buttercream on sides of cake (**C**), then cover cake with almonds (**D**) and refrigerate at least 5 hours. Before serving, dust cake with confectioners' sugar.

Nut Tips

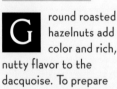

G round roasted hazelnuts add color and rich, nutty flavor to the dacquoise. To prepare hazelnuts, bring 2 cups of water to a boil in a medium saucepan over medium-high heat. Add 2 tbsp. baking soda, and 1½ cups unpeeled hazelnuts. Boil for 3 minutes (water will turn black). Drain, then transfer hazelnuts to a large bowl of cold water and slip skins from nuts with your fingers. Dry hazelnuts on paper towels, then place on a baking sheet and roast in a preheated 350° oven until golden, 15–20 minutes. Remove from oven and set aside to cool completely. When cool, put a small handful of nuts into an electric coffee grinder and pulse into a fine powder. Continue working in small batches, to avoid grinding nuts into nut butter, until all the nuts are ground. Grind 1½ cups blanched sliced almonds the same way. Use nuts in dacquoise or other preparations.

Croquembouche

SERVES 16

THE LEGENDARY French chef Marie-Antoine (Antonin) Carême (1784–1833) was noted for creating monumental pièces montées, or edible centerpieces. Among these was the croquembouche—whose name literally means "crunch in the mouth", for reasons that become obvious when you chomp down on one. Carême once proposed that confectionary was a branch of architecture; this extravagant dessert is a good illustration of what he meant.

FOR PÂTE À CHOUX:
12 tbsp. butter
Salt
2 cups flour
9 eggs

FOR FILLING:
1 ½ cups milk
½ cup sugar
4 egg yolks
3 tbsp. cornstarch
½ tbsp. vanilla
  extract
16 tbsp. unsalted
  butter, softened

FOR CARAMEL:
4 cups sugar

1. For pâte à choux, preheat oven to 425°. Combine 1½ cups water, butter, and ¼ tsp. salt in a large heavy saucepan and bring to a boil over high heat. Remove pan from heat, add flour all at once, and stir vigorously with a wooden spoon until mixture forms a thick dough and pulls away from sides of pan, 1–2 minutes. Return pan to heat and cook, stirring constantly, for 1–2 minutes. Remove pan from heat, allow dough to cool 5 minutes, then vigorously beat in 8 eggs, one at a time, making sure each egg is completely incorporated. Dough will come together and be thick, shiny, and smooth, and pull away from sides of the pan (**A**). Dip two spoons in water, shake off excess water, and scoop a walnut-size piece of dough with one spoon. Use other spoon to push dough onto a parchment-lined baking sheet. Repeat with the rest of dough, setting pieces 1" apart on baking sheet. Lightly beat remaining egg with a pinch of salt and brush each piece of dough with it. Bake until puffed and light brown, about 10 minutes. Lower heat to 350° and continue to bake until well browned, about 15 minutes. Allow puffs to cool.

2. For filling, bring 1 cup of the milk and the sugar just to a boil in a heavy saucepan over medium heat. Meanwhile, whisk remaining ½ cup milk, egg yolks, and cornstarch together in a large bowl. Slowly pour half the hot milk into

A

C

yolk mixture, whisking constantly, then return mixture gradually to milk in pan, stirring constantly with a wooden spoon until it thickens and just returns to a boil. Stir in vanilla and transfer to a bowl; cover with plastic wrap, and refrigerate until cold. In a large bowl, beat butter until pale and fluffy. Add cold filling and beat until smooth, 3–4 minutes. Cover and refrigerate until ready to use. Spoon filling into pastry bag fitted with a plain ¼" tip. Using a chopstick, gently poke a hole in the flat side of each baked and cooled puff. Fill each puff with filling (**B**).

3. For caramel, put 2 cups sugar and ½ cup water in each of two shallow saucepans and stir to mix. Cover and cook over medium heat until sugar turns amber, 15–20 minutes. (Lift covers to check color of caramel after 7 minutes. Sugar will become thick and bubbly, and then begin to turn amber. Swirl saucepans to distribute color. Do not stir.) Remove from heat. Reheat caramel when it becomes too thick. (Making caramel in two saucepans will allow you to re-warm half of the caramel, keeping it fluid, while you work with the other half.)

4. To assemble, dip top of 1 filled puff at a time in hot caramel using tongs or a chocolate-dipping fork. As you dip, place puffs glazed side up on a tray lined with plastic wrap. Form base of croquembouche with 12–14 glazed and cooled puffs, sticking them together with additional dabs of caramel (**C**). Add puffs layer by layer, using fewer at each level as if building a pyramid, to form a hollow cone. Allow caramel to cool slightly, until it is the consistency of honey. With a spoon, drizzle thin strings of caramel around cone (**D**).

Photography Credits

Our French Restaurants

FRANCE HAS a restaurant culture, the greatest in the world. France *invented* restaurants. Our first cookbook, *Saveur Cooks Authentic American*, concentrated on home cooks; there are plenty in this book, too, but we couldn't accurately represent French cooking without including professional chefs. In their restaurants, below, some dishes may no longer be available, but you're sure to eat well.

ALSACE

L'Écrevisse
4 avenue de Strasbourg, Brumath
(388.51.11.08; fax 388.51.89.02)

Soupe d'Écrevisses (*Crayfish Soup*),
page 65

Au Crocodile
10 rue de l'Outre, Strasbourg
(388.32.13.02; fax 388.75.72.01)

Baeckeoffe de Foie Gras
(*Potted Foie Gras and Vegetables*),
page 125

Aux Armes de France
1 Grand Rue, Ammerschwihr
(389.47.10.12; fax 389.47.38.12)

Volaille Fermière au Vinaigre
(*Farmhouse Chicken in Vinegar Sauce*),
page 189

Le Cerf
30 rue du Général de Gaulle,
Marlenheim
(388.87.73.73; fax 388.87.68.08)

Sandre au Pinot Noir
(*Pike Perch Braised in Pinot Noir*),
page 167

Maison Kammerzell
16 place de la Cathédrale,
Strasbourg
(388.32.42.14; fax 388.32.03.92)

Choucroute Garnie à l'Alsacienne
(*Sauerkraut Garnished with Smoked,
Cured, and Fresh Pork*), page 226

AUVERGNE

Grand Hôtel Auguy
2 allée de l'Amicale, Laguiole
(565.44.31.11; fax 565.51.50.81)

Filet de Boeuf au Vin de Marcillac
(*Filet of Beef with Marcillac Wine Sauce*),
page 206

BORDEAUX

La Tupiña
6 rue Porte de la Monnaie,
Bordeaux
(556.91.56.37; fax 556.31.92.11)

Soupe Paysanne à Boire et à Manger
(*Peasant Soup to Drink and Eat*), page
74; Salade d'Artichauts à la Ventrèche
(*Artichoke and Pork Belly Salad*),
page 112; Magret de Canard à la
Cheminée (*Duck Breast Cooked on the
Coals*), page 181; Chapon Farci Rôti
(*Roast Capon with Stuffing*), page 193;
Tarte aux Prunes Façon Grand-Mère
(*Grandmother's Plum Tart*), page 277

BRITTANY

Patrick Jeffroy
11 rue du Bon Voyage,
Plounérin
(296.38.61.80; fax 296.38.66.29)

Crêpes de Sarrasin (*Savory Buckwheat
Crêpes*), page 47; Crème de Potiron
(*Cream of Squash Soup*), page 69;
Cotriade (*Breton Seafood in Broth*),
page 149; Homard à l'Armoricaine
(*Lobster in Tomato Sauce*), page 153;
Kouign Amann (*Breton Butter Cake*),
page 292

BURGUNDY

Hostellerie des Clos
rue Jules Rathier, Chablis
(386.42.10.63; fax 386.42.17.11)

Fricassée d'Escargots au Coulis de Persil
(*Fricassée of Snails with Parsley and
Roasted Garlic Cream*), page 133

Hostellerie du Vieux Moulin
Bouilland
(380.21.51.16; fax 380.21.59.90)

Gougères (*French Cheese Puffs*), page 83;
Cuisses de Grenouilles au Beurre
Persillade (*Frogs' Legs in Parsley Butter*),
page 126; Pâtes Farcies de Coq au Vin
(*Coq au Vin "Cannelloni"*), page 186

L'Espérance
St-Père-sous-Vézelay
(386.33.39.10; fax 386.33.26.15)

Tourte de Groins de Porc
(*Torte of Pigs' Snout*), page 230

La Petite Auberge/Chez Millette
Planchez
(386.78.41.89)

Grapiaux (*Burgundian Crêpes*), page 48;
Oeufs en Bouillon (*Eggs in Broth*),
page 97; Boeuf à la Bourguignonne
(*Beef Stew Burgundy-Style*), page 204

Lameloise
36 place d'Armes, Chagny
(385.87.65.65; fax 385.87.03.57)

Mille-Feuilles de Grenouilles
(*Frogs' Leg "Napoleons" with
White Bean Sauce*), page 129

Ma Cuisine
passage St-Hélène,
place Carnot, Beaune
(380.22.30.22; fax 380.24.99.79)

Terrine de Foies de Volaille
(*Chicken Liver Terrine*), page 34;
Jambon Persillé Maison (*Parsleyed
Ham in Aspic*), page 40

CORSICA

Ferme Campo Di Monte
Murato
(495.37.64.39)

Soupe Corse (*Corsican Soup*), page 73

DORDOGNE

Le Vieux Logis
Trémolat
(553.22.80.06; fax 553.22.84.89)

Pommes à la Sarladaise aux Truffes
(*Sarladais-Style Potatoes with Truffles*),
page 137

LYON

À Ma Vigne
23 rue Jean Larrivé,
3rd arrondissement
(478.60.46.31)

Tarte au Citron (*Lemon Tart*), page 284

Chez Hugon
12 rue Pizay,
1st arrondissement
(478.28.10.94)

Poulet aux Écrevisses
(Chicken with Crayfish), page 190;
"Blanquette" de Veau
(Veal Stew),
page 217

Café des Fédérations
8–10 rue Major Martin,
1st arrondissement
(478.28.26.00; fax 472.07.74.52)

Gâteau de Foies Blonds de Volaille
(Chicken Liver Mousse),
page 37

NICE
•
Chez Barale
39 rue Beaumont
(493.89.17.94)

Salade Niçoise, page 105

La Merenda
4 rue de la Terrasse
(no telephone)

Tripes à la Niçoise
(Nice-Style Tripe) page 214;
Beignets de Fleurs de Courgettes
(Deep-Fried Zucchini Blossoms),
page 252

NORMANDY
•
Le Central
5-7 rue des Bains
Moreaux, Trouville
(231.88.80.84; fax 231.88.42.22)

Moules Marinière
(Mussels with White Wine),
page 150

PARIS
•
À Sousceyrac
35 rue Faidherbe,
11th arrondissement
(143.71.65.30)

Huîtres Glacées en Sabayon
(Oysters in Champagne Sauce),
page 44; Haricot d'Agneau
(Lamb Stew with White Beans),
page 233

Apicius
122 avenue de Villiers,
17th arrondissement
(143.80.19.66; fax 144.40.09.57)

Raie Raide au Beurre Clarifié
(Skate in Clarified Butter),
page 161

Arpège
84 rue de Varenne,
7th arrondissement
(145.51.47.33; fax 144.18.98.39)

Tomatoes Confites Farcies aux Douze
Saveurs *(Sweet Tomatoes Filled
with a Dozen Flavors)*,
page 299

Au Trou Gascon
40 rue Taine,
12th arrondissement
(143.44.34.26; fax 143.07.80.55)

Foie Gras de Canard Poêlé
aux Raisins Blancs
(Seared Foie Gras with Green Grapes),
page 122

Aux Amis du Beaujolais
28 rue d'Artois,
8th arrondissement
(145.63.92.21)

Boeuf à la Mode aux Carottes
(Braised Beef with Carrots), page 210;
Gâteau de Riz
(Rice Pudding),
page 295

Chez Clovis
33 rue Berger,
1st arrondissement
(142.33.97.07)

Crudités *(Raw Vegetable Salads)*,
page 29; Soupe à l'Oignon
Gratinée *(French Onion Soup)*,
page 55

Chez Maxim's
3 rue Royale,
8th arrondissement
(142.65.27.94; fax 140.17.02.91)

Tarte Tatin
(Upside-Down Apple Tart),
page 283

Le Récamier
4 rue Récamier,
7th arrondissement
(145.48.86.58)

Oeufs en Meurette
(Poached Eggs in Red Wine Sauce),
page 94; Foie de Veau Poêlé
(Sautéed Calf's Liver), page 218

Maison Prunier
16 avenue Victor Hugo,
16th arrondissement
(144.17.35.85; fax 144.17.90.10)

Bisque de Homard *(Lobster Bisque)*,
page 66; Sole Meunière
(Sole Sautéed in Butter),
page 156

Taillevent
15 rue Lamennais,
8th arrondissement
(144.95.15.01; fax 142.25.95.18)

Ris de Veau à l'Ancienne
(Veal Sweetbreads in the Old Style),
page 221

Willi's Wine Bar
13 rue des Petits Champs,
1st arrondissement
(142.61.05.09; fax 147.03.36.93)

Crème Brûlée, page 303

PROVENCE
•
Auberge de Noves
route de Châteaurenard, Noves
(490.24.28.28; fax 490.90.16.92)

Canard en Croûte d'Herbes et de Sel
*(Duck Baked in a Crust of
Herbs and Salt)*, page 176;
Asperges Blanches au
Sabayon à l'Huile d'Olive
*(White Asparagus with
Olive Oil Sabayon)*,
page 249

Le Cagnard
rue Sous-Barri, Haut-de-Cagnes
(493.20.73.21; fax 493.22.06.39)

Raviolis de Bourrache
(Borage Ravioli),
page 260

Hostellerie de la Fuste
Lieu-dit La Fuste,
route d'Oraison,
Valensole (Manosque)
(492.72.05.95; fax 492.72.92.93)

Tartare de Légumes
(Marinated Vegetable and Herb Salad),
page 246

Jacques Maximin
689 chemin de la Gaude, Vence
(493.58.90.75; fax 493.58.22.86)

Pétoncles Farcis à la Provençale
(Stuffed Scallops Provençal-Style), page 42;
Salade de Haricots Verts aux
Noisettes Fraîches *(Salad of Haricots
Verts and Green Hazelnuts)*, page 111;
Salade Tiède de Rougets aux
Artichauts *(Warm Red Mullet and
Artichoke Salad)*, page 114

Le Mas du Langoustier
Île de Porquerolles
(494.58.30.09; fax 494.58.36.02)

Gâteau d'Ail Confit
*(Garlic Custard with Chanterelles
and Parsley Sauce)*, page 30;
Dorade Farcie Grillée
(Grilled Stuffed Sea Bream), page 155

Relais Notre-Dame
Quinson
(492.74.40.01; fax 492.74.02.18)

Grand Aïoli
*(Vegetables and Salt Cod
with Garlic Sauce)*,
page 259

PYRENEES
•
Gîte Cal Pai
Cal Pai, Eyne
(468.04.06.96)

Épaule d'Agneau à la Catalane
(Catalan-Style Shoulder of Lamb),
page 234

La Formatgeria de Llívia
Pla de Ro, Gorguja
Llivia, Girona, Spain
(011.34.972.146.279)

Trinxat *(Catalan Cabbage and Potatoes)*,
page 262

Index

Table of Equivalents

THE EXACT EQUIVALENTS IN THE FOLLOWING TABLES HAVE BEEN ROUNDED FOR CONVENIENCE.

LIQUID AND DRY MEASURES

U.S.	METRIC
¼ teaspoon	1.25 milliliters
½ teaspoon	2.5 milliliters
1 teaspoon	5 milliliters
1 tablespoon (3 teaspoons)	15 milliliters
1 fluid ounce (2 tablespoons)	30 milliliters
¼ cup	65 milliliters
⅓ cup	80 milliliters
1 cup	235 milliliters
1 pint (2 cups)	480 milliliters
1 quart (4 cups, 32 ounces)	950 milliliters
1 gallon (4 quarts)	3.8 liters
1 ounce (by weight)	28 grams
1 pound	454 grams
2.2 pounds	1 kilogram

LENGTH MEASURES

U.S.	METRIC
⅛ inch	3 millimeters
¼ inch	6 millimeters
½ inch	12 millimeters
1 inch	2.5 centimeters

OVEN TEMPERATURES

FAHRENHEIT	CELSIUS	GAS
250	120	½
275	140	1
300	150	2
325	160	3
350	180	4
375	190	5
400	200	6
425	220	7
450	230	8
475	240	9
500	260	10

J. P. Donleavy's
IRELAND

Novels

The Beastly Beatitudes of Balthazar B
The Destinies of Darcy Dancer, Gentleman
A Fairy Tale of New York
The Ginger Man
Leila
The Onion Eaters
Schultz
A Singular Man

Novella

The Saddest Summer of Samuel S

Plays

The Plays of J. P. Donleavy

Short Stories and Sketches

Meet My Maker the Mad Molecule

Others

De Alfonce Tennis
The Superlative Game of Eccentric Champions,
Its History, Accoutrements, Rules and Regimen

The Unexpurgated Code
A Complete Manual of Survival and Manners

J. P. Donleavy's
IRELAND

In All Her Sins
And in Some of Her Graces

VIKING

Published in 1986 by Viking Penguin Inc.
40 West 23rd Street, New York, N.Y. 10010, U.S.A.

This book was designed and produced by
The Rainbird Publishing Group,
27 Wrights Lane, Kensington, London W8 5TZ

ISBN 0–670–81318–4

Library of Congress Catalog Card Number 85–41074 CIP data available

All the photographs in the book are from J. P. Donleavy's Archives
with the exception of the following: Ernest Gebler (page 121 above);
Stephen Hyde (page 220); The *Irish Times* (page 116 above and
page 136); E. Barrett Prettyman Jr (page 189); and photographer
Richard Simmonds (page 210) who the publishers would like to thank
for permission to reproduce their photographs.

The text was set by Wyvern Typesetting Ltd, Bristol, England
Mono origination by Butler & Tanner Ltd, Frome, Somerset, England
Printed and bound by Butler & Tanner Ltd, Frome, Somerset, England

To my Galway Mother
and
To my Longford Father

The latter whose comment upon Ireland
was

'They haven't got a pot to piss in'

I

The ocean beats pearl white against its high dark cliffs and spills a green tinted water on its sallow beaches. To look down from the skies, the tiny fields below are soft, silent and green in their inno- cence. From brown bogs and purple brighter moorlands, its streams and lakes shine silver. Upon the land that long knows how to tolerate suffering.

But to many of its native born winter non shivering inhabitants, it is a shrunken teat on the chest of the cold Atlantic. From which little of life's bare necessities and less of its joys or juices can be squeezed. And whose grey skies and sodden winds, force the mind to dream. Of other realms and to communicate with an almighty Gaelic god for whom this land alone is worthy of his blessings. And where, if only a horse could speak, we would know most about this citizenry.

Still, to more than a few, Ireland remains a glowingly sweet emerald vision having the fifteenth beer over some bereft bar counter at three a.m. in some outskirt corner of San Francisco, Hawaii, Boston or the Bronx. As patriotic and sentimental songs croak from drink sodden throats celebrating its heroes who fought and sometimes died for its flag. But rarely would it ever be a once bog trotter remembering his summer sweat in the seldom sun, pausing to spit again upon his hands, cutting turf back in a bog in that land. Or a once poor boy on a poor farm, who would at three hours past midnight, drive cattle ten miles through foggy darknesses to market and stand cold through a damp day to drive them back home again, unsold. It is a rare brogue whose vowels still purr lovingly com- memorating the land of his birth, for all its saints, its absence of sinners and its abundance of scholars.

But for many an innocent visiting foreigner, its once unspoilt green shores now enclose unsightlinesses of such stupendous multiplicity to be cited as an example to the rest of the world. Ruined cities with their ancient buildings toppled in decay. Street after street unloved and smashed to smithereens by the gombeen man. Plumbing, detergents and soft toilet paper have come. To leave a debris and litter strewn nation, already long past beginning to spew poisons all over its once clean grey skies. Of this, the land of the welcomes. But now of the packaged tourist. Who finds himself happily fleeced in the biggest clip joint in Western Europe. Ah, but this latter is only because the unsimple minded Erse need your money more than you do, and firmly believe you won't miss it, if they take more than they are entitled to.

The Irishman's faith in his own perennial poverty is as deep and unshakable as his belief in the foreigner's eternal wealth. For how could that latter stranger, across an inclement ocean and sea, afford to get here in the first place. But unlike most of the indifferent French or exacting Germans, the Irishman as he attempts to mulct you, will not infrequently murmur a compensatingly humorous turn of phrase or pretend to grin a smile that is on the lips but not in the heart. But at least such gladsome shallowness has made this island universally known for the friendly if not honest, disposition of the people. Who in recent years, since the advent of visual images beamed across the sky and landing to be seen and heard uncensored by the native naked eye, have become subject to one of the most astonishing social and cultural revolutions ever to hit and wreak near havoc upon any people of any nation on earth.

It all must have begun on one innocent day. In England. Where there is a corporation called British Broadcasting. This organization is the most amoral and to some large degree, fair minded, disseminator of information the world has ever known. And the Irish knowledge of the English language provided ready ears and eyes to see and hear the news of freedom of the flesh and mind. And the young, the eager and the frustrated set this conflagration of upheaval alight. Human nakedness had come. Along with aesthetic ideas out of the minds of agnostic men. Gods, other than the Irish god, made known. Four letter words and four letter deeds. In all their graphic technicolour splendour. Forcing many an aesthete who still lurks sheepishly in this land, and whose sensibilities outrage enough, to incite the founding of societies, not only for the prevention of cruelty to innocent grassland, trees and buildings, but also the prevention of cruelty to the spirit of Irish human beings.

And who am I to talk. Or explain. Or raise a finger to admonish, point or accuse. Or cast a first stone. Or say this land is not what it could be. Or should remain what it was. Or even murmur about the cunning gombeen man who might desecrate and sell off this nation and bring it to its derelict sorrowful knees. It is my nation. Mine. Where I am a citizen. Both by blood and convenience. Who became so, entitled as I always was by virtue of the Irish birth of my parents. I was for seven years educated here. While sheltering between times in the cloistered peace of Trinity College Dublin, I took my degree in drinking and harlotry out in the better pubs, at many an abysmal party, or in an occasional elegant restaurant, or even at an occasional stately home, where someone was usually being hammered on the head down the main staircase by a bottle of stout. Punishment given for having split an infinitive. And from this I then vanished. With my ill and random got credentials. To be in cities and places like Boston, London and New York. Or isolated on the Isle of Man. And then, years later, having walked into Fortnum and Mason's in London for tea one afternoon, my wine adviser Mr Young said in some surprise, 'Mr Donleavy what are you still doing here when authors have just become tax free in Ireland.' And only weeks later I found myself speeding up a pollution haunted highway from London to Liverpool. To take the mail boat and land in Dublin. Hopeful, in spite of all my history here, and what they did to *The Ginger Man* in Dublin, that I would upon returning to these emerald pastures, become a resident, and be tax eternally free for my future and past creative scribbles.

Not only from that above do I assume my right to speak, especially against those who would assume I have no such right. But knowing too, that my authority to so utter, is not only warranted but greater and more than most, descending as I do on both parental sides from ancient bog trotters back into the dawn of ages. And hold the name of such tribes for proof. But my privilege arises, too, from a voice oft banned and shunned within these shores but which has already spoken for more than thirty years, saying a song of at times bitter love, yet of love for this land.

I am a 'narrowback'. This I was early called by the novelist, poet and revolutionary, Brendan Behan upon first reaching these shores. It was a term learned by Behan from one, A. K. Donoghue, who like myself, had come to Trinity College Dublin following World War II. Donoghue, a Harvard graduate in Classics, was Boston Irish. And 'narrowback' was a term used by Irish born immigrant Americans to

My four Irish grandparents standing in front of the Donleavy barn in Co. Longford. It became a Donleavy tradition to be photographed in front of one's barn instead of the house. Alas most of the Donleavys had no barns in America, but most did at least have their pots to piss in.

refer to the first generation of Irish born in America of Irish born parents whose backs, broad from the old country, now toiled to rear the narrower backs of their children in the New World. Never having heard the term before, Behan relished the word, and I, as one then quite self consciously American, took it to be derogatory. Behan, then recently released from prison, and I, were that afternoon's joke being played upon us when we were introduced to each other as writers. A term, when then said in our conspicuously unpublished circumstances, was equally meant derogatorily. And not that many moments later, outside Davy Byrnes pub, Behan, his shirt open to his navel and the tongues of his shoes hanging out like a panting dog's, and I, in grey herringbone tweed, were facing each other to fight in the middle of Duke Street. As we squared off, Behan suddenly lowered his fists, and at his most carefully diplomatic put forth his hand to shake mine. To say, 'Why should we give them dirty eegits back sitting in there in the pub, who wouldn't even leave their drinks to watch us fight, the fucking satisfaction of thinking we had.' Behan and I, thereafter, if we did not ever become firm trusting friends, we certainly at least always remained close enemies.

Ah, but let us go back. To where I first ever became conscious of this land. It was inside a cinema at the foot of one of the highest hills in the Bronx, an area extending north of New York City, with pot holed streets and an odd large manor house, around which were still retained open space, and the neighbourhood was known as Wakefield. My very first awareness of Ireland came in the shadowy scenes of a film of Liam O'Flaherty's *The Informer*. To me, a small boy, Victor McLaglen the actor seemed massive, powerful and invincible. His shoulders heaving up under a great weight. And later, being shot by many bullets he went staggering undying along the street displaying a feat of endurance as his life ebbed away in death. And he then, and all these years since, reminded me of my own father. Who could throw a young bull down on its side or lift gracefully in the palm of his hand, a full grown man above his head.

I cannot remember another impression of Ireland until, having

This house was where I lived until the age of six in America. On top of one of the highest hills in New York and with the exception of a German family living on a small estate next door, most of the remaining immediate neighbours were Italian. But it was at the foot of the hill upon which this house stood where I saw the film of Liam O'Flaherty's The Informer.

In Van Cortland Park, The Bronx, my father, myself and my younger brother Thomas (T. J.) who latterly became a resident of Greystones albeit mostly secretly. Living as he did behind closed shutters as the sea spray battered the windows and he painted his pictures inside with frozen fingers.

moved away from Wakefield, a mile or two westwards across the valley of the Bronx river, to a small community called Woodlawn. These several streets intersecting a main street, and resembling a small midwestern town formed a place triangular in shape and cut off from New York on all three sides by two extensive parks, and a large cemetery. It was here in the front hall of our house on 236th Street that a telegram was delivered to my father informing him of his own father's death at the age of ninety three. As my father stood there, there were tears which I had never before seen in his eyes. And even as the event remained strange and unfamiliar, I was somehow conscious of something and somewhere which existed untouchable and unknown, far away out of my own world.

My father was one of the middle youngest boys in a family of fourteen. He and several sisters and most of his brothers had emigrated to America. Leaving land the Donleavys had occupied and still do, near Granard Co. Longford, as far back in the centuries as anyone can trace or remember. And my next consciousness of Ireland came when one of my father's brother's wives had died and I spent a late afternoon in a funeral parlour somewhere deep down town in this poorer part of New York City. I played or at least conferred with two cousins who were at their mother's wake. Who were trying to explain to me in the funeral parlour's lavatory that they were circumcised. Although I did not know it at the time, there must have been the Erse haunting ghosts within the tinted lit rooms and a banshee outside the window wailing under the thundering passing wheels of the elevated train. The world of sombre Ireland, where the memory of the dead is forever living, was hovering here. Amid the dark whispers within the words of fond recall. For someone, lips to lips, kissed the corpse of this still beautiful young woman in her coffin. And·I sensed, in that curious stretch of the Irish imagination.

That death
Is God
And living
Is unholy

II

In the ethnically mixed community of Woodlawn where I was growing up, one or two of my earliest playing friends' names were Irish, like Hennessy and Farrell, but more of my pals were Italian, German and even Dutch. With names like Briggi, Gerosa, Kuntze and Rotterhan. The friend Hennessy never mentioned Ireland. Indeed his first foreign reference was when he spoke his newly learned words of French to me. Vous êtes stupide. Italian was the other alien sound one heard in which one early learned to curse and profane. And as one grew up, conscious of being in one of the most fabled and talked about capitals in the world, not an Irish word or sentiment did I ever hear said. And even St Patrick's Day was everybody's day and many a Jew and Muslim sported a shamrock and wore a green tie.

But in the early years of the nineteen forties on a summer Saturday night on a windswept peninsula sticking out from the eastern shore of Long Island, my first full revelation of Ireland and the Irish unfolded. Reached by train across a long bridge of marsh and bay with islands and channels and names like Canarsie, Pumpkin Patch, Big Egg, Little Egg and Winhole Hassock, Rockaway as it was called, was a bereft long strip of sand dune on the shores of the Atlantic Ocean. It was here on a street full of bars, that I first heard a live Ceili band, saw Irish dancing and rubbed shoulders with the pure and simple Irish like myself. Two or three of my friends, champion swimmers, spent their summers here, working as lifeguards on these crowded sands which lay along the ocean front. The peninsula's length was cross sectioned by streets of summer boarding houses and a boardwalk along a mile or two of beach which could be jammed by New York's lower middle class poor in their thousands on New York's oven hot sultry days. Through open windows at night one could hear the crowded life packed in these wooden framed and porched houses. On a street, 103rd Street, saloons and bars were next

...ily. From the left, Donald, Carol and Alan, in ...raction and their father German. Donald, a ...ate me into boxing and wrestling which one ...iend and both brothers would gently threaten ...heir sister who was an early girlfriend.

...this, one of my first overnight unchaperoned trips, got drunk for the first time. And later, lurching in the dark on the boardwalk was nearly arrested by a benign Irish policeman voicing his concern that 'A kid drunk at your age is a disgrace'. And a young friend Richard Gallagher, upon his pale Irish skin got the worst sunburn of his life.

But I remember the fiddle playing and the strange dancing and jigs taking place in the centre of the large roomed saloon. The long bar, and the beer frothing as the glasses landed thump on the mahogany and upended down the throats. I found no pain in drinking as did everyone else, one glass after another. I met and danced with a handsome girl of raven black hair and blue eyes and a splendid smile. And was mystified by her presence here instead of at one of my more polite afternoon tea dances at Fordham Preparatory School where no girl had ever been as beautiful. Back in the city I saw her again. And went to a party down in the Irish ghetto where she lived. Finding it

Photographed here with two cousins, my father standing with his constant cigar to hand behind me, his brother Jim to his right. At this time I had just completed my first naval training and was later to get a fleet appointment to the Naval Academy and to prior attend the Naval Academy Preparatory School easily one of the world's strangest institutions of learning and where I first heard the name of James Joyce and wrote my first writing which ever received critically appreciative notice.

strange to be, as the saying was, among me own. And yet feel singularly alien.

My next awareness and the first awakening of an interest in Ireland came in the strangest of places. A unique school in the Navy. Throughout my relatively short service career I had become obsessed with not dying as an ordinary seaman swabbing decks. If I were to sacrifice my life for my country I wanted to do it as someone of some rank as high as possible and preferably as an admiral. I had risen to the low heights of second class seaman with a qualification of radar man. And had been assigned to an amphibious landing ship. I forget the reason now why I did not sail with her to the Pacific but my next ship to which I was assigned was a much more lethal weapon feared by both those at whom it was aimed and equally by all those aboard her. Such ship taking up its station off the beach at sea and armed with launchers and 100 tons of rockets, the vessel for three hours had the firepower of a battleship. The Japanese chose them as the first items to blast by any means out of the water, which was simplicity itself once they were hit. Although I always heartily lent my voice to the corps' song which graphically embodied its purpose and intentions, 'Off To The Beach Fighting Amphibians, We Sail At Break Of Day', I nevertheless preferred to command a flotilla of these ships, rather than have my life disrupted forever while merely sitting and watching a radar screen. When I heard about a chance to go to the Naval Academy, I rather think I jumped at it.

Although I had succeeded in the Navy in passing exams, both mental and physical, my academic record was otherwise unimpressive, not to say mildly appalling. In fact an officer interviewing prospective candidates to sit the Naval Academy appointment exam, point blank refused me permission, saying I had no chance against the records of other candidates he'd seen. It was a rare and perhaps the only occasion in my life I had ever verged upon pleading with someone. And was benefitted by having chosen a moment that this officer was in a desperate hurry to go out and play golf, and simply to get rid of me from the room, ended up giving me permission. Out of the many who took the exam on this base of 10,000 men, I ended up being the only one who got an appointment to the Naval Academy. Still to this day, I do not know what became of the two amphibious crews I left behind and who sailed southwest without me.

But there was before this, one other early factor of Irish influence in my life. Unlike all my other young friends growing up in America, I had an enlightened and wise mother who forbade soda pop, chocolate, fats and all American junk food and insisted they be avoided with the expression, 'You must eat something which will stick to your ribs'. So along with brown bread and other wholesome pure foods many of which were home grown and bottled by my parents, I was also fed upon oats out of a shamrock adorned, green tin imported from Ireland. My mother extolling to me that such oats came from the most fertile of ground, rained upon by the cleanest heavens and sprouted up in the purest of air. All of which distinctions the word Irish now became associated with.

However, the Naval Academy Preparatory School was where I first heard the name James Joyce. The school, formerly the Tome School for boys and taken over by the Navy, stood luxuriously in its parkland splendour in Maryland, precipitously overlooking the Susquehanna River and the tiny town Port Deposit which was

hidden with its single long main street pressed between the river and the steep rising hill behind, upon which the school stood. Having received an appointment to the Naval Academy, it entitled the appointee to attend an academic year to prepare for the final entrance exams to the Naval Academy. A Professor of English now a Chief Petty Officer in the Navy and recruited from the fleet, was our English instructor. This erudite droll gentleman who was widely acquainted not only with literature, but with a splendid variety of jokes, managed, in the context of war and the military, to enthrall an extremely intelligent but nearly deliberately illiterate class. For the most illiterate of whom I ghost wrote their required themes. As these were read aloud to the class our instructor remarked concerning touches of James Joyce he perceived in the writing. Shattered to know someone had already imitated me I repaired to the mostly deserted school library, and immediately searched out and read the little I could find mentioned of this gentleman. Who seemed described as a combination of renegade Catholic and former medical student who, as a blaspheming anti christ, profane and pagan, drank and caroused his way through Dublin with his cronies, and who had in a stream of consciousness written somewhat obscenely about his native city. I lost no time in looking up Dublin in the encyclopedia. From which I gleaned three principal superlatives. That Dublin was possessed of the world's biggest brewery, that Phoenix Park was one of the largest municipal parks in the world, and that O'Connell Street was one of the widest thoroughfares in Europe. None of these facts may have been true then or are true now but they, all three, remained fixed indelibly in my imagination and became the first adult things I knew about Ireland.

The war suddenly over, and on a spring afternoon amid the gentle rolling hills of Maryland, discharged from the Navy, I exited the gates of this naval base for the last time. But remained pleasantly haunted by the widest street in Europe. Imagining it as I did, lined with trees. A spacious boulevard upon which one could contentedly stroll or

(Opposite) *My mother in the United States. Although taken as she said, barefoot from an Irish field she was brought to America by a rich Australian uncle and her indoctrination there took place in the company of an elegant lady in private railway cars and the suites of famed hotels across America. My mother was never impressed by America's modern way of life or its wonder foods and I was always forbidden white bread and soda pop and fed on our own compost grown garden produce.*

stride, arms stretched out to the world. Wander in its biggest park or drink a brew from its vast brewery. I still vividly recalled the abdication radio broadcast of a King of England. And prior to this monarch's speech, the nine o'clock tolling of the bell, Big Ben. And the strange profundity it proclaimed. Aware that Europe was a more ancient place than America. And with a heavier accent on the living of life. Where, although one might not be encouraged to, a fart might be called a fart.

Towards the end of the war a few old friends were turning up. Some of whom, in military service, had been to Europe. And one with whom I'd been at prep school and who lived in the nearby community of Yonkers. While stationed in England he went on a weekend leave to Ireland. With some relish and amusement he described a Dublin pub. The closeted privacy of little cubby holes into which you might go to drink a strange black beer called Guinness. And that you could order things like cheese, sausages or a pickled onion. The mystery of the word stout which was lifted up to the lips and which I'd seen mentioned in Joyce's *Ulysses*, was solved. Somehow this brief description of a public house in Ireland made a memorable impression on me. I imagined somewhere safe, timeless, cosy and insulated from the world.

Except for my hearing of James Joyce and knowing that John Barry, Wexford born in Ireland, had distinguished himself enough to be called the father of the American navy, nothing else Irish crossed my sights during my brief naval career. But now having left the service it was time to try to go to college. With my poor academic record not much improved at the Naval Academy Preparatory School, I applied to various East Coast Ivy League American higher institutions of learning. And then to more obscure institutions further west as far away as Wisconsin, before I could get anyone to even consider to take me. As I was now nearly having to search across 3,000 miles and with the vision still vivid of my friend eating cheese in a pub in a stray beam of Dublin sunlight, and the widest street in Europe, I, out of the blue, asked my Irish Galway born mother, were there any colleges in Ireland. Her instant singular reply was Trinity College Dublin. Again I rushed to my tiny and local library for the address, which I discovered was simply that. University of Dublin, Trinity College, Dublin.

I wrote off immediately. Luck, combined with their unavoidable ignorance of American academic qualifications, which I must have attempted vaguely to glorify, had W. B. Stanford, my duly appointed tutor, writing back acknowledging receiving a testimonial from a former principal, and without further ado said that classes would begin on 21 October 1946 and that it would be advisable to arrive some days beforehand as it might be necessary to find accommodation in the city at first. And for the first time I saw the use of the word Esquire after one's name.

Ireland began to become a strange almost unIrish destination. Almost as if one might think one was going to the legendary gaiety and boulevards of Paris. At first I booked to go by ship. The word spreading fast of my departure among friends. Who thought the whole idea more humorous than anything else. In the boxing room of the New York Athletic Club, Commodore Manning, captain of the S.S. *America*, wrote me a note to take when booking my passage on that ship. Then, all set for Europe, suddenly a port strike occurred. And I found myself arriving at Idlewild airport, as it was then known, to go much more expensively by plane.

My departure presented what must have been two of the most enjoyable days for my father. As we gained speed down the runway for take off, the plane suddenly slowed, stopped, turned around and taxied back to the terminal. At some mechanical fault afoot, we disembarked. No one in those days left an airport until a plane had disappeared safely into the sky. So passengers were again greeted by their friends. Both travellers and all their guests were conducted into a lounge for drinks and to the restaurant for lunch and the rest of the morning, afternoon and day went by while they were lavishly unstintingly entertained by the airline. Until the flight that day was finally cancelled, and I returned home with my parents. Next morning there was again the day long drive across the Bronx and Brooklyn and the same thing happened half way down the runway and a similar day unfolded of celebration and meals. I stayed that night in the New Yorker Hotel. And an airline limousine this time brought me back to the airport where my parents again awaited.

For two whole days of the aircraft's delay I was conscious of my father's big hands wrapped around his complimentary drinks, his fingernails garden darkened with soil in contrast to the sleekness of the airport lounge. As stories were swapped in this predominantly Irish group, I could hear my father's spontaneous and uninhibited roars of laughter. And I should have realized that growing up in the vicinity of my father's brogue, Ireland was being inculcated into me without my ever knowing. For throughout his life in America, my father, except for his constant smoking of cigars, remained as Irish as Ireland. Even to the taking up of the writing of poetry. And in the way he walked and looked at life. Like a poor farmer surveying his cattle in the field. Just as we would both go on an evening stroll during our family summer trips while growing up, which took us through the mid west. And my father, his hands folded behind his back, his interest keen in all around him and his insatiable asking of questions of anyone friendly enough to answer as we walked the main street of a prairie town surrounded to the horizon by fields of corn and the lonesome wail of freight trains.

As the ice tinkled in the glasses of whiskey during that forty eight hour delay, my parents befriended several of the passengers among whom was an ebullient gentleman called O'Callaghan. This silver haired handsome man, known to his friends as the silver fox of Wall Street, was full of laughter and hand rubbing optimisms on this his impending return to Ireland after many years away. Underlying his rakish elegant American patina was a thoroughly Irish soul. One of those people to whose coat tails one can attach and fly behind. And as he had met my parents and from their many hours of airport reverie together, I was in a manner entrusted to him to be looked after on this bleak trip out into the sky of the Atlantic Ocean.

The flight took something like fourteen hours. Flying first north to land for refuelling as it was growing dark on a cold bereft airport at Gander, Newfoundland. Disembarking and walking across a chill windswept ground to what seemed a barren grey building, there hardly appeared any human life save for a man standing warming his hands at the glow of an open fire in a barrel at the edge of the airfield. Runway lights again lit, the four propellors on the wings of this great long hawk beaked fuselage, roared. To take off over such strange dark cold names and places as Loon Bay, Fogo and Joe Batts Arm. And fly bumping up into the heavens again. Ireland beyond assumed a dark bewitchment on the other side of the world. In the black October sky, droning on towards dawn across the deeps of the Labrador Current and the Gulf Stream Drift far below. Coifed, tailored, starlet attractive hostesses patiently dancing attendance upon every journeyer's whim. Up and down the narrow aisle of the smoky aircraft, the constant interchange of passengers calling upon each other in their seats. The growing exhilaration in the anticipation of Ireland. As if arrival there were the answer to all eternal problems and prayers. The clinking of drinks being lofted into mouths. Every hour or two O'Callaghan would come conspiratorially to my elbow to inquire if I were having as good a time as he was and encouragingly pat me upon the back. And then descending through the thick cloud with daylight flooding east, suddenly below, a broad estuary, tiny islands and then low hills, nestling lakes and ponds gleaming black and then flashing silver. The first browny green sight of those small meandering fields clustered about some white tiny cottage with turf smoke rising from its chimney on this windswept land that reached to the edge of the great heaving Atlantic Ocean.

There were cheers as we landed at Shannon. And there was at least one passenger who made as if to kneel and kiss the wet ground. As all Americans do they regard foreign officialdom as being some toy game the natives play. But one of the returned exiles who had not yet achieved the sophistication of this patronising attitude, was carrying a large bundle of Irish currency he had bought at a discount in New York and when asked if he had any currency to declare, confessed. Fetching up the massive wad of bills out of his pocket in a fit of honesty to have the lot promptly confiscated by bemused customs officials eager to oblige. Tears now in the exile's eyes as he announced that he could not find it in himself to lie to his countrymen. A much more worldly gentleman, O'Callaghan, commenting on this imprudent act of candour, that foolish though it was, he nevertheless understood the overwhelmed feelings of this fellow Irishman. Although he thought he might have better kept the money in his pocket and dispose of it celebrating and be sure that illegal currency or not, every customs man able to bend his elbow would join him in the nearest pub.

While awaiting another plane to take me on to Dublin, I noticed the big crystal grains of sugar in the bowls of the restaurant where the tables were covered in neat white table cloths. The thick slabs of bacon and gleaming, deep orange yolked fried eggs on a plate. The butter a golden yellow white. The soda bread brown with bran. Following breakfast, a sliver of sun suddenly shafted down between the sweeping clouds. Out in the intoxicatingly clean, cool, moist fresh air, I walked a short distance away from the cluster of single storied white frame buildings and along a road into surrounding open countryside. On my feet were a pair of black and white saddle shoes. Perhaps the first ever seen in Europe. The lane wound gently between iridescent velvet green pastures. To where I suddenly came upon a pond with three swans. In the lonely silence, their stunning eloquent whiteness on the gentle black water was miraculous and a moment of unforgettable beauty. Ireland in one of her graces, leaving for me to discover yet, her sins.

And the grey

Rains

Not yet sprinkling

In one's heart

III

There was the choice of an all day train or less than an hour plane to Dublin. And in my first of many Irish extravagances I chose to fly, joining the ebullient O'Callaghan who was exerting his delight in all directions and who was in a marvellous hurry to get there. It was on that flight that I first encountered what other American college friends I was soon to meet, referred to as the Irish 'hook' and 'crut'. Both chronic conditions interrelated as they caused and perpetuated each other.

On board the two engined propellor plane, sitting next to me, was a youngish man who had business at Shannon and was returning to Dublin. In telling him that I had come to Ireland to attend Trinity College, he immediately launched into a painstakingly offhand explanation as to how I had made an awful mistake in not choosing University College, Dublin's other and Catholic higher institution of learning, instead. His vague reasons did sound suspicious to me, but as we were bouncing around in the clouds and I had a moderate disposition towards getting airsick, one may have had other discomforting things to worry about. And I don't know how deep my heart sank or if it did, but I did wonder how my usually extremely wise Galway mother could have let me down.

In Dublin, O'Callaghan had a hectic social round to attend to, meeting old cronies, friends and visiting with his elderly father who lived with his sister, and he kept a taxi on tap as he sped hither and thither in and about Dublin and its environs. In a nearby suburb called Monkstown, I had found someone, recommended on the Irish grapevine to America, with whom to stay, a policeman, a massive gentleman, as they nearly all were in those days, and his attractive wife. A small house near where a church stood dividing the road on which roared the double decker green upholstered trams. In a cold, clean, neat, unadorned room, waking up to my second sample of tastily delicious tea, bacon and eggs for breakfast. Encountering, without yet knowing it, my first taste of Irish bemused curiosity which provoked a shy smile on the beholders' lips as they listened to the naturally optimistic American accent and had their attentions caught by the appreciably brighter clothes from the New World.

Still in an unrelenting blaze of enthusiasm, O'Callaghan was ecstatically continuing his round of visiting. One or two of his former associates in his younger days were now ministers in the government. And he took a delight in visiting them at their offices exchanging presents and getting an export licence for a side of bacon from the very heads of government. He was amused to recall their less resplendent days as patriots, but remembered the glamour of his own and his friends' rank in the War of Independence, as being that equivalent to generals. And now they had their own nice little nation, and had he stayed he nostalgically reminded himself that he too would probably now be a minister of state.

It was with O'Callaghan that I went to my first Irish country house. Speeding the dark roads on a Sunday night in a noisy taxi between high granite walls, the canopy of tree branches closing like the entrance to a dark cave ahead of us as the dim headlights faintly peered into the blackness. Till finally we reached a pair of gates, wheels crunching the gravel, swept past a small gate lodge to motor up a long drive through spacious parklands. An array of ancient cars parked on this great pebbled apron before this ochre yellow mansion. And inside surprised by its warmth and grandeur. The elegance of its circular black and white tiled front hall. The soft carpets, fires blazing in the grate. Guests in black tie. The flowing abundance of food and drink. And my own unconscious bemusement at the luxury one had not expected and the easy pleasant welcome of one's presence. As I voiced my concern to my hostess over my choice of university, it was unequivocally pointed out to me that not only was I to attend the most important and revered of all Irish institutions but even being so much as a student at Trinity conferred upon one a social entitlement second to none in the city of Dublin. And with relief and pleasure, one departed this beautiful lady in her long white satin gown, reassured that I could cheerfully look forward to my years at Trinity College Dublin.

In a Georgian mansion off Fitzwilliam Square, I was introduced to O'Callaghan's sister, a marvellous cook and hostess. O'Callaghan's father, a charming and still handsome man in his nineties, lay abed where he managed to read a novel a day and only laughed to say that occasionally it took him a day and a half. It was here in this Dublin townhouse where I first encountered sherry prior to Sunday lunch. And the sacred ritual of such things as roast beef and Yorkshire pudding with black uniformed maids scurrying back and forth to keep the chill from superlative gravies, roast potatoes and Brussels sprouts. And following the spongy sweet delight of trifle, to withdraw upstairs to the drawing room, where a black stove nestled in the white marble chimney piece blazed out heat while one lay back on the soft upholstered sofas to listen to Mozart on a gramophone. And where it might not be found impolite if at four before tea, one had nodded on a chaise longue, sound asleep.

From my temporary lodging in Monkstown I stepped out in a moist mild breeze on this my first official day as a student at Trinity. And walked past the small front gardens in a moment of morning sunshine, the smell of the sea in the air blowing in over Dublin Bay. Near the church at the fork in the road, I boarded the wood panelled and green upholstered tram. Climbing up its narrow stairs to the top of its two tiers. Able to look from the windows down into the passing walled green suburban gardens. Their monkey puzzle trees, laurels, rhododendrons and subtropical greenery verdantly proclaiming the respectability of the inhabitants. This utterly beautiful vehicle's bell clanging as it roared and swayed on its iron wheels along its shiny tracks, destined to come to a final halt at a tall pillar of granite on which stood a statue of Nelson on that widest of European boulevards in the city of Dublin.

I was not to know this first day that this road and route were to play such a significant role in one's Irish life. The tram turning right into Newtownpark Avenue, and abruptly left again parallel with the coast of the sea. Roaring past the town hall and a tiny house standing but a few feet beyond the weathered ancient stone cross which marked the pale. This house with one door and window opening on the pavement and a single window above on the upstairs floor, was to become an historic location in one's college days. The tram now dipped down into the village of Blackrock past O'Rourke's public house and up a hill again along the higher Rock Road where one could see down into a small bereft park and out across the grey waters of Dublin Bay to North Bull Island and the mount of Howth the other side. I never tired of this marvellous journey. And the sight of the funerals with their black plumed gleaming horses pulling the coffins which rested in peace behind the polished glass of the hearse. Either on their way to or returning from the Grange Cemetery, the horse cabs would be seen pulled up waiting outside a pub, the bereaved inside being refreshed. From the tram, too, one could peer into the odd uncurtained window of the row of substantial suburban houses along Merrion Road. Perhaps see an electric fire's glow on some fitted purple Wilton carpet which gave one hope that one's own feet, now grown so cold, could somehow hope to be thawed again. Or at least such interiors gave the assurance that there were more than a few in this land who had more than a pot to piss in.

High and mighty elegant hopes could be inflamed, too, passing through the great Georgian square of Merrion, enclosed by its soft red brick elevations and fenestrations showing over the tips of its central park tree tops. An American flag fluttering in the breeze in front of that Consulate. And mention on a plaque of Oscar Wilde's name on a house on the northwest corner. Dublin all in a cultural handful. For that so oft, ad nauseam quoted piece of information that Handel's *Messiah* was first performed in Dublin, happened just fifty paces away. Nearby I alighted at an intersection in Clare Street. Just beyond the glass canopy over the open stalls in front of Greene's book shop. Stepping for the first time on the great grey granite paving stones worn smooth with a hundred years of feet. A chemist's window full of a rainbow of bottled salts. A feeling that the morning was being born. More shop front windows, decorated with loaves of bread, a café, Johnson Mooney & O'Brien's, serving cakes, tea and coffee inside and where, together with students of medicine and natural science, I was to occasionally sit in the pale daylight from its ceiling skylights.

Directly across from the back gates of Trinity College stood a middle eastern architectural extravagance, an eastern mosque with pinnacles, which once upon a Dublin time, housed Turkish baths. Which should tell all that ever need be known about this Dublin city of bizarre dreams. The remnants of which dot every street, dispossessed monuments to fervently possessed hopes. Yet on a building's door nearly opposite the mosque is an oft shined brass plaque. One of the rare few things of high intentioned endeavour that remains comfortably unerased and still gleaming to the day of this writing.

THE MISSION TO LEPERS

Outside number 38 Trinity College and wearing the clothes I wore on my first arrival in Ireland, including black and white saddle shoes and holding onto the slung chains over which myself and other occasional undergraduates would, with belly bent, drape when returning from Dublin's pubs.

This brief stretch of street at the back Trinity gates also possessed an emporium for the treatment of teeth, the dental hospital. From whence I did, in all my time passing, always await a scream of anguished pain to emit from the darkened red brick building. But nary a sound ever emerged as I went in and out between the tall grey granite piers holding open these massive college gates. Through which, on this my first day, I stepped to confront a porter in his dark tail coated uniform, fox hunting cap on his head and who directed me forward to my tutor's office in Front Square, the other end of the college. Past these shadowy grey science buildings, wherein I would spend woefully few hours of my university years and those, all daydreamingly academically wasteful.

But I seemed more attentive in one building on a little rise on the left. Gold letters over the entrance proclaiming Pathology. Wide granite steps up to its oak doors. In there one did more than occasionally redden a spatula in the flame of a bunsen burner and bend over the oil immersion lens of a microscope to drop gentian violet stain upon some of these tiny organisms. Opposite on this back road into Trinity is the Chemistry building. And here amid the bottles

and bubbling, my hours were at their most bereft. I could never filtrate, titrate or make my experiments go pop like the rest of you. Certain was I that if I did mix together what I thought they said I should, there would be, if not a violently lethal, then at least one god awfully embarrassing explosion.

Standing a low squat building surveying the cricket pitch was the sports pavilion. Somehow always reminding me of a river steamer boat, which might, afloat, flags fluttering, take one on a picnic. Its tiers facing south and overlooking the splendidly mown grass. Many a time students collected there when spring mercifully came, to bathe in the warming sun. Within its clammy ground floor confines were the great tubs that cleansed mud from the rugby players. It had two showers which became the only place, that memorably cold first winter in Ireland, where myself and an American with whom I shared cold rooms could thaw in a sprinkle of hot water. My room mate, from Southern California, especially requiring hours standing in the steamy downpour. Indeed in his bedroom he lay abed every morning, eight hot water bottles from the night still packed about him and an electric fire perched on a chair faintly shining red rays on his damp blankets as he sipped restorative tea warming his long fingered hands around the green bowl.

Making my way that first day through the oasis of College Park enclosed by massive rhododendrons growing high up against the walls and iron fence along Nassau Street. Shutting out all but the roof and chimney pot tops and tram sounds of the city. To pass through into New Square. Its stark grey buildings to the south, east and north, and the mellow red of the rubrics to the west with its grey green slate roof from which chimneys reared against the sky. Suspended over the cobblestone gutter, the necklace of chain link fence strung round the square from pointed iron palings. Shadows cast by the branches of these ancient plane trees, the gnarled bark of their trunks twisting up from these lawns so flat, green and velvet. My whole life seemed to start here gazing out of my window at number 38. The street aglisten with rain. An occasional early morning fusty academic going

(Opposite) *A winter view of New Square Trinity College Dublin from the sitting room window of number 38. This glistening wet view of an empty college was the most frequent one seen out of my college windows. And it was always possible to identify a visitor long before he or she approached to knock on my door.*

to and fro, slippers shuffling in the wet, kimono held wrapped about him as he scurried from one granite open doorway into another. Not then nor during the many after years could I have ever thought that the pure Irish would ever get their hands on Trinity. To banish its elegance and traditions. Uproot its rhododendrons. Park cars in its sacred confines. And they have. But the ancient fabric of its beauty for the most part has stayed even that destructive hand.

With these black gowned students threading crisscross in Front Square this Monday, 21 October of Michaelmas term, undergraduate lectures in arts and science began. It was, too, according to the College Calendar, the last day for payment of half yearly fees without fines. As I made my way on the cobbles asking directions to my tutor's office, an autumnal sun brightening the grey stone and making the grass gleam emerald. Tall, weather whitened pillars in front of the chapel. And past an entrance in which was located the students' cooperative where, tucked in under the stairs, bread and simple provisions could be bought. My tutor's name so neatly writ white on black at another entrance. My feet thumping up wooden stairs to gently knock on a door on the first landing. Come in please. In the morning rays of sun a handsome wavy haired man stood in a grey pinstripe suit, waistcoat, white shirt and solemn tie, his quietly elegant manners bespeaking the civilized splendours of this university. To whose politely formal but friendly words I tried so hard to show I listened and believed devoutly all that he was saying. Welcome to Trinity. Thank you. He was the great classicist Regius Professor of Greek, William Bedell Stanford. Who had, despite his many charges and much more serious pursuits, marvellously managed to get me rooms in college. And a nice unAmerican touch, that I, a student of science should have as my tutor this scholar of ancient languages.

In the northeast corner of New Square and up a flight of stairs past a landing and behind four large neo Georgian windows were my college chambers. Set in the city like a semi precious jewel of peace and silence. With their giraffe tall ceilings they consisted of an entrance hall, two bedrooms, sitting room and skippery. Although with its own large front window, the latter was but a glorified kitchen with a gas burner, a counter, and a turf box. On a chair was perched a bucket of water. Which each morning was filled by a college servant from a tap alongside the slung chain in the college square. And then lugged up the stairs. I often watched this little ritual of my skip as he was called. His hand arest on the small iron spire of the paling post waiting as his bucket filled. Bicycle clips on his trousers. The brim of his hat down around the edges. Whose bald head one would only see when a lady called when he would, with pleasant military overtones, bow and click his heels to receive her.

My first and nearly last furnishing purchases were a mattress and blue blanket, a bedroom water pitcher, a wash basin, and providing one exception at least to my father's dictum, a pot to piss in. With no indoor plumbing in my rooms at 38 Trinity, one had to travel 200 yards to a semi open latrine. Constipation became an unpleasant condition if one wanted to avoid the chill wind and rain. Although in some rougher college circles there was evidence of urine stains down the college stone work. And the dawn hours might find a crunched up lump of one of the better English newspapers parachuting certain contents as distantly as possible away from the window out of which they came. And that first 1946 cold snowy winter in Dublin, a near warm place civilized with plumbing became of paramount importance. Towards which one set one's sights upon the moment of morning's first eye opening. And the nearest being Jury's Hotel just beyond the great pillars and curvatures of the old parliament building, out the front gates in a straight line a short way down Dame Street. In a side entrance down Anglesea Street one stepped up four steps to this narrow door of stained glass. To the left one of the most exquisite bars in all of Europe with its tiled walls and sombre cloistered interior, and ahead, from a turning in a cosy lobby, was the palm court with its wicker furniture and palms. And welcome warmth.

But there were a few marvellous comfortable compensations in college itself. Especially within the austere dignified walls of the dining hall. To which, engowned, one would set off evenings at seven o'clock for Commons. Convening in the vestibule with its two coal fires glowing against the brass bands of its grate. An eagle eye of a college porter noting each student by face who'd paid his quarterly Commons' Fund of three pounds thirteen shillings and sixpence. The dining doors opening. And the invariably hungry rushing in. Professors descending from the common room above where they had taken their pre dinner sherry, now assembled at the high table. A college scholar, whose free meal this was, rushing to mount the steps

1946 seated in my sitting room at Trinity, which except for odd elegances embellishing, which overflowed from James Leathers' personal bedroom, was generally kept like a military barracks. And because of its high ceilings and large windows was always uncomfortably cold through the winter. But it did occasionally heat up with antics normally forbidden in the college.

of the lectern to recite out across these heads, Latin grace with as much speed and immaculate pronunciation of which he was capable. A ritual closely listened to by other scholars for its every nuance of perfection. Beseatment with a loud shuffle of chairs. The sweating faces and darting eyes of young servant girls fetching great barons of beef up from the dungeon kitchens. Pushing the massive platters through the hatchway into this great room. They stood there catching their breath and surveying this assembly from which rose this loud throb of voices. These massive roasts placed on tables for the carvers to slice off the slabs of meat. The hustle and bustle of other college porters doubling as waiters flying with their laden plates between the tables. Steaming Brussels sprouts, turnip, cabbage and potatoes. A jug served of specially brewed beer made by Guinness, one to each table. Which led to heavy drinkers seeking to sit with as many teetotallers as possible.

There were musty dusty if not warm places to go in college. Two of the most conspicuous were The Historical Society and The Philosophical Society, located one on top of the other in the Graduates Memorial Building. I joined 'The Hist.' as it was called for the reason that I was told it was where newspapers and letter writing paper were available, plus a library, a silence room and a billiard room. But alas I only entered the Reading and Writing room once, feeling immeasurably ill at ease to go sit in view of others while reading a periodical. Then passing one cold gloomy winter evening I saw lights and heard voices in a back room. And found myself attending one of the Society's debates at which one nearly always heard apropros of nothing at all, reference to America as being uncultured. As I sat listening to this again expressed opinion this night, I was suddenly pointed out as being a member of the Society not wearing a gown as required and that the speaker should expel me for academic nudity which he did.

Forever thereafter I was never again seen at a college society but did make one bereft further foray to the Dublin University Gramophone Club, which held three concerts every term on a Friday evening at eight o'clock in the Physics amphitheatre, there to listen in its cool silence and on the hard benches, to Mozart on the gramophone. Later I did work my nerve up enough to peer through the window near the front of college into the quiet room of the Student Christian Movement during one of their every Thursday evening eight p.m. assemblies. Invited in, one did find solace among these kindly compassionate faces, knowing that these who tried so sincerely to discover the Christian attitude to every question which confronts man in his daily life, would never point a finger to the door to say get out.

But my rooms, then barren as they were, save for college issue of a sitting room table and few chairs, soon became a meeting place establishing its own society. Members pouring in each morning for cups of tea, and before, between and after classes convening. Parking their books and gowns while encouraging me to get up out of my cold bed and pour cold water into my wash bowl, pull on damp clothes and stagger off with them to have coffee.

The terms at Trinity extending to a brief total of eighteen weeks out of the year, presented to those living within these walls and behind these rhododendron shrouded fences, thirty four weeks of semi solitary peace to be pursued amid these quiet cloistered squares. To sit and stare hours of an afternoon away, from the sitting room window, out over the perspectives of the wet shiny pavement. With only an occasional figure passing in the college and a constant seagull or two squawking from roof gutters. The bell tower of the Campanile rearing above the slates of the Rubrics as if it were one of its chimneys. The evening glow of the gas lamps in the lonely enfolding comforting darkness. Here within this granite enclave, protected in body if not in mind and spirit. Many a morn, late afternoon and evening went by, kicking around life's imponderables. Conscious of this academic sovereignty holding one aloof and safe from the struggling troubles of the outer world.

Where among the shamrocks
One must find
One's own Irish pot
To piss in

IV

Unused as I was to religion being an identity, it took me some time to realize Trinity College was a British redoubt of the Protestant Anglo Irish. In this city full of Catholics. More than a few of whom aped and admired the English. And some of whom defied their Bishop's ban on Catholics attending within this verdured piece of central Dublin where British Protestants proclaimed their occupation. A not infrequent phenomenon of the strains of 'God Save The King' blaring out over the college walls as the West Brit students, turning up the volume of their radios, opened their windows when the BBC closed down their night's broadcasting. Collecting at the College front gates, politically aggrieved Dublin street shouters, who would batter at the big closed front portals to gain admittance as college porters within held them shut. And upon occasion when the pubs had emptied their inmates for the night, such person attempting fist and foot hammering admission was the likes of Brendan Behan, poet, playwright and patriot.

It was in this English, Anglo Irish atmosphere that my earliest point of view was formed of Ireland. But seeing it also through the American eyes of the handful, who like myself had arrived for the first time at Trinity. And hearing my first whispers from a Catholic professor at College revealing to me that he was a Catholic, here in this forbidden world for Catholics. But hastening, too, to tell that such a declaration of one's religion would not be held against one. Even so, that if I were in need of knowing who a Catholic friend might be to let him know. But amid Muslims, Hindus, Buddhists, both black and white, Quakers and Unitarians, rarely can I remember the issue of religion being raised within Trinity's walls. And certainly never outside at the idolatrous pagan parties which raged in their various venues throughout the twenty six counties and especially fulminated in this city of 300,000 mostly devout souls.

But the early concern of many of these arrived Americans from whom I heard initial opinions expressed about Ireland was not about religion, politics or sanitation but about money and food. As the foremost thing to befall many of them was slow starvation. U.S. government documents in triplicate in the hands of the Irish could be treated with the wry sceptical humour such complicated forms deserved, but as they slowly made their way across the Atlantic Ocean and through American bureaucracy, subsistence cheques on the G.I. Bill of Rights failed to arrive. And a few of these ex service-men now found themselves entering restaurants and announcing to the manager at the end of their meals, that they couldn't pay the bill. And were told, sure sir, that's no problem come back and pay it when you can. Just as they could be infernal in efficiency, and provided it wasn't a matter of religion or politics, the Irish could be sympathetic to an otherwise respectable gentleman temporarily caught in adversity. And one early learned that a strange unwritten law of generosity pervaded this land. And the biggest sin to be committed was that of meanness.

My first college invitation was to go and have a cup of coffee. Thus one embarked upon this sacred rite in Dublin. To be indulged either by morning, noon, afternoon or all three. Each café with its adherents. In my case it became Bewley's Oriental Café in Grafton Street which involved turning left out the front gates, past the Provost's House and traversing the city's cultural spine of Grafton Street. Paved with its wooden blocks aswarm with bicycles and off which variously extended Suffolk, Duke, Ann, Harry and Lemon Streets. Although there were cafés in these side street nooks and crannies, the élite coffee scented emporiums were all on the socially desired thoroughfare of Grafton Street. Where early morning gossip could be meteorically spread between the cheerful chattering of briefly pausing pedestrians. And where the wives of bank managers with light hearted things to think and do could flaunt their better than thou high heeled utter respectability.

Starting at the bottom of Grafton Street on the left, in a grey stone neo Georgian building, was Mitchell's. Definitely for the lady of society who'd been at a play the evening before, and carrying a catalogue from an exhibition of paintings, had just been to a fitting for a frock. Then further up, the glass table tops of Bewley's, its butter balls piled on plates, its stacks of fragrant fresh buns, its creamy glasses of Jersey milk and its roasted coffee smells perfuming the

Front Square Trinity College. The author his beard growing sparsely during his earliest days at Trinity and dressed in corduroys but having taken care to blacken the white of his saddle shoes which had caused many an unwary Dubliner to walk smack into posts and walls while staring at them and which once required the author to give medical attention to a girl knocked unconcious thereby.

street. This sacredly oriental interior was especially favoured by mothers whose sons had become priests. And by young ladies who were thinking of becoming nuns. Occasionally the tranquillity would be broken by a hungover poet rustling his paper who would sit examining the day's racing form at the courses while nursing in his celibacy his agonizing impure thoughts. Tucked away on other crimson banquettes were solitary men of the minor merchant class who secretly read recently banned novels and were experts at crossword puzzles. But I had repaired for my first Dublin coffee to Switzer's, down iron balustraded stairs to the warm and cosy basement of this, for Dublin, large department store. There, frequented by hockey playing lady students from Trinity and tweedy Anglo Irish matrons from the country, one luxuriated in the optimism pleasantly floating on the din of these animated voices.

But there were other fashionable cafés full of other more curious kettles of fish. And nearly next to Fannin & Co. suppliers of surgical instruments, was Robert Robert's at the top of Grafton Street. Where in the door past its cake counters and ground floor tables, it had a back section elevated up some stairs. This was the habitat of local accountants, managers of the better nearby haberdasheries, and a plethora of non practising physicians from out of the respectably prosperous middle class. But it was uniquely and especially full of aficionados of the Royal College of Surgeons in Ireland. These were a strange breed of medical student who despite growing grey, and many balding, remained anciently in attendance at this revered institution of medicine. Always affirming over their morning coffee that they could pass 2nd, 3rd years, 4th and even their final exams if only they could succeed in passing their 1st year, which, in view of their enormously accumulated sophisticated knowledge, now presented subjects which were so rudimentary, that they were now beneath them to retain as learning. Such gentlemen of surgeons invariably originated from modestly comfortable farming families out in the provinces who had one son a priest, one a dentist and a daughter a nun, and the whole family together mumbled the Rosary on their knees at night.

In a Dublin so full of charming chancers, these medically dedicated con men survived on their wits and the adoring women they attracted who had no option in their loneliness but to be gullible and sew back buttons on their seducers' shirts. But as perpetual apprentice physicians they were always ready with a smile to greet you, sporting their Aran Islands tweed ties and with their vast medical knowledge at their fingertips and never without a stethoscope in their pocket, would in their best bedside manner, slip upon a chair beside you, and order a black coffee as they borrowed their desperately needed early morning cigarettes. After their first deep inhalation, asking after your health and supplying an instant diagnosis and a suitably illegally scrawled prescription on the back of your bill which included his two coffees and plate of rashers and eggs. Ah, but the bedside manner would soon smoothly change to a more matter of fact and confidential comportment and in a quick shuffle of blandishing words, an attempt would be made to relieve you of legal tender. Preferably in the form of a big white British five pound note. Which in those days was majestically unscrawled in its own elegant flowing script. But if not that high a financial dimension you deign to loan on an immediately repayable basis following a certainty in the afternoon races, there came a rapidly diminishing politely mild pleading for a pound, a ten shilling note, and if no sign of paper money looked to be soon soothing their palms, anything at all, all the way down to a six pence would do. The latter at least being the price of one bottle of Mountjoy Nourishing Stout from that lesser known brewery situated in the north of Dublin near the banks of the Royal Canal. And seven bottles of whose brew you could drink, while saving a theoretical penny on each, in order to have an eighth bottle of Guinness costing seven pence. A routine religiously followed by the better poets stretching their imaginations and pockets of an evening.

But these strange perennial forever unqualified medical students did get involved in a final commencement of sorts, albeit non academic. Which would generally take place when a gentle moist breeze was blowing over Dublin. They would upon such a clement sudden bright and cheery morning, commence without warning to borrow at the drop of a hat as much as they could smilingly blandish in the space of one day from every friend and acquaintance met as they stretched their legs throughout the metropolis. Repayment due in the usual way of a promised counting out of notes over a bucket of champagne from the massive stack that was to be won on a guaranteed absolute certainty running in the fifth race at Leopardstown, a filly kept under top secret wraps the whole season who would explode from behind in the last furlong to overtake and fly past the winning post at one hundred to one. However these particular accumulated funds instead of being placed on this filly, went instantly to make a down payment purchase on credit of every vacuum cleaner available from every unsuspecting shop. These modern deposers of dust, marvels so recently new to the country, were either resold or pawned within the hour. The sale usually consummated by the perennial medical student providing his stethoscope to the victim to listen close up to the magical whirr of the impeccably reliable vacuum's motor. And this anciently apprenticing sawbones with his brand new tweed pockets stuffed with Lady

Laverys as the Irish Punt was then called, would be gone that night in a cloud of cigarette smoke and blaze of brandy on the mail boat to England to be ne'er heard of again. But sheepishly remembered enough by his ruefully admiring victims.

The epicentre of art and literature in its smoking, drinking, betting and talking attitudes, was also in Grafton Street. Forming as it did, the main hallway between the narrower corridors to the left and right into the cafés and pubs which in turn were like the rooms of a sprawling country house. It was the first thoroughfare in the world where nude streaking on two running legs was to become known. But at that censorious time in Ireland it required the perpetrator to sport the bottom part of a pair of pyjamas over the head and from this facial disguise peek through the fly while side stepping pedestrians, cyclists and vehicular traffic. Starting at Fannin's the medical supply depot near the top of Grafton Street, the streaker emerged from this revered black doorway flanked with windows full of bed pans, spatulas, forceps and microscopes, and giving the war whoop of the Seminole Indian, the naked speeder launched himself flying down past the Monument Creamery Café. Grabbing up a pre paid for fish from the grey marble slab of the fishmonger's and followed by suitable protesting shouts from an assistant would, waving the fish by the tail, streak by the jewellers' shops and the high quality furnishing emporium of Cavendish's. On that famed corner of Duke Street, it was incumbent upon the streaker to pause and hold aloft his fish and say aloud the whole of the Roman Catholic Act of Contrition. Such latter pause only forgiven if a member of the Garda Síochána was visible within thirty yards. The streaker then making for Davy Byrnes pub forty strides to the east where clothes and further disguises awaited in the gents. A fiver being duly peeled off as the award for this excursion. It was, of course, the first symbolic attempt of the intelligentsia to break the hold of sexual repression upon the country. But as always it was significant that no one present in the pub took the least notice of the event except to wrap their hands around the drink it was customary for the achiever of 'the deed of the nude velocity' to buy.

If Grafton Street were the main hallway in the cultural mansion of Dublin then Duke Street to the east was a breezeway to its preferred salons of the Bailey and Davy Byrnes as well as a highly frequented betting shop located mid way along its short length. There was also

Myself in front of Davy Byrnes pub which became a frequent place to visit in the early days of one's undergraduate life. Later, with the noise and the people, one did shift to the quieter privacy of Jammet's back bar and the cool beauty of the Shelbourne Rooms. Bicycles at the time were a major form of transport and the sound of draught horses pounding with their rumbling carts through the streets, was a daily sound of the city.

nearer Dawson Street a small Georgian edifice in the top floors of which few discouraging words were ever said against amusement and where many an astonishing post pub closing party raged. Davy Byrnes pub was what one might imagine to be a Victorianised twentieth century interior. With its curving pink marble counter decorated underneath with the sediment end of dark wine bottles. Along its walls were exotic Bacchanalian murals by Cecil Salkeld which seemed to glow in the subdued lighting and under which the habitués sat on soft crimson banquettes. But at the rear of the pub was one of the strangest of all strange places in Dublin called the Gilded Cage. Reserved for drinkers of spirits and champagne, access to which was through a trellis door in an iron lattice work. This exalted enclosure was furnished in burnished beige velvet covered stools and cushioned settees. Its polo coated cavalry twill trousered inmates with their silk and satin frocked ladies hesitated not, to assume the elevated status and essence of superiority which this revered inner sanctum conferred upon its habitués. As puff puff went the cigar smoke and pop pop went the champagne bottles like guns at the grouse shoot as all within here convincingly demonstrated their assets. And where by raising their vowels and laughing loudly, they assumed safety from any perennial medical student propositioning for a loan or selling a vacuum cleaner. And where to be sure such hapless gent with his stethoscope plugged in his ears would find all backs turned in his face as he hoovered between these indifferent legs.

The Gilded Cage was further insulated from questionable accostings or any temporary rubbing of elbows with beer imbibers, by being separately entered from a side lane off Duke Street, thereby keeping discreet these élite comings and goings. Eager social climbers eavesdropped on the whispered confidential revelations concerning Hollywood legends. And many an awesome snub was perpetrated here and ignominy delivered with the aplomb of a sledge hammer by these privileged inmates many of whom were current plaintiffs and defendants in large libel actions. Here, too, could be found drinking blond haired and nattily suited silk tied stockbrokers from the stock exchange who traded financially advantageous secrets with the owners of famed stallions and winning fillies. The only hazard being for these grabbers at life's banquet, that sometimes upon a late night exiting into a deserted narrow Duke's Lane, they might be set upon by gurriers lurking with pickaxe handles who would not necessarily take your money but would enjoy to the utmost as underprivileged Irishmen, if not militant socialists, to beat the living bejesus out of you and blind and choke you with the dust raised out of your own belted polo coat. And it was no use shouting out that you were a friend of the working classes.

Around each and every corner of Grafton Street environs there were other pubs and places and spaces to be sure. Within this kingdom westwards from the Shelbourne Hotel to Great George's Street, and south from King to Dame Street, the whole of the fashionable world then extended. Boisterous saloons of post rugby matches where spouting a sonnet or giving a favourable opinion of James Joyce would get you a fist in the gob. The Dawson Lounge with its narrow stairs down to its basement tiny bar and its upstairs squeezed full of not a few resigned poets and painters, convicted and sentenced to Ireland for the rest of their lives. On the outskirts of this milieu were the more peaceful neutral houses of refreshment to which folk repaired taking time out to avoid familiar faces or more often rehearse revenges while licking their wounds from the life and death contests of conversation. There were the confidential taverns, too, especially in the vicinity west of Grafton Street. Where the likes of certain of your Trinity College porters collected of an evening and where you might venture to discreetly straighten out a college indiscretion. But only a few paces further afield were the secret dens and snugs where conspiracies could brew. To fight for Ireland and drive the British invader out,except for the richer tourists among them. To loft and flutter the tricolour across the northern border. But to drink outside these boundaries other than being forced to by pub closing hours or in the emergency of your mother's death or funeral was a self imposed form of banishment which could shrivel up the soul and blow you away. Unless of course you were writing a novel.

And ah, too, in those days, the premier pubs were jammed tight, not only with native customers squeezing in the doors but with an invasion of curious foreigners not seen before nor known since. From Spitzbergen, from Ohio and Khartoum, from East Jesus California and even from Alcatraz. And many of whom were gentlemen who preferred gentlemen. Assembling with their wrists adorned and cigarettes held at lofty dainty angles. They were actors and organists. They were party givers and goers. Who merrily pranced and pleasantly preyed upon each other. With their homemade instant night clubs to which admission was granted for a bon mot or an armful of stout. Some of them held court in castles and country houses chock full of butlers and maids where one in utter centrally heated comfort could ooh and aah at the Meissen and Tiepolos. And the rare females mingling among them were lulus indeed. Much given to painting the male nude or exercising impromptu recitals on musical saws or clothed in nothing at all, with bosoms bouncing, entertain as they weaved hips flashing through an assembly, belligerently clacking their castanets. Highly welcome behaviour in this land full of suspicious ice cold virgins where hot women were hard to find.

The most serious part of Dublin drinking life was the timing. Especially of your degree of inebriation. Ten or eleven of a morn, stone cold sober, you would not want to set your own still faintly bleary eyes on many of these pub habitués in their depressions deeply hungover a marble or mahogany counter. But as noon passed and early afternoon progressed over a lunch during 'holy hour' when the pubs were shut, and the evening approached and the mind had grown rosy with tipple, these same faces avoided earlier, were by the verge of pub closing time more than made pleasantly palatable by the alcoholic confidences now being disclosed. And it was throughout the day a matter of musical chairs. Repairing first to a safe quiet pub where the initial tanking up with a more intimate friend could take place. To insulate from what would come later, and was in every Irish pub where a group of cronies were drinking, always a condition of your arriving presence. That those grouped there already long engrossed in the chosen subject of dispute, were in control of what was known as 'the snub'. A rebuff so lethal that nothing resembling it is known in the sadder annals of mankind. Each man present jealously guarding his small preserve already established by his opinions expressed on the urgent questions of the day. Usually imponderables chosen at random for their limitless scope of dispute. 'Does wood float' or 'Is the sky without clouds blue'. Entrance to such company was a very ticklish manoeuvre indeed, carefully taken step by step. And often easiest and quickest achieved by quietly pretending to be laggards drunk. For in this part of Dublin city there were few donkeys and pet horses upon whose back you might drape inebriated and be trotted home, and every accommodating understanding and sympathy was offered the man incompletely in control of himself. It helped, too, to spout a few quotes made by esteemed deceased figures from the world of science, literature and art, slurring your speech in the process in case of inaccuracies which would be pounced upon like a cobra striking a mouse. But if too embarrassed not to be in possession of your sober senses, you had but to lonely patiently wait. Till the buyer of a round of drinks, who would for that purpose among his cronies be the moderator of proceedings and would out of the corner of his eye assess the ripe time to finally invite you with the words, 'what are you having'.

If a snub remained chronic, the simmering victim was bound to finally boil over with epithets instead of epigrams renting the air. And as fists followed, it led to another condition arising, that of being banned and disbarred. Such edict being bestowed for obstreperousness beyond the call of erudite argument and the barman in all cases acting as judge and meting out sentence. Which could last a week to a month or six months to a year, depending upon the number of doors ripped off, bottles or windows broken. And could be indefinitely extended if prominent front teeth or eyes were knocked out or if enough stitches were sewn in the various injured faces to leave scars as reminders of the original mayhem. A general lack of heinousness in such battle could also mitigate in the length of disbarment but it helped too, if you were otherwise a published poet or race horse trainer. There were those, too, who were barred for life, and who usually declared such distinction as warning to anyone in their present pub who might be foolhardy enough to accuse them of splitting an infinitive. Alone exempt as a class of person from barring were gas meter readers being always regarded as innocent parties, well known to be the most benign of all peace loving citizens.

Most disbarment was usually finally purged following restitutions, contrite apologies and if necessary, intercessions by other pub habitués. But it was only ever certain that it was lifted when you found yourself served alone as a customer. For if you arrived with a group it was accepted that in the full glare of bonhomie to be asked to leave was too gross an embarrassment and at such times you'd be served with one drink till the discreet message was got to you that it was to be your last. Many protracted disbarments resulted in reimposition due to the over zealous celebration of its lifting. When the blamed again might resort to fisticuffs over the meaning of the word 'clarity', giving as one pub philologist did his own definition with a war cry turned into a physical sample, 'Clarity is that force without witticism given to this fist sent in the direction of your face, that when hit will have no trouble seeing stars.'

But let us out of the better bars, pubs and snugs and even out of the Gilded Cage, pop up a social notch or two to where disbarments were rare indeed. To just around the corner of Duke into Dawson Street and forty paces north along that boulevard. To take a sharp turn right up these steps under a glass canopy. Through swingdoors and enter upon the black and white tiled vestibule always pink tinted aglow by winter with a blazing coal fire. The smiling greetings of an ever attentive concierge to pause you pleasantly in your tracks. A porter or two to take and safely keep your parcel. And always a comely pair of girls at the reception desk to witness your passing and purring deeper into the interior. Strolling by the friendly splendour of the grand stairs arising under a crystal chandelier and Georgian ceiling to the cosy accommodations above. Bless yourself here, to now thankfully enter this, sanctum of all Dublin sanctums. An arena in spite of its access to the public, so exalted and spiritually enclosing in its private intimacy that to merely go there and sit was a loneliness so pleasant it put one aseat among the gods. This was the lounge of the Royal Hibernian Hotel. The most austerely and beautifully elegant meeting place in all the world. And long lain now a dismantled treasure entombed with the other ghosts of Dublin.

And go there I did to sit over many many a year. Where only spectres go now like do the sorrows that have passed in that place. But where once any paupered impostor merely by crossing his legs, sniffing his snuff and shooting a cuff, could assume the pretentions of a solvent prince. As so many of that charming chancer ilk chose to do then. And bask the day away under the smoked green stained glass ceiling dome from which gently the pale light descended upon the habitués of this room. Their love of it making them members of a private club. Its waiters and waitresses famed figures long endeared to its clientele who patiently tolerated even the most delayed attention from these ministers of refreshment. To whom a request was addressed, 'whenever you're ready'. And the response 'I'll be with you any minute now'.

The Royal Hibernian Lounge, although an atmosphere not to awe an American, would even to the most uncomprehending of that breed, finally make him find quaintly singular the eye of observation of gentlemen here found who surveyed all from behind their flashing monocles. And who spouted Anglo Irish vowels so echoingly haughty that they made the tables' glasses shiver and tinkle where they touched. Even I once, sitting innocently entweeded and perusing a sonnet on vellum, through a not so innocent temporarily phoney monocle sporting in my eye, had my reverie most appropriately disturbed. By a lady. She was a tall lady. Physically long of neck. From which six strings of natural pearls were displayed. She originated diagonally from the extreme opposite of the room expiring her breath as she approached. Her chiffons flying behind her in her own breeze. I was in fact obscurely just around the corner of an alcove utterly minding my own unbloody business. As she silkily swept in to loud breathing proximity with her long black tresses falling forward. She stood towering suddenly over me. As I in my chair sought to decide if I should politely arise, when she announced in some of the spiritually loudest words I may have ever heard.

'Sir, you are, as I am sure you may be utterly unaware, as indeed I dare to hope to God you are, wearing represented in the three stripes upon your tie, my family's anciently established and royally bestowed racing colours.'

Ever so gently closing my book of poetry, the contents of which in significance were quite beyond me anyway, I stood instantly. Bowed deeply. Fortunately without breaking wind as one is so wont to do on such occasions. Or indeed wanting to ask how much her pearls were worth. Then further without demur, I swept the offending neck wear instantly from around my throat and out of my collar and tried to rip it up but the damn silken thing was so indestructibly strong I crumpled it away in my pocket. And in yet a deeper bow apologized to the lady for being now tieless in her presence. To which she immediately trumpeted her comment for everyone not stone deaf in the lounge to hear. 'Better that, sir, than for you to continue to be an arrant impostor.'

I was for some next several minutes making the most ironclad of resolutions never to set foot in this pompously pretentious place again. With ladies loose who ought to be back inside their own iron barred stables. But even that vision did little to cheer me and I was descending rapidly into the deep despair that such incidents invariably devolved upon one, when suddenly there came the waiter to my table with an ice bucket containing a vintage bottle of Charles Heidsieck champagne with a scribbled name and legend on Royal Hibernian Hotel notepaper. 'Mocking Laughter in the last today at Fairyhouse'. As I knew what strange words such as these meant in Dublin, I instantly sent this short advice on a card with a suitable tip and a fiver to the concierge who popped with it the few paces to the turf accountant in Duke Street around the corner and such proverbial fiver was placed on 'Mocking Laughter' to win at twenty to one. And I found myself not only that day but on many a day thereafter.

Many the pounds
Pleasantly
The richer

V

The 1946 year of my arrival in Ireland coincided with one of the harshest winters on record. Past Christmas the snows were piled high and even the odd days above freezing point were chillingly damp and cold. The largest municipal park which had so first caught my imagination had massive long high ricks of turf upon which it rained and snowed. These sodden chunks of fuel with which to heat our chambers could rarely be lit due to their wet condition, and if ever lit would only coldly smoulder. In the tall ceilinged and large windowed college rooms, lying long abed mornings, one's frozen feet of the night before not ever thawing before dawn. The dry warmth of Bewley's Oriental Café in Grafton Street becoming the day's first destination. So, too, for the survival of chilled limbs, did I have the early, middle and the latter part of one's evening planned.

In the inner core of Dublin city and within a half mile radius of the centre of O'Connell Street Bridge, you never at any point were more than one hundred and thirty nine and one half paces from a pint of porter or ball of whiskey. Or your trusty bottle of stout standing in their hundreds on shelves ready for their corks to be levered out with a hand puller and a suitable pop. In the better bars were clarets and burgundies, pickled onions, sausages, boiled eggs and sandwiches of ham, cheese and roast beef. But always on the very edges of these blessings lurked the cold desperate reality of the city and its stark gloomy poverty only a stone's throw away. Begging for a penny or selling a newspaper, shoeless urchins, faces streaming phlegm, scattering across the grey glisteningly wet streets. Steeling one to the necessity of food and shelter. For which there was still yet another place of a different and albeit less haughty kind of bliss than the lounge of the Royal Hibernian Hotel.

Following my first few days at Trinity, it was a rare occasion that my social life ever permitted me to dine at evening commons with regularity. Being abroad in Dublin in a city where it quickly became

Two serious geologists, Frank Tuffy and Anthony Byrne, in College Park. These two gentlemen were always faithful callers to number 38. Frank Tuffy having been a prisoner of war, who in order to avoid typhus and death, daily had taken outdoor ice cold showers in the camp and was therefore able to tolerate my winterish rooms.

apparent that appointments were rarely made, and if made, rarely kept. One seemed to become involved in social occasions without beginning or end, time disappearing without warning, and I never seemed able to manage, in spite of the short walk and having already quarterly paid for the meal, to get back to college to dine. Out gallivanting in Dublin, one was invariably pacing oneself to abide one's inevitable and hopefully unsnubbed appearance later in a pub. For me, as evening approached, this often took the form of a long wandering walk through Dublin's by ways. And alone as night fell I would venture back to Grafton Street. Emerging gently around the corner and peeking north and south to spy the way was clear of any hungry, thirsty, qualified idle habitué of the College of Surgeons. Then taking a few bounding leaps across the street to number 72, a marvellous small mock Elizabethan building which housed in a floor above its cinema, a wondrous café.

This eating emporium was not a precinct where one was likely to deliberately or innocently infringe anyone's racing colours. Nor was such place licensed to sell alcoholic beverages. Its mullioned windows looking down from an elevation of brick and faded bruised strawberry hued stone. Inside its vestibule a stray customer or two buying tickets to a cowboy film set on a sunny prairie. And the second feature always a travelogue on venturing to the steamy jungles of Central America or somewhere bereft up in the mountain ranges of the Andes. Tearing myself away from the temptation of such entertainment one would go up the carpeted staircase variegated to prepare one above for this sombrely illumined room. Its tall ceilinged interior, like a galleried hall of a great country house. Its bill of fare hallowed in one's memory. Consisting totally as it did of variations under a theme of different names, all nearly amounting to exactly the same thing. Combinations of bread, butter, bacon rashers, sausages and eggs, fried, grilled, poached or boiled. Each described as either a 'Tasty Tea', 'Evening Tea', 'Tempting Tea', 'Afternoon Tea', 'Dainty Tea', 'Savoury Tea', 'Snack Tea', and one latter tea described awesomely in italics as 'The Gourmet's Tea' to which an anchovy on a piece of toast was added. Be that menu as it may, I agonized each evening over my decision, even at times calling after the waitress to change my order yet again. But with a scalding pot of tea, always devouring with gusto my generous stack of buttered bread, rashers, sausages and eggs.

In the faint light of its shaded little table lamps, more often than not one found the Grafton Picture House Café empty with no other customer there but myself. A screen in a darkened corner behind which an elevator brought food up from kitchens below. Upholstered chairs and banquettes upon which to sit under the lofted imitation beamed ceiling. The recessed wide sills of the fake Tudor windows and mock mahogany furnishings. All giving an atmosphere, albeit ersatz, of utter comforting permanence. Always whispers of the country girl waitresses upon my arrival. Their urgent reminders down the serving hatch to hurry up down there as that poor man's stomach is shouting that his throat is cut. Such was the solemnity of this place's marvellous strange peace that I never once but dined there alone. Nor even said to another soul where I was going or where I'd been. And I suppose if ever a place on this earth or throughout my entire life ever gave one solace it could not be greater than that given me on any one of the gloomy wet Dublin wintry duskingtides that I dined on a 'Tasty Tea' in the Grafton Picture

House Café, and read as I did in the evening newspaper the In Memoriams to those of Dublin's departed dead.

Just as the raindrops were breaking one's back the winter did end and the buds came out on the trees. At such time St Stephen's Green North became the other great fashionable boulevard upon which your better class of Dubliner might be met sprinkling threepenny bits to begging tinkers. Or eyes askance, stroll head high betwixt and between the more sheepish and ingratiating chancers who also hopefully tread here. The southwestern sun shone upon these elevations, lifting the spirits of those who passed on these granite squares of stone, pleasantly in sight of the park. And just to the left out of Grafton Street, one found Smyth's of the Green, an emporium of many exotic groceries to incite your dreams. In the next nearby door of number 7, you might attend to have your portrait painted by the society portrait painter of the day. A tall ample handsome gentleman well known for his silk cravats and who would conspicuously correct a grammatical error heard in French, Irish or English. In this same building, yours truly gave three exhibitions of paintings in the Dublin Painter's Gallery, a large skylit studio deep in the interior up a flight of stairs and echoing many an artist's aspirations. Here I had the nerve not only to outrage and make one's first artistic enemies but to also painfully embarrass friends. Some of whom were asked to lug my still wet canvasses of the female nude from my rooms in Trinity, and watched by many a celibate eye, to transport such work up the entire length of Grafton Street.

Anybody who was anybody, and this was always anybody in Dublin, was to be seen on north St Stephen's Green. Popping in and out of its clubs located in this terrace of massive Edwardian, Victorian and Georgian houses. Down the basement of one was the Country Shop selling Aran Islands' sweaters, and serving teas of home baked scones and home made jams where the waitresses were all from the better families. If not heading towards Adams the auctioneers to bid for an antique, then one was usually on one's way to the glass canopy extending its awning out over the pavement under which clients were protected from inclemency when entering the Shelbourne Hotel. Admitting the ladies but keeping the rabble out was always a great tradition of all doormen in Dublin and letting the right sort in, their golden duty. And such traditions were in no better place enforced than in these precincts. If the Royal Hibernian was where

Anthony Cronin, Gainor Crist and Tony McInerney at one of my exhibitions which frequently became the subject of much discussion due to my forewords in the catalogue. These gentlemen would delight to await and be present at the gallery when a violent member of the Legion of Decency would attack a picture with her umbrella. As, at one time of an attack all of these three were behind my reception desk, they each in turn got a swat over the noggin. While I was out having a drink at a pub.

One of my oil paintings exhibited in Dublin. These executed in a technique resembling that used for water colours and such paintings as this one may have ended up patching a fence in order that Ernie Gebler could keep a neighbouring farmer's sheep from breaking into his lush acres surrounding Lake Park. Gebler's motto being, in this case at least, farming should always come before Art. Especially his farming and somebody else's art.

you might while reading a sonnet be accosted for infringing someone's racing colours, then the Shelbourne was the hotel where you might be whipped unceremoniously with a riding crop for calling a hound a dog. For here you encountered the worshippers of the pursuit of the fox, attenders at point to points, lovers of eventing, race horse breeders, and last and not the least smelling of horse piss, Masters of Foxhounds.

Entering the lobby with its pillars, a lift straight ahead waiting in its wire cage to ascend you up the well of the mahogany balustraded staircase to wide crimson carpeted halls from which doors opened into tall ceilinged rooms that looked out over the tree tops of the park of St Stephen's Green to the purple heathered Dublin Mountains. Attached to a discreet wall of an inside hall downstairs were the current season's fox hunting fixtures. And you would never be noticed if you suddenly decided to neigh and raise your front hooves churning in the air to gallop around the hotel. As indeed a patron or two did when the doors of this élite hostelry were locked to outsiders for the night. And ghosts walk here too. Tiptoeing so as not to disturb the tourists. And so lonely now, for another world has come. From all over the world. In pursuit of speculation and seeking industrial exploitative opportunity. And those who haunted these environs with the passion of their lives. All of them are gone. Dirndl skirts aswirl. Silk kerchiefs flying from their sporty cars. Their pearls nestled on the cashmere of their twinsets and their long gentle fingers alive on the keys that made music on their harpsichords. They've walked with their shooting sticks and their country tweeds. Right out the door. Standing one last time sighing at the Green across the street. Before they step into oblivion. Washed away by the more plebeian waves breaking with Philistine inelegance upon this island nation.

Also in the vicinity of the Shelbourne's venerable location and within a stone's throw of each other were to be found two of the best and most ancient gentlemen's hairdressers in the western reaches of Europe. Where an appointment was akin to a knighthood. And where the intellectual flavour of conversation could range from architecture to agriculture or from ballet to greasepaint, with any amount you might require of Jewish, Irish or Scottish jokes thrown in between. But the funnier of these witticisms were always avoided in case hysterical laughter made one shake while one's neck was being close shaved. And for the same reason nary a contrary word was mentioned on politics or religion. From the ceiling of one coiffeur's, pulley operated rotating brushes were lowered to the head and hair and there spun to brush, massage and altogether invigorate the scalp. Under such treatment one emerged back into Dublin life a new and entirely refreshed man. Solicitors, Protestant bishops, barristers, physicians and wine merchants flocked here to be barbered and shampooed. Rested in bowls of scented waters, their hands awaited to be beautified by the lady manicurist. And I'm sure if I at the time only knew what they looked like, there were also to be seen ministers of the government who had only to make a hop, skip and stumble to reach here from the nearby Dail Eireann. Such gentlemen taking time out from this God fearing nation's business, could lean back, eyes closed in peace. And let us hope, their spirits as mine always did, purred in bliss.

Following a haircut and a shampoo and in particular a good wiping, drying and powdering deep in the collar and neck interstices to rid of the niggling irritation of minutiae of hair, nothing was better than at this five thirty crucial time than to return across Kildare Street to this redbrick grand palace of an hotel where by its side entrance one could discreetly enter. And tread hushed upon a carpeted narrow corridor and up a stair, across a foyer, down again, and through the residents' lounge of flowered soft sofas and out a door into the shadows to climb another stair, walk through another small hall, descend yet another stair and then from a stately vestibule enter the most beautiful and serene of all of Dublin bars, the Shelbourne Rooms.

Fabled for its airy ambience and white friezes on its pale blue walls, this was where your pretending and unpretending better variety of folk spaciously sequestered themselves within two large interconnecting rooms. Its wicker furniture and glass topped tables allowing for the easy crossing of knees. Savoury sticks, cashew and Brazil nuts in bowls. Its curved bar at which never more than three or four would deign to congregate, thus allowing for vowels to effervesce and the bon mot to echo. Its habitués, for fear it would seem frightfully forward, did not look you up and down till your back was well and truly turned. Then, by God beware of who your dressmaker, bootmaker or tailor was. Because this was, too, the winter launching pad of gentry for the provinces. Where came hawkeyed English and

American visiting masters of foxhounds to acclimatize their servants and themselves before subjection to the rigours and foibles of the Irish country house. And where they might, for a few days, kneeling nightly by their bedsides, say their prayers in some comfort before their necks were risked in some severe discomfort, braving walls, hedgerows, bogs and ditches out to the north, south and west.

In autumn when a chill descended or in June with summer suddenly warming an evening, one would go there to sit. Wrapped up in one's own loneliness and taking one's own comfort from the comfort of champagne. Viewing the ladies and gents in black tie and gowns as they appeared prior to dinner or a ball to stoke up their allégresse. Or as happened once when my fellow college lassies and lads suddenly sauntering in to drink before a dance, found me there. On this long mild evening in June. After the college races. On a Wednesday night. When all so hoped to make this sacred undergraduate occasion a social success. And one is somewhat sad now. To admit that although present in the Shelbourne Rooms lurking in my contented loneliness and albeit happy to cheer such fellow senior freshmen on over their drinks, not then, nor once did I, in all my university years, with the single exception of one cold rainy night at the Dublin University Gramophone Club, ever attend a college social occasion. Having been swept away invariably as I was, by the inexhaustibly teeming endless embroilment of life in Dublin by day and especially by night.

In Ireland in the immediate years after World War II, one was comparatively rich, and certainly richer than I'd ever been before and, alas, have been since. An allowance from my wise Galway mother was sent regularly without strings attached from New York, which was in frequent addition to my monthly bonanza cheque from the G.I. Bill of Rights. In the midst of my fellow starving Americans, my own way of life was led in some splendour. My stipend even being several times greater than my college servant's wage with which he respectably supported a small house, wife and clothed and fed four children. Under the banner of 'Incidentals Account with Trinity College' my bill for the quarter ending 1 March 1947, while incurring no debits for Baths, Repairs and Dilapidations or Punishments, amount to £18.8s.11d. For which total one was supplied with college servant, daily bottle of milk, quarterly rent of chambers and 'Commons Fund' of £3.13s.6d which provided one daily reasonably

From the Incidentals Account it will be seen that I took no baths, and incurred a tardy payment fine of seven and six pence. 'Commons Fund' each evening provided one with being served in the dining hall by acrobatically skilled porters who placed in front of one soup, a plate of meat, two vegetables and a sweet. A special beer brewed by Guinness was also available for the occasion. And it helped to find a seat between two of the better-mannered students.

sumptuous evening meal with its glass or two of beer.

In those days an orange coloured ten shilling note bought an evening's drinking of seventeen bottles of Guinness, or it could also provide nine pints of porter, or eleven balls of malt. And last and most of all, twenty bottles of Mountjoy Nourishing Stout. But prior to arrival at these party outposts where the drink flowed freely and without additional charge, there remained the custom at these counters of these pubs, of a strange ritual somewhat alien to me as an American. Of buying round after round. And voices heard, as one voice would say, what are you having. And another voice answering, no no, what are you having, it's my round now. There would then invariably ensue a mild insistence as to whose privilege the buying of the next round would be. Before I knew it, one's turn to buy a round inevitably came. Yet as I would offer, and make the attempt again and again, there came protests too numerous and apparently vehement, to subdue. And it was a long time before anyone even hinted that you were occasionally expected to threaten, shout and even shove and punch the opposition down. But one cannot imagine that even from the poorer among the group, that it would ever be severely held against one for not buying your round. Although it would surely be noticed and remembered till the end of time. For even with your wife and tiny numerous children at home starving as many were, not to be generous was the unforgettably unforgivable. Which would earn you the invariably resentful eternal sobriquet, 'He's nothing but a dirty no good mean bastard.'

Pub life almost entirely regulated one's own. At morning opening these meeting places would start to slowly fill with their habitués drifting in until reaching a peak of activity when holy hour arrived closing the pub between two thirty and three thirty. In the case of Davy Byrnes much of the company would retire across Duke Street to the Bailey Restaurant where the drinking could endure accompanied by food thought the least harmful to the thirst. By four thirty all were ready to decamp again back over the road. In a nation moving at the slower pace of Ireland, the only thing that was ever fast were the clocks in every pub. The bartender always ten to fifteen minutes prior to closing time noisily collecting glasses and bottles as he announced in ever more insistent and mock angry tones, 'Now please. Time now gentlemen please. Way past the time. Gentleman please. If you will.' This was the one moment of a bartender's and publican's day when he could indulge speaking in a voice hinting of a slight lack in diplomacy. Or even to take the liberty if not pleasure of leavening his voice with a tinge of severity. As everyone within sight and sound stood their ground assured in the knowledge that the remaining contents of their glasses was a sacred right to consume. I never once saw a member of the Garda Síochána in uniform enter to see that closing time was being observed. But I did encounter those in mufti quietly drinking away with the other dilatory customers, and sometimes silently deliberating into the foam of their Guinness as whether to take action or, as was invariably done, resignedly downing the contents of their glass and ordering up another one to further breech the licensing laws.

But as was with the likes of the Shelbourne Rooms, or even after the pub, if there was not the ball, there was always the shindy. The plans for which got whispered urgently from ear to ear as closing time approached. The succinct words being. 'There's a bash on.' Whiskey, in measures of twenty six and two thirds fluid ounces, gin in other volumes and even odd exotics in liquid quarts were ordered together with grey parcels packed with dozens of bottles of stout, and handed up and over the bar. And with such recently confided invitations one emerged with such groups ferrying such armfuls out pub doors. In the case of my acquaintances frequenting the thronged confines of Davy Byrnes, there was not far to go to pull further corks out of further bottles of stout. In fact not many yards as the crow flies or legs might wobble to a terraced redbrick discreetly anonymous Georgian building. With rooms on top of one another, a couple to each floor where the indiscretion increased as one ascended and where, under the motto, Bash On Regardless, the parties throbbed the night away. The more serious fights and arguments being engaged on the top floors from whence the losers could conveniently be fenestrated through an oft demolished window and land four storeys below in a rubbish heap mound of discarded rotting felt and disintegrating burlap. While much intermediary peeing might follow upon their heads if the revellers upstairs weren't more discreetly urinating down the balustrades to give just arriving visitors a taste of what they might expect should they ascend.

But let us not forget the slightly more serene post pub closing ritual of the Bonafide. In those days a term used to refer to public houses open after your normal licensing hours and permitted to give refreshment to the weary thirsty traveller. The rule being that such wayfarer had come some great distance on a dusty or more likely wet road and in passing on his way elsewhere and suitably parched, was craving liquid sustenance. Although there were your occasional two footed uphill and down dale pedestrian Bonafiders, more usually used a beast of burden, bicycle or automobile for such migrations. And with the customary plethora of people desperate to continue a night's drinking, this nightly nomadic pursuit was often a party in itself. Arms and legs along with the empty bottles from the previous pub, flailing and flying out windows. The boozing occupants hell bent countrywards in a din of epithets, the vehicle on its suspension rolling and pitching like a ship in a hurricane. Bumps and potholes on the road blinking headlights on and off as sane citizens out late on foot, hid behind thick walls and stout trees till such vehicles had safely careered past. And death, sadly, was not unknown.

Bonafides ranged around the outer vicinities and environs of Dublin. And south of the River Liffey this usually meant village pubs in the foothills of the Dublin Mountains. The beneficial aspect of such places and locations often being that verbal battles originating earlier in the inner city pub could blossom into full scale violence and take place in plenty of room. The aggrieved as it were, repairing outside to settle their differences in the late night peace and tranquillity of an untrafficked village street. Thereby permitting a large circle to gather around the antagonists either as spectators or as many invariably became, participants, engaging themselves in the battle when the circumstances incited. Usually this was when some poor unfortunate, ganged up on, bit the dust or mud, and prostrate was ripe to receive an additional battering of a boot in the ribcage.

It was an unwritten law that owners of vehicles used to transport to the Bonafide were to be left unharmed. Such persons usually were socially perched high as indeed only the financially better off members of the community in such post war days could afford to own a motor car. However such folk, as designated immune from bodily harm, were not estopped themselves from meting out punishment where they deemed it deserved. Their exemption from flying fists and feet being insured by several who would surround and protect such motorists without whom people could not get the ten or so miles back to populated civilization. There were, of course, occasionally present some of your gurrier folk without scruples who would attack anyone, and especially a more affluent automobilist. Such low types were fortunately not in abundance and usually were of a sort who

Tony Byrne and Val Hines taking time out during a geological expedition to Malahide, a lady student in the background. During such expeditions some romantically explosive situations were also explored.

ingratiated themselves in the company by spouting a verse or two of simple poetry purporting to be original from their own lips. And did then by their further pseudo intellectual blandishments inveigle to these Bonafide environs. However, once loose there in a general discord they could be depended upon to curse, swear and swing nail studded clubs and bring lead pipes down thudding on craniums. Thus adding a touch of true vulgarity, calculated viciousness and utter savagery to the mayhem.

But if in the night exterior, goings on went raging, the metacarpals splintering and the blood splashing in the puddles of water, there were always among such groups the peace lovers who continued their discussions and deliberations inside the pub. Reminding that this sovereign state was still a land of saints and scholars, who took no notice whatsoever of the sorrowful contusions being administered without. Indeed, so engrossed in their various schools of thought were they, that upon reappearance of the bloody faces of the maimed they might not even deign to examine the finer details of the carnage until the victors or the vanquished drew such attention by including them in an order for a round of drinks.

Ah but the open scope provided by the Bonafide was nothing in mayhem. Compared to the retirement for a bash in the venue of the country house. Many of such being houses perched precipitously on some edge or cliff over the sea. By the not curious coincidence that their owners were heavy drinkers of a sort who liked a marine atmosphere in their lives. Catching crabs or lobsters from the back garden or indeed availing of the convenience of a cold morning plunge in the ocean to sober up for the serious day's drinking ahead. But such architecturally spectacular places were usually the exclusive province of the hereditarily well heeled élite of the élite. In whose company there was never any need to travel far to risk your neck fox hunting. Often, too, such host would be a large yacht owner who would suicidally seek the life threatening hospitality of the Irish Sea and while frequently away in such a pursuit would leave his wife at home on the edges of the cliff. Who, as such ladies would, heading to town for cocktails and dinners, convene a few friends to return to her empty house. There to puff on hemp, foxtrot and drink in the spacious grandeur. And such battles as did there take place always began typically and innocently enough, invariably being merely an expression of opinion on an artistic matter.

One such famed evening erupting in this sumptuous drawing room when a dark blue suited gentleman in a bright red yellow spotted bow tie took exception to the slow pulsation of the music being played on the gramophone. And while the needle merrily passed over the record, he feathered his neck wear, shot his gold linked cuffs, ceremoniously opened his fly, and then in the pure, albeit faint, electric light of this evening, took out his appendage member, through which he commenced to pee upon the rotating plastic platter of fine grooves. The change in tempo from largo to a very watery andante instantly called attention to his act of disapproval from every quarter of the room. In which were present three members of the Royal Dublin Society and four members of the Royal Irish Automobile Club, the latter indubitably one of the most exclusive private clubs on the face of the earth. With suitable words of shock and dismay followed by those of chastisement, the seven encroached upon the perpetrator of the peeing to drag him away from the committing of this disrespectful nuisance which, as the pee percolated down into the gears of the turntable, stopped it spinning and caused the music to groan to a halt. However, as the culprit was dragged away he grabbed and pulled a priceless Gobelin tapestry down from the wall and as he and the ornamented fabric were tugged across the room he peed further upon the latter which incited an art-loving lady to beat him with her handbag wounding him in the head. Thus was first blood drawn.

The culprit of the peeing was otherwise than in his present behaviour, a jolly and agreeable person. And of all surprising things, was a young ship's captain and opera lover guilty of only censoring another's musical taste. But as came the increased volume of imploring screams from the other engowned friends of the quite beautiful hostess, these members present of the Royal referred to Clubs laid into your man goodo. The hostess herself, however, cared not a hoot about her tapestry nor music nor gramophone, and was equally casual as to whom she let tamper with her body, enjoying as she did men in any and all variety. Thus, she vehemently cried out to the disciplinarians to desist. Whereupon the ship's captain being unhanded, the hostess promptly took him by the hand and by a secret door to the back servants' stairs, up which both disappeared to bed. While meanwhile his spilt blood required that sides be taken, consisting of those who approved the urinary censorship and those who abhorred such musical interruption. However a disagreement concerning the period in which an Italian master had painted a hall painting was already providing a violent battle of unbelievable proportions among the rest of the guests in the front hall. Where sides were also drawn up. From persons, many of whom at the time, were innocently dancing and enjoying to look as they waltzed by these works of art. However, the folk who having been long enough in Ireland to know what raised voices meant, and hearing the loud commotion, tried to escape to the drawing room. From which latter, however, now came an equally forceful commotion. Signalling all that it was distinctly time to have one's fists, if not a cudgel, at the ready. But too late, as the warring factions from the drawing room now confronted the warring factions from the hall. And as the battle now gave rise to two sources of contention, no side knew what side they might safely be on. All present realizing it was every man for himself. With each taking a doubtful look at the other and in lieu of continued doubt, commencing to fight for their lives. Indeed if someone's back was turned and such person not previously having indicated which triangular side he was on, he was for the sake of prudency instantly chosen as an opponent. Usually a bottle of stout being wielded to baptize him as he stood. And if he continued to stand and the bottle did not break, he was duly hammered without blessing to the black and white tiled floor without so much as a murmur of apology for such unsporting unfair play.

Having Celticly hard skulls most victims of attack from behind were able to withstand at least the first onslaught. The bottle often breaking and such hardy gents licking the stout from their lips, enabling them to turn to identify the sneak attacker. And woe be unto him. For such assailant could be assured of receiving one of the most unholy of woolings. This famed Dublin chastisement consisting of the aggrieved gent knocking the treacherous chap to the ground and grabbing him by both his port and starboard ears and engripped also with a goodly handful of hair, then pounding his skull repeatedly on the tiles, while removing the hirsute plumage about his hearing appendage and shaking the living daylights out of his neurons.

With the resulting jungle drum cacophony of many heads now being thumped and banged the length and breadth of this once dignified hall, those still upstanding gave a good account of them-selves as the battle raged totally without rhyme and most certainly totally without reason. But always in the midst of such melée where the fists, boots and bottles were flying, one could catch the unforgettably calm sight of a philosophic gent perched somewhere above it all, safe from all harm. In this case one had but to look atop the main staircase and there he was. Smiling gently, sitting high, a bottle of champagne at his side, and sipping a glass as he quietly peered through the balustrade at the carnage below. The beguiling contentment upon this particular face clearly felt as a ravishingly attractive lady put her fingers gently through locks of his dark hair. Such folk as this philosopher might be thought to be, was not a barrister, solicitor or man in some context of the law. But in this case was a gentleman who dabbled in poetry and had in his earlier days carefully attempted to be only on the receiving end of handouts, but instead had received many a wooling for his opinions and had learned the lesson how to precisely remain a comfortable and uninjured spectator albeit a sheepishly guilty one.

The time was past midnight on this November night of the new moon. A sea wind shaking doors and windows. And a surf booming in the caves at the foot of the cliffs. The front hall marble tiles of this house like the opinions expressed upon them, were black and white only. Entry here was dramatically through great doors from an outer vestibule, a tier above. Indeed usually to get to such houses at all from the road you penetrated great dark portals in great granite walls and dramatically ascended or descended as one might to a sacrificial altar. In this case more than one hundred dark stone steps between mountainous rhododendrons, a sombre vista appropriate to the carnage now in full swing. Pilasters being chipped and smashed. Marble busts being toppled and cracking the tiles. Hepplewhite furniture flying. And everywhere transporting through the air were other and not much less valuable divers objets d'art. These missiles airborne with such abandon made it clear to even the members of the better Royally designated clubs and societies that no amount of their admonitions and civilized cautions had even a vague chance of according priority to the safety of the priceless antiques.

As windows smashed and drapes ripped, the wind blew a gale. Even wall niches were disfigured, and their marble busts toppled from their recesses. And now the sound of feet were heard pounding, running riot on the upper floors of the house. Ladies screaming as frocks were torn. Such mayhem always being a time to settle old scores, slanders and long sworn revenges. One well known eccentric beauty suddenly openly declaring as she exhibited her bosoms that the husband of every wife present had been at them and that she had the biggest nipples in Co. Dublin and was about to prove it. This increased the screaming as she made to rip open every other lady's bodice within fingernail grasp. But it did, as the many breasts present were revealed, have the effect of stopping the carnage and the blood splashing briefly. Allowing a dignified member of the Kildare Street Club to remind the combatants to come to their Anglo Irish, if not Irish, senses. And for someone to telephone for medical assistance. Duly the doctor did arrive. Qualified as it appropriately happened at the Royal College of Surgeons in Ireland. A gold watch chain suspended across his waistcoat, his elegant black case at his side as he stepped from the front door into the vestibule. From whence he could survey further and down upon this blood bespattered carnage strewn front hall. But before he could cut any gauze or get his stethoscope out, he dropped to the deck like a brick, felled with a heart attack.

The only place of partially untrammelled and seeming safety was a water closet adjoining the vestibule, the door of which was flanked by large potted palms. The good doctor was gently carried therein to be propped aseat upon the toilet bowl in order to keep at least his upper torso out of the wet. For a length of lead pipe had, as a weapon, been recently ripped from the lavatory wall and water was pouring out over the hall floors which were now aflood from this fractured pipe. Meanwhile, another sensible member of the Kildare Street Club summoned a second doctor. Who in turn arrived. Again with a gold watch chain and in an elegant blue pinstriped suit and sporting the subtle light blue, red, green and broad black stripes of a Trinity College graduate's tie. The doctor took one look at the carnage amid the strewn furnishings covering the length and breadth of the vast hall and then spied his colleague slumped unconscious on the toilet seat nearby. Whom, god help this poor latter physician and the fine cloth on the back of his trousers, which were residing upon such seat and to which he now adhered, being that it had only that very afternoon been freshly painted. And in an emerald bright green.

Trinity College graduates are among the most sophisticated of people and have long since gone out to distinguish themselves and triumph in all corners of the world. Especially those who have succeeded in the faculty of medicine. But this gentleman doctor so taken unawares, could not have imagined what was in store at this otherwise stately elegant home, and he stood rigidly in total shock. At least for the moment. For he too then did promptly become hors de combat, fainting backwards into a potted palm.

But who shall in this world ever say that such imbroglios do not befall even the most well and benignly intentioned of men in the best of country houses. For despite the unfortunate developments therein, to all these stately venues did proceed, in general, your usually better category of invited people. The semi pleasured class you might say. Who in the bliss of these mostly mixed husbandless and wifeless gatherings, convened to fight off the glooms of life. Albeit which frequently only deepened further in the close proximity of loose women and randy gentlemen. Requiring more bottles of stout and glasses of whiskey often accompanied by other alcoholic exotics whose headache making constituents were those derived of potato brewing. But which in the imbiber produced more arias, lullabys and cradlesongs. Which in turn somehow incited more insults and verbal lashings. For hours on end. Leading to these thrashings. When both battling and loving hugs merged into one another. And more times became tears and sobs. But at any stage it remained always unforgivable to go home. Commendable to wake in a heap somewhere. Bleary eyed in some strange cold room and lucky that your feet weren't soaking freezing in some mountain stream. Or in some thatched cottage or at the end of the anonymous hall of some great ancient house. Shivering under somebody else's coat. Dreaming a nightmare on somebody else's floor or sofa with the prong of a broken spring up a backside. Or looking for warmth in somebody else's arms. Wrapped around someone else's body or someone else's body wrapped around yours. And you knew you were well and truly arrived. In the free state sovereignty of boozers, spendthrifts, wife beaters, onanists and would be philanderers. And this indeed was, in the land of saints and scholars, an utter revelation of Irish life. Leaving this American so recently a newcomer.

Bewildered

In a complete state

Of moral shock

VI

The first of the doctors to arrive at the battle scene, who was a renowned fly fisherman, fortunately proved not to be dead but had only a minor heart attack, but did however have a shoulder dislocated as it required several party goers present to rip him off the toilet to whence the major part of the seat of his trousers was affixed in wet green paint. Of course, good Samaritan automobiles did ferry people back to be medically attended at the better hospitals in the city of Dublin. And indeed this coastal area, haunted with the legend of this battle that had taken place there, although it was never quite the same again, did eventually return to its normal every day exterior of peace and quiet.

But one had just cause to remember that night for in the very beginning of the melée I had been clubbed by a damn sneaky assailant with a stout bottle on the back of the head. Weathering the blow I turned to swear revenge, announcing loudly as I did so several of the bloodier battles of the then recently ended war. I'm sure my attacker had never been more than ten miles from Donnybrook in his life but I pretended such assumption to his having been present at Anzio, Bataan, Corregidor, Normandy and Stalingrad. And loudly inferred that none of these battles he'd been through, would, in the annals of violence, hold a candle to the battle that was now about to unfold about and upon him in reprisal for his diabolically dastard attack. But lo and behold, a distinct Dublin friend was already beating the bejesus out of him with fists, sending lefts, rights, and uppercuts to his jaw and bolos deep into his solar plexus.

It was my first lesson in Irish combat. That you did not sportingly present yourself in a frontal forthright manner declaiming to challenge your would be opponent and thus give him a gentlemanly chance of protecting himself. Nor did you stand anywhere mid scene with your back unprotected, gesticulating or uttering war cries or hysterically calling down the wrath of God upon one's foe. For unseen attack from the rear or an unguarded flank was the practised Celtic approach. Plenty of time to spout about comeuppance and fair play when you had your foot across your supine man's throat while he attempted to squeak out apologies between his gasps for mercy.

But there were other places. One resembling no pub, resembling no country house. Which if you couldn't find a venue by the sea suitable for late night social relations, you could, if you knew persons who knew the whereabouts of this locale, repair there for entertainment which was as various as it could be violent. Now over the years in Dublin there were many attempts to open up and run improvised gambling casinos and the like. Especially in the basements and cellars of the great Georgian townhouses. And indeed some were run. Roulette being played with a large ball bearing found somewhere, which was spun within the rim of an old discarded automobile wheel. The unreliable nature of the contraption often leading to disputes settled occasionally by someone found dead under such tables with a knife in the back. But never in the modern or ancient history of the Irish State was there anywhere at any time anything like Charnelchambers.

Perfectly describing the place, this name was uttered in awe from my own lips upon my first innocent visit there. Charnelchambers as it did, consisting of a series of cellar rooms located central in a once elegant Georgian Dublin square north of the Liffey. It was first where a charming cherubically rotund gentleman lived whose luxurious previous life had been reduced in circumstances and he was enduring an impecuniousness which had now prolonged beyond the temporary. While in his more undressed states, he was fond of reminding people that his Christian name was Basil, and from the Greek, meant kingly and royal. Afternoons he would be seen in the gilded cage of Davy Byrnes, the Dawson Lounge, or holding court in the public rooms of the Shelbourne and Royal Hibernian Hotels where he was devastatingly quick with both merry and unmerry quips.

Basil smoked cigarettes with a long ivory holder and spoke in what was then referred to as the King's English. To pay his own rent he initially took in carefully selected paying guests, many of whom were listed in The Almanach De Gotha if not Debrett. And who had, when their luck was down, repaired there as a temporary resort. Which frequently became their final one. Thus these chambers came to house princes, counts, moguls, black sheep, white sheep, and ultimately even members of the Irish Republican Army. Such was the irreligiously pagan nature of the place that it even with the latter, lodged the odd Orangeman and Unionist Presbyterian. And as Basil himself was a man who preferred other gentlemen, they too of this persuasion were frequently domiciled within. Ireland having become post war a fabled mecca for the more sincere elegantly cultured homosexualist. In fact every condition of mankind including sodomites, necrophiliacs, coprophiliacs, and especially erotomaniacs were to be in these dungeons finally found. It was overflowing too with the failed and bankrupt, the criminal as well as the contented insane. Even the odd honest to God gee whizz American from the midst of Minnesota could end up here. Although singularly short of hermaphrodites, it did in the course of its existence become the most astonishing place of festivity and mayhem ever invented. And did sadly leave many who wished it never had been.

It was upon a rainy wintry Thursday afternoon when I was having visitors to tea in my Trinity rooms, when an enormously tall eccentric gentleman with whom I occasionally played and lost one sided tennis matches, mostly due to the fact that he could serve a tennis ball at 200 miles an hour, arrived amidst the company with a breathtakingly beautiful blonde lady in tow. I was painting pictures at the time which, although she was too polite to condemn as appalling, she did at least admire my nerve. I thanked her for at least noticing them and expressed despair that it was the only way I had of spending my Sundays in a bereft, empty, closed up Dublin. And was then promptly upon the Sunday invited to call upon her. My enormously tall tennis serving friend had apoplexy on the spot. And nearly ripped her address out of my fingers. I was a little surprised to find reaching her residence in this highly dilapidated street, that one had also to descend down steep narrow stairs deep into a basement area where one had to rap one's knuckles on a rather shabby green door. I was agreeably reassured but not a little nonplussed when a corpulent, marvellously elegant gentleman appeared, answering the door with an ivory cigarette holder held high, scissored between the extreme tips of his first two index fingers. He was attired in what seemed some form of butler's regalia but with a gold chain hanging across his crimson waistcoat. I was not to know at that moment that after ten in the evenings following pub emptying time, he always greeted would be guests at the door, totally in the nude. With not only his cigarette holder stiffly horizontal but his private appendage as well.

Nor did I realize that by daytime Charnelchambers' seemingly open doors of these various rented crypts had to be padlocked and barred at night. But upon this swiftly darkening late afternoon these cellar rooms and former kitchens so vast, damp, dark and endless, and which extended into alcoves, wine vaults and coal bunkers, seemed anything but the setting for some of the most memorably exquisite social occasions I have ever attended. Housing as it then did this highborn lusciously curvaceous beautiful lady with such abundant radiant blond hair. Who having escaped Germans, Poles, Russians, and other middle European warring ethnics during the war, had now recently escaped a dangerously violent, alcoholic and highly eccentric Anglo Irish husband and was now in her straitened circumstances, secretly seeking solace there.

On this Sunday I followed the cherubically bubbling blond Basil clothed in his black jacket, crumpled white shirt and black tie, as he proceeded backwards through this dank dungeon to its very last rearmost room, while dropping the Princess' title every few steps. Basil, who astonishingly resembled a portly Hollywood matinée idol, had been an ace Spitfire pilot shot down over Germany who with one leg broken made his way back to England to fly again. But during the last weeks of the war further injury caused by a flying bomb repaired him to convalesce in Ireland. Now as the door opened he bowed and clicked his heels, as if one were being conducted into a sovereign's presence. And there awaiting me, seated within upon a chaise squeezed in her narrow damp cramped room, was this gracious Saxon skyblue eyed Princess. Her possessions stacked everywhere within and on top of everything up to the ceiling.

I was, of course, immensely anxious to enter upon the more socially less dangerous and preferably cultural side of activities in the Irish capital. Having now nearly every night at party or pub, had to fight for my life. And as a hostess at home to one on a damp, cold, winter Sunday evening for late afternoon tea followed by drinks at seven p.m., the Princess, albeit in her dank dungeon, was as much and more than I ever dared hope for. Basil, her landlord, continuing on my repeated visits to act as concièrge come butler rushing to fill a vase with water when I, desperately in love, also brought flowers.

These being an exotic bloom or two, by necessity lifted from the college botanical conservatory which housed such specimens. Upon these occasions the Princess baked the most exquisite scones which she served with whipped cream and her own home made strawberry jam. It was impossible to conceive of any husband ever battering or beating her. And my tall explosively serving tennis partner who had previously constantly turned up with dazzling foreign women at my rooms ceased suddenly to do so saying he was not about to introduce his love objects only to have various college roués run off with them as I had done with this cultured curvaceous aristocratic middle European beauty.

Of course I was merely lonely for the excitement of an intelligent female mind, and certainly no roué but I did most eagerly upon this particular and subsequent Sundays in my tweeds enter through the iron gate in the black fence which stood in front of this decaying Georgian mansion and proceed heart thumping down the steep iron stairs and trepidatiously knock on this basement door. Indeed even continuing to think Basil was the butler. As he would on subsequent occasions precede me through this first vast room, once the kitchen of the great mansion above, having already put a kettle to boil and arranged tea items at the ready to be delivered to the Princess at home beyond her door at the end of the long dark passage. Always enjoying to hear Basil's spiel declaimed in his exquisite vowels as he clicked heels and bowed.

'Ah how nice to see you again. And so soon. Her Royal Highness awaits. Ah and how good of you. Flowers. She'll be much pleased. I do wish more people were as thoughtful. And dear me. Shades of the African Congo. Dare I imagine. Orchids. How exotically surprising and pleasing. I think if someone were to bring me flowers, even a single tiny violet, I should swoon. Not on these damp stone floors, of course. But on the appropriate part of a chaise longue. And into desirably appropriate arms.'

Everyone, at least upon my first few occasions down in this dungeon, had damn decent vowels. The British accent then being used like a blow torch to cut a social swathe through all that was Irish. And even I, I must confess, undertook to subsequently overhaul and polish my own phonetics. As much from a sense of protective coloration as anything else. And it did undeniably ease one through the better places in town. But did little to impress the Princess who through her trials and tribulations had become somewhat socialistically minded. But not to the degree that this might have made her discourage capitalistic upper class men's attentions. Although sad as her countenance sometimes could be, the Princess would as soon as two or more gentlemen collected, rally her own aristocratic spirits, adoring as she did to be surrounded by her admirers. One of whom was already present on this initial occasion as I took a seat on the side of her bed. Coronets embroidered on her linen sheets, pillow cases and napkins. And just as I was discreetly examining such embossment between my thumb and a forefinger I felt my heel under the edge of her bed, knock against a nearly full porcelain vessel of urine. As it happened, a pot not begot in Ireland for it was a rare exquisite piece of Meissen emblazoned on its sides and cover with a coronet and her escutcheon. Which pot gave hint of chamber music to come. And in which, in view of my father's sentiments, I later took great pleasure to piss in.

The two orchids were placed on a Louis XV ormolu mounted marquetry poudreuse where the Princess kept a small altar and icon and where two candles flamed to illumine the room. We took China tea with lemon slices from her Dresden as she sat on a Louis XV giltwood chaise, reputed made for Madame du Barry. Sparkling were her one remaining pair of diamond and sapphire brooches being the most valuable of her few remaining unpawned possessions. Tea was always followed by a pure pot still Scotch whisky and fruit cake baked in the great stove out in the kitchen. Then my fellow guest Peter, maestro virtuoso, would arise. A gentleman who had long loved, worshipped and adored the very grimiest of Dublin pavements this Princess had been compelled to walk upon. And as you might know he was matriculating within that four foot thick granite walled bastion on St Stephen's Green, the Royal College of Surgeons. However, this brilliant student, unlike many of the balding perennial habitués there, had won exam prizes in midwifery and gynaecology and passed his first medical years with flying honours. He loved Ireland even as he abhorred the savage poverty and doom ridden slums where he delivered babies. An old Etonian as well as an ex Royal Air Force Spitfire pilot he was as exquisitely English as anyone could ever hope to be. Wearing his old school scarf, voluminously like a great boa constrictor around his neck, with the rest of its long length hanging down his back to his ankles. Flowing blond locks of hair framed a face so astonishing aquiline that women upon catching a glimpse of him were known to weep. And indeed Basil, fluent in Sanskrit, unleashed constant avouchments of love in this language which Peter embarrassingly understood. But these sentiments from both men and women were nothing. Nothing whatever. Compared to what happened to such ladies and gentlemen when Peter opened his violin case and brought forth his cherished fiddle built by Antonio Stradivari.

In her terribly tiny room, the Princess had strategically assembled us. Peter taking up the only unoccupied corner to carefully draw his bow back and forth in his rosin. And then tucking his fiddle lovingly between chin and shoulder, would with the faintest of frowns upon his brow, tune the strings. Beyond her heavily gauze curtained window which opened upon a tiny courtyard and outdoor privy, one could hear the rain splashing from broken gutters and gurgling in the outside drains. And if the gauze were parted one could see the rats scrabbling in the piles of debris. But here inside. Turf smoke from her small fireplace scenting the air. The whisky served. Peter began to play. All within and without becoming utterly still. In this hush now. As we listened. To the violin strains of Mozart, Brahms, Bruch, Dvořák. Played with all the warmth and exquisite tonalities alive in this gentleman's heart and skill.

Ah but inevitably. As such musical moment progressed there would finally find another Princess adoring member of this tiny audience appearing. Who out of one of the dark, dank, windowless wine cellar caves back along the hall, would now silently slip in the door. He was called Adolphus the Vicomte. And when whisky was poured at an intermission, Adolphus shuffling barefoot in slippers on the paving stone, would announce in his heavily accented but impeccable English.

'Your devoted servant madam. Brought forth from his abject hole by such wondrous music, apologizes to impose. And to you too, gentlemen, for my lack of sartorial elegance. But pyjamas somehow do, don't they, make one appear as if one were just arriving from South America, or in the case of their being silk, as mine happen to be, as if one were just departing to go there.'

Adolphus was a pale, thin, aristocratic titled black sheep from a family who forwarded a not unhandsome monthly emolument which would continue to arrive providing he physically stay forever and absolutely out of his native country. Although long a denizen of Charnelchambers, Adolphus preferred to live as much of his life as he could in the manner to which he had previously and sumptuously been accustomed. And did, upon arrival of his monthly cheque, have the Princess cash this for him and to summon a horse cab. Then in his slippers and a borrowed raincoat from Basil who sported it in his Foreign Office days, Adolphus thus covering his pyjamas would make his way up and out into Dublin life once more. Mounting the horse cab in which he would clip clop to the pawn shop to redeem his morning suit. Out of hock, too, would come his cufflinks, studs, shoes, shirts, tie and socks. Then taking off his pyjamas in a pawn shop cubby hole and folding them to rest in his repossessed attaché case, he would dress in his cutaway coat and striped trousers, stick in his pearl tie pin, and step out again to his waiting horse cab. The jarvey saluting as he held open the door.

'Ah yer honour, sure as the holy ghost himself never sneezed, youse is looking as great as the Protestant Bishop of Meath. 'Tis a treat to see and serve you. It is to the Shelbourne Hotel per as usual.'

Of course yours truly was, on a couple of late morning occasions, a passenger in such horse drawn brougham which took Adolphus directly to his suite already booked awaiting him at this renowned hotel. From whence each day the Vicomte would go racing and in the evenings dine within the comfortingly sprawling up and down rooms of the fabled French family's restaurant, Jammet's. Which had lace curtained windows and an entrance fronting on Nassau Street across from the Provost's back garden of Trinity College and the iron door for the use of College Fellows. But the restaurant could also be reached by a discreet dark alley just up and left off Grafton Street. If the Vicomte was not found here over pheasant and champagne he would be in attendance at dinner parties, balls and receptions, with as often as he could, the Princess in tow and might manage in this manner, depending upon his luck picking winners at races, for a week and at the absolute most a fortnight. But inevitably broke and penniless, paying his bill he would discharge from the Shelbourne, returning on foot to pawn his clothes and with the money buy sustenance to last until his emolument arrived once more and he was able again to emerge from his pyjamaed existence in his tiny, windowless wine cellar room in Charnelchambers.

But on musical evenings such as this, Adolphus would present himself, elaborately apologizing in his nightwear state. The Countess inviting him use of her giltwood chaise. Upon the edge of which he would contritely and solemnly sit. But from which he would inevitably rise in religious fervour, enthralled by the music of Peter's violin. The Vicomte's hand held over his heart as if it had been pierced and he was holding back the spurting blood. Which upon one occasion did come. When following a goodly amount of the Princess's Scotch whisky, and possessed by the beauty of Peter's playing, the Vicomte stood pressing and banging his forehead against the wall with such force that the skin on his brow was broken and the blood one thought would burst from his heart, cascaded instead out of his skull and down his face. As he would implore Peter.

'I beg of you don't stop. Play. Play.'

Except for a vision of the Blessed Virgin claimed seen by one of the more transient occupants, a devout member of both The Legion of Decency and Legion of Mary, little could be claimed of a religious nature in Charnelchambers. However, where the now departed member of The Legion of Decency had avowed witnessing his vision, indeed on the very site upon which the Virgin stood, miraculously a tiny spring was discovered flowing. But sceptics continuing to scoff until one night a Trinity College law student, short circuiting the lights, plunged the place into darkness and a life and death free for all. When suddenly a blue halo was seen glowing exactly in the niche where the original vision was witnessed. Sadly on this occasion disputes over who thought they saw the glow led to even greater mayhem. But other than this phenomenon such cultural and religious behaviour was rare indeed. For the later and now more historically associated activities down in these Charnelchambers of which I was not only soon to learn more, now dominated all. And yours truly was to be held accountable by many folk for their having ever started.

Nearly all the entrenched tenants of Charnelchambers were foreigners in this foreign dark land. And as adversity, inclemency and loneliness could do in Dublin, it wed many a man and woman together. In consolation if not in bliss. But meanwhile what one was more and more conscious of in Ireland was that most times in which a rare refined atmosphere created and prevailed, there would not be one Irish born earthling present. But plenty were there I'm telling you, one night as I lay dreaming in the Princess's arms and was suddenly awakened by a long agonizingly blood curdling scream. Like none ever heard from man, beast or woman which proved to be a herald of what was to come.

It was a Saturday. The Princess and I had been to the races and Jammet's. And I was a rather shaken man. For the night before, returning past midnight to my rooms and mounting the entrance steps of number 38 Trinity College, I had only gone a few steps into the dark hallway when I was grabbed from behind. I could feel my senses waning to unconsciousness in the process of being choked to death by an unbelievably strong pair of arms. I repeatedly slammed my elbows backwards into someone's ribs until, just as the voices of a celestial choir began to be heard, they finally let go and I fell gasping to the stone floor. In the dim light of a college lamp I saw the unmistakable figure of my tall explosively tennis serving friend running away along the cobbled gutter and by the slung chains of the quad. The Princess reassured me that only very few of her suitor boyfriends ever got that jealous enough to actually kill. But with the evening wearing on past pub closing time she thought it best I not for the meanwhile venture in the dark back to college. And, of course, I was glad to avail of the tranquil, blissful, peaceful hospitality of her bed for the night. And that I would be safe there, my head tucked in against her shoulder, an embroidered coronet pressing against my cheek and finally asleep. Till a different complexion altogether descended upon these subterranean premises.

Basil's impecuniousness had like many of his tenants now reached rock bottom due to his equal penchant for high and elegant if not riotous living in about the better Dublin social venues. Such pursuits requiring much more money than he managed to collect in his weekly rents. He had also recently taken up the expensive pastime of racing and with his blond locks newly rinsed, enjoyed to travel there by a rented chauffeured Bugatti Royale landau. On one such outing to the Curragh in this astonishingly long bonneted vehicle, Smyth's of the Green had provided a hamper crammed full of exotics previously unobtainable during the war. And with the Princess, the Vicomte and me invited along, Basil flicking his ash out the car window from his long ivory cigarette holder announced to his comfortable guests:

'But how good of you all to come with humble me to the races. Decent champagne, don't you think. And rather good smoked salmon. I must as landlord with such distinguished tenants, keep up appearances, don't you agree. Of course, darlings, tonight is the first of my ''bring and drink'' parties which I shall keep as brief and quiet as possible.'

The Vicomte in one of his dungeon incarcerated periods was, of course, shrouded in Basil's all covering military mackintosh, and a pair of Wellington boots. His pyjamas underneath with their strange light blue and vertically bright red striped colours catching many an eye as one cruised about the paddocks. On the mornings following these first shindigs Basil was able to collect together the empty stout bottles and with a barrow and a tiny barefoot boy pushing, would proceed to redeem them for cash at the pub. Admission to Charnel-chambers being, for those not already living there, a minimum two dozen parcel of stout or a bottle of spirits. But you might even, as one notorious entrepreneur did whose current girlfriend working in a butcher's purloined such, gain entrance with a couple of pounds of steak. And upon entrance frequently sold and bartered his remaining sirloins. He would also have in reserve sausages, dozens of eggs and bacon. These latter often ending up in the stomach of a particularly starving lady sculptress who would after repairing to a vault to accommodate this gentleman's prodigious biological urges attempt to sneakily conduct herself a great fry up on the stove. And would loudly announce upon finishing her gargantuan greasy feed, that she was ready to select the biggest penis present for dessert.

As the fame of Charnelchambers spread, the number of bottles needed for entry increased. But not all paid admission however. For there were those who were welcomed without hindrance. These were folk of the titled or discernibly upper classes, having in their gowns and dinner jackets just taken leave of parties and balls and in search of fashionable low life, sought to confirm for themselves rumours heard north and south of the Liffey and the length and breadth of Dublin. Basil receiving them in his nightly naked and stiff appendaged condition at the door.

'Ah my dears and darling intending débauchees. By your vowels shall ye be known. Or indeed if you're not speaking, then by a peek, my dears, at your better and further particulars when the ladies' gowns are up and the gentlemen's trousers are down.'

Never was there ever a shortage of potential entrants to Charnel-chambers. Ferocious battles often taking place at the door. Basil employing a docker or two from the Dublin quays to keep out some of the more objectionable types who would sometimes in a gang storm down the iron steep steps from the street, as even more would pile down the stairs behind them. But there were times too when some perspicacious people upon entering, took one brief look and were wisely instantly screaming to get out. As this reaction alone made them highly desirable to be made part of the profligacy within, such victims were often, utterly hysterical, actually pulled and dragged further over the threshold and the door locked behind them. Gurriers, aging newsboys, street walkers, amateur bookies, and others of poor reputations could only gain admittance in the company of someone known to Basil. And as many were known, Basil upon their flutes having played, few gurriers were ever refused admittance.

But as the nights wore on there was a variation on the theme of human beings that the Emerald Isle had not known before and may not have ever come to know since. In attendance, were hypnotists, carpet fitters, magicians, market gardeners, and upholsterers. These latter ready to cover anything in burlap which was all the rage of interior designers of the time. There were picture framers who would without hesitation perforate a canvas around your ears. Wrought iron craftsmen, and one who had actually made a cage to imprison virgins. Lady chiropodists, who would treat more than your long toe nails. Practitioners of acupuncture, one or two of whom, let me tell you, were up to their very own special kind of prodding. There were quislings from Sweden, Norway and Belgium. Safecrackers and spivs from England. Gas meter readers and earbitersoff. The latter so referred to as a group since in most battles there were those whose gnashing teeth would instantly go towards this hearing appendage. And many a chewed ear was found next morning on the Charnel-chamber floor. And even a pure black African gentleman who adorned in his princely robes arrived with a retinue of servants carrying pots of cooked rice and a cauldron of boiled chickens. And with three drummers and their drums in tow, by god would he do an Irish jig.

Sadly, to an altogether previously benign habitat of Charnelchambers there finally arrived wholesale violence within the precincts. For which one pleads forgiveness for having albeit in self defence, first perpetrated. It was upon a misty depressingly damp evening when the Princess and I were huddling together in her narrow bed for warmth. The Princess's pot to piss in at the time was out of action having sprung a leak. And having had much stout to drink out in a pub I was putting off the evilly cold moment of heading out into the rat infested courtyard to the latrine. Although I could put her silk dressing gown on over my shoulders, my feet would not fit into the Princess's slippers. So in the sockless clammy discomfort of my own shoes, I unbolted and unlocked the door and stumbled out into the courtyard inclemency to the dreadfully inhospitable water closet there. Upon my return from an extremely long pee, there was a strange man inside the room. He was attempting to further pull back the covers from the Princess whose bosoms were already exposed as she clung with one hand to an edge of a coronet embroidered linen sheet. For some reason a British rather than an American expression seemed to leave one's lips, attesting to the bias of one's life within Trinity College.

'Damn it, sir, what do you think you're about.'

As I was in the Princess's kimono the obnoxious gent assumed he was facing a push over cream puff transvestite. Many of whom had been recently featuring as late late guests in Charnelchambers. His reply to my inquiries was, to say the least, not only rude but objectionably suggestive. And concerned the possible three of us there and then doing something together. I then repeatedly, firmly but politely requested him to pronto depart.

'Like bejesus fucking hell I will you English pansy.'

The next thing I knew I was having my face slapped. Which, considering previous mayhems, was innocuous enough. But one thing I had already learned in Ireland was not to, on such moments as this, stand on ceremony. For your man without declaiming his intentions, had already lowered his head and was about to butt me in the solar plexus. Stepping a pace back as he charged forward, I gathered every ounce of my weight behind my right clenched fist. Circling it past my knee upwards and letting it flower into what was clearly the most unmerciful uppercut ever unleashed. Catching your man on the left cheekbone and parting his feet from the stone floor which took him over, without touching, the seat of the Princess's Louis XV giltwood chaise. As one does at such times, you notice a lot of significant things and one happened to catch sight of a jewel encrusted dagger which the Princess had in her hand. Of course as the man reeled out the door holding his face pouring blood I was horrified. But at least he was still alive as he might not have been had he tangled with the Princess. His silhouette lurching side to side along the hall and upon reaching the front kitchen your man fainted face forward in the doorway. Appearing as an actor might in limelight. With a bone crashing sound as his skull hit the stone floor. A cacophony of voices rose with the cry.

'By God who hit him with a hatchet, who hit him. Let's get the dirty fucker who did that. Up the Republic.'

This was the more sporting side of Charnelchamber life. Those who were physically aggrieved did instantly attract their champions who immediately sought to wreak retribution. However this moment was, put in its historical context, merely the beginning of many ensuing nocturnal carnages to take place in these cellar crypts. For when your man disappeared off to the hospital, the most awful slaughter of the innocents took place that night. The Vicomte happily for him being ensconced spending his monthly emolument in his one week splurge at the Shelbourne Hotel. The Princess even thinking her room had better be turned into an infirmary. Which suggestion I vetoed vehemently, as the thumps and bangs boomed against the door. For this mob of your gentleman's avengers out on their spree were already marauding into the various tunnels and vaults. Descending upon the trusting guiltless occupants there even as they lay asleep. Then dragging them out into the hall and beating the living daylights out of them. Indeed women found entwined with men also became innocent victims. The Princess's door however remained securely bolted and locked and reinforced with two stout oak timbers slotted into place. While the Princess inside professed no knowledge of anything outside to the belligerently inquiring voices. And I anxiously shivered in her protectively enveloping arms. Terrified as much now by the dagger she obviously kept somewhere handy when she was abed.

Although the previously peaceful nature of Charnelchambers changed to one of acrimony and animal viciousness, nevertheless occasional moments of charm were still to be enjoyed. Including one unforgettable evening when a considerable number of members of a travelling circus arrived. Such folk spent long months slogging on tour across Ireland's countryside, performing in cold, windswept and rain leaking tents and shuttling about in trailers and caravans. And down in these cellars they seemed glad of a little change to the home like intimacy, as it were. Albeit in the company of a notorious tinker widely known and feared as Lead Pipe Daniel The Dangerous who had shepherded them to Charnelchambers, laden with booze of every description. And it wasn't long before the place was festivity itself and literally jumping. With three midget acrobats bouncing around like balls.

The Princess and I undid her barriers that night, and indeed dressed as for the opera where in fact we were headed but instead with Peter playing accompanying airs on his violin we formed a select audience right then and there in Charnelchambers as all these circus folk one after another performed on the kitchen table. All except the Iron Lady, a weight lifter, who had the whole lot of us sit on the table as she commenced to balance it while elevating it two handed over her head until our own heads were hitting the ceiling and doubt as to our safety was being expressed. Next was Madame Splitcrotch the contortionist with one leg straight up and the other straight down as she spun like a top and then turned herself into several sorts and shapes of pretzels. A lady sword swallower who had not a sword with her, did her act in the most obscene but none the less impressive manner possible. Lead Pipe Daniel The Dangerous providing a personal priapus which made the Princess gasp in disbelief and which the lady swallower engulfed to its hairy hilt. While a mortified outraged Peter refused to play. Indeed he stormed out. Which was as it happened just as well. For moments later his Stradivarius might have had a bath in jets of water.

The gathering otherwise was having such a good jolly peaceful if bawdy time. With another batch of uninvited revellers arriving. Until most perilous of all, but at least seemly, the fire eater while digesting his flames set the kitchen alight, igniting the Hessian wall hangings with their pornographic tableaux. The pompiers were called. And as you might expect meanwhile, someone threw on a bucket of piss. Stinking the place to high heaven. As people all at once tried to get out and up again to the street, the front door became jammed shut. And there was a god almighty surge to the rear. Which met head on with Lead Pipe Daniel mid corridor. returning as he was from having had his way with a lady temporarily residing within a vault, who was a distinguished professor of anthropology referred to as Molly Of The Apes. Not only was Lead Pipe Daniel, the ape, grunting and growling with satisfaction, but he was also emptying a whisky bottle down his throat which could shortly mean one of the most vicious and terrifying people in the length and breadth of Ireland was about to act up. All six foot five inches tall and seventeen stone of him. Announcing.

'Ah God, one good woman fucked gives me such an appetite for another. And as an illiterate untouchable humble tinker I don't mind telling you I prefer the lady intellectuals.'

In spite of the yells of fire, Lead Pipe Daniel The Dangerous thought the mob was rushing him, and was instantly grabbing around himself for a suitable length of his usual weapon after which he was named. But thank God he was not near plumbing. Instead merely fists and boots left, right and centre were being landed, until mercifully the fire fighters arrived. Not only dousing the conflagration but everyone in sight. The Princess and I only being saved from a soaking by managing to get back into the safety of her room. And dear me there we stood in our evening finery. The Princess near to tears. With another barbarian head bashing, testicle twisting affray substituting for opera that night. For that was the trouble with Charnelchambers. No matter what innocent pleasantry was in progress it inevitably ended up in some form of diabolical grief. Which you were always damn lucky wasn't terminal. And reflected in Lead Pipe Daniel's oft quoted poem.

Bad as I am
I am not for nothing
Daniel the Dangerous
The Lead Pipe Maniac
Searching for truth and justice
All over the fucking zodiac

Ah but enough of recounting the mayhem. It should not be forgot that it was in Dublin where soda water was first invented. And in the sphere of human ingenuity lay one other of the most astonishing aspects of Charnelchambers. For down in these dungeons also collected together some of the greatest thinkers, axiologists, scientists, philosophers and moral tacticians of this or any epoch. Although the tenets of such schools of thought as Bishop Berkeley's Immaterialism were long established by this Trinity College man, the bings, zings and nerts of nuclear fission and fusion had only then been a few years postulated. Indeed in Dublin lived one or two who had taken the first steps to disintegrate the nucleus of an atom which brought the dawn of the atomic age. And which has now led to folk spying upon the quarks, ziffs and piffs zinging tangential off their innocent electrons. In fairness to such eminent persons one does not suggest for one microsecond that they hatched their theories or even visited or were within a mile of these notorious crypts. But begrudging sceptics should remember that it was within the damp night time walls of Charnelchambers where the more eccentric and some of the most brilliant of these great minds collected who promulgated conceptual essences which have since pervaded the entire thinking and drinking world. And when one such metaphysician was accused of frequenting this barbarian basement in order that he be able to consort with loose women and to booze and fornicate the night away in the company of other layabout waster whoremongers, he announced loud and clear for all to hear.

'And how better to think and speculate upon the concealments of the universe than to dip one's wick in the depths of hell where the sexual and intellectual temperature is at melting point.'

So, as blows, curses and slander flew, and women screamed away, or clustered in safe corners whimpering, there were still those Guinness stout sippers who remained resolutely discoursing in quantum physics, electromagnetic theory, wave mechanics and the acceleration and focusing of charged particles. But, too, could be heard less rarefied discussion concerning the causes of the occasional abundance and scarcity of ladybird insects in the environs of St Stephen's Green. Nor was the trivial mundane ever eschewed. The cause and frequency of rain in Ireland and the effect it had on the psyches of the natives was a recurrent theme. Which sadly led to more heads being wooled and broken than nearly any other subject ever mentioned.

As well as the brilliance there were those who were of an immediate practical bent. Especially a trinity of gentlemen better known as The Awful Three. Who perhaps more than anyone helped to bring the days of Charnelchambers to a close. Composed of a geologist mining engineer, a musicologist part time undertaker and a philosopher of no fixed occupation or address, these eccentric persons were always one expedient jump ahead of everyone. In a pair of boots the geologist was often seen at midnight tramping through Dublin's most fashionable shopping venue, Grafton Street, pushing a wheelbarrow aglow with a lantern and full of instruments of exploration, pails, hammers and chemicals. A confirmed absolute atheist pagan, this gentleman, so scrupulously polite that no one ever could find cause to upbraid him, took one look at the Charnelchamber floor from whence now trickled the spring sprung at the time of the appearance of the Blessed Virgin to the devout member of The Legion of Decency. The geologist dipping his finger in the water, tasted it and in a thrice he and his cohorts were wielding pickaxes to take up the paving stones and with shovels digging where he said his Geiger counter nearly jumped out of its box registering readings. And they duly proceeded vertically down. At the time one certainly did not know if these gentlemen would find their precious and rare metals. But certainly there was no fear of fire when the geologist and his two assistants were finished. For by god the presence of water was everywhere, with the whole of Charnelchambers aflood a foot deep.

The Awful Three did compensate Basil and his other tenants handsomely and as fervent admirers of continental aristocracy, they cemented a waterproof bulkhead across the Princess's and Adolphus's doors to keep their rooms dry. In due course they also provided those inmates who did not immediately flee, with an elaborate network of stepping stones. But continue to explore they did. Erecting a caisson around where they dug. Till finally in muddy exasperation both the Princess and Adolphus moved out. The Princess taking up a post as housekeeper in a large Irish country house with Adolphus as butler. The understanding being that when the Vicomte's emolument arrived he was to revert to being a paying guest. An arrangement which after the Vicomte's first week as a guest proved fatally difficult even in the ultra eccentric atmosphere of your usual Anglo Irish country house. As Adolphus when he should have been butlering continued to smoke cigars and drink sherry all morning while lying in the bath.

But the nightly visitors still came to Charnelchambers. Some of whom were rumoured to be international secret agents and counter spies. And who mingled among those, whose only claim to notoriety was to have pawned and sold their worldly goods in order to drink the proceeds and now didn't mind risking standing or falling into water up to their knees. But there did remain, too, a few diehard thinkers who felt wet feet helped them delve into the obtuse infinities of the universe. Some drunkenly submerging even as they spouted facts and exactitudes of specific dimensions. But Charnelchambers without its previous elegant tenants who contributed at least some charm and grace to the atmosphere, was now, more than ever, a dangerous place. Groups of glowering malcontents collected who, along with their slandering, gossip, revilements, backbiting and character assassination which always led to fisticuffs, now resorted to the far more lethal chastisement of dunking.

With the Princess gone I returned but once more to Charnelchambers on a late Sunday afternoon to hopelessly fumble in the water now seeped in under the bulkhead of her room, to search for cufflinks I'd lost. Not trusting the stepping stones I came in a pair of trout fishing hip boots. Basil was asleep in his vault, snoring and gently floating in a dinghy. I found myself disbelievingly standing among a handful of professional scientists and a museum curator who invited by The Awful Three, watched the excavation and the mud being removed from some precious ancient gold Celtic artefacts. There were as well a sideline amateur or two who were equally enthralled not only with the treasure trove but also with the engineering brilliance of this mining shaft which had now penetrated down into the bowels of Dublin city. Admittedly no one at the time in all the stack of mud and depth of water, was tussling with the subjectively distant unknowns concerning the innards of the atom. Or waving a frustrated fist trying to get their theories heard. Everything seemed to be perfectly normal as one listened to the learned comments concerning the gold chalices and bracelets, and to the crunch of the digging far below. And why shouldn't someone without planning permission quite reasonably be engaged in mineral and archeological exploration in the basement of someone's innocent building. Ah, but there was a reason. Which came without warning. As disaster struck. And methane gas exploded. All of us were knocked backwards into the water. The spring poured forth with a vengeance once more. And screams erupted to get out, get out. But by god in the hand of one of The Awful Three there were not only the ancient gold artefacts but the confirming sample attesting to the presence of the metal for which they were originally searching.

Amazingly no one was injured. The Awful Three immediately taking credit that this was so. Even to the ridiculous point of suggesting the safety factor of there being water into which one was blasted flat. Suddenly one could understand this Ireland, and from whence came its strange intellectual dynamics. In other lands and places, similar professional gentlemen would be confined to institutions for the mentally unusual or at least restricted to traditional modes of experiment and scientific reasoning cooped up in their laboratories. But here down in Charnelchambers the great minds instead could commune with these variously doomed spirits and from their melancholy quibbling could even derive verities to formulate an equation which would explain time. Or even find a cube root of an infinity which would explain space. Here where the air vibrated hot with the intellectual wattage of the habitués and profound perceptions blossomed from the mathematical purity of the wit. Especially concerning the origin of the next drink. But where even among the most erudite of these minds, no conceit or pomposity was ever displayed.

But pure science and its triumphs were not the only reasons for Charnelchambers' claim to fame. For down here too came great artists from the world of the theatre, mime, ballet, puppeteering and even papier mâché. And practising the latter was a gentleman who was the first ever to make replicas of the head of the Blessed Oliver Plunkett, long before his sainthood. These being sold to tourists by the entrepreneur who used to gain admittance with his steaks and sausages. And became the last man to remain in possession of Charnelchambers, taking the entire place over and installing a plethora of native born Irish. And was heard to announce shortly thereafter.

'By god look at that now, the British pagan while they were here kept it as neat as a pin. And now since our own have taken over, the place is a disgraceful filthy disgusting pigsty. And it's a fact, that what the Englishman doth hold together in beauty, the Irishman by god in violence doth tear asunder.'

Charnelchambers did indeed become even more violent than ever. With racecourse touts, newsboys and the friends and enemies of Daniel The Dangerous, driving away the scientific minds and lyric thinkers. And especially those who latterly became one of the first serious architectural preservation groups in Ireland. And had convened under the auspices of The Awful Three, and established themselves under the name, The Society For The Prevention Of Cruelty And Disgrace To Dublin. But the worst came upon the occasion of Daniel The Dangerous impersonating a priest and inviting an innocent group of young nuns from a convent to attend at the grotto of The Blessed Virgin. And upon their descent into Charnel-chambers the nuns were invited by the ecclesiastically robed Daniel The Dangerous to commit a grossly indecent act.

Ah, but then to remember it was where once such was the eminent comings and goings to this refuge for temporarily distressed gentle-folk, that many a newsboy through a long cold night fought to station himself just at the top of the steps. There in snow and rain selling his newspapers and opening and closing doors of the arriving horse cabs out of which your gentry either stepped or flopped. Sadly whenever one climbed up those steps one always recalled Charnelchambers before it had ever become a scandalous bunker of the damned. Remembering it upon my first occasions there as a place of peace and spiritual refreshment. The night haunted by the agonizingly beauti-ful strains of Peter's Stradivarius as those vibrating strings sounded their strangely painfully sweet chords which just as strangely made one weep. But making one in the glooms of life glad to be alive again on this Gaelic trolley ride through the universe.

But to Charnelchambers, as the Irish poured in, there came too, one who made Daniel The Dangerous seem but as a celestial choir boy. Wives deserting husbands to throw themselves at his feet. And husbands deserting wives, their jobs and vocations merely to listen to him speak. Evicted by other landlords, he even appeared with a whole family of three children. The eyes of these tiny creatures could be seen hiding in the shadows and watching. Until finally came the departure of Basil himself. Dear old wonderful Basil who started it all. And was during his last days posing nude for an English lady painter who specialized in studies of gentlemen. Especially 'The Male Rampant' as many of her pictures were called. And not that long after his portrait in full length and stiffness was completed, he one dawn nearly got murdered in his dinghy bed. For a remark passed, concerning the face of this new Irish tenant's wife. This taken as an insult by the aggrieved husband, who after a late night out in the pubs and Bonafides working up his appetite for revenge, came creeping in his socks into the small wine cellar cave where Basil slept in the bottom of his boat which now rested on the damp paving stones. From the door your man took a tiger's flying leap. Landing with a great earthshaking thump on his knees on top of the sleeping Basil's chest. Who woke to find a powerful pair of hands around his throat squeezing it to the consistency of a bootlace. Only just still alive by morning, Basil decided he'd had enough. Of fights, battles and blood. Of people of every hue, cry and description ascending and descending his basement stairs. With motives mostly malign. His destination was as far away from Dublin as the Kashmir Mountains. To whence he said he would go and forever stay. As far as humanly possible away from Dublin. And speak only ever again in his beloved Sanskrit. And where sadly one has learned he how lies buried. A brief epitaph upon his tombstone.

I did my dears
At least have the courage
Of my desires

VII

Had he lived Basil would now never believe that in the years following his departure there existed a committee invoking his name which had approached the Tourist Board to have preserved those notorious crypts of Charnelchambers as a national shrine as the Lourdes of Ireland. For as you might know the vasectomized and pagan Awful Three made not only a fortune out of their previous archeological finds and metal deposits but also bottled holy water and manufactured religious artefacts, rosaries, scapulars, and holy pictures. Selling all these as having been blessed at the shrine dug so sincerely deep in that dungeon. But so that they would appeal locally to the natives such artefacts were imprinted as having come from Czechoslovakia.

Ah, but before entering upon another subject not entirely alien to the one just left, you may well wonder who on earth or in all that mud and pain was the freehold or leasehold owner of the land below and the building above, of which Charnelchambers formed the cellars and foundations. And I myself always marvelled that whoever he or she might be, they could never be accused, as every other landlord in Ireland could, of being nosey concerning their tenants' morals and standards of behaviour. But as many of the great old Georgian buildings of Dublin, if not being knocked down, were falling down anyway, many a landlord could afford and did take the attitude, live and let live. And bloody well get as much rent as you can while the walls still stand.

In a place as small as Dublin secrets were hard to keep. But the identity of the free or leasehold owner of Charnelchambers remained a mystery. Until Peter, during one of our last nights down in the crypts, pointed him out to me. And I was astonished to find he was one of the few people in Charnelchambers outside of Peter, Adolphus, Basil and the Princess, to whom I had ever spoken, and indeed did so at some length. For I immediately took to this strange gentleman's kindly, most benign and seemingly religious demeanour, who was such an entirely different kettle of fish to those swimming around him in his cellars. Admitting, of course, some little bias in this, as I recognized him as someone who had bought two or three of my amateurish paintings. Being as he was a generous patron and collector who worshipped art in all its forms. And upon the occasions this gent had incognito appeared down in his own very premises, he always arrived alone with a bottle of whisky, stood alone and departed alone. And regularly wearing a light tan trilby hat, a drab mackintosh buttoned conspicuously closed at the neck and his hands plunged deep into its pockets. Because of the constant trace of a smile he wore he was referred to as Your Man Mona Lisa. And indeed by this name was he designated when I was first introduced. Basil himself never knew nor did any of his tenantry ever learn who he was. When he was asked and answered that he was a patron of the arts, it was assumed he was on release from an institution and with such aspirations would remain harmless enough.

The rent for Charnelchambers was collected every Friday morning by ten by a solicitor's clerk who wore a light tan trilby hat and drab mackintosh buttoned tight at the neck almost identical to Your Man Mona Lisa upon whose behalf he acted. Peter said he was an ardent music lover, but would disclose no further concerning his identity. But I did at least learn who it was this strange landlord had as one close friend. None other than my tennis playing partner of the 200 mile an hour serve who attempted to strangle me to death. But I did not yet know this when Your Man Mona Lisa stood at my elbow down in Charnelchambers when he in his first strange shy whisper quietly informed me.

'I am not particularly devout but do perform my religious duties as a Catholic. I am not a paederast, bigamist nor I hope a bombast, nor indeed any kind of curious person. For which in this most refreshingly liberal minded company I apologize. I am instead a shy individual to whom God in his infinite kindness, if not wisdom, has given a certain financial substantiality. I write nothing, paint nothing, compose nothing, sculpt nothing, invent nothing. But I do so enjoy to be here merely to listen to and merely watch those of you who do all these things.'

Of course, not one of these habitués present, that Your Man Mona

Lisa referred to, had so much as written a word, painted an X, sculpted a lump or composed a note in a millennium. Including, too, yours truly who had merely latterly achieved notoriety by embarrassing everyone in Dublin by exhibiting a collection of still wet paintings. Which some wiseacre referred to as being work of my sticky period and guaranteed fresh in off the palette. But the true nature of Ireland was slowly unfolding. The art of living here was to be alive and listened to. Or as happened more often, to be told to shut up and be all ears before you had them bit off you altogether. And while you drank, talked, sang, disputed or gossiped, you might merely mildly worry as to who would buy the next round. But by God don't stop to think you're anybody special or anointed because you write, paint, sculpt or compose.

To some modest degree one had oneself adapted to Irish behaviour. Ignoring the rain, chill and discomfort, and even indeed occasionally enjoying it. But you did finally wonder, where did you go among the natives of this land, noted worldwide for its charm and friendliness to the stranger, to find more than a handful of decent, fair minded citizens. Men and women free of their thick coatings of repressive obtuse bigotry which held them imprisoned by their thwarted erotic desires. A condition known as suffering from the crut. And after a sample evening in Charnelchambers where some of this crut was nightly chipped off, you'd wonder sincerely and deeply where were all the saints and scholars, for whom this isle was famed. Or indeed for the matter of that where were all your actual writing writers, versifying poets and composing composers. The answer was, by God, they were everywhere. And in their myriad abundance. In every nook and cranny of the civil service. Even the gas company. And all the branches of the government. And mostly, by evening, sitting inert, facing their blank pieces of paper.

And now to fully enter upon the subject not entirely alien to Charnelchambers. Welcome then to the world of Irish art and literature. From whence an abundance of world celebrated writers has come. Who in each case performed an absolute and utter miracle of survival. For such men and women were on every side met by opposition both public and private to all their words and deeds. Such scheming hindrance in more than half, perpetrated by their contemporary would be writers and artists. And a more bitter, resentful and treacherous crew you'd spend a hard lifetime's work trying to find. Who did by their backbiting and venting envy attempt to still these lyric voices. Causing them to gather up their written sheets of paper, pack their bags and go down to the Dublin quays to board the mail boat for England.

But some with their penned words so few, did stay. Drinking and betting in the city. They were the word counters, adding up each one they managed to gruellingly scratch out on a page. As an encouragement to go on. And above all not stop if once you've started. To have at least at the end of each day a page, a paragraph or a sentence. And to least of all worry about what it said. And be better off than those without words at all to count. Who stared hours, days and weeks away, facing the blank sheet of paper. Pulled from their fresh stacks of more blank sheets. Their sharpened pencils ready to scribble and their typewriters oiled, ready to tap. Those few who had such typewriters and those, less than a few, who had such oil. As there they sat in their ill illumined quiet back rooms. A neat pile of turf awaiting to be put on the just lit smouldering fire. And in these romantically inclined gentlemen's minds, great literature was already alight and living. Tomes lying open to their favourite pages. Chapters unfolding as they saw themselves in the image of other famed past writers. Perhaps more in the Russian manner than in the French. An exiled Turgenev rather than a coffee drinking Balzac. And tomorrow when they really got down to work and wrote all over that blank page and filled those in wait, the publishers would be clamouring. The presses roaring. The masses buying, borrowing and grabbing and reading your every word. The royalties pouring in from every corner and language across the globe.

But back here now in Ireland, here in Dublin, down this rhododendron leafy street in Ranelagh or Rathgar. The kimonos remained draped at the ready. As the long night grows chilled. And never further than an elbow away sits a pack of twenty of your pink packed expensively priced 'Passing Clouds' cigarettes. Ready to be puffed, and the smoke sent overhead, and the ash tapped in the ashtray. The woman of the house to whom you were eight years betrothed before you got joined in the grimness of marriage, has fixed supper. Placed on your desk under a warmer. Two veg, chunk of ham and peeled boiled potatoes. Under a cosy is a pot of strong tea. The wife has gone to make a novena. And without her nagging complaint, silence reigns. Because in this beyond, here in the suburban edges of Dublin in these shrubbery environs, the general respectability is such that not one of your neighbours wants to be observed doing exactly what the other is doing. Writing a book.

But above all never let it be said or even suggested that such native born and reared men in their kimonos and puffing out their 'Passing Clouds' are of no consequence as writers. Or indeed were not already part of the great literature to which they aspired. For, modestly unbeknownst to themselves, they were. They'd read every trumpeted classic author. Or at least prepared damn well to pretend they had. Or were primed with the lore of these famed authors' lives. In the image of which they lived their own lives and they were if nothing else, discerning critics. Their collective atmosphere hung over Dublin. They awaited, even as they shunned and damned them, to read the work of the handful of writers in this land who wrote. And they, above all, remained open minded. Ready, before they condemned, to listen to the composers who composed. Or quote the poets who versified. And they would upon a Tuesday come from near and far to lurk in the pubs around the central city. Standing at the edges of gatherings. And were, some of them, the men about whom the writers wrote. And the latter were, because they did, quaking in fear of libel. Because having managed themselves to chip off their crut and put pen to paper and push, they found they hadn't a good or decent word to say about anybody. And the pursuit of such grievance resulting from such ridicule and contempt, was a much sought after opportunity eagerly availed of, there being no shortage of lawyers in Dublin. Such legal action often being easy to pursue, for there was nothing like using your man's real name for the sake of clarity. And making what he fictionally did as scurrilous as possible for the sake of reality. And, by God, meeting as one would do every day at court with the newspapers full of it, did your battle against obscurity a damn sight of good.

But to the origins of the literary stirrings. Let us go. In those days you could find them all happening within a donkey's roar of Grafton Street. A sound, too, you could hear coming out of some of the more prominent of the protagonists. As they went from pub to betting shop and back. Their noses in the racing sheets in the hope of winning, and roaring like scalded animals if they lost. But if fortune was smiling you can bet they were in haste to be a mile away in a different pub from their impecunious cronies, buying each round for themselves in their contented loneliness. But literary life was not all wagering on the horses. Occasionally you could find discreet, cultivated, non roaring gentlemen. Central among whom was a young man with the simple name of John Ryan. He had surplus to his needs what few people in Ireland had in those days. Namely and plainly money. His was a face I saw again and again at the various better and more respectable bashes. But to whom I had never spoken further than being introduced forty nine times. His behaviour never ostentatious nor even apparently rich. Then it was upon one Saturday autumn morning on the way to the races at Leopardstown that I, in the company of a friendly gentleman of another plain name, Pat O'Reilly, who, known to everyone, for he had been an Irish champion ballroom dancer, called at a large country house, Burton Hall. We were shown by a black uniformed, white aproned maid upstairs and along a corridor. As the door opened to a large comfortably furnished bedroom, faint sunlight streamed in the window after rain. In front of a white marble chimney piece stood an easel with a massive portrait of Wolfe Tone in the course of being painted. The picture was carefully marked off in squares to copy from a photograph similarly marked off. Ryan stood with his palette and brushes and for the fiftieth time I was introduced to this indisposed young gentleman recovering from a nasty bout of 'flu. It was to be my first serious, sober encounter with the Irish world of art. And I was memorably stunned to here find this gentleman so far away from the social turmoil of Dublin and content in his own solitude.

John Ryan seemed entirely different from your usual run of Irish folk. In his rakish tweed jacket and often a bright cheerful tweed tie loosely knotted at the collar of his silk shirt, his casual neat cleanliness alone, just following the war, bespoke of at least having some wherewithal. Quiet, unassuming, unfailingly polite, Ryan pleasantly listened as other people spoke. And only when they were finished their say would he then gently and equally pleasantly tell his own amusing story. Underlying every turn of which would always be an abundance of Irish irony. And I became one of his ardent listeners. But then, too, my ears would have pricked up at the mention of anything to do with writing, or indeed mention of that name James Joyce which had so much to do with my coming to this land in the first place. And suddenly in some astonishment after all the mad endless parties, I discovered through this gentleman, there was another

John Ryan in front of 38 Trinity College Dublin. Ryan was an early frequent visitor and would decorate with drawings the tiles of my fireplace as we would talk with James Leathers and others and sip Guinness late into the night. Ryan said there was nowhere else in Dublin he enjoyed to visit more than the monastic ancient enclosure of Trinity.

world in Ireland, an actual Irish world of culture. Albeit occasionally if vaguely connected with the sort of comings and goings one had encountered in the dungeons of Charnelchambers. But a world where fists weren't always flying and where you wouldn't, instead of listening to Mendelssohn, get a violin wrapped around your throat.

Before leaving Burton Hall that day we took Madeira in the music room and Ryan sat to the piano and played 'The Lark In The Clear Air', a piece inspired and composed in the vicinity of this very chamber. As the name of Joyce came up, Ryan appeared to have an astonishing knowledge of this man, his life and his work. He had all his books and a recording of Joyce reading from *Finnegans Wake*. And as nearly everywhere one ventured in the city of Dublin bespoke of him, Joyce was a frequent topic of conversation. Ryan knew the streets, the doorways, pubs and people Joyce wrote of. Some of them still alive and if not kicking at least ready to quaff a ball of malt or a pint as they would reminisce of this exiled author. Each scrap of information eagerly sought. Such places as we ourselves frequented as Davy Byrnes, the Bailey, conjured up stories and the ghosts of this man. Even places as anonymous as Clontarf and Sandymount reverberated with awe and atmosphere at the mention of his name. Of course Joyce knew Dublin in more tranquil times. When the like of Lead Pipe Daniel The Dangerous was not at large. Nor folk like The Awful Three. Nor indeed Brendan Behan or the American from Ohio, the saintly Gainor Stephen Crist.

Ryan too had a familiar knowledge of the one or two actually living and published working writers of the day such as Samuel Beckett, the scholarly, brilliant cricketer, product of Trinity College. Who had already transported himself from these shores. And of whose work 'More Pricks Than Kicks' I first heard mentioned down in the vaults of Charnelchambers. And which title in the context of the place, I associated more with penises and feet shod in hob nailed boots which were landing in your ribs, than with the sharp prods of misfortune. It was one of the first works I'd heard of produced by a living Irish writer, whose words in no way resembled a tourist brochure. Or sounded as if the author were covered all over in crut.

There were too, of their sort, what one might even refer to as salons in Dublin. These, not your legendary type where tea and sherry were taken aseat on your Louis XV chaise longues in elegant drawing rooms with your established notable men of letters in attendance. But your more rough and ready venue where someone's teeth might be pulling the cork out of a bottle of stout. Even so, these latter coarse textured parlours were more than occasionally frequented by scholarly gentlemen of astonishingly accumulated erudition. And one such salon was established right there smack in Grafton Street. Right in a building owned by Ryan's family business, the Monument Creameries. And in these premises, paying little or no rent, Ryan would allow the odd friend in pursuit of art to stay. In some comfort too, as there was a fitted green Wilton carpet, hot and cold running water, lamps, chairs, couches and other amenities. And some of these occupants were later to distinguish themselves in the fields of poetry, writing, painting and even sculpture. Making Dublin's most fashionable street the unlikely source of fine art.

But studded elsewhere over Dublin, were other ateliers in which thinkers, writers, composers and painters were lurking. And to these Ryan would periodically pay a visit. Occasionally, I went in his company. Always prepared for the no less than bizarre. Finding that such places would inevitably be crammed with the unbelievable. From venomous reptiles to birds of paradise. Or perhaps, safer less exotic amenities, but thought precious to these gentlemen in their fields of endeavour. And more than once involving the less than salubrious. Which in this case concerned an enormous pile of turf in the corner of the room in which was established a not inconsiderable compost heap. And into which went all this gentleman's bodily functions, plus left over potatoes, tea leaves and slops. In order to complete the life cycle therein, various vegetation and fungi sprouted on top. As calling time was usually prior to lunch, one tried as inconspicuously as possible to hold one's breath. For although our host claimed his manure pile to be without odour, and indeed would in proving this stand over it and deeply inhale several times while his fists beat on his chest, nevertheless one did nearly keel over from an utterly lethally disagreeable fume. The other tenant of the building being a wrecked car repairer who occupied the garage below and was usually wearing a mask as he sprayed vehicles. But then as our host served tea, burned incense and played on a small organ, music of his own composition, the stench miraculously and completely disappeared.

Ah, but back to the absolute eye of the hurricane, the address of 39 Grafton Street. Beneath which too emanated the smell of a renowned fish shop. This Victorian brick edifice stood across from the golden frieze of Woolworth's Five and Ten Cents Store. And Ryan's family business occupied it as it did several other Grafton Street buildings. Next to the fish shop on the ground floor was a large Monument Creamery café, which served meals and had both a bakery and grocery. Next to it, one entered a narrow hall and climbed up a flight of stairs. It was here at the top that one turned left to a suite of rooms Ryan had established for himself. The front room over the fish shop he used as a studio and back as a reception room and office. If a drink were needed in the pub as it invariably was following anyone's meeting one another for more than three minutes, folk would only have to descend the stairs, step out across the street and walk twenty yards to the corner, turn left by the exotic furs displayed in a window and proceed past Tom Nisbet's painting gallery and into John McDaid's pub. Which advertised 'Where the drink is efficacious and the conversation effervescent'. Slowly but surely this converted church at 3 Harry Street with its cold, barren, lofty interior, its grim downstairs lavatory and a back door out to a side lane, became an established meeting place for poets, painters, writers, and various

Interior McDaid's pub. Centred seated together and fourth from left Tony McInerney, Randall Hillis, Brendan Behan, Gainor Crist, and extreme right Desmond McNamara the puppeteer and sculptor and first frequenter of McDaid's. This astonishing photograph taken by one of Dublin's roving photographers was later obtained by Randall Hillis and may stand as the only photographic record of such intellectually sophisticated gentlemen all having an unrehearsed drink together.

chancers and con men, the latter who, poor souls, erroneously thought such people worth associating with. Although this public house had a bemused owner and an extremely pleasant and understanding bartender, the only one in Dublin to have ever bought yours truly a drink, nevertheless this big grim room to have become celebrated in any manner, was a mystery to all who went there. But it was certainly a place where many an insult and snub was delivered and fist thrown, and many a lady's tear was shed.

There was, all over Dublin plenty of space and time for the outspoken word. But by God to put it in print you had no shortage of troubles. And for a sincerely lyric word, the only possible outlet was the literary magazines. One such *The Bell.* The sound of which was then fading. And to which I submitted an early poetic effort. To finally have it rejected. But not ignored. Harry L. Craig who worked on the magazine and whom one later met in the pub Davy Byrnes, recalled my name and the poem. This handsome well built gentleman said he had not only read it but even thought of publishing it. Of course already having experienced in Ireland what was generally known as plamoss, one disbelieved him on the spot but appreciated his attempt at mitigating the first kick in my literary teeth. Which, of course, in my brash fulminating omniscience, had left me utterly stunned and horrified.

Yet I soon came to learn that I might have been lucky. For the gossipy stories in the world of belles lettres did spread and reach my ears. Concerning the kind of Dublin editor one might unfortunately encounter. Who, hung over from the night before in the company of the literati, was usually late to work of a morning or more likely afternoon or indeed didn't show up for days at a time. And meanwhile might have left the likes of an aspiring literary gent named Brendan Behan minding the office. And such folk suddenly blessed in their jacket pockets with a blood pudding and sausage or two ready to cook, would not hesitate to stuff the fireplace grate with manuscripts and putting a match to them, would boil a kettle for tea and when the fire was roaring hot, scald their sausages stuck on the end of any handy fountain pen. And when such culprits were tackled for such acts there would be a plausible reply.

'Ah, I'll grant you, it isn't the kind of encouraging rumour young hopeful writers are likely to take comfort from hearing. But as it was myself cooking me own sausages and someone else's manuscripts doing the conflagrating, sure I'd like you to tell me if you can think of a better way of advancing up the literary ladder.'

But one problem you never had in Dublin. Was advertising yourself as a writer. Which could be done on nerve alone and was achieved as fast as you could split an infinitive. For if you didn't declare yourself you could soon have someone else sarcastically doing it for you. The mere careless mention of owning a pencil and piece of blank paper could make you the day's if not a lifetime's victim of ridicule. As had happened on that encounter with Behan in my earliest Irish literary experience when we were first introduced, and were unaware of the gathering's efforts to make such occasion their first big uproarious laugh of the day. With neither Behan nor I thinking it at all funny. Indeed as I recall again, my fists were already tightening as I confronted this mildly belligerent unkempt individual with his great shock of black hair and a broken and twisted nose nearly snarling on his face. And over the years one was to know Behan, his chest was nearly always blazoning from a stained and soiled open jacket, his crumpled shirt open to the navel, and his belly thrust out over a belt barely holding up his baggy worn trousers. But it was his stumpy fists and fingers with which he gesticulated while stammering that gave Behan an almost benign and endearing comportment that bespoke of him as a writer. In contrast to his incidental companion Lead Pipe Daniel The Dangerous, another proclaimed man of letters, his bellowing voice spouting his poetry which Behan would sometimes write out for me in my notebooks. Taking a mischievous delight in the fact that this great violent monster feared everywhere could pen adoring lines to the Blessed Virgin Mary. Albeit Lead Pipe Daniel would in his poetic vision have her situated somewhere up a tree and would, while singing his paean of praises to her be unable to avert his eyes from looking up her holy robes which resulted in the poem's last lines being invariably sacrilegious.

But then Behan himself could be a violent man, having served time for the attempted murder of a policeman and always ready to break a pint glass on a pub table and shove the resulting jagged edges in your face. In spite of this, he was just as quick to make peace as happened in our first encounter previously mentioned, squaring off in the middle of the street in front of Davy Byrnes when Behan could see I meant business. At the same time, having already become much familiar with armed and unarmed combat in Ireland, I had already taken a quick glance behind me for any accomplices sneaking up to wield a bottle on the back of my head. And was also careful to stay out of range not only of his fists but also a flying kick in the balls. My usual precaution being to sense the first flicker of movement in one of my opponent's muscles. At which moment I would feint with a left and then unleash a straight right fist to concuss central on the nose of such pertinent face. But suspicious though I was I did shake Behan's hand when it was put forth.

'Ah, there's no need to fight. Why should the pair of us out here beat the bejesus out of one another to the satisfaction of the eegit likes of them inside. Sure I'm a writer. And I meant no harm in calling you a narrowback. But I can tell by the way you're ready to fight about it, that you're a writer too. And fuck the ignorant bunch back in there who wouldn't know a present participle from a hole in their buried mother's coffins. Come on, the two of us, we'll go somewhere and have a drink. And we'll tell the story around that the both of us were so fast at getting out of the way of each other's fists, neither of us could land a punch.'

This was literary Dublin. Without a sign of a book in anyone's hand and where the spoken word was your ready claim to fame. Where no one would ask, as they would in America, if you had anything published. And if you did, how rich did you get. Here, if you dared, you could stand up and declare yourself. And know that the ridicule would spread far and wide behind your back. But at least you could be in your own eyes what you said you were. As I dared to be in this city where there already existed a few published writers and poets. Patrick Kavanagh, conspicuous among them. This man, his powerful arms folding his big farmer's hands across his chest walked the streets like a battleship plunging through the waves. And with whom pedestrian encounters were quick and decisive. Mostly amounting to a few salvoes from his sixteen inch guns. Which blasted at you if you were not too timorous to acknowledge him with some kind of greeting, to which was his invariable reply.

'Have you got a pound to give me.'

'No.'

'Well fuck off then.'

My rooms at 38 Trinity College became a salon of sorts. Even Behan turning up. Not in search of conversation but to buy guns for the I.R.A. whose seller, unbeknownst to me had asked to store them on top of my clothes cupboard where they lay for some time in a great stack under thick wrapping paper. But in more peaceful pursuit, John Ryan would appear on many a cold winter evening. Sit content hunched in front of a pathetic fire and while talking, draw pictures on the tiles of the fireplace as one talked. Sharing these rooms and often in the company, was James H. Leathers who quite literally was held by all who came into contact with him as being the most charming man ever to set foot in Dublin. From Los Angeles, California, this six foot five inch tall unhurried American, who was not, by the way, my strangler, nor did Leathers ever play tennis or take any other strenuous exercise, but was instead a collector of exotic gems, Icelandic literature and lover of music, theatre and ballet. Daily he would prowl the auction rooms buying books and pictures. And he had commissioned a Celtic silversmith to put some of his jewels in settings. Leathers also took a keen interest in Irish folklore and its

James H. Leathers in his leather motoring coat descending the steps of Trinity College dining hall. This extremely tall and ultra shy gentleman with whom I shared rooms, and whose company was sought by hosts and hostesses alike all over Dublin and who turned one's Trinity rooms into a social mecca with his legendary charm, had no equal. For which one was indeed glad as this human insulation he attracted prevented both Leathers and I from freezing to death during one of Europe's coldest winters.

homespun industry. Even to outfitting himself in Aran Islands' sweaters and socks. And appearing one day in pampooties. The latter a slipper sandal of undressed cowskin sewn together and tied across the instep. Which raw and nearly still bloody was not suitable for dinner parties. As my painting career started dead centre of our college sitting room, Leathers, having unearthed himself from beneath his nightly covering of hot water bottles, would appear late in the day a cup of tea warming his hands, and striving to make as diplomatically kind as possible comments on my painting efforts. One of his more extreme statements being.

'Ah, I see you are rather more this afternoon than yesterday clearly painting with a rather fuller brush.'

However Leathers' presence attracted people from all walks and kinds of Dublin life. Both men and women, all of whom, struck by the strange magnetism of his company seemed content merely to be silently in his presence. Indeed many a friendship came asunder as some of these folk fought bitterly among themselves vying for the privilege. His bedroom mornings could be packed to overflowing with tea drinking and cigarette smoking visitors. Whom he would receive while he lay supine head and shoulders propped up on pillows, working up his fortitude to brave the cold in getting out of bed. It was indirectly Leathers who led to my coming across many a modern writer whose existence was then unknown in Ireland. For one of our visitors who sought out his company and who, liking the free and easy nature of life in our Trinity chambers at number 38, moved into Leathers' vacated room when the latter finally could no longer take the cold and damp and returned by slow boat to California. This next occupant of Leathers' room, a Michael Heron, not only brought his own charming company into the premises, but also his collection of books. Of such authors as Henry Miller and Albert Camus, whose work and names were acknowledged elsewhere in Europe and hardly heard of in Ireland.

Other callers at number 38 quickly made the influence of America evident. A. K. Donoghue, and Ray Guild, both from Boston and Harvard. Douglas Usher Wilson, James Hillman. All of these recently arrived on these shores. Each making his own not inconsiderable impression on the natives. Hillman on stage in a public college performance, gave a sample of jitterbugging never seen before. Wilson made his impression with his own brand of philosophy, cutting through Irish crut on every side. And to all forms of evasion and equivocation, including my own, he could be heard to thunder.

'You're talking through your paper Irish asshole.'

But perhaps most influential of all was A. K. Donoghue. This classically and politically minded gentleman introduced a strange behaviourism in the land. Resembling that of Wilson's who, also a Bostonian, came from the upper ends of society as Donoghue did the lower. And Donoghue's contribution was that of spoken honesty. First evidenced by his appearance in a pub when asked by the round buyer what he'd have to drink. Donoghue's blasphemous reply,

Kilcoole Village. The road up the hill led to Mr Poulton's pub. The road to the right was to Kilcoole station a mile away. And the lane between them to the right of the village shop led, as the crow would walk, another mile or so along to my cottage.

which had never been heard before in the land, stunned the entire public house and many a public house for miles around. When the immortal words were uttered.

'I'll have a sandwich.'

By now I had established for myself a tiny speck of notoriety in Dublin. More by one's fists than by one's paintbrushes. Meanwhile Ryan had begun a literary magazine called *Envoy* at 39 Grafton Street. And within this one publishing entity did much of Ireland's then literary world concentrate. Further in my own pursuit of painting survival I had bought a smallholding along the coast of Wicklow at Kilcoole beyond the pretty seaside village of Greystones. I would on occasion come up to Dublin. Usually calling on John Ryan at his studio which now also acted as an office for his literary enterprise *Envoy* magazine. For Dublin then these offices were luxurious indeed. Desks and fitted carpets. A gramophone and other comforts. And even the practically unknown personal instrument of a telephone. Kavanagh could often be found there by mornings read-

Surrounded by my chickens and scratching a living from the soil which Patrick Kavanagh rightly defined as entitling me to being called a phoney. Kavanagh, a small farmer knowing full well that any American could climb aboard an aeroplane and a few hours later, having stood under a hot shower could then sit down to bacon, eggs, sausages, pancakes and maple syrup back in the good old U.S.A. And God, there was many the odd moment when I wanted to do just that.

ing snippets from submitted manuscripts to which his invariable reply was.

'Rubbish. Utter drivel and the most appalling nonsense I have ever had the disinterest to read.'

Of course Kavanagh hadn't read more than four words of a single line but would fling the offending pages back where they came from. And upon this occasion and as the door opened a manuscript of my own hit me in the face. Kavanagh at least had the good manners to apologize. And knowing that Kavanagh had been a farmer or at least from a farming family I took the opportunity to avail of farming if not literary advice and asked him about growing potatoes. He looked at me with his most brilliant portrayal of sceptical disgust.

'Ah God, I suppose now you've got an acre or two.'

'Four acres.'

'Four acres have you. And I suppose you've got chickens.'

'Thirteen.'

'Thirteen have you. And I suppose too you've got cabbage, their leaves sparkling of a morning with dew.'

'Six rows.'

'And you're wading twice a day through the nettles and docks to fetch a bucket of water from the nearby stream.'

'Five times a day.'

'And I suppose it's a nice little three room cottage with a hedge around it and you've got a cow to milk and a patch of strawberries ripening for June.'

'I have.'

'Phoney, phoney, phoney. Utterly phoney. The whole thing is phoney. Nothing but phoniness.'

Kavanagh shook his fist as he shouted and lurched in his mock high dudgeon like a ship pitching in a storm. One saw the truth of his remarks knowing that this simple way of life had cost a fortune in education and existed upon a small private emolument arriving every week from an attentive mother and that I had come to this peasant land with my nice big American pot to piss in. And I laughed outright at his wisdom. But what he did not know was that I had taken my college mattress out of Trinity and placed it on a door torn off one of the cottage rooms and this stacked on bricks was my bed. And that I had found an old face of a rusted shovel in a hedgerow, cut down an ash sapling and shaped and fitted it as a handle. And with this same spade, dug a basin in the tiny nearby stream from where one fetched water. But as I left the office of *Envoy* that day. Still laughing. Kavanagh turned to talk behind my back.

'That man's no phoney. Sure if he were he couldn't laugh at what I said.'

I wasn't exactly

Guffawing

And Kavanagh left me

Feeling

Phoney enough

I can tell

You

VIII

Popular American tunes took three to five years to arrive in Ireland, making it altogether marvellously nostalgic to hear them again and be reminded that there was escape if escape were needed from this creature comfortless land. But before the world of art conspicuously reared its more than occasionally chastising head, and the desperate struggle for survival began to be fought, there were many other pleasant moments to be had in these early germinal days in the latter half of the nineteen forties. Which in this perennially poor land, once unforgettably havocked by a great famine, gave plausibility to the drawling nasal tones of an American accent which by itself spelt wondrous riches westwards across the seas. Such speech having long been the symbol of carefree wealth as bespoken by Hollywood movie sets, exterior and interior, and flashily elegant costumes both voluminous and scanty. Add shiny rooms, silk curtains, and steaming water pouring out of gold taps into big tubs bursting with bubbles and blondes, and you have an appropriate sample of what long queues lined up to see in the cold wintry rain on a Dublin Sunday afternoon.

But there did exist the occasional oasis from physical adversity. Attending upon the races, one would invariably repair to some nearby country house. And in the case of going to Leopardstown in south Co. Dublin it was cause to visit John Ryan's mother's house of Burton Hall. With Ryan's father dead, his mother single handedly ran the Monument Creameries. This for Ireland was a large business consisting of a string of more than twenty shops selling butter, cream and eggs throughout Dublin and environs and included two of the bigger cafés in the city. With John Ryan, a young painter with a strong interest in writing as well as politics, Burton Hall became unwittingly an accessory to these aspirations. Providing the antithesis to Dublin's desolate dens of iniquity. The most contrasting element being not only Burton Hall's sumptuous setting, interior grandeur and furnishings but also Ryan's stream of spectacularly beautiful sisters. Who could produce one highly pleasant shock after another as they appeared when least expected out of the various mahogany door frames and glided into the music room, drawing room or library. To beseat themselves in these splendid settings spreading flowing gowns on the vast Axminster rugs. Their charmingly attractive mother, chief of this dynasty, was an early collector of Jack Yeats's paintings. And these massive wistfully sad pictures with their figures aswirl in palette knife slashes of colour, of men in mists out on bog lands, at country fairs, and race meetings, always brought the wild cold mystery of the Irish countryside into the room. And beneath such a picture, I overheard Ryan's mother, as her children and their myriad friends unstintingly feasted in the lavish surrounds about her, laughingly rubbing her hands at her front hall blazing Christmas turf fire.

'I'll be glad when the festive season is over when instead of spending money I can get back to making it.'

Few Irish people have ever been far from hard times. Which always lurk in mind no matter how good present times are seeming. And in an Ireland where most were of less than modest means, Mrs Ryan was generously tolerant and indulgent especially of those who might reasonably be thought not to have a pot to piss in. And you might meet anyone at all at Burton Hall, from a university professor or Hollywood star to a gas meter reader, and of which latter there were plenty. Dublin, because of its intimate size, could find you knowing people much more quickly than you ever got the chance to forget them. And soon enough you'd find there was hardly an unfamiliar face in sight. I had made several of my earliest visits to Ryan's house before I realized a beautiful girl, Cora, who had become a girlfriend was also one of Ryan's sisters. Nor did I know that a silent gentleman of wry wit in the rare times he spoke, called Patrick and in whose company I spent many a long partying night when I would try to coax more from him than an amiable nod and smile, was also a Ryan brother. But this was the first I was to know in friendship of a world of the rich and prosperous and the purely Irish Irish. And to and from this large yellow ochre Georgian mansion one did more than occasionally go.

Surrounded by tree lined country lanes and set in its 200 acre park, Burton Hall in itself was a cornucopia. A hundred head of Guernsey cows grazed in gently rolling meadows. A champion pedigree bull tethered in a field by the drive awaiting to serve. Acres of walled vegetable and flower gardens. In long greenhouses glowingly golden peaches were ripening. Asparagus leaping from their beds to point their stalks at the sky. Artichokes splashing out their large thistle leaves around the fresh purple of their budding fruit. In the Hall's basements were vast, and even for Ireland, nearly inexhaustible wine cellars. A fleet of cars in the courtyard garages. And along with the family's cheese making, bakeries, chocolate factory, tobacconists, Burton Hall and its servants could supply your usual seven course feast without stress or strain or the morrow's impoverishment. Indeed, awake next morning under silk eiderdowns, your breakfast tray would groan with your sizzling sausages, rashers and eggs, toasted soda bread, marmalade, butter balls, coffee or tea. But prior to one Sunday evening when Leathers and I had been impromptu invited to stay to dinner I heard a mildly exasperated John Ryan saying to his sister.

'Cora, for god's sake see they don't serve us with the cured sides of a pig and the sunnyside up reproductive product of farmyard fowl.'

But there was plenty enough of your champagne in the library and your elaborate wine flowing dinners with *pâté de foie gras* on the Dresden. All put before you on the gleaming mahogany and with savouries before and after the entrée as you surfeited under these sparkling crystal chandeliers. And your vintage ports and special pale old brandies, followed by plans for late night excursions. With a wise Mrs Ryan insisting her trusted sober chauffeur drive us in her Daimler through this green sleeping kingdom of high granite walls and hedgerows to the ballroom dances, counties away. With rarely a light on the landscape to be seen. And you might be back again in a day or two. After another dinner in a different house. Another ball in another ballroom. Another hooley. More noise, more people.

To this place of comforts Ryan showed no favouritism in issuing his invitations to parties and the fearsome were invited along with the well behaved. Even though the former were definitely a bevy of them that doth drink from the finger bowls and doth wipe their knives between their teeth. But they would, like anyone else with a mouth on them, quaff barrels and bottles dispensed from the schoolroom under the servants' stairs. Brendan Behan came in his spectacular déshabillé. Even The Awful Three. But the latter were respectfully requested by the butler to leave their picks and shovels outside. And too there were aplenty, gatecrashers who would not take the hint that there was doubt about their welcome. I even recall seeing Lead Pipe Daniel The Dangerous, who normally would have had a romp wreaking havoc of endless and antique proportions, and who came in a suitably dark suit he'd stolen from an undertaker's, where he was temporarily employed dressing the corpses. But Ryan had a curiously sobering and calming effect even upon Daniel who did nothing more daring than to sing like an angel a song he'd composed.

> I may be
> In many quarters
> Known as Daniel The Dangerous
> And I don't want to be simplistic
> But believe me folks
> All I am is violently artistic

Ryan, although busy enough in his own life, was thoughtful and kindly in his patronage. And would in deserving cases even install the temporarily impecunious in Burton Hall. One such of whom being A. K. Donoghue, the introducer of blatant honesty to Ireland. Where lies had for so long reigned as being the truth told for the time being. Donoghue a first generation Irish American said he had come upon this personal philosophy when one of his young Catholic friends in Boston had said to him that if he told his mother the truth that he didn't believe in God, she would drop dead. Donoghue went immediately home where his mother was ironing in the kitchen and said, 'Hey ma I don't believe in God.' His mother without looking up from her ironing replied.

'Is that so, pass me that sprinkling bottle.'

Donoghue now in Dublin had awed all by his candour. With an encyclopedic knowledge ranging from plumbing to the classics he applied the telling of the truth to myriad subjects ranging from Irish politics to his own sex life. Whereas in a Boston bar he would have received a quick fist in the gob, here, among this bourgeoning group of intelligentsia, he was at worst greeted with encouraging amusement. And now when he continued to ask for something to eat when he was offered something to drink he often ended up with his requested ham sandwich with two pickles on the side. Even Brendan Behan, who usually took the stage and filled and shook it where e'er

A. K. Donoghue on the right and Tony McInerney on the left standing in Front Square Trinity College and en route to Bewley's Oriental Café for a morning coffee where no gap of silence ever occurred in the conversation.

he went, grew quiet and listened attentively in the presence of Donoghue. But as this crut crunching Harvard gentleman skewered many a sacredly held Irish pretension, his penchant for the truth did less than help him find continued food and shelter. And recently arrived in Ireland on the G.I. Bill, Donoghue had not brought a pot to piss in nor had he a recent cheque from the American government to buy one. And when an admirer was congratulating him on the observation that it was the ice age and not St Patrick that kept the snakes out of Ireland, Donoghue reflected that all his spoken truth had done for him was to bring him an agonizingly prolonged lack of women, sex and money.

Ryan, ever conscious of the survival difficulties of people he admired, and solicitous of Donoghue nearly starving and without somewhere to live, invited him to Burton Hall to sojourn at length. But advised that it would be best while doing so if he were to stay out of the way of the mother. Which in such commodious mansion seemed a minor problem, but Ryan said was best guaranteed avoided by accompanying him into Dublin every day and returning in the evening. But Donoghue disliking pubs in general and some of the more boisterous company Ryan occasionally kept with the likes of Brendan Behan, chose instead to stay the day in these lavish surroundings. Polishing off an early served breakfast tray. Late afternoons submerging in a bath he refilled to the brim twice with the heaps of endless hot water and drying in blanket sized fluffy clean white towels fresh off their heating rails. And throughout the day silently descending the deep carpeted grand staircase to choose from among the many books in the library and ensconce himself in a moss green upholstered George III mahogany armchair next to Mrs Ryan's Queen Anne writing desk. Just as he would prop his feet up on a foot cushion placed on a black and gold laquer centre table, Mrs Ryan would come walking in. Leading to the inevitable exchange of words two or three times a day as Donoghue would make to put down his feet and get up out of his chair.

'O sorry, do you want to come in here.'

'O no. Sorry, do please stay where you are. It's quite all right.'

Donoghue then repairing variously to the other reception rooms to which Mrs Ryan in search of privacy in her own house was now also fleeing, arriving only to find the ubiquitous Donoghue already there. Then in rapidly vacating such spots, Donoghue in a tiptoeing panic of avoidance seemed everywhere. In the hall, vestibule, schoolroom and conservatory, and still helplessly confronting this gracious lady. But as astute servants were in observance, suddenly Donoghue's breakfast did not arrive. Nor was his bed made, nor towels changed nor fresh flowers put on his various bedroom tables. And the message sank in. In a swift change of venue he became resident now in Ryan's studio and office at 39 Grafton Street. With another bigger and better drama about to unfold. At four in the morning. When after hours of a battle with a rat sheltering in under the bed taking place. And Donoghue finally trying to shine a torch upon this rodent in order to take aim with his shoe and hit it a fatal belt in the gob. Outside down in the street a patrolling guard saw the light of the torch flash across Ryan's front room studio ceiling. Immediately the alarm of a serious theft in progress was raised. With now more commotion outside and then inside. Donoghue in his nakedness peeked to look out the window. To see Grafton Street and the sidewalk in front of Woolworth's five and dime store aflood with police. Who, from the sound of another disturbance in a back lane to the rear of the building, were there, also staked out, hands at the ready for imaginary guns. Of course with its adversary otherwise occupied the rat's nerve increased and it now ventured to escape running along the wall skirting under the rear window, Donoghue now letting go with one of his shoes. Which overshot the target somewhat and with a loud shattering of silence in this wee hour of the morning, smashed through the window. From which the guards now expected to see at least the nose of a Luger project and spit bullets. When they announced by loud hailer that unless he came out with his hands up, they would open fire.

'Don't shoot. I'm a Harvard graduate.'

At four twenty three a.m. Donoghue, one shoe still raised in his hand, proceeded down the carpeted stairs and nakedly emerged from the literary portals of 39 Grafton Street. Repeating again and again in his best pronounced American, his academic qualifications as the best insurance against being gunned down. The guards levelling their Browning automatics as he stood on the pavement in front of the stacks of cakes displayed in the window of the Monument Creamery Café. From the top of Stephen's Green more guards advancing north in a phalanx down Grafton Street. As two more military units came around the corners of Chatham and Anne Streets advancing south. The fire brigade, bells in the distance clanging also on its way. It now began to rain. And one of the police upon snapping on handcuffs on Donoghue's wrists held behind his back, commented.

'Well you could sure use your cap and gown now.'

John Ryan, meanwhile, back at Burton Hall was woken in his sleep and motored into the rescue. Finding his barefoot guest shivering wrapped in a blanket in a police cell not that far from the scholarly granite walls and high iron fence of Trinity College Dublin. But it did not take long before Donoghue was back enjoying what he could in this ancient Danish city. Choosing his daily favourite spot at one of the cool, white grey marble tables in Bewley's Oriental Café in Westmoreland Street. Where he could have a delicious black coffee with two small jugs of cream, a butter ball and a spice bun. And read his admired columnist Myles na gCopaleen in *The Irish Times*, who frequently alluded in his daily pieces to classic matters wittily expressed in snippets of Greek and Latin.

In the strange micro macrocosm of Dublin I had found you could achieve all sorts of things, especially if you were a foreigner. And it infinitely provided scope for an amateur to dare enter into and embark upon a career in the world of art. My first step having come about one morning when I exited from my rooms at Trinity and strolled out into the city to take coffee, when I had also taken in an exhibition of Jack Yeats's paintings at the Victor Waddington Galleries in Anne Street. Impressed by the prices and delighted by these marvellous extravagant whorls of colour, and myself hardly capable of drawing an imitation of a triangle never mind a circle, I bought some paints, brushes and canvas. And in the centre of my sitting room at 38 Trinity College I set up an easel and commenced painting. As the rumour spread of my activity I was visited almost immediately by an English lady artist outraged that I had not spent the usual fifteen years in Florence at the feet of contemporary masters. She swept in. And in front of several visitors who although mystified, were at least up to that moment gently sympathetic to my efforts, the Bloomsbury lady stood floor centre in her tweeds and loudly declared.

'You are my dear, so obviously presently in your celluloid penis stage. And I fear will clearly remain there. How dare you presume to paint. I rushed here immediately I heard. How utterly dare you.

Private Showing . . .
OF
PAINTINGS AND WATERCOLORS
BY

DONLEAVY

AT
7 St. Stephen's Green Gallery,
MARCH 15th—3.30 TO 6.30
EXHIBITION FROM MARCH 15th

(Above) *The author's then wife, Valerie with Michael Heron her brother and the author, at the author's third Dublin exhibition at 7 St Stephen's Green when more of the paintings were dry than they were at previous exhibitions, and when I was falsely being accused of hogging Dublin's cultural limelight.*

My drawings on my invitations were occasionally commented upon to zoology class by my Professor of Zoology and Comparative Anatomy, James Brontë Gatenby to whom such invitations were always sent. This world famed zoologist would always point out a dorsal or ventral liberty or two I might have taken with my morphological contours.

Private Showing . . .
OF
PAINTINGS AND WATERCOLORS
BY

DONLEAVY

AT
7, St. Stephen's Green Gallery, Dublin,
JUNE 8th — 3.30 TO 6.30 P.M.
EXHIBITION FROM JUNE 8th—22nd, 1950.

When five years of my life have been spent in the Prado painting reproductions before I took the liberty to put a brush stroke of my own upon a canvas.'

I, of course, out of humility broke one of my cheaper brushes in two. Trampled a nearly empty tube of flake white and was seizing my canvas off its easel when the English lady continued in a less accusatory voice.

'Well, since you've started to make such a fool of yourself my dear, don't for God's sake now stop. By being an even bigger fool and with the sort of nerve you've got you're simply bound to be some day not laughed at. Which, of course, if you don't mind I am about to do right now. Ha ha ha.'

John Ryan had now married as had I, both of us to tall, dark and beautiful women. Still keeping my rooms at Trinity, but fully combating what was to become country life in the raw in Ireland, I had now conceived my first story in an empty compartment on the train ride in from Kilcoole along the coast to Dublin. Where one looked out and down from the edge of the Killiney cliffs over the grey green of the Irish Sea. I wrote 'A Party on Saturday Afternoon' which was later published by John Ryan in his now established *Envoy* and over the objection of his other editors. But also with the enthusiastic encouragement of my other first fan, one of Ryan's beatifically beautiful sisters, Kathleen who had become a Hollywood film star in such films as *Odd Man Out*.

I had now also given my second exhibition of still wet paintings in the painters' gallery at 7 St Stephen's Green, writing introductions to the catalogues and availing of my own brand of Donoghue's blatant honesty as I did so. My foreword did not make people drop dead but they did sure as hell lead to a lot of begrudging and growling. My first foreword was concocted in part from my correspondence at the time and entitled 'From a Letter'.

In front of Dockrell's on Great George's Street they paused and his friend A. K. Donoghue said, 'Donleavy, shut your mouth and let me give you the entire truth in one sentence. The land is the basis of everything.' Donleavy was impressed, Donoghue being one of America's most monumental scholars and so Donleavy rushed back to Trinity College and made decisions. Firstly, he wanted to paint, secondly he would give up Trinity, thirdly, he would go to the land from whence all things came. He fled Dublin with a rolled mattress, a beautiful wife and a tin trunk containing an axe, blanket and frying pan. Then things began to happen. Peas were flung into the soil, followed by cabbage and potatoes. Donleavy searched the countryside for stones, lifting them he built a studio. Things were damp and cold and winter evenings long and lonely, but people like Doug Wilson would come out with his sleeping bag and have a chat. Month after month things were happening. Concrete floors were laid, furniture made, hedgerows torn down. Valerie made clothes, curtains, sowed flowers. Chickens arrived but the horrible things refused to lay and things looked desperate for a while, then Jim Hillman, a conscientious American, wired a chemical compound that made chickens make with eggs and sure enough, the American miracle drug began to work and prosperity settled, a great protective cloak. The spiritual warmth of the country, a morning birdwatch by the sea, the sound of salmon caught by the seal, the swallow's sexual song, and towards evening a read in the papers; an hour's tragedy during sunset; Horace Bones murders his illegitimate offspring in the Wicklow Mountains; Mrs Muldooneen, the landlady, serves arsenic in the spuds to several Anglo Irish Trinity students; Joe Ireland crosses the border, sabre between his teeth, baby Power in his pocket, shillelagh in one hand, the Sinn Fein Rebellion book in the other and establishes a stout-taster's post in the North; and A. K. Donoghue, having left Ireland because of lack of food, gets stones in his kidney because of too much food in America; and in all the pubs, across the expressionless face of Ireland, stand the still poised figures and a bottle of stout – the dictators, the poets, novelists, inventors, geniuses, gourmets, business tycoons, painters, politicians; a word in your ear and the cry of all Ireland, 'What will you have? A bottle?' And all the time Donleavy was painting.

As insults and complaints rained and a letter of mine appeared in *The Irish Times*, my exhibition did give me my first taste of fame. As I saw pouring into the gallery a stream of folk who in testing the wetness of my canvases were adding their finger prints. And amazingly some only came in to buy, for sixpence, one of my catalogues. In which I was serving up my own dish of what I hoped was the heartfelt truth. But Donoghue was already gone. However, upon his last ditch stand before he departed the shores of Ireland, he did at least establish The Irish Republican Publicity League at 39 Grafton Street and appoint himself as its secretary. Attesting further to the supreme tolerance of John Ryan whose address this was, albeit that he himself was sympathetic to Donoghue's espoused cause. Which was to fund a movement and purchase flags, and guns to make Ireland whole again. And Donoghue, searching out the best sounding Irish names in a Boston telephone book, sent off to America letter requests imploring aid to such cause. After hundreds of mailings and some few hungry weeks during which he got no replies, one finally came back with a modest donation. From an Italian gentleman who had just taken over the Irish pub to whom Donoghue had addressed his appeal. Evidence enough that not many of the sons of the ould sod gave a good god damn about the political plight of Ireland. Not to mention that of a totally destitute would be patriot.

Donoghue's dawning departure was the end of an era. And of the first bemusements with this land. In which very few could afford to remain. Finally one starving afternoon Donoghue presented himself across the street to the Woolworth's café. Which was up the stairs on a floor above that where they sold their wares and into which one could daily stare from John Ryan's studio. Donoghue, ordering a double pot of tea and a spread of your usual bacon, sausages, tomato and fried eggs and upon golfing these down, he called for the bill and put up his hands to tell the waitress.

'Shoot me, I can't pay.'

And sadly, just following by one week Donoghue's departure, there came a letter from a sympathetic friend in Paris in which was enough money to allow him to further survive and espouse his nationalism. And for such acts of kindness one to this day still remembers the man's name, a Stanley Carnow. And regrets that he never got a thank you reply, for Donoghue the non recipient had through the good offices of the American consul already secured free passage on a rusty cargo ship and was in a hurricane at the time, being tossed like a peanut all over the Atlantic waves.

Better funded people like James Hillman and Douglas Usher Wilson set off on their own grand tour of Africa and the Middle East. But ah. As well as myself, there was one other gent who remained. None other than the saintly calmly contented Gainor Stephen Crist. Who was nearly the counterpart of Donoghue. Raised in Ohio in the middle of the Middle West where his father was a prominent doctor. And where he was an indulged only child. Simply put, Crist revelled in Ireland. Attesting to certain abilities perhaps lacking in those who left. Salient among which was one, that of being able to obtain goods on account where e'er he went. Which was into grocery shops, pubs and department stores and even into the American Embassy. Crist in addition to being a refined American, had an astonishing resemblance to the Duke of Windsor and was also possessed of what could be described as an English accent. These added to his plethora of other social and moral advantages and being able to present himself in the at least sleeker and as yet untarnished garments of the new world, allowed him to effortlessly cut a swathe through Irish life. Except perhaps for one early unfortunate incident. When he had sent a grey herringbone tweed suit to be dry cleaned. Which duly returned, having been thoroughly washed and laundered. With the sleeves shrunken half way up to his elbows, the trouser legs half way up to his knees. And the garment nearly squeezing him to death.

Except that they left every customer pissing in debt, most Dublin pubs if they resembled anything at all, resembled banks. Stout mahogany doors, frosted glass windows etched with legends, 'Whiskey Bonders, Sherry Importers'. And constantly conducting transactions of handing over your pound note to have a Guinness or ball of malt deposited in your belly which in turn were guaranteed to give birth to dreams in your brain. Some pub owners were the nearest thing one could imagine to a priest presiding over his faithful flock. Listening to woes of the weather, racing, or the shocking price of petrol as they might listen to a confession of sins. Dispensing forgiveness as penance was paid in the price of a stout or ball of malt. Entering to take a pew. Kneel to adore this god and perform with these sacred liquids, the religious ceremony of quenching thirst. In this land where all of life had finally to become lived in the mind. And where there came no better man to do that than the eminently contemplative Gainor Stephen Crist. Who was able to do nearly the impossible, that of running up credit in an Irish public house.

Crist in sizing up Dublin and liking to have at his disposal liquid refreshment at all times and especially outside of pub closing hours, had to confront two problems, one of time and the other of money. In the first of these he paid a visit to a distinguished lawyer and man of letters, Terence de Vere White, to inquire concerning the establishing of a private drinking club in Dublin. Of which he would be the first founding member, Chairman, Grandmaster and President and who knows, even occasional bartender. One imagines that Mr de Vere White had cautioned upon the licensing difficulties and expense of such a venture for Crist failed to pursue the matter. However, he remained extremely concerned that he would ever be without a drink

(Right) Gainor Stephen Crist with his first wife Constance in front of my rooms at number 38 Trinity College. My name just legible painted in white on the entrance behind us. Constance, being one of the few of the many like myself and Crist who braved the academic world of Trinity, but who succeeded in getting her degree.

(Left) Crist at the side gate of Trinity from which he is exiting to pawn an electric fire. This saintly expedient gentleman on this day had resolutely made the decision that money for a few pints and ball of malt in the pub would keep him as comfortably warm as any electric fire. And as he said, the steam from his piss could prove it.

through the mere lack of money. And to this problem he paid his next attention. Elaborately biding his time in those strategically situated public houses that took his fancy, and wherein he prepared his carefully devised protocol. He would attend at the pub for two consecutive days and then arriving on the third, always shortly following morning opening, he would upon taking his first drink and paying for it, then present to a nonplussed barman, an extra ten shilling note. Explaining it was in repayment for the other night when without warning he had run short of cash while having a few drinks with friends. The barman, always a practised politician in facing any customer, but not recalling the incident, and facing this gent distinguished far beyond your usual calibre of your average American, and further faced with the dilemma of telling him he was mistaken, usually took the ten shillings. Which for any bartender could be a matter of relief that the principle of restitution was being observed in a city like Dublin where to incur a debt always meant you were leaving for somewhere and not returning soon. In any event bartenders had already found that this plausible gentleman's bon-homie was such that it often involved every customer in buying a substantially greater number of drinks, so that it became a profitable matter to nod back when Crist said put that round on my bill please. Thus did one of the greatest American drinkers ever to hit Ireland and pop back a ball of malt, prepare for his financially enforced dry days. And dear me, who is to say that such debts although they grew astronomically and unwieldy large, were not in their every penny always repaid in full. For Crist had not only enormous compassion for his fellow man but was an absolute stickler for fair play.

But even Gainor Crist was not without his difficulties in other areas of obtaining goods, particularly those of a rubber quality. For upon presenting himself in a chemist's shop for the first time to buy contraceptives, and making his condom request known, the chemist blessed himself, turned candy coloured purple and red and then knocking over his counter of laxatives and other highly in demand eliminating aids, not only retreated into the back of his apothecary but pushed his two young lady assistants before him. And as a nonplussed Crist persisted in his inquiry the white coated gentleman stood in the rear doorway of his premises shaking and speechless until his offending customer had left. Thinking this was a mere aberration of an overworked druggist Crist tried again, but with similar results, only this time the chemist became violent and threw a box of sanitary towels. It was not until the third attempt that the chemist, aware that he might have an errant tourist on his hands did at least, while firmly showing him the door, say that such unmentionable things were not for sale in Ireland. Crist being a man fond of family also had a further concern too for the consequences of the lack of contraceptives. For in the birth of a child in life threatening circumstances he heard that in Holy Catholic Ireland it would not be the mother who would be saved, but the new infant.

Crist ever fascinated by religion if not politics, was very largely instrumental in bringing to my notice aspects of Ireland I might never have come to know, due to my own absorbing fascination at the time with wine, women and song. Crist was an extremely politely precise gentleman. Indeed upon first ever confronting him in the Pearl Bar in Dublin he was already wearing a sweater belonging to me and was profusely apologizing for a small stain he'd got on it. Explaining he would only wear it till exactly five p.m. when he would take it off. The sweater, which Crist had on in some photographs posing as a male model had been borrowed for him by his brother in law Randall Hillis. It was from this connection to his first wife's father, stationed as a clergyman in the Irish north, that Crist first brought to my own attention the phenomenon of an Orangeman. Describing to me as he did these formidable men and boys who marched thumping great drums and who sang their songs with delight and fervour, of being up to their knees in Catholic blood and up to the knees in slaughter. Crist taking a nearly satanic delight and amusement that these two groups of Christian religionists could so oppose one another with such unChristian repugnance. His interest in this extending to Catholic martyrs as well as Cromwell who was responsible for slaughtering so many possible ones. Crist gloating to draw attention to the phenomenon of the strange similarity between the identically preserved ancient heads of both the Blessed Oliver Plunkett and that of Oliver Cromwell. And on this issue I would find Crist on many an occasion comfortably sitting in his sofa chair waging his own personal war against the crut. Which would take the form of writing a number of varying letters on the subject of the likeness of the heads, to the editors of the daily Dublin evening newspapers, *The Evening Herald* and *The Evening Mail*. Crist always remaining immune to the fact that such letters went unpublished.

Crist who was fond of saying, 'I taught Donleavy everything he knows', was essentially correct, especially concerning much of Ireland. But as I deliberately avoided storing knowledge, much of what Crist conveyed to me, did then, and has certainly since, vanished from mind. As an American, Crist spoke of wielding what amounted to a so called double edged sword in this land. Which by one's accent and tolerant outlook allowed one to assume alliances on nearly every religious and political side and enjoy a congenial fraternity right up and down the rungs of the jealously guarded Irish social ladder. An American could also identify when necessary, or pleasant, with the British ruling class, or the Anglo Irish or the Dublin suburban upper, or slum lower or working class. Leaving one totally free to associate among and even eagerly agree with either bigoted rabid Protestants, or crut encrusted Catholics or indeed with the odd mystified but invariably smiling Hindu or Mohammedan who had found his way to these shores, usually to medical school.

If anything, Crist himself was possessed with a triple edged sword. For, unlike any other American at Trinity, he could spend endless hours in the company of any Dubliner in a bar, and transform even the most lacklustre of these into electrifying company. Often by merely listening in concerned head shaking agreement to every word your man spoke. And in short order, and after a few pints of stout, these previously colourless repetitive pub stage Irishmen could even be moderately entertaining. But Crist out of Dublin and in the countryside, could wield even more astonishing transformations in some of these pub habitués. Which I discovered in an instance, when in the middle of a Trinity College summer afternoon, I was accosted by Crist as I exited along New Square from my rooms at number 38. And to which he immediately directed me urgently to return. To fetch my toothbrush. For he was inviting me to his country residence in Kerry. I was not to know then that it was to take us five days walking and hitch hiking in any and every direction to get there. And that I was appointed to buy all the drink on the way and spend nearly the total of three days and whole nights in various pubs. Each time, upon my suggestion that we should proceed, Crist's hand would come to stay me upon the arm. And as the man to whom he was talking would continue to ramble on as he had done for the three previous hours, Crist would also say, 'Mike, wait, this man knows something. Listen.'

On this same night, and finally dislodging Crist from his crony, who had sold his farm piecemeal to drink it, always prefacing the point by recounting how he would, cutting hay, go to the hedge and look down the road and lay down his scythe and then sell the field. And on his donkey cart would come and go to the pub till he'd drunk the proceeds. As Crist listened, this gentleman still had his donkey and cart outside into which he would fall unconscious that very night and the donkey would take him home. But Crist and I had nothing similar and I found myself with him utterly out in the middle of nowhere, finally coming across a fairground where Crist in a feat of strength rang the strong man's bell with a wooden hammer. Impressing a girl nearby whom he then insisted on escorting home because she said her father would beat her unconscious for returning so late. He set off with her cross country over the fields and I was left waiting half the night outside the fairground after it had closed. Crist duly returning. Armed with his usual stout bottles, having, by the dishevelled looks of him, either chastised the girl's cruel father or led his daughter further astray. But Crist's mood serene. We lay down on the side of the road to sleep. And as the sun came up breaking through the mists to wake me, there he was, sitting, shivering in the dawn chill in his shirt sleeves, his arms wrapped around his knees, and benignly content as he stared out into the green hushed silence. Both his sweater and jacket draped over me to keep me warm. I knew too, that anyone disparaging me behind my back, often justifiably, sad to admit, would find Crist giving them a 'wooling', pounding their heads on the floor until they made their apologies. Although he had other reputations frequently deserved, this man from Ohio was one of the most kindly, compassionate and saintly of men. And whose wearier sentiments in those days were occasionally voiced.

'Life in Ireland is a fight with the heavyweight champion of the world. But they don't let you lie there, knocked out, they throw water on you to get you up to knock you out again.'

At the end of our long journey, to a house overlooking Dingle Bay, we arrived to find Constance Crist, Gainor's first wife and their first baby daughter, Marianna. Petra, as Crist referred to his wife, was British and as directly outspoken as she was an extremely attractive sensual lady, and never averse to letting the Irish know what was on her mind. And I'm not sure that she wasn't even the originator of the word 'crut'. Were her anger to be aroused sufficiently, she was not afraid to publicly voice her critical opinion of Ireland or the Irish. As I heard her once not unreasonably do to the entire passenger population riding on the top of a Dublin tram. Who seemed actually to sympathize instead of attacking the pair of us. But equally she could be as charming and humorous as the Irish themselves when she chose. She it was who first introduced her husband to A. K. Donoghue when she met Donoghue sitting next to her in the American Embassy. And single among the three of us, at Trinity, as strong ladies can and do, she was the only one to attain a degree. She sang many an old song to us and as we all sat on the hillside of the mountain where we had climbed to picnic by a black lake, she would tell strange haunting tales of punishments, ghosts, tortures and murders in an ancient Yorkshire castle in which she grew up. Her voice so laughter rich in the rare June cool, clean sunshine. As we three lay there, the larks above ascending singing.

Into the same stunning

Blue

Under which Crist lies now

Alone

In an island grave elsewhere

So far

From this Ireland he had come

To love

IX

The small house on a hillside overlooking Dingle Bay to which Crist had invited me had actually been rented by a gentleman who was instrumental in Crist's first introducing me, a confirmed theatre hater, to the actual live world of Irish stage drama. Where again one encountered the presence of one of these foreign catalysts who made things happen in Ireland. It was my first ever evening at the Gaiety Theatre, a place which much later was to cause a more considerable incident for me. I attended in the company of Crist, who was there to see a friend of his perform. But as it turned out as it usually did on most of these occasions, Crist was early to attend and late to leave the theatre bar, resulting in nearly the whole of the play being heard in the distant background. But I did at least catch a brief stage sight of Crist's friend performing. In a scene where he rushed out of the wings to stamp his feet, and shout suitably impressively while flinging a paper on the stage. His name was George Roy Hill later to become the distinguished film director.

Hill, of partially Irish origins, was another Middle Western American. Having been at Yale, he was an ex Marine fighter pilot whom Crist, as a sailor in the U.S. Navy had first met when volunteering in a Florida bar one night to do Hill a favour. Hill was then taking his last steps in flight training and Crist was a naval yeoman who assigned the various pilots to their various examiners in flight tests. Crist overhearing Hill at a bar say he thought he might fail, introduced himself and informed Hill that it was possible he could assign him to a lenient examiner. All of which happily happened and Hill got his wings. Then more than 3,000 miles away and fully three years later, in the front square of Trinity College Dublin, Crist spotted again this familiar face and introduced himself.

Hill like Crist was from your distinctly better sort of American background, indeed of the Brahmin class. Tall, dignified and handsome, Hill wore a bowler and walked Dublin's streets accompanied by a properly rolled brolly. But he was not to be mistaken for someone unable to give a strong account of himself when called upon. As proved when he wasn't long first in Crist's company. When both their very capable fistic abilities were put to the test. To the point of attracting the attention of the Garda Síochána. If there was any certain thing these two men had in common it was that neither would suffer to witness insult to a lady. And it was such an instance, of a disparaging remark being made by someone as to the abilities of a distinguished lady of the theatre, Ria Mooney, that a battle of two against four ensued in a village street with Crist and Hill victors, having avenged Miss Mooney. But both then being apprehended by the Garda Síochána in the process.

If Crist was among the few who could succeed in running up credit in a pub, then Hill was the other astonishing phenomenon as one of the rare men who was not forced to finally flee Ireland with his tail unfirmly between his legs. For Hill was one of Dublin's few American success stories, not only acting in this play at the Gaiety but producing it as well, the play being a hit and making money and Hill able to go off and sojourn in Paris. But Hill had not been entirely without his difficult moments in Dublin. Indeed, as had other Americans, he reached the actual point of starvation. But having sworn a principle to himself not to rely upon his family or anyone else for support he attempted to subsist upon what was due him on the American government's G.I. Bill of Rights. But the non arrival of such emolument, as it had for Donoghue, driving him to Woolworth's for a plate of bacon and eggs, so too did it force Hill into the Red Bank Restaurant, one of Dublin's best and most expensive dining venues, and fully in keeping with Hill's own standards and background. Hill having there his first full meal for nearly a week. But with your usual half bottle of Chablis with the smoked salmon. A Bonne Mare with the filet mignon and a Bearnaise sauce. Creamed spinach, with your butter anointed boiled baby potatoes. And all followed by a whipped cream decorated chocolate mousse and an Irish coffee. Asking for the manager, Hill was quietly wiping his mouth with his linen napkin and sipping his drink when he arrived. Hill explaining he could not pay the bill but would do so upon the first opportunity. The manager benignly taking the whole matter in his stride and inviting Hill to another Irish coffee compliments of the house.

'And I quite understand your temporary impecuniousness, sir.

And certainly we remain appreciative of your continued esteemed patronage.'

One has the temerity and fondness now to recall Abraham Jacob Leventhal, or Con as he was mostly called, a Jewish gentleman, Dublin scholar, wit and man of letters who was also the patron saint of Americans on the G.I. Bill attending Trinity College and whose mouths he more than occasionally helped fill. Leventhal, bundled up in his tweeds, sat behind his desk in his ground floor office in Front Square, his window overlooking the cobblestones and the velvet grass. There was much sober bemusement on his face as chilled starving Americans entered his presence and took a moment's respite by a rosy coal fire in his grate. He was asked favours and approvals which sometimes were gently questioned but never refused. Although I knew then nothing of this gentleman's literary abilities or associations, I marvelled at his patience and his unhesitation to sign these endless bizarre in triplicate documents confronting him. And which he so often would do in the clear certainty of the applicant's unentitlement. His was a shy, unassuming way, and the reference to him as Con Leventhal was thought to have come about with his frequently prefacing his sentences with the phrase, 'When I was on the Continent'. But there is no question that when Con was on the job as registrar, many an American neck did he save including my own, by merely saying.

'I do think I sign here, don't I. O yes. And on these. In a trinity, of course.'

These were all matters happening in a country where one was wont to complain about many things, but you could never say you were constrained by documents. Over which rules were broken and exceptions made at the sound of a brogue, and where a gesture or a smile could get you a lot more than a writ. Although, by God, some of your smiles and gestures were not of the best and plenty of your writs wax stamped and emblazoned were served flying all over the place.

There were no documents and not much cash upon us on the impromptu toothbrush trip with Crist to the west. But it was my first extended stay in the Irish countryside. Kells Cove was no more than a house and cottage or two at the end of a path between boulder built walls and overlooking a tiny inlet on Dingle Bay. The nearest transport, a mile and a half away, was reached by a rutted dirt lane leading up to where the main road ran and at where a once daily train

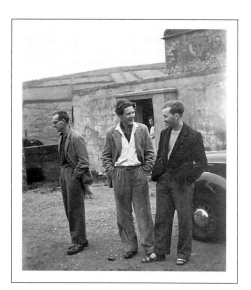

Gainor Stephen Crist, David O'Leary and John Ryan on the Dingle peninsula. 'The West's Awake' was a frequent cry and when made in Dublin usually meant that all those in hearing distance would set off towards the Atlantic like lemmings and would often walk the entire way.

stopped in each direction at an isolated unmarked lonely spot at the foot of a dark rising mountain. On the main road there was a grocery tucked into the side of the hill, where Gainor Stephen Crist, Esq. already had opened an account for your best of bacon, eggs and tea to be supplied. And there was a pub. Two miles away across the fields as the crow flies and as Crist and I stumbled. Such forays necessitating a wet foot slog across treacherous bits of bog and upon an inebriated return it was a life risking venture. The nearest town was Cahirciveen another seven or so miles to the southwest along the coast. Crist, who was a ferocious walker, could transverse those miles in no time, twiddling his thumbs nervously in front of him as he did so. And waiting patiently as I would shout for him to let me catch up. But once he did stop dead in his tracks to call me up from behind and ask me to investigate something on the road ahead. It was a dead bird. Crist grew nervously white as the blood drained from his face. And I watched him detour down into a ditch, climb a wall and wade through nettles to circumvent this area of the road where the dead bird lay. I once asked him what would he do if a dead bird came to him in a box.

'Mike, I would kill the man who sent it.'

Cahirciveen itself on this sunshining day reminded me of a main street of Western cowboy territory. And as one entered it on foot, striding centre of the road, the curtains twitched at the windows.

News of your arrival would have already reached the other end of the town. Where Crist was heading as he always did to a post office. If not to send something then to see if something desperately sought had arrived. Cahirciveen, although a spooky town, was one of Crist's most favourite places. Not least for its reputation of having more pubs per population than any other half square mile area on earth. Except for the church and Garda Síochána, nearly every other building and shop, no matter what else it was for or sold, had a board supported between two barrels as a bar. Everywhere we entered the corks out of the Guinness bottles went pop. Thus producing an ambience much to Crist's liking. We set off to walk the seven miles back and for some of it got a ride standing up in the rear of a lurching donkey cart which a young monosyllabic boy was driving. Who was suspicious and shy of his strange passengers. But as Irish custom would have it, you could not pass without offering a lift to another on the road. And back we came. Down the winding, twisting, stony lane. Through the trees the sound of a brook in this glen. Back to the bliss of this little house. From which you had only feet to take you somewhere. Only a candle to light your night. A bucket to hold your water from a stream. A turf fire to cook your meals. Nothing to get up for tomorrow. And no need to do anything today. Cloaked in this protection. With the West awake. Like strange, unseen lightning and unsounding thunder. Premonitions shimmering, tingling in the air. The haunting deathly strangeness. Of the hush out across Dingle Bay.

Ah, but let us not forget there were full blooded born Irish Irishmen living in Ireland. Robust of spirit. Brave in adversity. Randy in appetite. Thirsty in drinking. Right fisted and left footed in fighting. Ready always as a sacred duty to do you a favour. Or be on your side when the chips were down. And one of the first of whom I met through John Ryan. And his name Tony McInerney. McInerney was about the closest you could get to your Irish country gentry of the time. From a farm on the banks of the Shannon where their fields sloped down to its edge. The house nestled in trees and approached by a drive through front gates. From such respectable, comfortable background McInerney and his brothers proceeded to the best schools and into various professions as did Tony into the field of accountancy. He was one of the first to appreciate Donoghue's imported honesty. Smilingly listening to that iconoclastic latter gent blow holes in the myths and disembowel long held Irish beliefs and spout his stream of insights and observations for hours at a time. McInerney finally maintaining that one of his cherished ambitions in life was that upon getting his inheritance he would take Donoghue to the West and sit him on the end of Slea Head. And with the next parish being America across the Atlantic and the great waves slamming the cliffs below, to listen to him for the rest of his days. But alas when McInerney did get his inheritance, Donoghue was gone to America and McInerney went instead to Paris. In the company of such always readily available universal tourists such as Crist, Behan, and Michael Heron, my Trinity room mate. But on the same occasion McInerney also saved my bacon on the very eve of my first marriage. Where in front of my prosperous in laws and under some scrutiny due to my artistic bent, I was standing without a bean to my name, unable even to buy a wedding ring. When that very morning an envelope arrived containing a sheaf of money and a cryptic note. 'You never expected to get this did you.' It was money I'd loaned him on a trip to the West an entire year previous. And such sums then usually being treated as a gift for life. With this manna from Ireland, Valerie, my wife to be, and I travelled into Bradford and there I bought a platinum wedding band.

For political reasons McInerney had been interned at The Curragh. And he still moved with that strange curious gait of a man who was following someone or being followed and which Behan was so fond of parodying in his characters on stage as the raincoated gunman, collar up, surreptitiously moving. McInerney, although capable of adding up a column of figures in the blink of an eye was also an insatiably scholarly man, as incurably curious as he could sometimes be unrelentingly stubborn over an opinion. Although accumulating cultural knowledge was not my forte, it was McInerney who exposed an Ireland of traditions and he who had secured the pampooties for James H. Leathers. But it was astonishing how well one could know someone like McInerney and yet know so little about him. As one day I thought I had the absolute well thought out brilliant solution to his life. One morning putting it to him upstairs in Bewley's Oriental Café in Grafton Street.

'Tony, why don't you get married and have a family.'

'Mike, I already am and have three children.'

And as well as having a talent for fatherhood, McInerney was full

(Right) *Tony McInerney on the banks of the Shannon near where his family's farm sloped down to the shores and where we spent much time whiling away many an afternoon. Someone like McInerney, either on the streets of the city of Limerick or the lanes of the countryside would, every short distance be stopped to pass the time of day with one acquaintance or another. Making for a powerful network of communication from coast to coast.*

(Left) *McInerney at Kells Cove, Co. Kerry, as a father. In our Dublin days together it was some years before I knew McInerney was married and had children and not until I suggested this as a solution to his life did I learn that he had already taken the step.*

of many others. When we first sat down to play chess and I who could already defeat the formidable likes of Gainor Crist found myself on this board being slowly but surely outpositioned and systematically routed. And McInerney finally putting me in checkmate, spoke up at my shattering dismay.

'Mike, you mustn't think you're still not a great chess player. Interned at the Curragh for three years, playing every day, I could beat everyone in the place. And against some of them, a Russian Grand Master wouldn't stand a chance.'

It was by happenstance with McInerney that I ended up living where I did when I fled to the land and struggled there for survival as his and my forefathers had done when there was nowhere else to go. McInerney, after his grand tour of the Continent with friends, still had a remainder of his inheritance left and was looking to purchase a little farm. And one day I accompanied him on his search. Out along the Wicklow coast. To a bereft, flat, strange, barren stretch of bogs between the land and the sea. McInerney upon reconnoitering this four acre plot with its corrugated iron bungalow shrouded by its overgrown hedges, its old slate roof cottage in disrepair and lean to shed and a small stone barn, decided it was not suitable for him. I already had, following my marriage, attacks of anxiety concerning one's survival. In spite of returning to Dublin after my wedding richer than I had left. But it was upon my then wife Valerie renting us a bed sitting room in which there was merely a bed, a stove and a sink and that the w.c. was on a landing out in a semi public corridor, that I panicked. Having been brought up in reasonably large houses in America, I had till that time little idea that people lived in such limited circumstances. The claustrophobia struck me with a sledgehammer profundity. And to such degree that I found myself returning that night back to my commodious if primitive rooms in Trinity.

By the time I was aseat in my sitting room in number 38, my heart was palpitating in what I thought was a serious heart attack. Struggling to the door, holding desperately to the bannister as I descended and hoping desperately that my 200 mile an hour tennis serving opponent wasn't lurking there ready to jump me. I emerged safely from the open hall and to the terra firma of New Square and summoned two students in the distance to assist me. They, of course, at first thought it part of a playful joke but my increasingly plaintive cries finally convinced them. Fortunately they were rugby players and each catching me under arm lugged me on my quavering legs to the front gate's porter's lodge where a taxi was got to take me to the nearest Trinity College affiliated hospital. On the way I remember recalling a similar taxi in New York when I'd cut my arm in a fight and the taxi driver refused payment for what he said he regarded an emergency. But there was on this occasion no hesitation on the part of the taxi driver to make sure he got his fare from a man clearly dying in his tracks. Searching in my wallet for the money I was nearly angered enough to stretch your man out flat on his back. Slight proof that I wasn't quite dead yet. I vaguely recognized the young doctor on duty from Trinity's medical school who put his stethoscope over my heart and announced in some surprise.

'There are few patients I've ever examined with a heart sounding anything near as healthy as yours.'

But such catastrophic event and the realization that kind parents and kind governments weren't going to support me for the rest of my life drove me to buy land. The source of all and where I at least could die standing on ground in which I could be buried cheaply. And it was my very rich father in law, who made it possible. His name was John MacMichael Heron. Whose custom it had been to give expensive canteens of silverware to all his friends' children upon their weddings. And my to be mother in law, who had discreetly discussed with me one morning as to my assets, concluded I had neither those nor prospects. And I seemed even poorer upon disclosing that I had a small allowance from my own mother. Suddenly invitations were rushed out all over Ilkley and beyond throughout Yorkshire. To an impromptu cocktail party to celebrate our wedding. John MacMichael Heron lay these days in his bed, ill. I had got him to take up painting and he overnight began to produce a series of talented attractive well crafted pictures. And with him I played chess and spent much time fascinatedly listening to him telling me stories of his struggles and triumphs in his business career. His advice about my staying to live in Ireland was simple. Buy Guinness shares. Ireland to my in laws being a distant place where perhaps the only acceptable respectable thing about it was its famed brewery, Trinity College Dublin, its wartime plenitude of beef, butter, bacon and eggs, and its race horses.

Upon the evening of the cocktail party I was summoned to my father in law's luxurious mirrored and rosewood panelled bedroom and was handed a cheque. Which at first I hadn't looked at and then later was entirely staggered to view in highly pleasant disbelief. And then as the cocktails were quaffed and the canapés downed, from nearly every guest came more cheques. And now just back from a brief paid for honeymoon at Kettlewell in the Yorkshire Dales and having at six thirty p.m. been destitute save for a pound or two left over from McInerney's returned loan with which I had bought the wedding ring, by eight thirty p.m. I was staring in my continued disbelief at the sum total of the astonishing cheques in my hand. Of course, everyone in this rich community of Ilkley thought it was a shotgun marriage to a ne'er do well claiming to be an artist on top of it. And certainly one felt the slight resentment since every mill owner's son for miles around had assiduously courted and tried to marry one of the stunningly beautiful Heron daughters. The last of whom was now to vanish to Ireland in the company of an American not only without a mill or factory but also conspicuously without a pot to piss in.

My first mother in law at my last Dublin exhibition. This brave lady with a sense of taste would always indulgently buy one or two of my pictures even in the blaze of adverse publicity and accusations of such efforts being not only still wet, but tasteless and obscene. Of course, in truth they were really not half bad at all.

Michael Heron in his gents' natty suiting. His father upon seeing how he lived in our rooms at Trinity sent him immediately to the tailor and haberdashery in order as he suggested, he maintain his dignity. Heron senior being a prominent Bradford wool merchant.

But having now enough money to buy at least a pot did nothing for the terror I felt for my future in Ireland. And upon that day with McInerney and looking around this bereft and forlorn gathering of buildings, I thought I had nothing to lose in making an offer for what appeared to be a basic necessity in life. No doubt thinking there was money in things like chickens and pigs. Plus around one, all was green with space to breathe and move. Instead of being abjectly incarcerated in a bed sitting room paying rent on somewhere to be you did not own. But this was back to Irish peasantry. And I recalled an earlier day when Michael Heron's father called to our Trinity rooms long before I was ever a prospect of marriage to one of his daughters. With this elegantly tall, professorial looking gentleman arriving, wearing a gaberdine raincoat of his own design and manufacture. His son Michael was out and as he waited there, looking about him, his suit lapels hand stitched, and trying to appear unconcerned at the sight and condition of the college sitting room which I was then using as a studio. Crusts of bread, open milk bottles on the table among my paints and brushes. As he kept repeating.

'Well, you're young, you're young.'

But a day or two later in the pedestrian joy of a Dublin morning I met Michael Heron walking up from the bottom of Grafton Street, a silk Trinity scarf flying from his neck. He'd been to the haberdasher's and was utterly transformed out of his previously baggy and unkempt clothes and was now sartorially resplendent in your best gent's natty suiting from the top of his trilby hat to the tips of his brand new shoes from a reputable bootmaker's. It appeared that his father, utterly shaken by his visit to his son's rooms had given him a large cheque with which to refurbish his appearance if not his college living conditions. The cheque being handed over with the words.

'Michael, I'd like you to keep up your dignity.'

Heron in those days, from an English public school and previously at Cambridge and a wartime serving British naval reserve officer, had been before the war sent by his father, in view of his expanding business, on a grand tour from Sweden to Corsica and from France to Russia. Heron ending up speaking many languages fluently but more than anything relishing strange cities and the writers and poets who lived in them. Although familiar with Paris, Rome, Stockholm and Berlin, the city he was coming most to adore, was Dublin. Patiently and even indulgently accepting its hardships and impecunious life. Haggling at length with the old ladies at their stalls over a pound of tomatoes. Heron, as well as his rooms in college, kept another place out in Dublin. And many an evening we walked up Great George's Street in its direction. Visiting pubs, one or two of which had literary connections but usually bore no trace or commemoration of these. And at a fork in the road of Camden and Charlotte Streets we would end up drinking the early night away in the pub then called The Bleeding Horse. And, albeit indirectly, it was through Heron and later meeting his sister and then his father, and followed by Gainor Crist's insistent counselling that I should marry that I ended up being driven to become an American imitation of an Irish peasant. And according to Patrick Kavanagh, a full blown rural phoney.

After long, stubborn haggling, when even the estate agent shook his head in disbelief at my refusal to budge from my offer, declaring finally that if the price were any lower the vendor would be out of his mind to sell. Terence de Vere White solicitously handling the sale. And even he thought £350 for three buildings and four acres had to be a reasonable bargain. And like happens at every country fair all over Ireland the estate agent uttered those words you hear at the verge of attempting to finally consummate a deal.

'Would you split the difference now that stands between you?'

Although the vendor was back in the village of Kilcoole I split the difference. The agent and I drank on it in the lounge of the Grand

Hotel in Greystones. I signed a caretaker's agreement and practically the next day, my college servant Noctor and I lugged my possessions out of my college rooms and out Trinity's side gate into Pearse Street to the bus whose last stop was Kilcoole. Without knowing it, I had come to one of the strangest places in all of Ireland. A patch of land just raised above the sea, a vacant landscape north and south with the Wicklow Mountains rising inland to the grey pointed peak of the Sugar Loaf. Waking in the morning to find myself listening to a donkey's bray and then half shattered out of my wits to see this animal's hoary head peering at dawn in our cottage window. It was the month of February. But a kinder one than usual. Although I still rose shivering from a wet mattress. My newly wed wife more mystified than complaining. Coping with cooking on an open fire and lugging water from a stream. Asking only to be able to own a cat and go take an occasional bath for a shilling at the Grand Hotel.

I was now in Ireland literally dug in, body and soul. And venturing to Dublin I would on return progress through St Stephen's Green and up Harcourt Street to its elegant granite station to come home by train. In order to stop at Kilcoole, one had to go up to the engine driver before leaving and make the request. Kilcoole surely being one

Valerie going to fetch the milk along the entrance lane to the cottage. It was along this muddy path that Behan went to the pub a mile away, carrying a suitcase full of my shoes and throwing a pair away into the field on the right as soon as they got wet and then putting on a dry pair. All easily done as Behan never wore or tied up shoelaces.

of the loneliest train stations in all of Europe. And where it was chosen to land guns in the time of the Troubles. It was a straight mile towards the sea from the village and four miles beyond Greystones. From where the sand and pebble beach went as a twin wavering ribbon with the white surf and a line of telegraph poles stood along the tracks like little pins stuck in a map. With hardly a habitation on this stretch of coast, farther south beyond Kilcoole station was yet another ten miles of watery bog called The Breeches. On windy, wintry days alighting on the station itself, half built on stacked great cast blocks of cement to hold back the sea, one was swept by the spray of the waves. The train tootling its whistle to abandon you there as it now made its way down the track to Wicklow town. Leaving a ghostly loneliness in its wake. I would then, jumping from stone to stone, have to negotiate a narrow path which led half submerged through a bog and past a tiny shrouded neighbour's cottage where lived a Mr and Mrs Smith. An astonishingly handsome couple both in their middle eighties and retired from Dublin. Behind their tiny gate they

Valerie, Patricia and John Ryan in the early days before improvements at Kilcoole. These two elegantly beautiful ladies in these primitive rural surroundings still seemed able to effect a garden party air of Henley and Ascot. Their host having abandoned his dinner jacket was now with rolled up tattered sleeves fighting the world with hammer, spade, brush and pen.

With Valerie in a field at Kilcoole, the Irish sea in the background and the leash of a visiting pedigree dog in my hand which might have symbolized my last contact with the respectable world. In those days one cannot imagine who might have owned a dog which might needlessly compete with the eating of food stuffs.

were enclosed in massive shrubberies. Their big blue grey cat Snooky, who was a marvellous ratter even with his balls cut off, sat like a sphinx on guard. The bog extended into their garden and came within yards of their front door and their chickens pecked and wet their claws in it. Their tiny three rooms were stuffed with their big pieces of mahogany Victorian furniture. And here is where they would stay to live out their lives. Sometimes walking four miles along the track to Greystones and back.

Strange stories, rumours and mystery surrounded this area. Grey Fort, a large mansion, stood empty just across the fields. Where Marconi was reputed to have once lived. As well as an AngloIrish family called the Hamiltons. To the north was a large estate in ruins with the remnants of fine brick barns and a massive walled garden. The builder of it said to have been shipwrecked on the shore and returned from America to build his home there. The area also seemed to have found other odd foreign folk like myself settling on this boggy coast. And my first lessons of the Irish countryside and being an imitation peasant farmer were learned here.

I had also come to Kilcoole with a steamer trunk full of fifteen suits and twenty pairs of shoes, two of which were for playing golf. I had a beaver collared polo coat as well as other extravagant and inappropri-

(Left) *Myself, Douglas Usher Wilson and Michael Heron at Kilcoole early 1950. The cottage behind, prior to any improvements but in which, over dinner and wine, many a late night discussion would take place in front of the fire. During which Douglas Wilson would invariably declare that I was talking through my paper asshole. Which I hope by now has at least hardened up to cardboard.*

(Right) *Michael Heron seated, Douglas Wilson, holding open a book in his hand and James Hillman looking on, a luggage case full of my books and documents is being perused. To the left lies my first efforts at a garden with my first mechanical farming implement, a wheelbarrow. And these visiting gentlemen are standing on the first lawn I ever mowed. Or pissed on.*

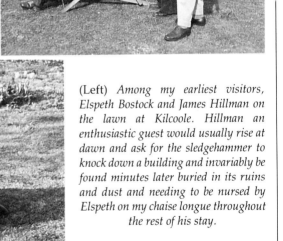

(Left) *Among my earliest visitors, Elspeth Bostock and James Hillman on the lawn at Kilcoole. Hillman an enthusiastic guest would usually rise at dawn and ask for the sledgehammer to knock down a building and invariably be found minutes later buried in its ruins and dust and needing to be nursed by Elspeth on my chaise longue throughout the rest of his stay.*

ate garments. The nearest my hand had got to holding a farm implement or tool had been in wielding a squash and tennis racquet. And above all other things there came something else new in life, my first country squabbles. And in this overnight I reverted to being as suspicious and paranoid as any peasant farmer. In my continued battle of survival, my reputation for a short temper and tough dealing soon spread. And was even used as an example as far as the village as an expression for people to say to others, 'Why don't you go down there and try that on the American.' Of course some did. To find me standing there with pitchfork, scythe and axe at the ready. But I was still painting my pictures which were now being exhibited a little less wet than they were previously. And at the same time I was still writing my forewords. Which were now far less optimistic. And under my heading, 'From Notes And Letters'.

We are not dead yet. Where there is life there is success. Two days until Christmas, the most vulgar and vicious time of the year – the time of the big kill, adultery and commerce when only the child has any purity or love. I have just come from a pub where they are drunk and fighting. In Ireland friendship is on the lips but not in the heart. The past six months I have been as bitter as acid and suddenly feel sad. When you're sad you don't want to fight the system and when you stop fighting the system it's time for the big sleep. When hatred turns to love, the will to kill is lost and that's bad in these hard times.

Recent reports from cosmologists have kept me on the philosophical jump. It looks as if the whole set up is tumescence and detumescence; bloom, blossom and seed. Is it any better to know. It prevents the blunders of giving to the poor or of having the fear of not giving. It teaches you the lesson that the integrity is in your own heart and in no one else's. Ireland has everything which is too much of nothing. It rots and kills the enlightened and corrupts that which is born original. Much better to dream of Ireland from 3,000 miles away. In the climb to disappointment, I feel a need of love and trust, but I have only met with calculation which is of money and faithlessness.

The animal wants its back protected and to eat. Man is that animal and when he has eaten, he deals in art and artifice, and it becomes lie and compromise; a soft, ingrate murmur of accents and incomes. They tell you to have Horace Ictericton, Bart. open your show, it will get a picture in the paper and give the opening 'class'; this is the universal feeling, the feeling to which all animals respond; the great aesthetic communion without body odour. Where do we go for love?

As outspokenness does in Ireland, it is first met by silence. Then the forces collect. Then the whispers. To see how they can shut you up. And then drive you out. But as a foreigner they always figure you're going to go soon sometime anyway.

As a matter of fact and publicity I did get a picture in the newspaper. Large and central and conspicuous on a page of *The Irish Times*. And coming into Greystones' train station as I did then to catch the train, parking my small red van across from the local garage of Watson and Johnson, there were awed gasps from various folk from whom one might buy a newspaper or apple. 'I didn't know it was your wife.' And clearly one secret was manifest right there, nearly on the spot where the Irish patriot Eamon de Valera was once arrested, that the whole of the neighbourhood for miles around assumed I was living in sin. Not least because of our young age for marriage. And that there were 'goings on' in the isolated 'down there' at Kilcoole.

Greystones was a small village with tiny fishing cottages still tucked in between some of the larger Victorian houses. It was with its tiny harbour cloistered and safe on an otherwise exposed windswept coast. It had what was unique in Southern Ireland, a large Protestant population and its most prominent social core was that of the modest-sized Grand Hotel. Its panelled comfortable interior of public rooms and a sun terrace overlooked a croquet lawn on its sea side where the morning sun arose out of the Irish Sea, and warmly, on such days, bathed this palace like place, flanked each side north and south by a collection of respectably commodious houses. Greystones was also possessed of a unique area known as The Burnaby. Crisscrossed by tree lined roads, with large houses within their lawns secluded behind high hedges and evergreen sub tropical shrubberies, this tranquil purlieu was as close to an English suburban elegance as one could get. And its inmates, if not Protestant, were then many of them of an ilk best described as Protestant Catholics. These highly respectable refined folk were prosperous professional and business owning people who made up the population of altogether one of the most attractive communities in the whole of Ireland. My own mother, sojourning at the Grand Hotel and one day having visited me at Kilcoole and then taking her afternoon stroll, came by a house being sold on the sea front. Taking tea with the lady owner who then removed the For Sale sign out of her window as my mother bought the house that very afternoon.

My mother's house in Greystones as it is today and lived in by my sister Rita. The two upstairs side windows stare directly down the bereft coast towards where one had settled near to Kilcoole. For five years alone behind its shutters closed against night and the sea sprays, my brother T. J. painted many of his hauntingly marvellous paintings.

Bathing in the chill waters at Greystones harbour. This idyllic setting was one to which one would frequently gravitate either to sit on the rocks in the sun or, late at night during a storm, to witness the mountainous seas crashing against the sea wall.

In my studio at Kilcoole with the early manuscript of The Ginger Man *and an early painting on the wall above my makeshift desk the top of which was a door torn off a cattle shed. It was upon this desk that Behan's manuscript of* Borstal Boy *lay next to that of* The Ginger Man *while Behan wrote his editorial comments in the margin of* The Ginger Man *manuscript. Although Behan thought that the book would shake the world, there is little evidence on the author's face that he so believed.*

Inland Greystones extended to merge with an equally attractive village situated further west near the Glen of the Downs, a hamlet on a hill called Delgany. Again with an attractive small hotel, marvellous Protestant old rectory as well as having an elegant Catholic curate who was also the distinguished painter, Jack Hanlon. And many a famed French artist's glowing picture hung in the shadowy gloom of his small reception rooms. As one went south from these two pleasant places there was along the coast, an area of Wicklow populated by a myriad variety of nationalities from all over Europe, from Dutch to Russian. Most finding their way here after the war. Just up the lane from me an Englishman from Leicester bought and cleared an acre and turned it into a market garden. Having that morning at four a.m. collected his vegetables from his holding, washed them in the stream and then rode with them on his bicycle twenty miles to Dublin. Because of the fine quality of his produce the merchants at market would await his arrival. And then cycling back, this wiry battling self educated and intellectual man would go for a swim in the cold sea and walk there by my studio chewing a raw carrot. Hearing my typewriter one day he made me a present of an old dictionary in which among other things I found the word 'Papaphobia'.

It was here on a June day and in a sun porch I'd built that I started to write *The Ginger Man*. My occasional visitors being James Hillman, Douglas Wilson, John Ryan, Tony McInerney, Anthony Cronin and last but not least, my first literary protagonist of all, Brendan Behan. But the latter's first arrival had been on one of the rare occasions I was away. I returned to find the oil stove blackened along with every pot in the place. And was confronted by disarray on every side as if a robbery had been committed. Which it seemed it had for there was the mystery of all but one pair of my twenty pairs of shoes gone. It did not take long to find out who the culprit was who'd unlatched a window and climbed in. Stepping out to my studio, I found there on my makeshift desk, a manuscript lying next to my own manuscript copy of *The Ginger Man*. Picking up the crumpled, stained and wrinkled sheaf of pages and in just turning a few I could see from words such as peeler, nark and screw that the setting was that of a British correctional institution. And as I was holding in my hand the manuscript of *Borstal Boy*, I recalled that day outside Davy Byrnes, Behan's proffered hand and his words 'Sure I'm a writer and you're a writer too.

And fuck the
Ignorant bunch of them
Back in there'

X

With my then wife Valerie away, I proceeded on my own that day at Kilcoole to clean up the shambles of used pots and strewn furnishings. Then later that afternoon covered in dust and sweat I heard whistling coming down my long entry lane. And I went out to my front gate to see Behan in his shambling duck walk approaching me. Sockless as usual, and sporting an unlaced up pair of my shoes. I asked him where were the remaining pairs.

'Ah Mike, now I hate the countryside. I hate cunning country ways. I hate country people. And I nearly hate getting my feet wet just as much. Sure I knew you were already out somewhere in a pair of your own shoes yourself. So I took a bag full of the rest of them you weren't needing and wore a pair till they got wet on the way to the pub. And a bloody soaking wet walk it was too. As I went along I had to fling the wet pair into the field and put on a dry pair. You'll find them with no bother. Start there just over the fence is your first pair. And the rest every fifty yards or so up to the pub.'

Behan always had a favourite question for Valerie. Asking her to think of who she would rather be married to, himself or Gainor Stephen Crist. Behan although conscious of Valerie's English and finishing school background was at ease with her clearly unaffected ways, and he always felt free to make his visits out of the blue. Although one wouldn't encourage Behan to do your housekeeping, his own background in English Borstal and prison was treated by him as the same as having been at Eton or Harrow. And despite his expressed distaste of the countryside he enjoyed to come to this strange isolated piece of land. Where you could shout, cavort and sing. He had already read most of my then manuscript of *The Ginger Man*. Taking out his pencil as he did so and marking suggestions and corrections in the margin as he went along, finally signing the page to which he had read. He said it was a funny funny book but his voice

Valerie sitting with her favourite cat in front of my first improvements to provide a painting studio and later a study where the first chapters of The Ginger Man *were written. The window and the primitive wall above and below it, built by me.*

grew grave and serious as he spoke of my reference in the manuscript to the white death, which is how I described that resulting from tuberculosis. In reading bacteriology at Trinity and attending pathology lectures in the medical school I was at the grim autopsy performed on a young Dublin girl. And as the pathologist pointed out these various internal tubercular lesions and spoke of this disease I became aware of how rife it then was in Dublin, especially among the slum poor. I could see that my all enveloping mention of it, if not in a harsh and clinical manner, was nevertheless upsetting to Behan, who talked so openly, albeit privately, about his other medical and even venereal problems but who regarded this disease with a phobic concern. And he said I should play down the mention of it.

Behan as a visitor was uncomfortable stopped too long in one place. And he was anxious to progress further afield, especially if guaranteed to keep his feet dry while being transported on wheels. Mechanical devices had already begun to play a disastrous role in one's Irish country life. In America one had never even looked in under an automobile hood at its engine, never mind trying to join up

The author with his motor car formerly owned by the Bishop of Meath and striking a pose of the artist as a bohemian and aggressive young man, whose family's motto had become, 'I'll thank you not to fuck about with me you low cur.'

wires and take nuts and bolts off and try to put them back on. Still existing hand to mouth I had dared just then to buy second hand a car formerly owned by the Bishop of Meath. Disposing in the process of a red unreliable and very old Ford van. Which at first I could start mornings by pushing myself and jumping in. And then had to wait for the mailman on his bicycle and later even the assistance of my extremely strong neighbour, a farmer. But my Austin Eleven had a little black button one pressed on the corner of the dashboard and as one did so the engine would leap into life. And Behan and I were soon on our way touring the countryside. Driving first to the town of Newtownmountkennedy. Behan, like a pied piper entering the village, singing and talking to everyone on every side and drinking there in a pub. Then driving up the steep hill to the brim of Kilmurry, a table of land from where one could look down and distantly out upon the Irish Sea. And feel that Ireland was the very centre of all the universe.

There was then living and writing, another author in Ireland. This one full fledged, published, accomplished, and already achieving that one unforgivable thing above all, that of being rich by it. This gentleman was Ernest Gebler. Who had emerged from the same slums as Behan and remembered this little boy who swam bare arsed as he himself had done in the waters of the Royal Canal. Gebler, a tall, slender, high domed, taciturn figure had written a book about the story of The Mayflower and that vessel's journey to America and its landing on that shore. Which when published became not only a bestseller but was bought by Hollywood. Gebler had in successive steps moved back to Ireland from London where over a period of years the book had been written. And from a house in Dublin's suburbia he had now taken up residence on an estate overlooking Lough Dan, called Lake Park. In the lee of these bereft wild heather clad and boggy hills, this commodious lodge with a porch had two large reception rooms either side of its front hall, a stone flagged kitchen and several sprawling bedrooms. Its rearmost wings nestled against a pine forested hill and were built around a splendid enclosed cobbled courtyard of barns and stables. And in its sylvan isolation it was a paradise.

I had first met Gebler whom I now knew for some time as a distant neighbour, at a dinner party given by one of the more glamorous of Trinity's undergraduates, a David O'Leary. This astonishingly handsome, cultivated young man, despite his name, was the son of a British Army General and he delighted to bring together people whom he considered were the butt and at their peak of resentful gossip in Dublin. O'Leary had flatteringly put me head of the list. Gebler, due to his recent golden literary windfall, was not far behind. Gebler had also written an enthralling novel of Dublin slum life called *He Had My Heart Scalded*. And as he stood now boss of a great estate he was bemused to see Behan. But perhaps not as delighted to watch and listen to him as he cavorted running riot chasing servants, goosing the cook and conspicuously swimming naked in the cold, still waters of Lough Dan. Gebler was then recently married to a young American lady, his first wife, who literally was of fabled Hollywood, being the daughter of two of its stars. This strikingly handsome girl was a sensation as she arrived in Ireland, and stunningly tanned in her dazzling clothes, set all the Irish gentlemen who saw her alight. With her marvellous voice she and Behan listened to one another singing songs. And we spent an alternately tense and blissfully amusing afternoon here in this rambling shadowy house so neatly and pleasantly secluded with its tea pavilion in its walled ladies' garden. And where once, as I helped pile a load of turf in a barn, a workman confided to me.

'Sure that fellow Adolph Hitler, don't be believing any of that old rubbish he's dead. He's alive and well and living in Wicklow. Hasn't he been seen yonder more than once in the pub without his moustache.'

In the abstemious Gebler household the whiskey and Guinness were not flowing as fast and furious as Behan usually liked. And our next port of call on this Odyssey was to another writer, and too, a painter and horticulturist. We drove from Roundwood to Annamoe and to the house of Uplands also on the side of a hill where lived Ralph Cusack. No two people were more opposite nor more fond of one another than the mostly charming Cusack and the frequently obstreperous Behan. As the result of some brief conversational difference they could in turn hurl upon each other foul abuse and then fall tearfully contrite into one another's arms. Cusack, a talented painter and writer, was a man of almost painful sensibilities. As a music lover extraordinary, he would hold his brow listening to the great horn of his gramophone projecting symphonies out into the room from the top of his concert grand piano. Cusack, a serious bulb fancier, grew tulips, both importing and exporting these around the world and like Gebler had a pot to piss in. He was also the author of a hauntingly strange novel steeped in the obfuscations of Ireland and Dublin.

That night there was, as there always was, a party. Leaving Cusack's in a plethora of goodbyes, of tears, and hugs we went on our way through the Glen of The Downs in my blue Austin Eleven. The night cool summer breeze blowing a smell of wild garlic in the open car windows. And as we left the whole wide Wicklow world behind Behan was talking about *The Ginger Man*. About how although it showed the Emerald Isle in an unflattering light, that the book was an act of love for Ireland.

'Mike, as many as the kicks as you give us in the arse in that book, let me tell you I would consider it an honour to be ever mentioned in its pages.'

I chauffeured Behan and as he demanded we stopped in pubs on the way, where he would sing and astonish the habitués with his quips and burlesque. Pouring pints over his head while reciting various statutes from British law. Finally we arrived in the rough, squalid streets of Dublin's Night Town. Entering pubs there where Behan knew all the inmates as well as they knew him. In the corner snugs Behan urging me to hug all his old ancient lady acquaintances, grandmothers long retired from motherhood and its desperate struggle of survival. Behan whispering in my ear as he'd push me into a cackling old lady's arms.

'Mike, she was these forty years now as dedicated as any nun, selling her arse for a few bob down the quays, to buy a bit of bread and tea for the childer and she's deserving of a heartfelt squeeze now at the end of her long ordeal. Come on, give the old girl a decent and better kiss and embrace than that.'

Entering a great Georgian tenement not that far from the summer stench of the Liffey we climbed rickety stairs to a party held in an ancient, tall ceilinged room groaning with the weight of people and dense with cigarette smoke. Behan singing a stream of patriotic songs, frequently changing the words to others less patriotic which would incite mayhem among the fervent nationalists present. But Behan, as the roaring mouths and fists approached, was always able with a quip or two and a ready sympathetic laugh to hold off such assaults. And in his best Dublin accent mollify the aggrieved patriot and implore him to see the joke of the matter. And Behan, although an I.R.A. man, had strange opinions not usually associated with the southern Irish cause of ridding the North of its border and the supremacy of the northern British Protestant. And he confided more than once to me.

'Mike, let me tell you about the Orangeman. There's no better human being on earth. And if it were a choice between me own and one of them as a friend, I'd have the latter on my side any day. A brave and noble people.'

Behan this night was now filling a pint glass full of every conceivable drink available at the party. A mixture of stout, sherry, port, gin and whiskey, which he then topped off with poteen. Putting the glass slowly upended in one movement to his lips and swallowing it nearly to the last drop. Which he hadn't quite reached as he suddenly like a tree felled collapsed backwards unconscious on the floor. Standing next to him as he did so I could hear faint screams from somewhere below. Occasioned by the ceiling underneath being dislodged down upon an innocent, recently wed couple honeymooning in bed. Blamed for Behan's misdemeanour and now surrounded by an irate host and most of his guests, I was unpleasantly requested to dispose of the body. Behan, no light weight, was lifted up and put across my shoulder and I lugged him down three flights of stairs and tipped him in upon the blue leather rear seats of the car. Driving in the early dawn back with him to Wicklow. Waking in my damp morning bed, I heard someone out around the house talking to the cows who had broken through a fence onto the lawn. It was Behan whom I'd left asleep in the back of the car. Now awake he was advancing playfully to pet an already angered bull on the nose. Rushing naked out of bed I grabbed a pitchfork kept nearby for such emergencies and ran out on the lawn just as the bull's pawing forelegs were scooping up sods and sending them flying into the sky. Behan thinking this the beast's invitation to play.

'Ah, don't harm the poor creature, Mike, he means no harm.'

The bull charged the pitchfork and with a hook of its horns into the prongs sent it flying out of my hand and as I jumped behind a wheelbarrow full of weeds it, too, promptly was the next to go skywards, the weeds raining down on Behan like confetti, upon whom the realization had also dawned that he had better run for his life. But as he always could at such dire times, he had ready a merry quip.

'Ah Jasus, Mike, for the love of the Salvation Army would you keep the horns of that ton of bloody beast away from rooting me up the hole out of which all of me wisdom comes. And wait till I get me feet back into the pair of your bloody wet shoes and run.'

But barefoot Behan had already to flee around the corner of the car as the bull charged and removed the left back fender off that dignified vehicle. Behan skedaddling knees in the air, as he went shouting curses through a patch of stinging nettles and threw himself up on top of a hedge of briars. The roaring bull in close pursuit as Behan finally clambered up a young ash tree. I followed now trying to distract the bull away, hammering its massive heaving hindquarters with a shovel as its horns tore into the bark of the ash tree. The milling cows in their curiosity at last coming to one's rescue. Surrounding the bull and with a pair of heifers one on each side of him I was able to drive the bull in the herd, away. Behan, a devout proclaimed atheist in conversation, was on this occasion perched up in the ash tree, praying loudly to the Almighty for deliverance.

'Let me tell you, Mike, for a moment there, I did not think that my redeemer liveth.'

When things had calmed down later in the morning, and the sweat of Behan's anxiety had dried he suggested we go down my boreen to the sea. Old Mr and Mrs Smith who, hearing this singing, roistering voice coming at them across the fields and seeing Behan before seeing me, fled into the safe confines of the hedges around their cottage and locked their gate. It was only when I caught up and stood between them and Behan that they would show their faces. And, as I introduced him, Behan who could be charm itself when he chose, made his boisterous overtures to this dignified elderly couple.

'Now it's no mystery to me eyes that the handsome pair of you find the country living for all the bogs, the mad bulls and bats at night, much to your liking.'

When we reached the beach upon this cloudy, cool, grey day Behan took off his clothes and, running down over the stones and pebbles, plunged into the white, foaming, freezing waves. His great black shock of hair bobbing about as he frolicked like a seal out beyond the pounding surf. Leaving me standing in terror on this treacherous shore that I might at any moment have to jump out of my shoes and dive in to rescue a suddenly drowning Behan. And the sound now of a faint whistle reaching us. Far in the distance down this bereft coast I could see the tiny emerging dot of the train from Wicklow town. As it grew louder and closer it was a signal for Behan to come up out of the waves. And charge up the beach to stage centre on the pebbly sand. Legs spread wide, he took up his position, at the side of the tracks as the train approached. Arching his shoulders back and projecting his belly and privates forward. Penis in hand, he waved and shook it at the train's passing windows. Where I could see an occasional newspaper raised suddenly up in front of a lady's face and be just as quickly held aside for an eye to peek out. But not to say that among the wagging fingers there weren't also some laughing faces.

'Ah, Mike, I am showing them me scars of war.'

The site of Kilcoole station which was not much more than a piece of raised ground so designated. The tracks go towards Wicklow town and the beach on the left was the one upon which Behan nakedly cavorted after a cold dip in the sea, to entertain train passengers on their way to Dublin.

Behan was fond of describing and demonstrating venereal evidence of his penis having undergone wounds and mends. I did tell him that with my beard, the only one at the time in the whole of Ireland, I was known all over the district not to mention in plenty of parts of Dublin. And that there'd be a train soon coming in the other direction chock full of members of the Legion of Decency with coils of unanointed rope to string the pair of us up on the cross piece of a telegraph pole. And Behan always quick to accuse one of any sign of petty provincialism rounded on one.

'Now, Mike, if I had an erection, you could say I was being provocative but the fact that I was in a natural state of me own flaccidity, sure what bloody harm is it to wave me flag of procreation and stimulate the conversation among the passengers. Coming up this coast all they're able to look at on one side is the sea and the other the bog. And sure most of them anyway wouldn't know what it was I was waggling in my hand a'tall.'

Behan coming back up the fields came into the cottage with a roaring appetite. As I looked about to see what there was to eat Behan asked would I mind if he were to look after himself. Requesting only to have a big bowl, which he then spied, taking it down from the shelf and with his soiled sleeve, wiping its foot deep and foot and a half wide surfaces rim to rim with an elbow. Busying himself around the room, he collected various ingredients beside him on the table. Pouring in flour and baking soda on top of eggs he cracked then crunched and dumped in shells and all. Next came cornflakes, oatmeal, left over mashed potato, spoonfuls of marmalade, and strawberry jam, a banana broken in pieces, and tomatoes. And still the ingredients were added, a pint of milk poured on, slices of bread crumbled up, salt, sugar and ketchup, cocoa powder, a gobbet of honey until Behan turned around.

'Mike, what's this in this jar, I don't want to use anything that would ruin the flavour.'

'That's Horlicks, made of your pure pleasant ingredients.'

'And you don't mind if I take the rest of this tin of peaches here.'

Behan spooned out half the jar of Horlicks, shovelled in a spoonful of beef extract, sprinkled on vinegar, poured olive oil and over all squeezed a lemon. Taking a large wooden spoon he stirred the mixture to a paste, pouring in milk and water as needed to make it nearly liquid. Then as he had with his pint mixture of drink the evening before, Behan lifted the bowl to his mouth and with three brief interruptions for breath, swilled down the entire lot. Finally smacking and licking his lips as a beam of sunlight shone upon him in the window. And Behan turning around and seeing the astonishment on my face.

'Mike I always like to look after me health. And I'm a great believer in the Irish principle that more of something is better than less. And that if variety is the spice of life then why not have plenty of that as well.'

Behan disappeared off to my studio to collect up his manuscript of *Borstal Boy*. In which many songs and verse appeared. Behan maintaining the advantage of such was the space you could leave before and after each, thus with fewer words necessary to write to fill out the page. Behan always, as he did, would heft a manuscript in his hand, estimating its weight and then would proceed to calculate the number of words, choosing a page and with his little stub of a pencil, counting down the lines and then the words across and then his fingers flicking over the pages to the last one upon which he would scribble down his figures and then frowning in his act of multiplication would with satisfaction announce the result just as a farmer might, assessing the number of bales of hay stacked safely in the barn. An analogy, alas, which was as near as ever describing Behan's associations with country life. On this late afternoon standing at the corner outside my studio, and as Behan would in such profound moments of written words tabulated, he out of the blue became serious on another serious subject.

'Mike I regret as others might not that I have been sentenced to death in my absence by the I.R.A.'

'I'm sorry to hear that Brendan.'

'Well it's not as bad as it would be if I were sentenced to death and it were carried out in my presence. I have this little bit of the present geography situating me here to be thankful for that I'm not in my coffin. And now I'll tell you another thing. To your credit and not mine. I was behind your back complaining to McInerney that there you were bringing him bags from this place of old dirty potatoes and cabbages for him to use to feed his kids and that you wouldn't be that fast or generous when it came to buying a thirsty man a drink in a pub. And McInerney turned on me and nearly tore my head off, saying it was more than the fucking likes of me or anybody else had done.'

But such was Behan's concern for my present safety that it was only as he was leaving after four days, and singing me a small bit of commendation if not praise, that he made his announcement about the I.R.A. and that they were presently in search of him in every nook, cranny and pub of Dublin and might have already drawn their own conclusions that he was out peacefully sojourning in the countryside. And so informed, would acquaint with the friends he knew there and might now at this very moment be advancing belly down from every direction across the fields with Thompson sub-machine guns and gelignite ready to spray bullets and blast me, Behan, the whole place and both our manuscripts to kingdom come.

I had in those country days periodically gone to Dublin, arriving off the train at Westland Row Station and walking down its ramp into the city's dust and grit and the puddles of rain on its dark grey granite pavements. Often to call upon the sprinkling of people one still knew holding out in their various redoubts. And especially McInerney whose number of children had increased. And as often, too, one would take a solitary walk as I had done many a night out of my rooms in Trinity. Heading along Tara Street and turning down the Quays of the Liffey. Finding now that Dublin's sad, strange loneliness could overwhelm one. Making one recall the earlier days when occurred respite from the grim chronic poverty and hardship abroad in this city. The most memorable interludes being the arrival of the odd American coal ship in the Liffey river. With on board, its pouring hot showers, clean sheets and American accents and bountiful amounts of food. And Ray Guild, a former Harvard football star and scholar, who had accompanied Donoghue on a whim to Ireland and who was writing a doctorate when not freezing in the damp cold, managed through his and Donoghue's abilities as cooks to temporarily serve in this capacity while the ships were in port. And upon one vessel, its Greek cook confidentially whispering to Guild about Donoghue.

'Hey, who the hell is this guy you brought with you. He speaks aristocratic Greek, like he was a prince from a royal Greek family or something.'

At such times, knowing that one was being slowly driven out of this land, one could overwhelm with homesickness for America and its fabled prospect of plenitude. On these ships then arriving its officers would prove to be great hosts, providing food and drink for parties arranged in Dublin. To which myself, Donoghue and a handsome lady attracting Ray Guild would go. And where one could listen to a Shakespeare quoting black ship's steward who when asked how he was liking the city was quick to sum it all up.

'Hey man, there ain't no action here.'

But then just as quickly he would wax lyrical about his dream to one day transport a little package.

'Man. Just ten pounds. That's all it's got to weigh. Then one night after we've docked in the States, I just walk off the ship with it. Just one little package of that stuff they call heroin man, and I'm fixed for life. And then I'll just be able to sit back and enjoy this guy Shakespeare.'

But now out in the Irish countryside the freedom of being without a fear of reptile fangs strolling through tall, sunny, flowering meadows was to be enjoyed. Or the unworry of bears lurking in berry patches or awakened in their lairs in the outcroppings of rocks. And even

In my studio at Kilcoole. One found painting a much more congenial way of life than that of an author although it was the latter calling which I found necessary to indulge to get recognized in the first. And of course ended up persisting in the second.

where in America as a boy, once lost in the woods, it was a great old, giant, shaggy, grey Irish wolfhound who led me back to civilization again. Dublin now became dingy in contrast to one's growing affection for land and the clean aired countryside. And a growing distaste for the smoke and grime and falling down walls of that unnurtured city. Finding, too, that the love of Ireland lay under its grasses in its ancient bogs, and across its heathered hills. Upon which a man could walk, smell, touch and cherish their colours and textures. Unlike those I had known in America where one was always conscious of lethal things like spiders in dark corners and venomous snakes in tall grass. Here a safe Wicklow morn arose out of sweet mists off the sea and turned clouds pink high over the hills. The cock crowing. Swallows and swifts streaking the sky. The sound of a drip of moisture from the cottage slate roof hitting the ivy leaves. The ground silvered with dew. The air softly damp and cool and the first bee of the day buzzing.

My second summer at Kilcoole there came a crop of bountiful hay which my local farmer Farrell cut for me and which by hand I raked and put in cocks, trying topsy turvy to make and sculpt these as I went. And then an old established auctioneer advertised and held an auction. To which only one old, shrewd, nearby farmer came sourly denigrating the quality of my hay as we walked from cock to cock. Sitting then on the first stone wall I'd ever built waiting patiently for me to capitulate my reaping into his hands at a giveaway price. Which, in my crushed desperation following all my sweating hours, I was nearly on the verge of doing. But the wise auctioneer advised we not sell and hold the auction the following week. And when I told my farmer neighbour Farrell that the old farmer had said my hay was poor he commented.

'Well you'd soon find the hay would be good enough after he bought it.'

And the elder farmer Mr Farrell then showed me how to rake down and restack my cocks to a rainproof peak on top and how to pull away the hay from the base to make an eave and keep the bottom of the cock dry. Reaching then underneath and twisting the hay into roping to which could be tied a string that went up and over the cock and was joined the other side. This done, north, south, east and west to prevent the cock falling or being blown over in any wind. Telling me that any farmer, seeing the cocks firmly held down and sitting dry and safe, would conclude the hay was well made and could survive the rain and he could come back in his own time to collect them.

When the next time of auction arrived the old, shrewd farmer from up the road waited back on my wall again. And fortunately two more customers arrived. To whom I was now able to give an erudite guided tour. Demonstrating the weatherproofing of these now neatly raked and tied down cocks. And finally the bidding was begun. As usual with no bids. But then following the auctioneer's voiced impatience a bid came and the escalation was swift and furious and the price rose to a dizzying delightful figure. And somehow one felt one had won one's first great victory over struggle and adversity on this verdant isle.

And the lesson

Never while you breathe

Give up

My paintings prior to being transported in for an exhibition in Dublin. Probably some of these just completed, are drying in the sunshine. The stack of cement blocks were to form the walls of the sun porch I was to build on the cottage. And there can be no doubt that I did bitterly struggle to survive on the ould sod.

XI

My love of land came out of Wicklow. Growing up in America its terrain always seemed wild and anonymous and that you were always exploring but never lingering, and where in wandering you might get lost. Whereas in Ireland land was something you knew, touched and felt belonged to you, and into which one would one day melt away.

The village of Kilcoole was by laneway about three quarters of a mile distant or a half mile as the curlew flew. With its great looming rock jutting out from the hill on which the village was built. It was said to occupy a point at which tinkers had gathered camping on a common over the centuries. Beneath the rock in a small graveyard with ruins of a church, a vampire was reputed buried and upon whose grave the grass never grew. In the same way a forlorn air of mystery seemed to hang over this village and the countryside around. Where on the verges of the narrow sheltered lanes tinker families erected their tiny tents under which they slept. One day walking to the sea, I saw a small child playing along by the bog, on an embankment alongside a stream. As I walked by a little distance something made me turn and look back. And now suddenly the child was nowhere to be seen. I ran, returning to where the child had been, to find it was now face down immersed in the stream. I lifted the child out and emptied its mouth of water and it seemed unharmed, carrying it back soaking to its tinker parents who were some hundred yards away squatting on the grass around their fire, eating. I was referred to and thanked as the man with the beard. And long afterwards and even many miles away from Kilcoole in another county, wherever I would pass tinkers on the road, and they would see me and my beard, a greeting and blessing was always saluted to me. A reminder of how good tidings as well as gossip could travel and be remembered far and wide in this land.

On the brim of the Kilcoole hill there operated a local grocery store with a pub in the back. A Mr Poultan, a genial gentleman and his wife had bought this business and settled there. He was a ranking officer in the British forces who'd survived the Burma death march and had vowed then that if he lived he would go back into the world and be just the simplest of men for the rest of his days. And it was a strange atmosphere indeed to enter his village pub and have this pukka sahib serve one from behind the bar. But, as many other older and similar stories sprang from this curious coastal land. Towards Greystones one of my favourite walks was to Ballygannon across this flat low stretch of terrain. And along this empty seashore was the most haunting of all places. The outline of an avenue from the beach still remained where it was now half covered in bog. Leading from where a shipwrecked gentleman had made his way to the spot upon which he'd built a bijou redbrick strange, now a remnant, of a manor house with its exquisite redbrick barns and its vast overgrown walled gardens of boxwood hedges where cattle now roamed. One would return over the fields again with the plaintive curlews flying in the evening dusk, sounding their long lonely whistling cries, and feeling as if coming back from 10,000 miles away in another world. And somehow more contented to continue the days and weeks of one's solitude.

Ernest Gebler, who owned 200 acres to my four, and was an eccentric farmer to say the least, was my nearest erudite neighbour. And my isolation was occasionally broken by visits to this fellow recluse with whom one would talk half the night away over tea and the odd whiskey in his sitting room. Driving there up the steep hill to the windswept tableland of Kilmurry from where one not only looked down upon the fertile green of Ireland and its grey sea but up out of it into the universe. And beyond to this remoter wilder moorland countryside. Turning down a narrow dirt lane through gates and into a grander drive to sweep up in front of this sprawling house sheltered in the trees. Once as Gebler and I were standing in the forest upon the side of the hill looking down on the roofs of Lake Park, I asked him what he felt about his extensive tract and if he felt a sense of ownership over the large whole of it. And Gebler put his fist up against the nearest tree.

'Every bit of this bark, tree trunk and the branches. And all the shrubs and blades of grass that grow anywhere on these acres. I feel every particle of it as mine.'

An aerial view of Ernie Gebler's former estate as it was in 1951 overlooking its Lough. The house sprawlingly comfortable and nestled in this stunningly lonely beautiful spot, was the setting for many an all night conversation with Gebler whose writing efforts would begin following a midnight milking of cows and our discussions which ended as I retired to bed usually at three a.m.

Over my tinier piece of land my own feelings were the same as Gebler's. And although he was smiling at his own words, I knew Gebler meant what he said. Even to lying prone on the red, white, and black colours of his Meshed Beloudj rug in his front hall, the door open, and his high powered rifle aimed with its telescopic sights at distant sheep of a neighbouring farmer's who, when their noses were ready to go breaking through to dine in Gebler's greener pastures, they would feel the breeze of a bullet pass their nostrils, fortunately for them, triggered by a brilliant marksman.

Gebler being a night writer had organized his cattle and cows on the same lines. Sleeping till late morning or into the early afternoon when he would then take his leisure tinkering with his classically elegant cars. Their engines tuned to such superlative perfection that one or two were only started when he removed their spark plugs and with an eyedropper squeezed a preparatory oil into their cylinders. Or we might go walking the hills, shooting, and after late supper, approaching midnight, go with a lantern out to the barn to milk his cows. In the ancient mustiness talking of every subject under the sun and the moon, even to the then unheard of possibility of transplanting mint condition livers, hearts and eyeballs in place of those become the worse for wear. Confronting only a problem when considering the brain and the close to home prospect of new for old testicles. And standing once while the milk was singing in the pail and the moist wild Wicklow winds howled outside, I was telling Gebler that some of my favourite reading came in the matrimonial columns of the evening newspapers. But that my most favourite perusement of all was the lyrically saccharine In Memoriam poems of the obituary column. And on this thunder rumbling, stormy night in the white light of the Aladdin lantern, Gebler turned to look up at me, a smile slowly coming across his face.

'Mike, you're looking at the author right now. I got seven shillings and six pence for each one of those I wrote. They were put in a book so that the bereaved could select one which was then printed along with the death or remembrance notice in the newspaper.'

And in nearly the same practical way Gebler's career had begun. His Czechoslovakian born musician father had, when he was early growing up, prosperously written and played piano music in cinemas to the silent films variously in Ireland and England. Although travelling from place to place in a Rolls-Royce, young Gebler never attended schools and ended up having to teach himself to both read and write. As his father's occupation ended with the coming of talking pictures his parent now poorer became a musician with the Radio Eireann Symphony Orchestra and the family ended up in the slums of Dublin. In the big, old, Georgian tenement house where they lived, Gebler came across a pile of old magazines in the hall in which were stories he found he could imitate and then send and sell for a pound a piece to various religious periodicals. When his supply of inspiration stacked in the hallway finally ran out, he was driven to having to entirely invent and write in a new genre himself. As his recent found profession widened and flourished, his stories getting longer and his plots thicker, Gebler as a budding author became more ambitious, deciding he would now write a novel. Having meanwhile got himself a job as a movie projectionist, he took up part time residence in this tiny cubicle in the back of a cinema in Camden Street. Not least because, in setting to work on the landing outside his family's tenement flat, and as the months passed and no money materialized, Gebler's mother walking along the hall would, as she approached and passed, growl down upon his back.

'You'll never make a penny out of doing the likes of that.'

Removed to his black, airless nook Gebler continued his work, writing on sheets pinned to the inside of his coat which were then laid over his knee. As a reel of cowboy picture would run out and screams of protest would erupt from the audience Gebler knew it was time to change the reel on the movie projector. But often not before an irate manager burst in upon Gebler who would then stand up, closing his coat with his guilty manuscript disappearing under his jacket. Gebler shaved, washed and sometimes slept in this tiny projection room. Till one afternoon a letter from a London publisher arrived containing an advance of one hundred pounds for his first novel, *He Had My Heart Scalded*, a sad vivid story of Dublin ghetto life. Gebler packed up his shaving gear, slivers of soap, his dictionary and a few possessions, buttoned his coat, put on his cap and walked out the door. Leaving the fans with the first reel running of a Tom Mix cowboy film but which upon this occasion would not be changed when they shouted and stamped their feet to send the irate manager charging into the projection room.

Gebler was a disciplinarian for himself and those who chose to share in any way in his life. An early impecunious friend was once allowed a bed in a Dublin tenement room Gebler had rented. A chalk mark being drawn down the centre of the floor where Gebler ruled that his paying guest scrub and clean his area up to the line. And following his first novel's publication and the subsequent going out of business of the publisher, Gebler in his exacting orderliness immediately set to in the direction of another goal. One day an old book fell open at his feet and he saw on the page the word Mayflower. He discovered no historical novel had yet been written about that voyage, one of the most momentous events in America's history. He decided he would now write something which could become a bestseller and make a lot of money. Gebler boarded the night mail boat from Dublin to Liverpool and took the train from Lime Street Station to Euston in London. Down a basement in Kensington and at the British Museum, Gebler now embarked on years of work. Then one dawn morning, having had for sustenance to borrow a bottle of milk from a neighbouring front stoop, an hour later, gnawing on a crust of bread, a letter arrived. From an American publisher and containing a cheque. This time for 1,500 dollars. He climbed up out his dark room into the street, and every twenty or so yards, took the cheque out of his pocket, looked at it and threw his head back and laughed. He did this circling the Round Pond in Kensington Gardens till other park users brought him to the attention of the keeper. It was the first drop in the bucket which was to fill to brimming and make him a rich man.

But also such riches, as they did then and still do, brought many an Irishman with a pot to piss in, back to Ireland. And soon Gebler was in residence on his estate of Lake Park. This brooding windswept Wicklow hill which descended down through an ancient oak forest to the shore of these glisteningly black waters of Lough Dan. The tyres of vintage Bentleys, Bugattis, Delages humming on the pebbles up the drive. Roses perfuming the walks of the ladies' garden. Neat rows of potatoes, carrots, turnips blossoming. While Gebler sat at his typewriter in his study, a blazing turf fire burned in this sprawling lodge to shun away the damp and chill. And his mother had come to stay. Whose footsteps he now heard coming along the hall at the nearing of midnight just as he had settled down to work through till dawn. This sound approaching made the hair stiffen on the back of his neck as he awaited, hearing again those words hammered down upon him those many poorer years ago, 'You'll never make a penny out of doing the likes of that.' And which words now never came as his mother shuffled off to her sumptuous bedroom where a servant had lit the candles and had laid a hot water bottle to warm her feet between the linen sheets.

Gebler, voluminously read, was self educated in spheres that would astonish a Trinity College scholar. He was readily possessed of a knowledge of the world's everything from chemistry to physiology and from astronomy to astrology. But he had an irreligious disrespect for other areas of the fine arts. Which alas may have only been confined to one's own exhibited wet paintings. Two finally dry ones of which his first American wife actually bought. But which were both not long after used by Gebler to stop up gaps in his hedgerows to save his having to use nose tickling bullets to keep his neighbour's trespassing sheep out. But Gebler in the hard solitary world of writing remained much better disposed. When I, a year or two later, having gone to the United States and returned with the unpublished manuscript of *The Ginger Man*, Gebler upon reading it offered to support me till I'd completed some of its rewriting and the book found a publisher.

Despite the Irish being a highly disobedient race, an advantage when you yourself, a law abiding citizen, wanted to break a rule, it was nevertheless during these days that the other smaller and meaner spirited world of Ireland was then beginning to press upon one with its narrow minded, bigoted and bitterly resentful ways of its banned books, banned films, papers and periodicals. With much less money than Gebler to sustain me I was confronted with the wisdom of escaping the desperate sour restrictions of this isle. The manifesto foreword to my last exhibition ringing in my ears and the dream of America, land of one's birth and upbringing, growing brighter westwards over the ocean. It seemed that Irish born and reared men like Behan, Gebler and Ryan had antibodies in their systems to fight the spiritual afflictions and diseases of Ireland where you cannot fly off the handle or you'll be doing it all the time. But I was, too, to be a father. Of my first son. And Ireland had a fear. Always of bungling. That comes of dumb indifference. And my first wife Valerie had already removed to the Isle of Man where my eldest child Philip would be born.

My last act was to pack up my paintings in a great black box and deliver these to the station at Greystones. From whence they would solitary go on that lonely train ride along the coast where Behan might still haunt, shaking his prick at them as they passed. Meanwhile Gebler came down from his mountain lair. And we spent an afternoon haggling over my possessions which he bought one by one. I had sold my few acres at Kilcoole for nearly three times what I had paid for it. But had spent upon it three years of work. The sadness of selling lessened when it was bought by a pleasant, charming couple, a then Wing Commander Towell in the RAF and his Trinity educated doctor wife. I was astonished to see an odd tear in a couple of my neighbours' eyes as I said I was going. Leaving this land upon which one had scratched in the soil and where one had found it so hard to stay alive and finally realized one couldn't.

Gebler and I dined sumptuously at the Grand Hotel that evening following our bargaining session. And having so niggardly beaten down my prices all afternoon, he was now contradictingly generous, dissipating his potential profits as host on the splendours of our meal. Which we took amid the refined, mostly grey haired habitués

Kilcoole as it is today. The old stonework and my later building efforts merging as they return together to the Irish landscape, into which one can sink more gracefully than into any other on earth. And with unnoticed speed.

of this place. Who strolled the sea front, took lunch, tea, dinner and sat knitting or watching croquet on the lawn. These enviable Protestant married couples repeating their few words they had already without effort said to each other ad infinitum times previously. Gebler and I taking the house's oldest palest brandy to drink, toasting my departure as we sat back in the cosy comfort of our chairs.

'Mike, you'll be back. One day. Don't worry.'

But one is not finished yet with Greystones. Where now stood my mother's house. For there was Josie the barber in a tiny little kiosk of a building near the train station to whom I many a time went to have my hair cut. And great tonsorial artist that he was, he always knew if someone else meanwhile had touched or meddled with my hair. And nothing passing his window ever missed his eye. And after I'd long left, my brother T.J. came to live in my mother's house and winter there four winters. Testing the warmth as he moved from room to room behind its shutters on the sea front, being battered by the waves. The bellowing wind and flying spray shaking the windows and flapping the slates on the roof. And T.J. one day in his polite conversation getting his hair cut inquired about Josie's after hours' activities and discovered that as well as downing a pint of stout or two, he often did a barbering job on the recently deceased who were in need of sprucing up with a haircut. And T.J. thereafter, not taking any chances and not wanting to seem too particular, bought a set of clippers and scissors and comb to be thereafter reserved for sole use upon himself while still alive. And T.J., after many long talks and discussions, asked him once what he wanted out of life. And Josie said.

'I just want one simple little thing and I only want it after I'm gone. And that is for somebody somewhere to just remember me once and raise their glass to me in a drink, and say this one's for Josie.'

And it is in the same easygoing nostalgia that I now recall another Irish gentleman whom one had known these years and who was last to see me off to the Isle of Man at the airport as I was leaving Ireland. Ubiquitously brave, and without an ounce of literary or artistic ability or indeed even an interest in appreciating such, he was of such cocksure nerve that could enable him to sell a dozen grains of sand to a man who owned a beach. His Christian name suitably was Valentine and his surname Coughlan. And as many an Irishman can, Coughlan could simplify the whole story of his life in just a few sad but unselfpitying words. Always full of cheerful fight, he would weather all embarrassments at my wet painting exhibitions. In the case of someone sticking their fingers in my cobalt blue he had a turpentine hanky ready to cleanse such grasping organ. He stood faithfully by my little pile of exhibition catalogues assuring that a sixpence was deposited in the plate on their purchase and that few would escape buying one. This boyhood friend of Tony McInerney's was an Irishman who could serve as the symbol of all Irishmen, stage or real. We had become fast friends having begun such friendship at the end of an almighty fight in the middle of Duke Street outside Davy Byrnes on the same spot where Behan and I had confronted and first shook hands. The battle having resulted from my having caused his life to collapse in an almighty shambles.

I had met Coughlan on what was an attempt at having a polite gathering after pub closing one Dublin evening which had all begun innocently enough. With John Ryan in attendance who was at the time still of the status of a much sought after bachelor. Coughlan knew of a large prosperous pub in the outer environs of the city where in convivial musical surroundings licensing hours were stretched. In the always highly optimistic company of Gainor Stephen Crist we set off. And after an extended evening at the bar downstairs with many a song being rendered by the company, the publican who lived in an elaborate establishment above issued an invitation at closing time. Ushering us all carefully selected to the back of the premises and up the stairs. And in a large, heavily furnished Victorian room we were plied with trays of drink and food aplenty by the publican and his eager to please hefty sons. Suddenly out of a door there appeared four attractive ladies in their crinoline décolleté party dresses, each upon introduction taking up a position beside a gentleman. Crist, ever the man to be well behaved unless finding it urgently incumbent upon him to be otherwise thought that at last he was being introduced to a world of Dublin of which he had heard rumours but was always too busy in other activities to take time out to investigate and he very much warmed to the occasion. Concluding that he was at long last comfortably ensconced in his first real Irish house of ill fame. Aided and abetted as songs and music burst forth and John Ryan danced with one of the prettiest and bosomiest of the ladies. Crist leaning over to me to confidentially confer.

'Mike, I think tonight we're on to something entirely new and different.'

As was my wont on selected occasions I occasionally called a spade a spade and I affirmed to a purringly contented Crist that it would appear we might be there to entice to bed for payment. And to show we were not reluctant sporting gentlemen I announced over the loud sound of the music.

'Yes, it would appear that tonight's the night for fornication.'

The latter word which I had regarded as being discreet in the circumstances had not left my lips before there occurred four seconds of absolute silence instantly followed by roars as the first lunges were made and blows struck. For these were the four attractive respectable daughters of this publican who were by an hospitable host being brought forth from their purdah to delight and enthrall us, representing as we did unattached males, the only true one of whom was John Ryan, but who was at least better known than most to have one of the finest pots in the country to piss in. It was only the miracle of

Coughlan's split second brilliant diplomacy and strong arm intervention that a death or two did not take place in this house that night, and
only an aspidistra in a pot crashed broken on the floor.

But it was following the publican's daughters' discreet retreat and
our departure that the real trouble happened. Having so disastrously
blotted my copybook and disgraced my dearest friends and had all of
us thoroughly embarrassed and ushered forever out of that house,
and having thereby had Coughlan take pity upon my mortification,
he hospitably invited all of us disappointed back to his flat situated in
a highly respectable purlieu of Dublin. Coughlan newly and recently
married to an attractive lady, was a product of Ireland's best schools
and came of its best society, having taken up a modestly important
position in a large draper's. An outstanding bridge player and
Ireland's champion whistler he had long assumed respectable mem-
bership in Dublin's professional class. However, despite being strait-
laced, he could be irreverently honest and surprisingly outlandishly
generous. But, as would happen on these occasions, Coughlan
arrived back at his flat to find that a gathering of well bred lady bridge
players invited by his wife had not yet departed. Viewed as a happy
occurrence as two of them tended to be jolly and stunningly attractive. But Crist, as he was wont to do, had already attached to our little
party two ladies and their attached fancyman who pretended of all
things to be a Baron from Liechtenstein albeit with a thick Dublin
accent. But all three were clearly of doubtful character and intention
and had been picked up on the street just outside the pub of the
recent gross misunderstanding. It was not long before one of these
tough latter ladies attempted to stab yours truly in the eye with a
lighted cigarette with some accusation of impropriety usually
deserved while I was enjoying my higher spirits. However, as one
did not strike ladies, and taking umbrage, satisfaction had to be
exacted from their fancyman who had provoked the attack in the first
place and was already calling me unpleasant names. The battle
among us began. Gainor Crist, always a stickler for fair minded
justice, could also be mediator and peacemaker, but on this occasion
decided instead to be referee. Knowing somehow that peace was not
to be had at any price nor at this particular time, he announced.

'Make room please. Please make room for the combatants.'

Crist had astonishing faith in my fistic prowess, nearly to the point
of acting as my manager on the edge of any fight and even taking side

bets. He was himself one of the strongest people I'd ever come across but rarely had I ever witnessed him engaging in fisticuffs when it was simpler to just shove me out into the fray while he saw to it he got the best odds and saw that no one was undeservingly hit in the haggis. The thunderously noisy mayhem having begun with furniture flying, windows perforated and ladies screaming, it was not long before the attentive landlord of the building heard the uproar two houses away down the street where he lived. And he promptly came rushing in voluminous dressing gown and slippers and tasselled nightcap through a downpour of rain to knock on the Coughlan door. Which was opened by the impeccably polite Gainor Stephen Crist to whom the landlord now addressed his inquiry which suddenly became hysterical for just at that moment the body of an entire person came bursting through an aperture that had once been a glass window in the front elevation of this neo Georgian building.

'What's going on in my house, stop this immediately.'

Crist in his grey herringbone tweed jacket, grey flannels and other if well worn respectable ivy league garments, stood as he often did in the attitude of a saintly seer which, of course, he was, and replied to his anxiously overwrought inquirer.

'In exactly five minutes you are not going to have a house.'

To this now stunned person in his wetted nightwear whose mouth was speechlessly very wide open, Crist bowed and quietly closed and then ominously locked the door. For this innocent gentleman in his present inclement nightmare and shut out from his own building, was merely attempting to get a fair return upon his reasonable investment. But such folk, no matter how honest and just they might be, I heard often called a gombeen man. A term which I learned was used over the length and breadth of Ireland, to refer to a tolerated but unliked and sometimes bitterly despised species of individual usually engaged entrepreneurially in a small business and who in running a shop or renting a house became the creditor of his customers and tenants who in the purchase of bread, butter, milk and eggs or in accumulating unpaid rent, went ever deeper into debt. And it always surprised me that such usurious but hard working and meticulous folk were by the Irish at large invariably regarded as fair game. And on a night like this when, slightly sooner than it was precisely predicted, the flat, its bathroom, kitchen, bedroom, drawing room and its flight of ceramic ducks ascending across the wall and other sitting room contents therein, were demolished, it was considered that any property owner had this coming to him. Crist especially being one long practised in aiding and abetting débâcle befalling landlords. And the respectable blameless Coughlan was subsequently swiftly evicted and sued.

As I was the accused prime mover in the event, Coughlan went looking for me in every pub all over town. Reasonable enough as, through no fault of his own, except his generous hospitality, he had been deprived of his happily married nest and most of his breakable chattels which had previously perched decorously under the roof once upon a time over his head. Rumour of the impending fight as it did in Dublin spread rapidly and far, now taking on the proportions of an eagerly awaited world heavyweight championship. Crist taking bets at seven to one that Coughlan would not last through the first ten seconds. The height, weight, reach and wins, losses and knockouts of the contenders in previous fights being discussed in every pub within crawling distance of Grafton Street.

However for me, a fervent peacelover, it was quickly becoming a nightmarish prospect as Coughlan, not meeting up with or finding me, was now planning a late night assault upon my college rooms at number 38. My difficulty there being that I had in another melée, already smashed the lock and half broken down my front door through which free entry to my chambers might now be made. And as I now expected any time past pub closing for an enraged embittered Coughlan, who was indeed a heavyweight and a schoolboy boxing champion, to come thundering like a bull into my hall, and charge across my sitting room and splinter in my bedroom door, I resorted to the expedient adopted by the Princess of Charnelchambers who secreted her dagger near her through the night. And I stuck my sharpest dissecting scalpel in the side of my wardrobe in ready reach in order to at least have someone else's blood flowing along with mine, in case I were jumped upon while my legs were immobilized under the bed covers. This in the Emerald Isle being a favoured position in which to catch an unwary adversary. But, alas, attempting to sleep with one eye and ear open and freezing with my blankets half way down, only resulted in entirely sleepless nights and on the third when morn came I got up enraged and instead went looking for Coughlan.

Dublin in this respect was a turn of the century cowboy town of the

American West. Where, with your fists as six shooters, you headed along Grafton Street, wondering which one of the sidestreet saloons into which you might go might have you confronted by the fastest gun. And indeed if you were at all known as being such yourself there was no shortage of those growling nearby sizing you up. With my singular beard and resembling a sad faced Jesus Christ I was a marked man all over the city. And wherever I went in my holy conspicuousness, inevitably I was accosted, at least by someone brave enough to mutter under his breath. But more than just frequently someone would come roaring into my peaceful presence shouting, 'Are you him.' But with Crist so eager to take bets biased in my favour many an occasion was settled by being bought a drink. But upon this midday I found Coughlan in Davy Byrnes. The two of us retiring to the gents where I pronto requested him out under the sky. And all finished peeing and then without a single soul in witness except dumbfounded passers by, Coughlan and I had it out up and down the centre of Duke Street.

In the interim of spending his days searching for me Coughlan had also lost his job. But no man anywhere was as adept as he in surviving or, as he ultimately would, in prospering. But in these days he took up residence in the faded redbrick hostel of Iveagh House down Bride Street. Refuge of the male indigent where a cubicle for the night could be had for one and six pence. And whose noisy, boozy, cigarette coughing inmates were chastised by Coughlan to keep up their self respect and 'don't go out looking like that and giving our city a bad name to the tourists'.

And as all good things did in Dublin then, as they still do now, the latter establishment had its origins in Guinness and the profits of that great brewery. But Coughlan being attractive to the ladies had several stationed around Dublin supplying him with porterhouse steaks and other accompanying edibles. And nothing him dismay as he would entreat me not to waste my time worrying. But his most wonderful attractiveness was his calm indifference to painting, sculpture, music and literature. All summed up in one remark.

'Guff from eegits.'

Never without his gents' natty suiting, and white detached collar over his vertically striped shirt and enclosing his neatly knotted tie, Coughlan could enter any establishment and brave his way past any human obstacle. At a word, nothing was ever past his being able to get, or at a request, see a deed was done. Among his personally favoured accomplishments in derring do was his expertise at, as he called it, honest smuggling. For whenever there existed a profit to be made from one land to another, Coughlan was within the hour in transit with a roar of laughter. Once, with a large brown leather valise in his hand, approaching a customs man. Coughlan pretending he was carrying a great weight, which he was, struggling to get the piece of luggage up on the customs man's counter.

'There are 2,756 watches in this valise and because I wouldn't want you to think I was importing 3,000, I would be pleased if you would let me open up for you to count them for yourself.'

'Well that's fine now. You just move along there now, we're busy enough counting. '

The customs man chalking his mark on Coughlan's case, as he light as a feather now lifted the great weight down from the examination table and waltzed out on the terra firma of the docks with his declared 2,756 watches in tow, duty free. And the selling of which would make him many the thousands of pounds richer. Deservedly was Coughlan later to become one of the greatest of charming villains ever to antagonize British justice.

And I can

Hear

Him now laughing

Even as deeply

As he may be

Safely

In his grave

Counting his coins

XII

Starting on my long journey back to America I had gone for my last and favourite walk in Dublin as I had done so many evenings from my rooms at Trinity. Heading out along Tara Street where the opening words of *The Ginger Man* began, and past the baths where many a Dubliner repaired behind these dirty red bricks to get rid of his bodily grime in the big steaming hot tubs. At Butt Bridge turning down George's Quay and City Quay past the Guinness boats, and the chug chug of their barges and the mountains of barrels stacked on the cobble stones. Gangways up to the moored ships. Always thinking the pubs looked bereft and lonely but knowing by their steamed over windows that inside they were alive with dock life. Past the church indented discreetly in from the quay where a Dubliner might go to confess the worst sins of impurity.

As one reached Britain Quay ahead lay Dublin Bay. And here I would then cross over the top of the locks of the Grand Canal basin and come to where the Dodder river emptied into the Liffey. In the water always several floating dead cats or dogs. Attesting to the more than occasional Irish ambivalence to animals, which alas I admit to inheriting. Walking along the Dodder banks these waters flowing with such sewerage always reminded of the death and penury in Dublin. Now one would climb up steps to Ringsend. Where near the bridge the elegant name of Shelbourne was up on a pub. If one were to sail out on the mail boat to Liverpool it was this isolated south bank of the Liffey along Pigeon House Road that one would see. A sad empty loneliness and the last vestige of Dublin before reaching Liverpool.

Sometimes I would instead of crossing the Dodder, walk past the gas works and along a street called Misery Hill. Where in my college days I would stand for many long minutes peering into the stygian interior and watch a man perpetually there illumined by pink orange flames, shovelling coal in a furnace. I ventured here, a solitary pedestrian, and never encountered another lurking soul. But once, as it was growing dark one evening, I was nearly murdered. When instead of crossing to Ringsend I walked back along Hanover Quay beside a wall of high coal bunkers. Suddenly something made me look up. And there, a few feet above my head, standing on top of the bunker, a figure loomed with a stone raised to throw down on top of me. Who may have ended up dropping on his own head for, as I looked, he lost his balance and disappeared falling back into the coal. But it was always after such excursions out into this barren bleakness of Dublin that one would come back again into Trinity's academic cloister, the gas lamps faintly gleaming, and the choir's music from the chapel chasing away the winter damp air. And know that one never ever wanted to leave this peace and serenity.

Departing at the airport to Coughlan's waves, I flew away to the Isle of Man. Which, like the moon is to the earth, this Manx island outpost is to Ireland. A neutral independent place where the Irish need not feel they were among the British and where on holiday they

Myself having breakfast with Michael Heron on the garden terrace of my mother in law's house where she lived until her death. Life in this house, with my mother in law a brilliant hostess and Michael Heron a connoisseur of wine and food, was possessed of considerable bliss and would always turn my greying eyeballs glistening white. Tea at four, sherry at six thirty, dinner at eight and the sound of the sea round the clock.

Philip Donleavy and Valerie on the road outside the house once lived in by my mother in law at Port e Vullin, Isle of Man, and the wall below which lay the tea garden. Philip, always an acute observer of life, being about eighteen months old at the time.

could feel unwatched and freely breathe unshackled from the wagging finger and whispering voice of crut. Coughlan saying as we shook hands.

'Mike, the only thing wrong with the Irish is they think they own the country. But they're quick enough to get out of it when it suits them in the pocket book. And return only when the mother or the father is dying. But then after the funeral a few of them get stuck for months and years afterward like some lost, wet fly stuck in the gluey sap of a tree.'

On the Isle of Man after a picnic on the edge of the high cliffed headland Niarbyl Point, where one looked out across to the Irish mountains of Mourne, my son Philip was born following a quickened journey back over the mountain road to Port e Vullin in the north of the island. Relieved of my struggles on the land, I now reverted back to my former undergraduate ways and collapsed pleasantly into luxury and leisure, courtesy my now widowed mother in law who always bravely bought one or two of my drier paintings. One breakfasted in a terraced alcove under a palm tree, the sea breaking upon the beach beneath the garden wall. Late mornings motoring for fittings to Kaighen, my Manx tailor. Gâteau and Earl Grey tea at four, sherry medium dry at six thirty. But soon from this temporary easeful civilization, I was to return to Dublin. Flying from this Manx small airfield to sojourn a couple of days at the Shelbourne Hotel before taking the train to catch the ocean liner *America* at Cobh. Thence to cross the Atlantic to New York as my own parents had done. And of which my mother had said.

'One minute I was but a barefoot girl in an Irish field and the next I knew I was on Park Avenue.'

And now with an heir, arriving back in Dublin. Where it was always an eager Irish inquiry to know of children and especially of how many you might have. In from the Wicklow countryside Ernest Gebler arrived in his fur collared, long, leather motoring coat to take tea at the Shelbourne Hotel, his MG sports car parked across the street. I could sense that even he, in his own professed love of this land and despite his entreaties that I should not go, hankered himself for the promise of the New World which had already bestowed upon him so many riches. On that morning's walk in Dublin I kept thinking that around each and every corner I would find again some trace of the faces, laughter and voices which made life live in this city and whose buildings and streets had a way of making you feel it was yours. And that the streets would speak. The granite paving tell of the feet trod there. Alleyways whispering out their sad sorrows of cold embraces. Pub walls repeating all their tales. The calumny, backbiting and lies that begrudgers spoke. The scheming revenges keeping alive energies that would otherwise die. The envious burdened by their resentments, shuffling through the city avoiding looks and eyes. But all of them even more than the buildings and streets, were part of the sad and betimes glad soul of Dublin.

Crossing the ha'penny bridge from Bachelor's Walk over the Liffey, swans cruising beneath, I walked towards an old granite archway, realizing suddenly that Ireland was a state of mind I now carried with me where e'er one might go. Of words said and listened to and dreams promised. Then as had happened in all my previous years abroad in Dublin I met coming around a corner Randall Hillis, a brilliant law student now graduated and Gainor Stephen Crist's brother in law. He was on his way to the hospital to attend upon an old army friend who had come for the first time visiting to Dublin and who had suddenly taken ill and died the previous day in hospital. The deceased gentleman without living relatives had known no one in Dublin but Hillis who was now having to arrange his funeral. Planning to meet that evening for a drink, Hillis said he would later be going to keep his friend company in the hospital chapel where the funeral director had arranged for the coffin's vigil. That night I walked with Hillis in the wet, cold, winter darkness to this lonely death through these bleak back Dublin streets. And already one saw the sad desolation in the pale light of this hospital's window placed in their chill walls of grey stone. Inside, a black habited nun whisperingly directing us along the bare halls to the stained glass windowed chapel door. A low murmur of voices from within. And a startled Hillis entering to find the chapel full. Mourning figures kneeling and praying and votive candles burning. In the wax scented air we knelt at the back, watching these strangers pay their respects to the coffin. And as one of the old ladies blessed herself from a font of holy water nearby, Hillis, as she was leaving, inquired of her if she were a friend of the corpse.

'No, your honour, but whoever he is his soul couldn't be the worse off for the saying of a few of my humble prayers.'

Hillis was quietly pleased with the befitting event of this lonely friend who had come half across the world to see him, and had, as he wouldn't anywhere else, grievers to escort his final parting this earth. And next morning in this other world of Ireland, where gaiety, feigned or real, reigned and elegancies formed settings for another way of Irish life, I retired to the lounge of the Shelbourne and resting back in its flower decorated, deeply soft chairs, one ordered from an always slightly distracted flowing, grey haired waiter a bottle of champagne. To toast a bon voyage to Hillis's friend. Whose funeral was then happening at this eleven o'clock on this hotel's busy morning. Where folk arrived from foreign parts scrutinized foxhunting fixtures posted in the hall to which they were en route. Their monocles flashing as their haughty voices cut the air. Strutting and striking superior poses in their tweed suitings. Boy pages with their slicked back hair singing out names through the public rooms. Lunch aromas wafting from the kitchens. My old pal of the 200 mile an hour tennis serve coming to call. Keeping his life a secret as he always kept it. His magnificent vowels explicit and shy. Keeping his sentiments away from alien listening ears and prying eyes he knew so well were

Randall Hillis at Kilcoole aseat on the running board of the Bishop of Meath's car. This steely nerved gentleman who had fought the war in the Canadian Army had survived days of bombardments trapped above the beaches of Normandy, was responsible for doing the first proofreading of The Ginger Man *manuscript.*

eavesdropping and watching all over Ireland. These citizens so full of curiosity just like their cows and horses. To find out what you're up to. And then to see if there is any hope of making you fall flat on your face. But then later rushing for the train as it was about to leave for Cork, one's dire thoughts concerning this land were again retracted. The station master was about to sound his whistle and drop his green flag which, upon seeing us, he now held waiting behind his back.

'Ah, now, take your time we wouldn't let the train leave without you.'

But however briefly, one was soon to know too, in the obtuse sense, that one was back in Ireland. For following this long train journey on a rainy dark day on the Irish five foot three inch gauge railway track to Cork westwards via that strange stop Limerick Junction outside Tipperary town, we arrived at our hotel and had repaired to the dining room. To there, upon the white table cloth, unavoidably have tomato soup, mashed potato and stew, strong tea and custard. The well meaning waiter, in his stained, soiled white jacket, the sleeves rolled back from his wrists, hovering at the table and dipping back and forth several times like a cobra ready to strike before he would put a plate on the table. And then suddenly, just as we were about to begin our meal, Valerie sensing something amiss suddenly got up from the table and rushed back to the room. To there find that the maid had laid a raincoat over a sleeping Philip's carrycot. Had it not been for Valerie's premonitions and having not wanted to leave him alone, Philip would have smothered.

It was a departure now after seven years in Ireland. And in the soft mists, the drops of moisture streaked the train window as we rumbled along the coast of Great Island, from Cork to Cobh. To this town of steep cobbled streets and its old weather worn houses. Gulls squawking and alighting in the sea breezes as we took a tender out to the great black hulled liner *America* sitting majestically high on the water. Climbing aboard into its bright lit warm corridors. All shiny new and spic and span in its cabins. And with a trumpeting horn of the ship echoing back from the surrounding hills we sailed out upon heaving swells of the Atlantic Ocean southwestwards down past the old Head of Kinsale, past Cape Clear and the Fastnet Rock. And knowing that northwards was passing the last point of Ireland. Slea Head of the Dingle Peninsula.

On board the ship to be thrown instantly back into America. And the slow awakening to the shortcomings of that land. Where, returned isolated to the wastelands of my own romantic Bronx, I was soon to best get to know the Ireland I was leaving. Which before the next year was out became the only place I wanted to be, again under its rain and again feeling upon my hands its enduring loamy soil. Arriving, I met and talked with previous American born friends of Irish origins, and could see that the succeeding generations had never erased in the New World that indefinable look, skin, and cast of face that still reflected under their quizzical countenances the ancient suffering of this race. One did not know how scientifically explicit to be to their curiosity as to what it was like over there. Unable now under the weight of seven years of moral shock to repeat my first rose hued impressions. Or to tell of Ireland's uniqueness. The prevalence of vaginismus, among the female population. Namely the painful spasm of the vaginal muscles which in Irish women prevented the penetration of the penis. And thought to be the greatest cause of non consummation in the land. Attributable to a combination of raging tyrannical fathers, the Irish Catholic religion and the taboo of the body's sensuality. Yet one had, in one's moral American innocence, come upon, in just one evening down in the latter day Charnelchambers, more penetration and more fornication than you could wave a crucifix at. Such observations were, of course, always subjects for Honesty Night back in the old sod when the drink had stirred the passion to spout truth aloud and instead of singing praises to the sparkling silver streams, shimmering rainbows and green boreens, declarations were made as to the god awful crut encrusted misery of that bloody country.

As this year passed, having returned to the United States, with the manuscript of *The Ginger Man* growing thicker, one became increasingly homesick for the land that gave this book birth. But who should one day turn up out of the blue, but the man who had in the first place imported honesty to Ireland. A. K. Donoghue was back in Boston now prospering giving accent lessons among other things to those who wanted to speak the King's English. His inspiration in this pursuit coming from Trinity College's Anglo Irish who, if they were not in the squares of college conversing, would then be wielding such superiority out in the wilds of Ireland high up, boots gleaming upon a horse. And in this latter recreation Donoghue was already daily taking riding lessons. Meanwhile I was branded everywhere as an Englishman. My father telling a friend that any day he expected the Union Jack to be flying from a flag pole top of the house. But then not many days later I was reassured to overhear in a downtown Sixth Avenue bar a self proclaimed authority maintaining that the best English in the world was spoken by those at Trinity College Dublin. As my accent was just about the last asset I had now in the world, I was cheered. For the dreams of America were turning rapidly sour by the hour. Ireland for all its impoverished liberties and encrustations of crut that one had railed against, now loomed as a heaven beyond heaven. And if I could not as it now appeared, survive America, Ireland was the place where I would rather most go to die.

And lo and behold, hot on my heels and the growing holes in the backs of my socks, who else should arrive but that traveller most intrepid, and the eternal patron saint of tourists, Gainor Stephen Crist. Deposited upon this North American shore with his own débâcles in tow. And carrying recent tales of the old sod, convoluted and entangled as only Ireland's embellishing gossip could make them. There was in his life now a new lady Pamela O'Malley, later to be his second wife, who from a family in Limerick was a foxhunting equestrian as handsome as she was elegant. And a lady who exemplified the best in Irish women, that of braving and surviving the foible strewn paths taken by foolhardy men. Crist arrived, too, with the essences of Ireland, its familiar names, and long unchanging land and cityscapes to which I was now clinging to hold afloat one's spirits on this continent so massive and anonymous. That crushed from you not only your voice but every vestige of your pathetic identity. My father telling me that getting on television would get you somewhere, and as I hardly had car fare to get on a bus, I had to dismiss this unlikely prospect. But one suspecting and even knowing that if you were able on the airways to scream coast to coast into every American ear and stand stark naked on your head clapping your feet in front of every American eye, you still would be erased from every American mind a few seconds later.

And yet, America did have some pockets of tranquil repose. A. K. Donoghue, in early childhood growing up in this land with his Irish born parents, thought then that he was alive and well in Ireland. Overhearing his mother and father referring to Paddy over beyond in the meadow milking the cow and Bridget barefoot braving a muddy ditch collecting eggs. Donoghue was nearly seven years old when suddenly he one day discovered from his taunting friends that he was in fact in Boston, Massachusetts in the U.S.A. Nevertheless he was able to reply to his scorners with 'Pogue ma hone', which was the Irish for 'Kiss my arse'. It was this same recalled world of Donoghue's Irish parents to which Crist and I found ourselves holding in this nightmarish land. We both of us American born and reared were now indelibly attached to that country where we had only spent a handful of years. My own mother whenever reminded of the day of her departing Ireland, her eyes would fill with tears. For she was suddenly chosen from among her sisters and brothers to travel to America in the company of a rich Australian uncle. Her family gathered on the platform of the tiny train station enacting a scene repeated so many times all over Ireland, leaving those remaining behind red eyed with their grief as another young one among them left for the New World. Years later my mother saying, 'Never feel sorry for me, that I left.'

But in my own sadness now my whole being was yearning for the hills of Wicklow and the shafts of sunlight slanting out of its low skies along its coast. Instead of where I now languished, holding up both head and fist to the then raging coast to coast witch hunt to ferret out communists. My beard automatically proclaiming me one, despite the most fervent of capitalist souls purring within my impecunious person. Both Crist and myself felt isolated. He more by the loss of his glasses and his impatient demands of strangers to read signs. On buses and trains there invariably came mutterings in my direction and sometimes even remarks shouted back from the safety of the subway platforms as the train doors were closing. But I was not that long suffering due unexpectedly to a disquieting event. A gentleman, Willie 'The Actor' Sutton, a number one wanted famed bank robber was indentified on a subway train, and a few days later the identifier was shot down dead. Not only was I no longer muttered at but I had now merely to step into a crowded subway car, and would find it comfortably emptied out at the next stop. And any offending look requiring only a glance to send the perpetrator scurrying away.

Crist had located himself in an apartment on Long Island along Queens Boulevard overlooking the teeming highway. He had built himself a wigwam over his bed into which he now retreated for days at a time along with gallon bottles of Chianti and a stock of photographs he borrowed from me taken in Ireland and upon which he would gaze for hours in tears. As America closed in on me in ever tightening circles, I increasingly romanticized about my return to Ireland. Thinking of peninsulas found on a map whose headlands slanted out from the southwestern coast into the Atlantic Ocean and which I felt were remote and whose grasses were of soft green over which the moist mild winds blew and whose moorlands and meadows were sometimes swept with sun. And where I could taste being alive again. And if I were demising as I deeply, sincerely and self pityingly believed, how softly, how gently would the arms of that earth enfold and surely rest me in peace.

Whenever Crist's and my previous associations with Ireland became known, there was no explanation that would satisfy anyone as to why one did not have a brogue, never mind the American accents we were both born with. Finally it was simpler to merely say one was educated in England. And skip explaining all those centuries of marvellously wonderful Anglo Irish civilizing influences, and which were so intrepidly maintained within the high encircling walls of Trinity College Dublin. Where not only lofty vowels were elegantly spoken but where brollies unfurled in the rain, and bowlers were tipped in greeting and reasonably clean collars, shirts and socks were worn with only one or two holes and were only mildly disintegrating unwashed a month old. But at least now the Irish could be seen bathed spruce and fragrant in America and free of most of their chains. But there were the many still among them and who had not successfully realized their dreams in this land, who were even more blindly bigoted than the countrymen they left behind. And as a once shunned and hated race themselves, were busy hating and shunning the wops, coons, and kikes and others, who could be discriminated against as they had been as micks. Suffice to say my own father, as all Irishmen tend to do who have ever counted cattle and driven them to sell at a fair, put the entire blame for whatever was wrong in the U.S.A. on Wall Street. Ah, but nary a single prejudiced word uttered against those whose ethnic origins were English and who had perpetrated the centuries of Irish oppression. They were now the approved neighbour next to whom the Irish were glad to move and whose example of upstanding well groomed citizenship they might even emulate.

But the pace of my ebbing in this land was increasing. Just as my resolve was not to acquiesce to its witch hunting fear. Having daily to point out to all those daring still to speak to me, and who, implying political disloyalty, asked why I was growing a beard, that I was doing nothing, and that they were in fact shaving theirs off. I recalled now people like James Hillman, and Ernest Gebler who had each warned me of such a return. Ireland for all its faults and sins and lack of pots to piss in had been fatal in reawakening seeds sown by ancient peasant forefathers. Everything in America now was seen in terms of Ireland. Where gossip at least saw to it that you had ear witnessed news of eye witnessed misbehavings beyond the hill, or over in the next town or parish. In America all was the corrosiveness of the unfamiliar, of the so many faces unknown, and each disguised by resembling the other. Gebler, that sage man, had said America was a spectacular country but that Ireland was a beautiful one. He even went so far as to suggest that not everyone in the Emerald Isle was a backbiting, whispering gossip and waiting with a hook to wrap its sharp edge around the unwary carnal committer of sin. But as there was no touch or feel in America of being alive under its sky, I needed less and less convincing. And the sounds Gebler made, exhorting to

American born Irish. The old sod can always be seen upon their faces and the indelible stamp of this race never fades, not even when such sons with such faces have the biggest of all big pots to piss in.

fly back to where the wind and the rain sang a music like harp strings and where my forefathers had sprung forth, became louder and louder.

Except for the strengths lying dormant in my written words of *The Ginger Man*, my spirits were gloomy and hands weak with their uselessness. No hope to fight back against this massive country into which two centuries and Ireland's poverty and famine had poured the dispossessed. Where bullets flew by accident as much as they did when fired in murder and robbery. Black widow spiders in the shadows, copperhead snakes in the grass, sharks off the shore. And upon lonely Bronx and Brooklyn wastelands, bodies were dumped riddled by holes in rub out executions. The sound of my speaking voice was stilled. I found myself reading and cherishing every vision in Tomas O'Crohan's *The Islandman*, and Patrick Kavanagh's *Tarry Flynn*, bringing me living back to Ireland with it each day becoming more and more my dreamed of future refuge.

When I dared now to meet Crist he would inveigle me to places like McSorley's pub which emulated the Irish tradition of men only. Its sawdust covered floor and its plain interior granting some solace as one munched a raw onion slice on a slab of rye bread and washed it down with a beer. Evidence enough why so many American pubs are Irish named, albeit, this of McSorley, perhaps, originating in Scotland before it did in Ulster, but Irish enough for me all the same. To the other pubs we went, Crist and I with our Anglicized accents were invariably accosted as seeming foreigners. Having then to listen to our fellow Americans singing the praises of this land and what a great country we were privileged to be in. Unlike one's response on an Honesty Night back in Ireland, Crist brought sober silent reflection to these inquiring voices to whom he merely had to reply.

'Have you looked at the faces.'

But all was not banjaxed. Donoghue had spoken of Boston. Its bricked, paved, walkable streets. And all his lifelong Irish connections. The quiet, sombre elegance of Louisburgh Square where he'd first seen the splendours of space to live in from the vantage point of one of its kitchens where his Irish born aunt was a cook. And where a graceful lady of English ancestry patted him on the head and said, 'And whose little boy is this.' He told of Boston's West End ghetto, its family bakeries and family undertakers, and its cheap rents and food in this pleasantly livable city. And not that long later, at the end of that summer one was there. In a tiny dark flat, behind a disused shop front with windows opening out on a bleak dark courtyard, a patch of sky just visible vertically up. Little was Irish down these shadowy, narrow, garbage strewn streets. All seemed Polish, Jewish, Lithuanian and Hungarian and God knows what else.

As the weeks went by, the only Irish I met in the Irish town of Boston were Donoghue's closest friends, Lizzie and Julian Moynahan, who like Donoghue himself had Irish parents but unlike him were never under an illusion of growing up in Ireland. Products of Radcliffe and Harvard, these two handsome people with their charm and stunningly sharp intellects were the fortunate heirs to much of what was commendable in America. Having its humanity and generosity but also able to avoid its bleak bland conformity. Both tolerant observers who were not alarmed to be politically or religiously irreverent and were prepared to remain fervent backers of the underdog. Two people at least who were a reassuring flowering from their forebears who had in their coffin ships tumbled on the waves to this land.

And on an afternoon in Boston after one of my many sleepless nights I lay back in this shady sultry silence to nap a moment to regain energy enough to go back to my makeshift desk to write. For there was an Italian woman upstairs constantly day and night nagging at her husband and son and who had suddenly shut up and must have either taken cyanide or hung herself. I was listening to my pulse throb in the space between my ear and the pillow when suddenly I was transfixed. The palest purest music seemed to come drifting in my open window. I turned my head towards a fence separating another courtyard towards which I had often looked and from where just peeked the leaves of a poplar tree I could just barely see. The strains I heard were those of 'The Lark in the Clear Air'. Last listened to as I sat within the brocaded finery in the music room of Burton Hall. When John Ryan played it for me. And whose own windows looked upon those soft green acres of parkland. And not upon a bleak sewer sour courtyard. I thought I'd finally cracked, unable to take the struggle any more, and had been long gone upwards somewhere floating in the infinity of the celestial blisses. But as this unbelievably welcome soothing sound continued to reach my astonished ears, and then came the music of 'She Moved Through the Fair' with its sad words singing of death and disappointment, I knew somehow I was not deceived. And with my eyes closed, never did such a glow of hope give light so bright down in that dark tomb where no sun shone and bedbugs scurried across the floor.

My sensibilities in this ghetto enclave were not entirely alone. I had often passed an iron barred gate which led down a narrow passage to where a tree grew in a tiny curtilage called Poplar Court. In the adjoining alley beyond the wooden fence was living a Harvard professor. This gentleman was never to know how he had nearly saved my life as he continued over the weeks to play these traditional Irish melodies and make my struggles during this bleak summer tolerable. For my only other small comfort was an ancient Jewish gentleman who always, as he went past me on his way to the synagogue, and as I sat taking a few minutes break on my shop front stoop, would reach to tweak my cheeks to say 'What do you do in there. What is such a good yiddish looking gentleman who speaks so fine like you and makes tap tap with a typewriter noise, doing in such

This old white house at the top of the hill in Woodlawn the Bronx, became an outpost upon my first return to America from Ireland. The three front bedroom windows above the sun porch was where many pages of The Ginger Man *were written and it was also where Gainor Crist stayed as a guest in fleeing the horrors he encountered upon his own American return and where he bathed his forehead in balm with the shades pulled down in case someone was taking a bead on him with a gun.*

a terrible place like this. You no speak. You no explain. But don't worry, I ask you on my way back again.'

Ah, but in Boston, true to its nature, a publisher in his summery shirtsleeves on another sultry day pointed at the manuscript he had placed farthest from him on the floor near the door and said 'There's libel and obscenity in that book and we would be tarred and feathered were we to publish it in Boston.' Thus did the moral overtones I had been so used to in Ireland, follow me now to this New World. And clearly make themselves felt in what was one of the most Irish Catholic cities in America. If one had to suffer such things here why not go back and tolerate them where the breezes blew soft and moist and warm and were sometimes stained with sun. With peace so wild for wishing where all is told and telling.

And I did. Return to Ireland. Even if it were as brief as only staring down into the waters of Cobh harbour. And back in New York and no longer writing *The Ginger Man*, I continued to read each day away dreaming we were already back on the hillside overlooking Kells Cove in Kerry. Even the eternally patient, long suffering Gainor Stephen Crist had had enough, escaping as he had been doing from one nightmare to another and the next always a greater one. And I was not to know as he lay upon his bed at that famed outpost of that white house in Woodlawn atop 233 East 238 Street, New York, that he too was plotting to escape. I squeezed lemon in the warm water with which he now bathed his head. People were looking for him all over New York for various misdemeanours which were always well meant by Crist at the time they were committed. In a brown paper bag he carried a length of rope and piece of cheese. And upon his head he wore his thick, woollen Aran islander's hat. In an Ireland steeped in crut they might indeed make life a fight with the heavyweight champion of the world and revive you only to knock you out again. But there, beaten though you may be, they at least let you live. Here sudden death was everywhere. On the highways, a million cars streamed ceaselessly. The nation never stopped, day, night, midday or midnight. Even an unbelieving Gebler in his hotel when first visiting New York, got up from bed every hour to look out on the highway along the East River waiting for the cars to stop. And through the night they never stopped. In a letter from Ireland he wrote now speaking yet again as he always did, of weather, of colours, of the warm waiting stillness, and the soft heathery hues under the grey grey of its skies. A farmer in the distance shouting at his cattle and the echoes wafting back with the coconut scented perfume of the golden gorse.

The manuscript of *The Ginger Man* was thick and heavy between its grey cardboard covers. Crist in his yellow tie and faint green shirt would open it up across his chest and occasionally chuckle. My brother T.J., taking a peek, said if that ever gets published there'll be lots of lamp cords in under suburban closet doors. My wife Valerie and son Philip had already lofted into the sky eastwards and were back on the Isle of Man. Even some Americans were now encouraging our escape. After a night partying downtown with Crist, my wrist was ripped open when my fist had plunged through a pane of glass. And I stopped speaking. To a world that was so utterly indifferent to my voice. Gebler from Lake Park was saying get out even if you have to walk on the waves. And I would do, to get my hands to touch and dig again in the ancient loams of Ireland.

It was upon a February day. A sky cold and heavy with mist. The faint sun glowing pink. Chauffered by my parents I made it to the pier. Over these last days the shades of my room were pulled drawn to the sill. I boarded this ship sailing for Liverpool, via Cobh and Ireland. With relief one stood upon this deck, the ship ready to sail. Its horn in a throbbing blast echoing back from across the Hudson and the New Jersey shore. Beef tea was announced to be served in the garden lounge. Stevedores lifting the massive hawsers from their iron capstans and the great ropes of hemp splashed down into the water, were being winched back up on the ship. Then came an astonishing sound. And a voice I knew so well. Heard now as if I were dreaming. Feet pounding down the pier. And the black coated figure, whose sudden miraculous appearance I could not believe. A suitcase in one hand and his trusty brown paper bag banging against his knees as he ran, shouting 'Wait for me'. None other than that magic saintly man, Blessed Gainor Stephen Crist, clambering up the gangway just as it was being winched ashore. For this Dutch descended, honorary Irishman had disappeared without trace days before I left. Hiding out all night on subway trains, travelling last stop to last stop with his luggage in tow all over the city. And now fleeing back towards the ancient remoteness of Ireland and to the eternal follies of Dublin which certainly upon that embarkation day neither one of us thought we should have ever left.

To come

To this new world

Land

Under a sun

Bleeding with

Sorrow

XIII

It took eleven days on a storm swept Atlantic for the good ship *Franconia* to cross the ocean. Putting into Halifax Nova Scotia while the tail of the hurricane moderated. On this seasickening journey more than half the crew were laid low but Crist, his stomach impervious to the pitch and roll of the ship, was, unperturbed as ever, striding the deck with his nervous quick walk and was sometimes the only one in the dining room golfing down plate after plate of abandoned food, especially the smoked salmon uneaten in first class. He even won the Ping Pong tournament but lost against me when we'd played chess. Passengers collecting about to watch these titanic struggles during which I would mime the disaster I intended to visit upon his various pieces.

It was early on a chill morning, a misty rain falling, when from the deck of the *Franconia* I watched Crist debark upon the bobbing tender to take him away across this grey bay to the green shore of Ireland and land upon the granite pier at Cobh. His blue Aran islander's hat brightly conspicuous on his head as he stood on the tender's stern and waved back up to me on the ship. I was not to know but it was as close as I was to get to Ireland for some time to come. Weeks later via the Irish network of gossip I heard the unbelievable tales of Crist's complicated detouring journey northwards to Dublin which took him two weeks instead of one day. Typical of an Ireland where a stranger could in moments become an ancient friend and involve you in the rest of his life.

As there had been for me as a painter in my wet painting period, I realized that there was no future for me as a writer in the small, embittered, destructive, literary world of Dublin and Ireland. In my continuing struggle to survive and parked temporarily on the Isle of Man, I finally moved to London. But not before there had been a considerable imbroglio with the self elected protectors of a young Irish girl with whom Gebler had taken up. This new attractive lady, full of laughter when not full of tears, had broken away from the Irish

Son Philip in the front garden where a hammock swings and where tea was being taken under the palm trees when interrupted by the arrival of the Irish vigilantes looking for Gebler. When such violent incidents were not in progress the Isle of Man was an idyllic sub tropical if windy paradise.

prescribed way of life. And from behind a chemist's counter was overnight coping with her new role as the friend of an acclaimed author and was staying without the blessing of marriage as a long term guest in his manor. Edna, as she was called, was the product of a respectable Irish farming family from the west and convent schools, and arrived with Gebler at The Anchorage, Port e Vullin. This splendid house of my mother in law's perched in its gardens nearly sat on the waves. With my mother in law in India, we took tea in the garden under the sub tropical palm trees. Suddenly out of the blue a Manx detective arrived inquiring in general about the weather which was agreeably bright, balmy and sunny. Then other folk came in two more laden cars. Full to the brim with pure Irishmen. Plus a bishop from somewhere. At first it looked like the arrival of friends and a version of a family reunion and with the detective acting as equerry I decided to leave my guests with their guests and repaired back up to my study whose window faced out upon the sea and where I was writing a revision of *The Ginger Man*. Suddenly I heard screams from Valerie.

'Mike, come quick, come quick, they're beating up Ernie.'

Daughter Karen in the front garden where the door through which the author exited to defend Ernie Gebler is in the background. And Karen, who shares her mother's passion for cats, sits on the edge of an old well turned into a flower bed.

I leaped from my desk, papers flying and jumped down the stairs, taking off my jacket and a heavy sweater. I went rolling up my sleeves as I ran through a hall. Depositing my watch on the dining room table as I sailed across that room. I could hear the young lady Edna sobbing somewhere. And I increased speed out through the kitchen, already throwing shadow boxing blows to warm up my arms. I raced along a conservatory passageway which led to the front gate and a large door in a wall from which one could proceed by a slipway down along the side of the house and which sloped to the sea. At the bottom, caught between the high garden wall at his back and a railing fencing him from the waves, was Ernest Gebler battling for his life as six or so folk rained blows and kicks upon him. Above me as I turned out the door I spotted a seventh acting as a lookout on the road, and who saw me coming. I had no idea that the tongues had been wagging across Ireland over the association of Edna and Ernest. Or that those who abhorred such had banded into an army to end the relationship. But I did know that if people back in Dublin had doubts as to whether I could write or paint, the one thing no one seemingly disputed was my being able to give a decent account of myself in an affray. And the cry of warning was raised as I sallied forth down the slipway.

'It's him. It's Donleavy, he's coming.'

'You bet your bloody Irish arses I am and I'm going to kick the living bigoted shit out of all of you.'

Of course I may not have said 'bigoted' at the time. However, I remember trying to be positive sounding in my purpose as it at least would deflect some of the acrimonious attention being paid poor Ernest Gebler. And I knew by the expression, 'It's him', that my violent reputation had preceded me. But even as I approached Ernest who was as strong as an ox, and could snap his sinewy steel muscles like a whiplash, he had already flattened prone one of the six on the slipway and had just sent a fifth with an uppercut hurtling skywards, arching head first and feet last over the railing into the sea. And as I reached them I was able, in an authentically Irish manner, to level one more with a grossly unsportsmanlike blow just to the rear of his right ear while this victim's back was turned. One of the three remaining, turning to scream.

'Don't hit me I'm an old man and I've a Friday left to make of the nine first Fridays.'

As the latter gent, who admittedly wasn't in the springtime of his prime, was trying his damnedest to gouge one of Gebler's eyes out, I had no hesitation in unleashing an almighty boot up his backside to send him pitching forward on his face as he was scuttling away up the gravel slipway to escape. This seemed the signal for the two gents remaining and facing the two of us, in what now could have been a fair fight, to promptly speedily depart. One having to proceed hopping on one foot for Gebler had firm hold of the other. It was at this moment that I spied two more figures who were all this time lurking behind a wall in reserve but now thought the better of leaping into the breech as their cohorts limped, hobbled and crawled as fast as they could to their cars. The rear being taken up by the chap Gebler had sent flying into the drink who with the copious amounts of seaweed hanging down around his ears, now resembled a female impersonator transvestite. Clearly the intention of these unannounced visitors had been to beat Gebler to within an inch of, if not entirely extinguish, his life. And in the present rout of this gang of Irish beating it up the slipway, and me still outraged by such bullying behaviour, I had no hesitation in landing further kicks here and there on the various backsides. On the road at the top of the slipway and in the blazing afternoon sunshine and peaceful buzz of the bees in the honeysuckle, the bishop from somewhere stood with a crucifix and rosary blessing himself and declaring I thought, most unfairly and inappropriately.

'O dear God, I pray thee to deliver the pure and innocent of us from evil.'

As the culprits of the attack leaped back into their cars and disappeared up the road and over the headland in a cloud of exhaust, and Gebler finished thanking me for saving his life, I counted six teeth on the slipway and quickly ran my tongue searchingly back and forth in my mouth. Happily neither I nor Gebler were missing any. And Ernest, a genius with home remedies, bathed his cuts and bruises while comforting this pretty and entirely innocent girl who, sobbing before, was fortunately now, as I gave ringside descriptions of the infighting, able to see the amusing side of the matter and was half falling off her chair laughing and adding her own embellishments with her lilting brogue which could so melodiously coin a poignant phrase or make observations in fresh new words in her inimitable Irish way.

Of course, the young lady Edna was not only charming but also innocent of the culpability being alleged by the ostensibly well meaning vigilantes out to save her good name and to prevent her from being led astray by an international author and to put her back on the previous good path laid down for all well bred Irish country girls. In any event, Gebler was, for all his sometimes dour qualities, one of that rare breed, a consummate gentleman. And fully deserving of the battle fought to save him from the unjust punishment intended. But the Irish in revenge never give up, or at least not until you marry the girl. Which Gebler finally did as his second wife. And alas, another talented Irish writer came into being and to ultimate acclaim. Years later it did make me remember how, before the latter lady achieved her recognition, she had been made to suffer obtuse ridicule at the hands of some of Gebler's contemporaries, pretenders to artistic sophistication who, ready to pounce, lurked resentfully in the bitter world of Irish letters. And to whom I once announced.

'You are making fun of a young lady who will one day be the literary queen of England.'

Of course, the young lady could well take care of herself and certainly needed no help from me but I was full of such bizarrely grandiose predictions and never wasted an opportunity when I felt they could be expressed, not for a second thinking that any of them could ever come true. As indeed a few did. In any event as Gebler was already a literary king it was easy enough to throw titles about. Especially as I was pretentiously as possible readily assuming them myself. One never knew for sure who all these volunteer vigilantes were who landed out of the blue on the Isle of Man, but they did represent a faction and a mode of action frequently employed to stamp out any carnal impurity that might be thought afoot and publicly affecting the morals of the female citizenry of that land. And one knew such contingent could be gathered in a thrice by merely a whisper in an ear in any pub, especially if the perpetrator of such alleged debauchery had a foreign sounding name. And so had I come, in my little interim, away from the old sod, into contact with Ireland and the Irish again.

Not long after this event I debarked from this pleasant little island to London. Former denizens of Dublin like Desmond MacNamara, and Valentine Coughlan were there from whom one would hear the usual recent Dublin stories. Such as the news that modern criminal methods were being introduced to Ireland. And a couple of apprentice criminals with a bomb timing device were robbing a bank. And had this night driven their car around the block again and again awaiting the explosive charge to detonate. But then seeing nothing happen they then parked. And, lo and behold, who should come walking along but a member of the Garda Síochána who, viewing this suspicious pair three a.m. in the morning sitting in their vehicle outside a bank, ventured to inquire as to what they were about. And as they were explaining that they were merely deep breathers, out taking in the night air and minding their own business, the bank's windows blew out in a blaze of flying glass.

But now, settled in England I was as far away from Ireland as you could be, down a working class Fulham street where nary any soul thinking of the betterment of his social position and future, would dare to venture. And a young British élitist, son of an Oxford don, once walking with me through Kensington suddenly stopped in his tracks.

'I'm awfully sorry, my dear chap, but I cannot proceed farther, you see we are about to enter the borough of Fulham and I never walk there.'

There were other snobs but it was now left mostly to the Irish and those of past Irish association to visit me. The most consistent of whom were a Glin Bennett and a Davy Romney, both former Trinity medical students who'd become physicians, and were later to distinguish themselves in that profession. Desmond MacNamara came by bicycle bringing his own pillow to sit on my hard chairs. And Randall Hillis, with whom I waked his lonely friend, not only came but even moved nearby with a stunningly beautiful, genuinely Irish wife.

But there were other Irishmen, too, with their own special brand of snobbery. And on a Christmas day, holed up down my grim street in Fulham, where instead of fresh westerly winds down from the Wicklow Mountains I had now the tall chimneys of the Fulham power station looming, unleashing their clouds of smoke. Valentine

The author in his former Fulham sitting room as a first settler and social untouchable long prior to Fulham becoming fashionable and its residents acceptable. One former Trinity College friend at the time remarking upon discovering where I lived, 'Ah we've all changed. But he hasn't.'

Coughlan, full of his usual optimistic bonhomie, had come for this festive day's dinner. Which was not of your usual goose or turkey but of rabbit. For the occasion I had invited another single male Dubliner to my table and whose arrival we awaited. As nearly an hour ticked by, and my hungry son Philip, and tiny daughter Karen and wife Valerie were growing anxious to eat, Coughlan asked me did I by any chance at all tell this awaited guest, as I had told him, that I was having rabbit for Christmas dinner. I said yes, I had. And Coughlan drew his chair up to the table and gave a grunt of contempt.

'Well tuck in your napkins now and dig in your forks and start eating for you'll be waiting till beyond next Christmas before the likes of that bloody snob looking down his nose shows up.'

Then I recalled that this person of an Irish name and ancestry had been born and raised in England. But certainly there was a true Irishman arriving when Behan would occasionally show up. The two of us often setting off on a walk covering miles and miles, meandering in any direction across London, discussing as we went all matters pertinent and impertinent to our world, and to the world's world. Behan often, as my own father did, stopping to talk with anyone along the way digging a ditch or building a wall. Inevitably by evening we were in some pub near the London offices of some Irish newspaper. And on one such occasion we finally did have a fight. In the middle of Fleet Street. Battling back and forth and stopping the traffic. And finally being temporarily arrested. Behan, as an ex inmate of Her Majesty's Prisons, already persona non grata in the United Kingdom, seemed to know how to placate a British bobby and not further compound our felony, and ten minutes later up a Fleet Street alley the two of us were let go. Next morning while I was out, Behan with a red swollen nose and black eye turned up at 40A Broughton Road with none other than Lead Pipe Daniel The Dangerous in tow. But first the two of them had already visited my local library where they pretended to inquire after my address, the librarian telling me later in hushed tones of the incident.

'I didn't think, Mr Donleavy, that you would want me to release your address to these two particular gentlemen.'

In true Dublin style Behan wanted to borrow my typewriter. And Lead Pipe Daniel The Dangerous clearly intended to pawn it. My wife Valerie resisting their supplications. But Behan did help *The Ginger Man* to at least get published in France by telling me on the night of our fisticuffs, of The Olympia Press in Paris. Later, when the book managed to get its first reviews with its publication in England, and just as one's Irish associations were slipping, and over those particular long months when I was nearly more banjaxed than ever with litigation looming with The Olympia Press, Paris, over *The Ginger Man*, there suddenly came out of the blue a letter. The theatrical critic Kenneth Tynan, who was also a film script editor for Ealing Films, was writing to say he'd thought *The Ginger Man* a marvellous book and did I really hate films as much as Dangerfield suggested and that if I would think of something that could be put on celluloid my dialogue would be a godsend to British films. These were ecstatically encouraging words to hear while impecuniously tightly squeezed down this small Fulham side street. And there were no doubts in my mind that I had in the last five minutes entirely revised any previous loathing I may have had for films or Hollywood and was now, if I had not ever been previously, a fervent lover of tinsel and celluloid. At our meeting in his lavish Mount Street flat, Tynan, a cigarette dangling between his ring and small finger, admitted some possible Irish ancestry, and said, just give me an idea, tell it to me now or write it on a match cover or back of a postage stamp and provided you have no aversion to large sums of money we'll drop a contract through your letter box.

My mind, quicker than it seemed to have ever worked before, duly conjured a story concocted out of one I'd heard of a returned American making a trip to the west of Ireland to recover money left in a will. This idea, as Tynan had suggested, was duly scribbled on a match cover. And along with my dreaming of the free openness of Ireland and a film to be set there, a cheque came. Once more I was on my way back to that island land bringing with me a new pot to replace the old one I had been pissing in which had incurred so many recent leaks. Much needed, especially in a nation where, in the history of pissoirs, you will never find any so dismal.

I had answered an ad in a London Sunday newspaper, to rent a house in Connemara. Setting off from London with Valerie and a family of my two children, Philip and Karen. Arriving at evening after a long day's journey by train and boat, to at last come between those familiar enfolding arms of land around Dublin Bay. Howth to the north, Dalkey to the south. One's memory ringing with other names. Clontarf, Blackrock, Rathmines and Booterstown. And there was Dublin, dirty and grey. And now changed forever because A. K. Donoghue, purveyor of honesty and Blessed Gainor Stephen Crist, patron saint of tourists in Dublin, were both gone. Yet if only as pale substitutes for these two eminently volatile gentlemen, one did still see a few familiar faces passing like moveable landmarks upon the street. As if one were opening an old favourite book, the pages faded, but the words still there saying exactly the same.

And there were those other faces of sadder men, the poets, the novel writers, lurking figures who made their solitary excursions through their city. Casting an eye perhaps at a Jewish gentleman, inspiringly insane in the middle of Grafton Street who over so many years so benignly and brilliantly directed rush hour traffic. He was still there on this day as we took the train from Westland Row Station to cross the midlands to Galway City. An even bleaker place than Dublin. Where we were met and taken to an hotel and given dinner by my hospitable landlord. Who insisted on paying the bill and then drove three hours, mile after deserted mile over the curving road through a lake and pond dotted boggy Connemara. Its moorland landscape strewn with stone and grey granite outcroppings. My intrepid landlord leaning over his steering wheel to see ahead in the lashing rain drenching this endless loneliness. And to my question had we much further to go.

'Well, it wouldn't be much further now.'

Beyond Clifden and finally, over a dirt and rutted road and in an even more deserted landscape with the bleakest of darkness upon us, we arrived in the downpour to an isolated house in the wildest of wild places. Indeed, it was out on a peninsula reaching into the Atlantic Ocean, such as I had dreamed about. And stepping out of the storm swept black night, one was suddenly standing in the hall of this cold massive Georgian edifice. One's breath white on the air. Where nothing seemed to matter now except remaining warm and fed. In the gloom a staircase rose up to these giant bedrooms. One already felt a little haunted by the space enclosed within these thick walls, and the large brooding Victorian furniture. My imagination measuring a dining room fifty feet long, thirty feet wide and twenty feet high. Our exceedingly courteous and solicitous landlord promptly lit a fire or two to drive away the damp and cheer up our spirits. But none the less in my worry I fell asleep thinking that one's children could be found chilled dead in the morning. That is if I weren't found first. But when I did finally fall asleep and awake again, a surprisingly mild morning sun was streaming in the window. I could hear singing elsewhere in the house and I went to investigate. And there across the hall, was Philip. Already having the circus time of his life jumping with cliff hanging daring from one bed to another in his room. Later the two of us were happily playing soccer together in the cavernous front hall.

I set up a desk to write upon in a large sun porch that jutted out over the front door. Able to stare out miles over this windswept wild countryside. Where tracks led over the stony little hills to magically golden coral beaches. I could see six mountains and what appeared to be a lake in front of the house, but was in fact the Atlantic Ocean. Looking out on this landscape I wrote the film script of *The Rich Goat*, and began in this vast silence my second novel, *A Singular Man*. No visitors, no telephone, no newspapers. And with no radio, no connection to the outside world. But occasionally up from behind hedges and disappearing around walls were human faces and shadowy figures. Someone that first day of arrival was being buried. In an anonymous grave like the others in the cemetery which were unadorned but for a slab to mark the foot and head and a pile of stones covering the rest. A reminder that here was an earth which, as quietly as a flower blooms and its petals fall, could take one back into its bosom.

One morning in my sun porch workroom while I was staring down on the small field in front of the house, I saw the neighbouring farmer come running in the gate from the road. Philip and Karen were playing on the grass at the other end of the lawn and my neighbour shaking a raised hand at the sky and pointing up as he shouted.

'There's a dog up there. There's a dog.'

And apprehensive as the wildly gesticulating farmer approached in the direction of my children, I ran out into the hall and shouted down to Valerie in the kitchen, to call Philip and Karen as quickly as she could into the house. And out of the way of this obviously insane and possibly dangerous man. Who, as he now went back onto the road, was repeating his observation about this bow wow which he thought was barking high in the heavens. Meanwhile and later that day our landlord, providing us with a radio, also arrived with the news that the Russians had put a dog up in a space capsule orbiting planet earth. And isolated out in the bleak beauty of this ancient land one learned that the rest of the world had entered the space age.

And it was here that one came back to Irish ways. Indifferent to time, stoic to discomfort and calamity. A newspaper ordered from town came. It would at least be of a recent date, and at most, maybe a month old. But on the outside only. For inside, fattening the thickness of the edition, were other pages of some ancient date and from a newspaper of a different name and even of a religious or sporting nature. To me who did not want to know any recent news if I could help it, such random assembled out of date newspapers were a godsend. However there were other drawbacks of a different nature. A piece of pork ordered came delivered dipped in methylated spirits to disguise its very high and smelly nature. So too did come last year's biscuits and last year's coffee. But it was nothing to kill you as the natives thought a tomato, onion or fresh vegetable might. Ah, but why be fussy when one felt absolutely and contentedly at home. There was salt fish, potatoes and cabbage and the squirt of a bit of milk out of a cow and cream churned into butter. Not a stone's throw away there were the clear, clean Atlantic waters tumbling their foaming waves on these golden shores. To which one strolled each day. A local recluse always following along jumping behind stone hedges and outcroppings to hide and watch. There was, too, the strange phenomenon of excreta precipitously deposited on the peaks of stones in salient places such as forks in the road and especially along paths and lanes where it would confront the traveller and where villagers were sure to pass. Obvious to all that such could not have been pinpointed there by dog, mule or other beast but a human one.

The postman could be seen miles away on the hillside on his bicycle coming with the mail. And one day in answer to a card I wrote to a London friend, Christopher Logue.

Connemara
Sunday

My dear Christopher,

Come and visit. There are not many blades of grass out here but what there is, is counted by the population every morning. There's not a sound of anything anywhere except wind and rain and the odd donkey. The place will give you a jolt, at least the silence. You may not have sheets or enough covers on your bed but one hopes to keep you unchilled in the heart. The most bizarre bunch of fantastic faced people are here. The curiosity in their expressions makes them look mean. Maybe some are.

But when not doing their disappearing acts or standing on their heads clapping the mud off their boots, the natives seem by their toothless grins to be friendly enough when greeted. Others, the 'queer' ones, board up in their houses and come out at night. But by day some have not been seen for twenty or thirty years. When I asked what they did with themselves locked away with their windows covered over to the light, I was told they read by candlelight. What, at first, I couldn't imagine. Except old newspaper accounts of the sinking of the *Titanic* which are abundant here. But then on the front stoop yesterday came the news that at least one of them was reading a book called *The Ginger Man*. Which may account for some of the wild riotous laughter which woke me way past midnight the other night. This morning one of them (not a reader, I'm told) was buried and the countryside was smiling ear to ear as Irish do when another green greedy mouth is dead. So I leave it to you to come if you can.

Christopher Logue duly arrived smilingly after his long travel. Already with tales of prostrate drunk bodies on the mail boat and someone leaping overboard in a suicide. But at least by that evening he had got some amusement watching me in order to amuse Philip and Karen who were being bathed in a portable bath in front of the turf fire in the dining room, while I pretended to be a Roman gladiator, mop as a spear and with a silver sauce boat off the sideboard on top of my head.

Of course, Christopher Logue with his penetrating blue eyes and eccentrically aristocratic face and who with a long black flowing cloak out behind him as he careered on a rented bicycle about the winding hilly roads, was a lot stranger looking than any of the natives. Who indeed fled at the sight of his approach thinking him a reincarnation of a poet they thought was known by the name of Yeats and was long dead. Logue creating a sensation for miles around, as he swept down hillsides like a great raven, his bike bouncing over the stony road and his cape flapping behind him as he pedalled across the countryside while his splendidly booming voice declaimed his poetry out on the winds.

Christopher asked me why people seemed to shrink back as if in fear of him. And I told him tales of the power of a poet. That such a man in making his verses could compose one of ridicule to bring down upon those causing his displeasure, a curse repeated and recited down through the generations. Logue, a man of extremely practical inclinations only smiled to indulge what he knew were my frequent highly embellished exaggerations, but meanwhile he was surviving well. Mary, the girl who worked in the house and who would walk to Clifden seven miles away on a Friday night to attend a dance and walked all the way back, was amused with this gentleman who could go laughingly booming his voice through the halls and especially with his putting unsmoked butt ends filling up a jar in his bedroom. Logue meticulously saving these to remake and smoke the remnants reconstituted in his hand rolled cigarettes and which he could puff upon during the long train and boat ride back to London. And upon the eve of Logue's departure Mary had thrown the whole lot away. Collapsing in fits of laughter when she heard why Christopher had been saving them. However something else was to happen when Logue was leaving and returning his rented bicycle to the man in the town from whom he'd got it, and who seeing a few mud spots on the fenders and alleging other damage, now stood at the top of his stairs refusing to give Logue back his pound deposit. Logue then remembering what I'd said about the power of poets in Ireland. And just as your man was standing stubbornly shaking his head no in reply to Logue's loudest demand, Logue pointed an accusing finger up at him.

'I am a poet and I shall make up a verse that will ridicule you and all those belonging to you down through the generations.'

Before Logue could turn and leave, a crumpled up pound note landed at his feet at the foot of the stairs. Clearly out there in the back and beyond, and if not among the untutored and savage, it was at least still believed by the worldly astute that ill fortune if not damnation could be brought down upon you by the ancient power of poets.

Before *The Rich Goat* could be made, Ealing Films got sold. And except for one unforgettable event, a long gap of ten years was to occur after my sojourn this early winter November 1957 in the west. But on 26 October 1959 two years later, I was to be back briefly again in Ireland and certainly sooner than I expected. This time in the wake of the London production of *The Ginger Man* transferring to Dublin. Which no doubt was encouraged by quotes, one of such was attributed to Harold Hobson of the *Sunday Times*. 'There are two modern plays in London through which blows the wind of genius. One of them is Brendan Behan's *The Hostage*. The other is J. P. Donleavy's *The Ginger Man*.'

I was on this occasion to learn something about Ireland I suspected and which I had already expressed in one of my forewords, 'In Ireland friendship is on the lips but not in the heart'. But somehow I did not ever believe it possible that the emnity would ever come out into the public light. When news of a transfer of *The Ginger Man* stage production to Dublin reached me, I was delighted but thought it the ultimate act of bravery or madness. But to at last bring back to this land, this work to where it had found its origins, seemed fitting enough, if not even a vindication. Then with a couple of verbal first night protests, the storm clouds began to gather. At the final curtain were demands to make cuts. The cliff hanging moments on the second night taking place in the theatre owner's office when the production might have at any second been called off. The tension mounting each succeeding day as the newspaper word spread of this distasteful, repulsively sordid evening which was an insult to religion and decency. As the hours went by more tickets being sold, the audience increasing and queues forming down the street in front of the theatre. The secretary of the Archbishop arriving and then departing to the comment of Richard Harris, the play's star, 'There goes a battleship'. Following the third performance the play was finally taken off. In disgracing themselves yet again, the Irish had finally done it. For the first time in Irish history, they had stopped a play playing on the stage.

I had already seen *The Ginger Man* survive its way past countless publishers' rejections and then censors in France, England and the U.S.A., almost as if *The Ginger Man* could wield a curse against all who opposed or stole or ridiculed its words. But in Ireland I was to find a vast convoluted instant conspiracy spreading its secret silent tentacles in all directions and especially to every corner of Dublin city. It was clear that no public contrition or prostrate beating of one's head on the wooden blocks of Grafton Street could assuage the emnity. Telephones went dead. Hostile glances came from every side. One was followed upon buses and upon foot. A narrow minded intolerance welled up so vast, widespread and deep that it could hardly be called intolerance at all. It was the natural condition of the people described so long ago by Gainor Stephen Crist as the Crut. But it was now more like an electric wire plugged into everyone in the nation to whom intelligence reports were being hourly made to provide a glowering sea of threat. The only antidote to which was to

GAIETY

Telegrams: "GAIETY," DUBLIN. SOUTH KING STREET, DUBLIN. Telephone 78000-8
Proprietors: THE GAIETY THEATRE, DUBLIN, LTD.

COMMENCING MONDAY, OCTOBER 26th, 1959

Nightly at 8 p.m. Matinee: Saturday at 2.30 p.m.

THE DUBLIN PLAY THAT STARTLED LONDON !

SPUR PRODUCTIONS LTD. in association with
THE DUBLIN GLOBE THEATRE COMPANY
PRESENT

RICHARD HARRIS
IN

THE GINGER MAN

By J. P. DONLEAVY

WITH

ROSALIE WESTWATER
GODFREY QUIGLEY
GENEVIEVE LYONS

"There are two modern plays in London through which blows
the wind of genius. One of them is 'The Hostage.' The
other is 'The Ginger Man.'"—*Harold Hobson, The Sunday Times.*

Directed by PHILIP WISEMAN   Settings designed by TONY WALTON

PRICES: DRESS CIRCLE, 10/-; PARTERRE, 7/6; GRAND CIRCLE, 4/- and 6/-
NOW BOOKING 10 a.m.—9 p.m.

(Left) *This was the poster which, all over Dublin, disappeared within hours when* The Ginger Man *was forced off the Dublin stage by the intervention of the awesome power of the Catholic authority wielded by the then Archbishop of Dublin. This single poster was rescued by Tony Walton who had the presence of mind to grab it prior to leaving for London, and which he later bequeathed to me.*

(Below) *Richard Harris as Sebastian Dangerfield conferring with Isobel Dean as Miss Frost over a choice of sausages. Harris' rehearsals were as dramatic as his performances and were full of realism, and even merely reciting his lines had been known to stop traffic outside his flat in Earls Court Road.*

get word out to the outside world. But in attempting to alert foreign newspapers all our telephone calls were blacked out to and from London's Fleet Street. Subterfuge was everywhere. Not one of these enemies would reveal themselves into the light. There was even a fear that one might be trapped and prevented escape. Except that one knew too that they would be more than glad to see one go and rid Dublin of *The Ginger Man*.

John Ryan throughout was there, a friend in need if only to be just one sympathetic voice in the battle headquarters of the Bailey Restaurant which he then owned in Duke Street. Even Behan whose destinies and mine seemed temporarily to coincide, was there drinking soda water and somehow in his strange way was making amends with me, perhaps for no other reason than our infrequent meetings these past few years. Patrick Kavanagh, himself previously the plaintiff in a libel action headlined across the entire nation, was still ready to raise his voice in the praise of the prevention of public cruelty to authors and playwrights in this land that had now practised it for a century. 'In a mini metropolis long dead, Donleavy has at last set the city alive once more.' And as I walked out of the Bailey, I did hear another Irish voice.

'No wonder Ireland has long been the loud laughing stock of Europe, full as it is of the most insufferable narrow minded eegits.'

With no bands or flags there to see us off, we at last had made it out to the airport. A slightly eccentric friend of Ryan's driving us dangerously fast, making it unnecessary to look behind to see if we were being chased. Richard Harris, as Irish as anybody and the star of the play, was crumpled up brooding in the front seat of the car. He had declared he would play the role on top of an orange crate in the middle of O'Connell Street Bridge and break the jaw of anyone who objected. And Harris, as strong as two oxen, faster than a leopard and bigger than most, had to be believed. Indeed he more than anything else may have saved the author from being strung up in the fly space of the Gaiety. And now Harris was planning to fly with the script to Rome. To either give the Pope a reading of the play in St Peter's Square or else just deliver a piece of Harris's outspoken mind. 'If the Vatican is running Ireland and the Pope is running the Vatican then by God I'm going to put in my two cents to run the Pope.'

In order that no impurity reach the natives I had suffered exactly the same treatment as many before me. But at least I could feel free of these shackles clanking and subduing the voices that had nowhere to speak and nowhere to escape. Always knowing Ireland was a country in which it was best to be a foreigner, and be forgiven not knowing of its obtuse tyrannical repressions. And being an island from which you must take a bigger step to leave than you would a country where a train takes you across the border to another land. It was one wonderful, bright and cheerful feeling of freedom to step off that plane in London. Even realizing that I might never set foot on the old sod again.

But meanwhile the first inklings were manifesting of something that was happening to the world. American culture was spreading to population hordes everywhere, conquering and changing all in its wake. And in Ireland, banned though it may have been, they were, even as copies fell apart, reading *The Ginger Man*. And news of the words 'Will God ever forgive the Catholics' was out. Television, breaking through the custom barriers, had crossed the Irish Sea and was alive in front of Irish eyes. Which were bulging with insatiable curiosity. To stare at such immoral flesh and listen to such immoral words. I had briefly travelled to visit my mother then staying in Greystones and to overnight call on James Hillman temporarily residing in a mansion high up in the hills of Co. Wicklow. In my Dublin hotel room returning from a morning stroll I suddenly came upon the maid and a porter looking sheepishly guilty. And later I found a filmscript copy of *The Saddest Summer of Samuel S* missing from my luggage. Even all these years later, the conspiracy was still alive. But then on the same visit I had strolled through Dublin. And received the first of what were to be many taps on the shoulder, following which would come an inquiring voice.

'Are you J. P. Donleavy who wrote *The Ginger Man*. That's why I came here all the way from the U.S.A.'

When I went to visit some of my old haunts, the first of which was Jammet's, I found it closed and gone for good. Then a strange and curious sight in a main Dublin street. In a shop window a public protest at corporal punishment given in a Catholic school. Photographs of weals on skin. Something had changed. Voices were speaking to be heard. I strolled then to the Bailey bar and restaurant which was still there but since sold by John Ryan. As I ordered a half of draught Guinness at the bar in this large room jammed elbow to elbow and full of smoke and din, a voice somewhere away in a corner began a slow chant which slowly spread until booming in my ears my name was chanted on everyone's lips. And here anonymously in Dublin where the eye of conspiracy was upon me once more, I suddenly found myself triumphantly conspicuous. Not as the butt of resentment and glowering emnity but in the acknowledgment that here all around me were now Ginger Men and Women. Thinkers for themselves. And maybe even grateful for the spiritual favours received from the Blessed Saint Sebastian Dangerfield himself.

However as the chant of my name continued I was only able to wryly smile and quickly depart, leaving my drink behind. Sorry that in one's long reclusive isolation I had become too timid and inarticulate to show my appreciation and shake some of these ladies' and gentlemen's hands. But aware now that at least and at last and indeed, something was happening. In these minds behind these younger faces if not brighter smiles. And if they had not newer and better pots to piss in at least they might leak less. Where now in this ancient land of saints and scholars.

Among

The zealots and philistines,

The crut

Was being crushed

And forgive

Me

If I blow my

Own horn

With just a tweet or two

For it is at least

Of my own

Melody

And sweet to hear

XIV

Back in London and variously on the Isle of Man, nearly all my direct contact with the Irish had vanished. Valentine Coughlan still stacking up his secret riches in coins and Swiss bank accounts, would telephone me for front row opening night tickets and show up at my plays in a vast limousine full of his guests. And once asked me to write a poem for him to win a poetry contest. Which I did and he lost. I tried religiously each afternoon to take tea, even as late as it might be, and to desert at least for a couple of hours, my eyrie in a tall block of flats near where the hangings at Tyburn took place. I delighted to refer in general to the building as 'Tax Dodgers' Towers'. Such name due entirely to a single inmate who one morning when his driver had brought round his gleamingly new powder blue sparkling Rolls-Royce convertible to the front entrance, had irritatingly said to this chauffeur who was about to jump out and open the door for him.

'No, not that car, you silly, the black one.'

And from the same lofty heights, I had now for some years revelled in walking the streets of London, actively taking pleasure that no Irish zealot pedestrian here would dare point an accusing finger and assert that there be me passing upon such pavement, a known defiler of religion and outrager of decency. And alas, more than frequently, I was to be found at Vespers, in many a Catholic and heavily Irish church, listening to the singing and music. But a remaining Trinity College connection, A. K. Donoghue, former importer of honesty to Ireland and previous loud advocator of cunnilingus to be practised by the Irish male in the interests of the Irish female, would occasionally fly in to visit me from his haunts in mid continental Europe. Spending long festive evenings telephoning old friends, located now across the world, like the Moynahans and a doctor pal Ned O'Rourke to whom one would sing an Irish air or two into the mouthpiece. And one night descending twenty floors I watched Donoghue at this midnight walk out and away from the building to take the underground to

The author himself in his dentist's modern 'Tax Dodgers' Towers' during these balmy days and working up his appetite for the rare vintages and rare roasted beeves ferried up from Fortnum and Mason's. Having been so low for so long in one's life the contrast of being up high, delighted one. And, of course, everyone in such buildings did pay their taxes.

another outpost I kept in Fulham. From this great height one could see over the rooftops into the deserted streets beyond and there I suddenly saw a figure weaving a block away and out of sight to Donoghue, and who then came around the corner to confront him. Donoghue pausing to listen a moment to this only other late night pedestrian, then promptly going on his way. Next morning I asked on the phone about the encounter.

'It was, believe it or not, out of the ten million in this pagan city, one of me own, a drunken Irishman asking me for a handout.'

Due to some accumulated litigations on several continents I had carefully selected the location of 'Tax Dodgers' Towers' to be certain of no such encounters and that no one unless in a passing airplane could look in my windows nor would know where I was. Nor could I, by descending deep into a garage and getting in a car, alas only a

*A. K. Donoghue in 'Tax Dodgers'
Towers' or 'Dentist's Modern' as he
preferred to call it. Where he would
come for our lavish evening meals
and around the world all night
telephone calls to old friends, and
then depart back to Broughton Road
where he would stay.*

Daimler, be seen coming or going. But upon the actual day of moving in, I went into a pub, which although around the corner, I could directly see down on the street below me from my study window. In its saloon bar, I had just sat down contentedly in the bliss of my privacy when a melodious Irish voice, somewhat Anglo to be sure, erupted.

'Give that man sitting over there a drink of whatever he wants.'

The gentleman speaking was a Trinity College Dublin man, Michael Mussen Campbell, later Lord Glenavy. When this charming, welcoming gentleman asked what I was doing there, I dared not tell. For a start, not only was this Michael Campbell's local pub next to which he lived, but also a frequent literary meeting place, for Campbell was an accomplished and reputable Irish writer. For a long time afterwards I skirted this street, not to avoid the excellent company of Campbell but merely in the interests of the continuity of my reclusive privacy.

But ironically over my time there not once in the years did I ever again confront the engaging Michael Campbell but instead it was I who invaded this pleasant Irishman's privacy something awful. Being able to watch down upon his house and witness his arrivals and departures and be sure that among them there would have been some nostalgically nice face I'd known from Dublin. And always in my dull slogging afternoons I found pleasant distraction wondering what Michael Mussen Campbell was doing. Which, as I was mostly desperately glued to my typewriter to pay numerous lawyers, enabled me to keep track of the social seasons. To suddenly see him on his stoop in morning suit and top hat and know he was off to Henley or later with a bevy of friends and a limousine arriving, to know he was departing for Ascot.

It was upon one of these sunnier days when I would set off innocently south across Mayfair that the momentous moment came that brought Ireland back into my life. Mr Young of Fortnum and Mason's stopping me at the tinned soup counter with the revelation which at first I couldn't believe until I saw it imprinted in the highly respectable journal of the *Economist* whose offices were only a strong man's stone's throw away around the corner from Jermyn Street. And to which I repaired for a copy immediately following tea. There it was in black and white. This emerald green nation, the first in the history of nations, legislating to the exclusive benefit of artists. And money, if you could get it for written words, composed sounds or colours drawn, was yours every penny to keep. But of course in hearing this tax law, and once banned and twice banjaxed, I did think that it could be a ruse. Not only to get me, and others like me back there, but once innocently and securely dug in, to then hear said 'Now we've got you, you bunch of dirty minded bastards. Not only are we going to tax your filthy artistic earnings but we're also going to arrest you and put you in prison and burn all your bloody obscene books and manuscripts.'

But perhaps not. Brian Friel, the distinguished playwright, laughed when I told him this. And said that if anyone deserved to benefit by this law, it was me. There has been subsequently, an odd scare or two, but in a land which has undergone a sweeping revolution greater than any that has ever occurred to any people on earth it may be that freedom of speech and expression is here to stay. For since those days of the stopping of *The Ginger Man* and when that book was long banned, at last like a thousand other books it is freely available once more and there has been no need for Irishmen like Richard Harris to be ready on stage to give battle to an irate audience who at any moment might up from their seats, and pour at you over the footlights. When you would hear that perennial cry which put in Patrick Kavanagh's words would be.

'As a Catholic and an Irishman and a fucking eegit, I object.'

Ah, and what else did happen to the Ireland to which I returned. Besides half of it falling and being knocked down in a shambles over which many a greedy gombeen man licks his salivating chops. And where once antichrists were doomed from pulpits to burn to a crisp in hell. Where, too, there was no lonelier scene on the face of this earth than a Protestant evangelist preaching, that their redeemer liveth on a Dublin street corner. Many is the time, merely politely sympathetic, I paused to listen. These days such a sight is even lonelier, for no one is there now at all. The nation strains breaking from its shackles. Coming asunder to imitate the rest of the world. And it was the naughty amoral English, once again, who did it. Who broadcast their nudity, contraception and divorce. Their amoral words and modern ways arriving upon the innocent of this land unstoppable and unseen across the sky and descending through the antennae that reach high from every rooftop. And which, by God, you'd think might be shaking above as if copulation had only just been invented below. With hardly a mortal sin left to commit, a barrier has been raised between those former faithful and their moral custodians who have for so long been a massive power established in their grey dour buildings of Maynooth, planted on the lush green Meath countryside. But to where, too, the like of me has since been invited to say what was recently on my mind. And not once did anyone, censor, zealot or philistine, shake a fist in my face. Sad, too, now that this ancient religious culture with its plainsong, black refinements and sacred ceremony, has not been able to shield from the new inelegant gods who spawn their tastelessness and vulgarity. But then who was to know that so soon there would come the revolution.

It did sure long seem then that one would not ever again be back in this land of its now faded saints and scholars where the religiosity of the people had exchanged for garbage disposal, television and cars. I learned that my mother in America had, when de Valera was asking for money for this nation, given it, and too, that years later it was repaid with interest. And now that I was back in Dublin town fresh from 'Tax Dodgers' Towers', I, too, was looking for a loan. My bank in New York telling me they'd opened a branch in Dublin. To which I went to submit my further and hopefully better particulars. To find

Levington Park. The author's home at the time of writing in Ireland where with nine bathrooms, indoor swimming pool and eleven toilet bowls he finally has a pot to piss in.

my banker a fan of *The Ginger Man* and who, in taking a look at a picture I held up of a house I wanted to buy, said.

'Is that it.'

And I was handed a cheque book with such pleasantly casual ease that I nearly then became too terrified to use it. But nerve returning soon as I headed out once more on these streets upon which one had so often wandered previously on their grey wet granite pavements. And finding that Sebastian Dangerfield was walking everywhere before me. To begin my life again in an old familiar land. Where only in Dublin could you see a man pass oblivious to obstructions, with his nose buried in a book. And another on a park bench reading a tome opened on his knee. Who as I passed, jumped to his feet, cursing in high dudgeon and then sat back down again to peruse his page further which again incensing, had him once more up pacing in a tight circle. Where else in the world would you hope to find such serious readers. I then listened to the mellisonant, elegant voice of the estate agent, Dennis Mahony, rude in health, ready to laugh and in his stout country shoes and tweeds, was delighted I'd come to Ireland. And who, as I autographed a cheque and bought a house,

The author and his present family who occupy Levington Park consisting of wife Mary, son Rory and daughter Rebecca seated on her rocking horse.

gave me a copy of *The Ginger Man* to sign. And then charmingly to protect my interests, even against him, brought me to one of the best lawyers in town. And where the monocles flash under its skylight, we took glasses of stout in the Royal Hibernian Hotel. I had a pot to piss in. And it felt warm like the feel that Dublin once had and was now felt again.

The house where I first went to live was Balsoon House, on the banks of the Boyne near Bective Bridge. With its ancient ruins and cemetery this house was built on a site historically connected to the Ussher family, founders of Trinity. And then I moved to Levington Park, a mellow stone mansion where James Joyce came as a young man and stayed to walk in its halls. But here now as Ireland is, and upon whose verdant lands so much of the outside world's tawdry has descended, there were graces still. Remaining alive even among all those past sins.

On my first trips into Dublin one still felt that sense of stirring anticipation remembered of leisurely late mornings years ago when setting off to Bewley's Oriental Café out the gates of Trinity College. In the city where abject domestic circumstances never prevented your being alive and well out in the pubs and coffee houses. But now I came upon destitute, ragged, homeless scholars slumped over their books seeking only the warmth of the National Library. In a dark, sombre, noonday pub silent habitués were sitting over their pints watching an American film projected upon a big screen, the mystification with the modern world still written across their faces and buried deep in their souls. Here and there on the streets, one could see the phenomenon of the trusted and prosperous well groomed refined Protestant Catholic. Ladies and gentlemen who on a sunny day might be seen tweedily passing into the Royal Irish Automobile Club, perhaps one of the best preserved small enclaves of privilege remaining in Dublin, where very little now endures. For the buildings, they tumble down in this city. But there remains at least the perfection of the purple dark tops of the distant Wicklow Mountains rearing at the end of many of its longitudinal streets. Upon which, wisdom is still being uttered. A swaying gentleman on a corner with drink taken admonishes the passing pedestrians.

'Who the fuck is Ireland. You'd think listening to them talk that it was one of them.'

But there was wonderfully one of them. An Irishman in an

Forty years on from the days of Trinity and coffee in Bewley's, Tony McInerney and Arthur Kenneth Donoghue seated on the porch of the author's house, Levington Park. McInerney tendering the proverbial shilling and Donoghue pulling his forelock and the conversation never ceasing.

expensive Irish restaurant who finished his meal and jumped up and got a headlock on the owner and yanked his head down and pushed his face into his just rendered bill, and said 'Now you eat that and tell me if you think you've been overcharged.' And indeed there remains wherever you go that uncomfortable feeling that you are going to be cheated or lied to, and then the strange relief and pleasure when you're not.

I went to visit Behan's grave. And appropriately enough, in view of the publicity he had while living, it was unmarked. But now there's a headstone and his epitaph is proclaimed along with that of Joyce's, Yeats's and other such giants of literature. All reared up now to become tourist attractions. Their images on sale, the houses they lived in adorned with plaques. Bringing many a foreigner's voice to be heard and their cameras' shutters to click. And at least turning one of these authors, previously obscene, into a latter day saint.

I sit at a desk sipping China tea and lemon, chewing a blend of toasted cereals, nuts and seeds in an English made crunchy bar. And where from that same country across the water, evensong broadcasts on the radio. A late summer's rain spatters against the windows. The sun comes out with the chirp and chatter of swallows. A dove hoots. No snakes. No poison insects. No death in a shadow where you may reach your hand. Just old mouldering graveyards for their dead and for the living, the heritage of chickens and pigs once running around their parlours. And where unlit bicycles and cars still go in the dark. A benign earth to which earthquake tremors and a crematorium have only recently come. Adding at least a little doubt to the belief of the people that Our Lord preserves Ireland above all other nations.

I go to walk high on a lonely deserted hill with a church and cemetery from which one looks down on Lough Owel. Protestant names here fading away on the stones. A foal gambols near its mother sheltering by a wall in a field. As autumn comes, the foxhunting élite will gallop by. The weather forced the Irish to put their hope in heaven and made their bowel movements come at the end of day. This fair skinned nation raging alive, kicking asunder its ancient chains. Where once its sour grapes were boiled in bile. Now it advertises across the world its hospitality and friendliness. This land where time cannot fly. To which the stranger comes. To be fleeced or fooled by the smiles. A nation from which so many fled, now crawling with its human race. But no more do comely maidens dance at the crossroads. Or potato diggers pull their forelocks. Yet there is more to tell. Out here nestled in these midland hills. The air scented green. Ancient friends awake out of their deaths to shake a hand. Walk together across the meadow. Keep your voice down. The grass has ears. To hear your secrets said. Beyond these eastern rainbows. Under which at last this pot. Doth be. To piss in.

Where the brooding
Heavens carry
Their veils of rain
To hide all her sins
And keep her safe in her graces